PASSIONATE

NOMAD

The Life of FREYA STARK

Includes a new Epilogue by the author

Jane Fletcher Geniesse

Praise for Jane Fletcher Geniesse's

PASSIONATE NOMAD: THE LIFE OF FREYA STARK

"Geniesse tells Stark's story straightforwardly and without fuss, allowing her eventful life, rather than a lot of commentary on it, to produce a lively and flavorful narrative. . . . The woman who emerges from these pages is a complex figure—heroic, driven, lonely, and entirely human."
—*The New York Times*

"Fascinating . . . [Geniesse] has achieved, in the end, an admirable focus, at once critical and sympathetic. The portrait that emerges is a subtle and generous one."
—*The New York Times Book Review*

"*Passionate Nomad* is a work of nonfiction that reads and sings with the drama and lilt of a fine novel. The story of Freya Stark is stunning, inspiring, sad, funny, unique, moving. Jane Fletcher Geniesse tells it straight, but with a care for delicious detail and a sympathy for the characters that makes this a truly special book."
—JIM LEHRER

"Geniesse helps us understand why a woman of genius was wildly unrealistic in her personal relations."
—*The New Yorker*

"*Passionate Nomad* is a thorough, vividly written account of one of the twentieth century's most intrepid travelers."
—LARRY MCMURTRY

"Compulsively readable . . . [Geniesse] has done a thorough job recreating the life of a woman many consider to be the last of the great romantic travelers."
—*The Plain Dealer* (CLEVELAND)

"Geniesse has made an inexhaustibly spirited and entertaining story of [Stark's life] . . . A just and generous portrait of a truly remarkable woman."
—*The Observer* (LONDON)

"*Passionate Nomad* is a lickety-split read, fun, fast-paced and exciting. . . . Only real life—and a remarkable biographer—could have fashioned a character as fascinating as Freya Stark."
—PETER BENCHLEY

Also by Jane Fletcher Geniesse

FICTION

The Riches of Life

NONFICTION

The Attorney's Appetite

The New York Woman's Directory (contributor)

Living Well (contributor)

Passionate
Nomad

Passionate Nomad

THE LIFE OF FREYA STARK

. . .

Jane Fletcher Geniesse

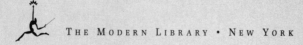

THE MODERN LIBRARY • NEW YORK

2001 Modern Library Paperback Edition

Grateful acknowledgment is made to the following for permission to print both
    published and unpublished material:
John Murray: Excerpts from the personal correspondence of Freya Stark.
    Reprinted by permission of John Murray.
John Murray (Publishers) Ltd.: Excerpts from the following published works of
    Freya Stark: *Beyond Euphrates, The Coast of Incense, Dust in the Lion's Paw,
    The Furnace and the Cup: Letters, Vols. I and II, Letters from Syria, Perseus in
    the Wind, The Southern Gates of Arabia, Traveller's Prelude, The Valleys of the
    Assassins,* and *The Zodiac Arch.* All excerpts are reprinted by permission of
    John Murray (Publishers) Ltd.

Library of Congress Cataloging-in-Publication Data

Geniesse, Jane Fletcher.
    Passionate Nomad: the life of Freya Stark/Jane Fletcher Geniesse.—Modern
Library ppk. ed.
        p.   cm.
    Includes bibliographical references and index.
    ISBN 0-375-75746-5
    1. Stark, Freya.   2. Women travelers—Great Britain—Biography.   3. Women
Orientalists—Biography.   4. Great Britain—Biography.   I. Title.
CT788.S72 G46 2001   910.92—dc21 [B]   2001030460

Modern Library website address: www.modernlibrary.com

Printed in the United States of America

2 4 6 8 9 7 5 3

Frontispiece: *A portrait of Freya Stark, by her parents' friend and fellow painter,
    Herbert Olivier (courtesy of the National Portrait Gallery, London, and
    Mrs. Theo Larsson)*

Title-page photo: *Freya Stark in Lucknow, India* (Dust in the Lion's Paw, *courtesy
    of John Murray)*

Book design by Barbara M. Bachman

This book is dedicated to the memory of

Joseph Francis Fletcher (1934–1984),

Professor of Chinese and Central Asian History,

Harvard University. He was a gifted scholar whose

command of Slavic, Arabic, Turco-Mongolian, Tibetan,

Manchu, and Chinese languages gave him a clear

view of that vast but scarcely understood region

whose borders run from the Caucasus to the China

Sea. Edward, Bob, Tom, Julia, and I miss him.

He was the best of friends, my brother.

Acknowledgments

My extended adventure at the side of Freya Stark has left me indebted to many talented and generous people on both sides of the Atlantic. First, there would have been no book had my dear friend and editor, Kate Medina of Random House, not encouraged me to write it, endured my slow start, and finally put me in the hands of her wonderful colleagues: Olga Seham—whose sensitive commentary was invaluable—the legendary Sam Vaughan, the indispensable and gracious Lee Boudreaux, and Barbara Bachman, Robbin Schiff, Deborah Foley, Benjamin Dreyer, Susan Brown, and all the others who made the experience, and the book, beautiful. I am deeply grateful to them all.

A corps of unmatchable friends helped me in countless ways: Wren Wirth, Wendy Benchley, Madge Huntington, and Edmée Firth read the manuscript, and Edmée translated all of Antonin Besse's letters, a heroic task done with nuance and flair. Dr. Lois de Menil translated and encouraged, while Noelle del Drago undertook an interview for me in Switzerland. When Henry Catto was our ambassador to the Court of St. James, he and Jessica threw a grand party at Winfield House that broke the ice among Freya's friends. The invitation from Dr. Helena Lewis to speak at Harvard was a grand stimulus, while Alix and Tom Devine, and Susan and Peter Nitze, on a variety of research missions abroad, provided lively company. Forde Medina encouraged with pesky questions; at a shaky moment, Tim Wirth sent flowers; and with exquisite timing, Peter Benchley intervened to see that the book title was right. Dr. Betty Ann Ottinger, Dr. Arnold Cooper, and Dr. Judith Nowack provided psychological insight into Freya's character. My thanks also to Ann Banks at the Fishers Island Library and to the librarians at the Humanities Research Center, University of Texas, Austin, the Library of Congress, and especially the Middle East Institute in Washington, D.C., where Betsy Folkins pointed the way to many good sources, and even after relocating to Iowa gave the manuscript a careful read, as did Nameer Jawdat.

In Paris, Antonin B. Besse was consistently helpful and supportive. In London, my husband and I found a true friend in Barclay Larsson, whose family has long been entwined with the Starks. Together with her husband, Theo, and son, James, the Larssons' generosity has been boundless.

I also discovered how loyal the Murrays of the John Murray publishing family are to Freya's memory. Jock and Diana let me interview them a number of times, and John and Virginia, in addition to patiently responding to numerous inquiries and requests, gave me their generous permission to quote Freya's own inimitable words from works published and unpublished. They were seconded by Michael Russell, who published eight volumes of Freya's letters, and the writer Caroline Moorehead, who edited them after her mother's death. It has been a pleasure to know her and benefit from her memories and those of her brother John, whose parents, Alan and Lucy, were such close friends to Freya. I loved every Harrod's take-out lunch given me by E. C. Hodgkin, as well as his wry wisdom. Pamela Cooper and her son the Honorable Malise Ruthven were both helpful and delightful to know and contributed many insights, as did Xandra Hardie; Peggy Drower Hackforth-Jones; the Viscount Norwich; his daughter the Honorable Artemis Cooper and son-in-law Anthony Beevor; Hermione, the Countess of Ranfurly; Veronica Bamfield; Doreen Ingrams and her daughter Leila; Sir Isaiah Berlin; Ambassador Boris Bianchieri; Lord Sherfield; the Marchioness of Cholmondeley; Countessa Anna Maria Cicogna; Nigel Clive; Hugh Leach; Richard and Bridget Sawers, who invited me to see Ford Park; and Sarah Bowen of the BBC, who shared her thoughts and sent her radio program on Freya. Special thanks to Colin Luke, whose documentary films on Freya's last adventures are hilarious and touching, and to Molly Izzard, Freya's English biographer, who both heaped documents on me and treated me to a fascinating afternoon at her lovely house in Tunbridge Wells.

Of Americans who remembered Freya, I am grateful for the time and memories shared by John Beach, Evelyn Lambert, H. C. Bailey, Jennifer Hamilton, John Guest, and Helene Sullivan Walker, for whom Asolo stirred such poignant memories.

Many others here and in Europe shared their memories and/or gave help: Susan Mary Alsop, George and Lucy Adams, Sir Philip and Lady Adams, Mark Heathcote Amory, Rosie Rodd Baldwin, Giorgio Bastianon, Janet and Henry Berens, Betsy Birch, Franco Boido, Jane Boulanger, Jac Chambliss, Mariela Camara, Zia Chishti, Harold Costello, Missy Crisp, Contessa Mariuccia deLord, Jacqueline de Chollet, Joy de Menil, Contessa Laura Loridon, Elizabeth Drury, the Dowager Lady Egremont, Emma Menegon, the Duke of Grafton, Patrick Leigh Fermor, Lady Henrietta Fitzroy, Lord Gibson, Sir Martin Gilliat, Charles Harding, Father Donald Harris, Derek Hill, Lady Marie Noelle Kelly, Nadia Lavalle, Lord Boyd of Merton and Lady Boyd, Sir Mark Lennox-Boyd, Osyth Leason, Gertrude Legendre, Professor Seton Lloyd, Felicity Longmore, Alexander Maitland, Jan Morris, Joanna and Freydys Murray, Ned O'Gorman, Princess Osman-Oghlu, R. G. Penson, Leslie Perowne, Caroli Piaser, Alan Punchard, Meaghan Rady, Sir Frank and Lady Roberts, Lady Joan Robertson, Jim and Pam Rose, Sir Steven Runciman, Sheridan Russell, Sir Michael and Damaris Stewart, Lucretia Stewart, Wilfrid Thesinger, Colin Thubron, Thor and Virginia Thors, Mario Valmarano, John and Susanna Vernon, Richard Waller, Lavinia Wallop, Lady Teresa Waugh, Lavender Goddard-Wilson, Francis Witts, Sir Paul and Lady Wright, and the many, many others who buoyed my spirits over the long haul.

My children, Tom and Julia, who long ago ceased asking "Freya who?" in favor of affirming faith and enthusiasm, were a joy to be with when they could come along. Lastly, especially, and above all, I thank their gallant father, Robert, who through thick and thin has been my champion, my strong oak, and my dearest traveling companion.

Contents

Prologue

On a gray, wet Tuesday, the twenty-eighth day of an exceptionally rainy September in 1993, a duke and a duchess, a countess, three viscounts and their viscountesses, three daughters of two former viceroys of India, as well as innumerable lords and ladies and knights commander of the British Empire, parked their umbrellas in the vestibule of St. James's, Picadilly, in central London. To the strains of organ music, they stuffed their dripping mackintoshes under the pews and settled down to listen. They were joined by a distinguished crowd of Oxford and Cambridge dons, journalists, ex–foreign officers, representatives of the Royal Geographical Society, the Iran Society, the Royal Asiatic Society, the Royal Society for Asian Affairs, the Council for the Advancement of Arab British Understanding, and assorted other institutions.

These were friends, admirers, and former colleagues who had gathered for a memorial service celebrating the life of the famous explorer and traveler Dame Freya Stark. On January 31, 1993, Dame Freya had reached the age of one hundred years. On May 11, in her beloved home of Asolo, in northeast Italy, she had died. From across the Atlantic, *The New York Times* announced the news in a magisterial obituary three columns long, pronouncing her a "consummate traveler." In Italy, where Latin exuberance could be expected, papers called her *la regina nomade,* the nomad queen.

In the months after her birthday, the English press had been celebrating the career of the "intrepid," the "legendary" Dame Freya, whom the writer Lawrence Durrell had declared a "poet of travel . . . one of the most remarkable women of our age," and *The Times* of London described as "the last of the Romantic Travellers."

When friends congregated in Asolo to bury her, they chose from the glittering array of medals she had been awarded the seal of Sister Commander of the Most Venerable Order of St. John of Jerusalem to place about her neck. This is the order that looks after travelers and pilgrims on their way to the Holy Land, and Freya had always told them, "I like to feel a pilgrim and mere sojourner in this world."

But such a comment was far too simple to explain the complex nature of Freya's wandering. Why, friends always wondered, did she seek remote and dangerous places, and above all, why did she want to go alone? What drove this audacious, exasperating, and admirable woman who was ultimately awarded with a knighthood by the queen of England? She had been exploring little-known regions of the Middle East since 1927, when she slipped through the military cordon surrounding the rebellious Druze in the mountains of Lebanon and was apprehended by the French authorities, nearly sparking an international incident. A few years later, living in Baghdad, she scandalized the British colonial community with her insistence on consorting with "wogs." In Persia she discovered a hitherto unknown fortress that had belonged to the ancient cult of the Assassins and nearly died in the attempt. But the book she wrote about it revived an interest in Islam's secret societies, and because she had also corrected His Majesty's Survey maps in both Persia and Luristan, she won the Royal Geographical Society's Back Grant for her cartographic accomplishments, the first of many honors to come.

By 1935, when the Royal Air Force was called to make a dramatic rescue in the desert after Freya had attempted to find a buried Arabian city, London was at her feet. And so was the British Foreign Office when she slipped into hostile northern Yemen in 1940 and undermined an Italian effort to make that isolated country a base for their aircraft. With her prodigious success in creating an anti-Axis propaganda network that stretched from Cairo to Baghdad during the war, Field Marshal Lord Wavell, at the time chief of Middle East Operations, credited Freya with reducing sabotage against the Allies on the eastern front. But when the British Ministry of Information sent her to the United States in 1943 to warn against the dangers involved in imposing a Zionist state on Palestine, the bruising reception she received deflated something in Freya's optimistic spirit, and friends knew she was not the same.

Freya wrote thirty books on her adventures, including four volumes of autobiography and eight of published letters, at a time when stupendous changes were taking place in the Middle East. They captured a magic world of harems and caravans slowly giving way to a harsher modern reality. Freya saw it all, probing the differences between East and West, and striving to bridge them with understanding and sympathy until she emerged as one of Britain's outstanding authorities on the region, admired and praised by men of influence. All her life she was almost feverish in her restless pursuit of Knowledge, relishing the dangers encountered along the way. She claimed that she found confronting danger a way of "passing through fear, to the absence of fear," always the essential ingredient for the truly adventurous.[1] In 1950 Vita Sackville-West, reviewing one of Freya's books, said: "I suspect you of being a born pirate, of being a born smuggler too, if life had cast you into a different century. . . . I am the sparrow watching your eagle; the mouse lying between the paws of your lion."[2]

It would seem that Freya's life propelled her from one adventure to the next, almost as if by accident. As opportunities arose, she seized them boldly, making the most of what was offered. In the beginning she did not have a specific goal, other than wanting to be a writer—and, above all, to be loved. Yet in the end love was the one thing at which she failed, despite a series of ardent attachments to men of talent, and she remained convinced that a damaging accident she suffered as a child had ruined her looks. Both her childhood and youth had been difficult, burdened with poverty and loss, and she emerged from those formative years voraciously needy, prepared to use others with all the dexterity and force of her powerful nature. Resilient, exuberant, and exceptionally charming, she nevertheless carved a life that was rich beyond what even she could have imagined and that, when all was said and done, was truly her greatest work of art.

Afflicted with periodic illnesses; struggling to find the money to pay for her extravagant taste in houses and clothes; courting and being courted by intellectuals, generals, politicians, and socialites, Freya inspired a whole generation of younger travel writers because she looked for the underlying truths in all she saw. Her style, poetic and sometimes even mystical, was stunningly original, and she left behind a body of work unequaled in its perceptions of the remote peoples who make up the Islamic world. Those seeking a better grasp of the special nature of Middle Eastern societies still find these travel classics invaluable. In the end, however, it may be not her travel books but her vast archive of vivacious, marvelously descriptive letters, alive with whatever mood and condition she found herself in, in whatever obscure corner of the world, that will stand longest as Freya's contribution to literature.

Freya never lost a rapturous sense that the earth and everything on it were marvelous. "The word ecstasy is always related to some sort of discovery," she once wrote, "a novelty to sense or spirit, and it is in search of this word that in love, in religion, in art or in travel, the adventurous are ready to face the unknown."[3]

This, then, is the story of a true romantic. Those who gathered in church that wet Tuesday in 1993 were bidding farewell to a woman of phenomenal determination and curiosity, who believed life could be sublime and drove herself to wander like a gypsy in order to make it so, her ecstatic gaze trained on the next horizon.

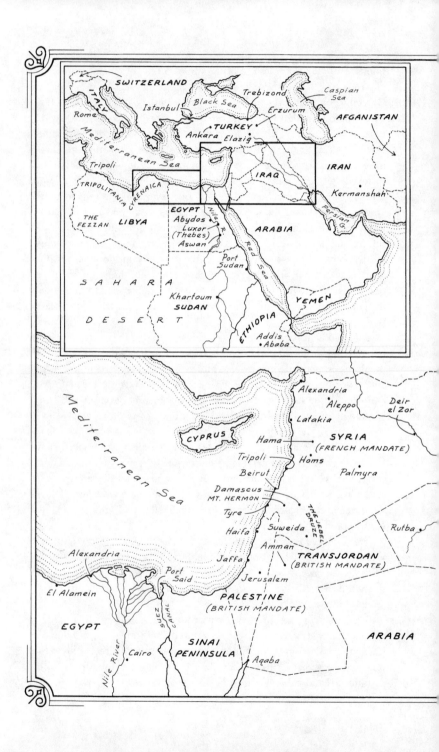

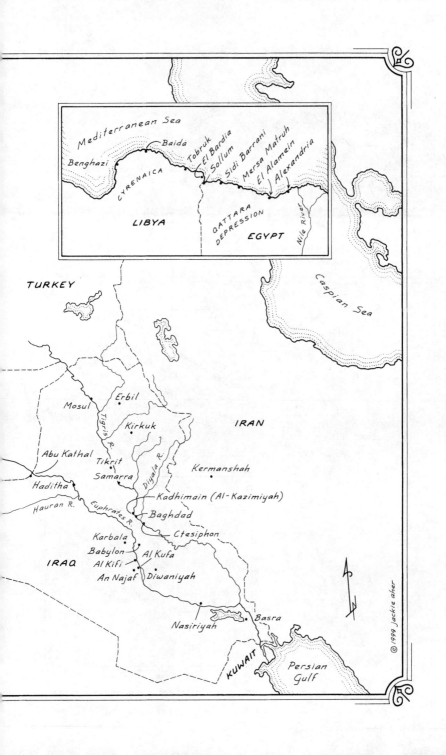

Mediterranean Sea

Baida
Benghazi
Tobruk
El Bardia
Sollum
Sidi Barrani
Mersa Matruh
El Alamein
Alexandria

CYRENAICA

LIBYA

QATTARA
DEPRESSION

EGYPT

Nile River

TURKEY

Caspian Sea

Mosul
Erbil

Tigris R.
Kirkuk

IRAN

Abu Kathal
Tikrit
Samarra

Diyala R.

Kermanshah

Haditha

Hauran R.
Euphrates R.
Kadhimain (Al-Kazimiyah)

Baghdad

Karbala
Ctesiphon

Babylon
Al Kufa

IRAQ
Al Kifi
An Najaf
Diwaniyah

Nasiriyah
Basra

KUWAIT
Persian
Gulf

© 1999 Jackie aher

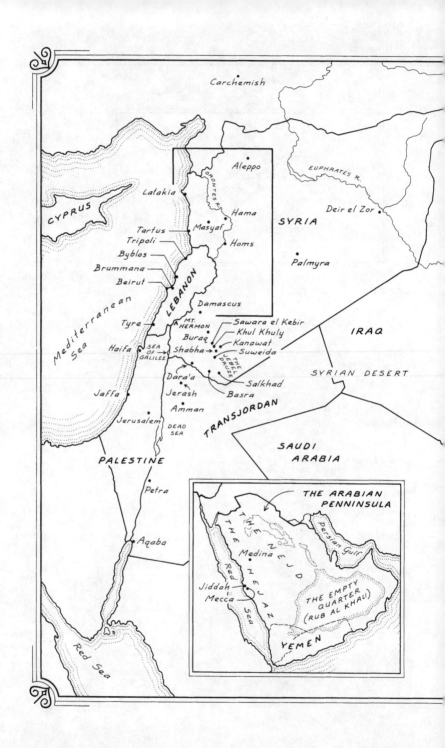

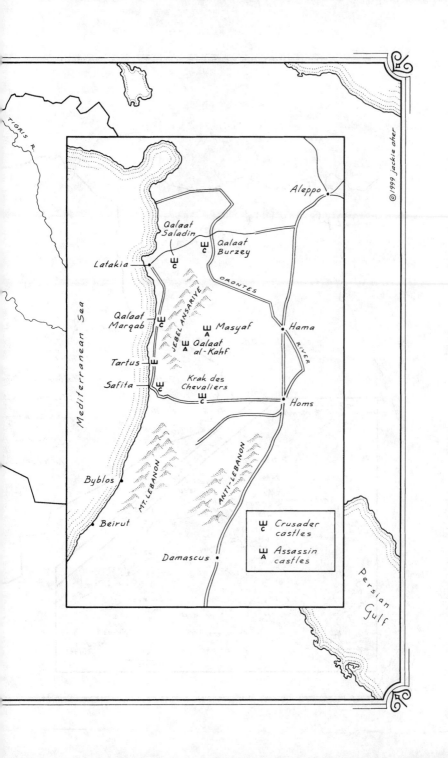

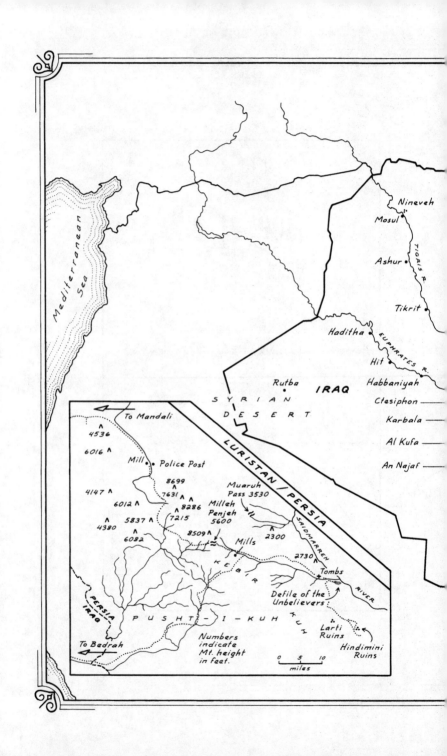

Harsin
7775
7800
9207
Gian
Nehavand
1210
Mianabad
7313
6100
6870
NEW MOTOR ROAD
Varazan
8204
Varazan
Pass
7060
7240
Darreh
Gizaru
ITTIWAND
NURALI
Qal'a
Kafrash
Gamasiab
Pass
Gatchenah
Valley
Beira
Numbers indicate
Mt. height in feet.
0   5   10
miles

NORTHWEST LURISTAN

Alishtar

Erbil

Kirkuk

Sulaimaniya

Samarra

DIYALA R.

Kermanshah
Nehavand
Arak

Mandali

Al
Kazimiyah
Baghdad
KEBIR KUH
Khorramabad
LURISTAN

PERSIA

Bedrah

Babylon
Dezful

SAIDMARREH R.

Diwaniyah

Uruk

Ur

Basra

Persian
Gulf

© 1999 jackie aher

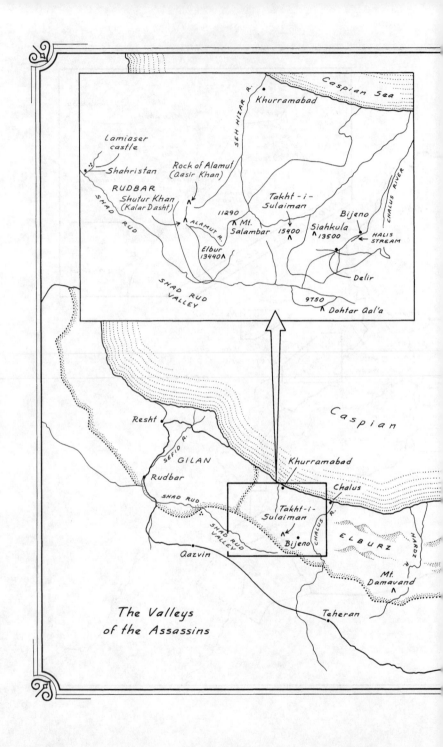

The Valleys
of the Assassins

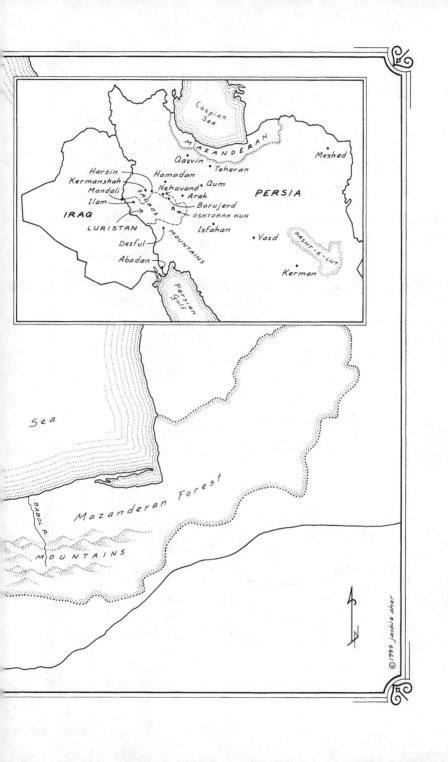

© 1999 jackie aher

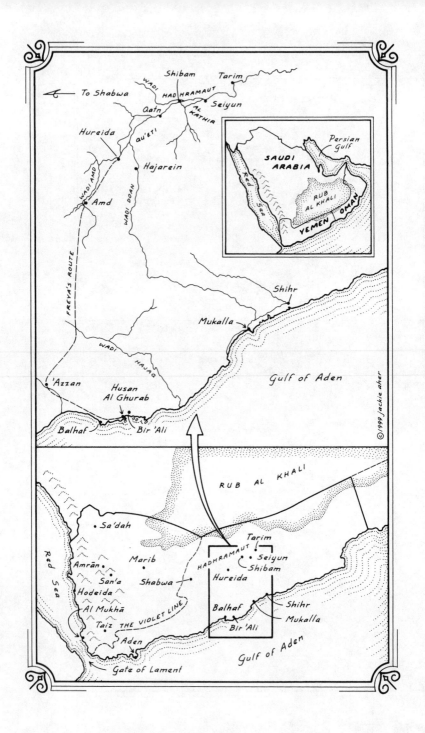

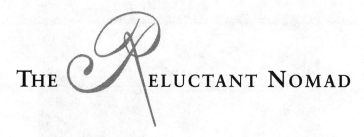

THE RELUCTANT NOMAD

*If one had to live in prison for many years, with nothing
to look at but the wild, a tuft of yellow grass perhaps with the
southwest wind moving through it, a clump or two of heather
and the sky, such a tiny view, so restricted and yet alive, would
mean more than any artist's masterpiece.*

—PERSEUS IN THE WIND

*The five reasons for travel
given me by Sayyid Abdullah,
the watchmaker:*

*To leave one's troubles behind one;
To earn a living;
To acquire learning;
To practice good manners;
And to meet honorable men.*

—A WINTER IN ARABIA

Freya at age twenty. From her earliest
years, books were her refuge.

CHAPTER ONE

The Beginning

> *The chief thing the traveller*
> *carries about with him*
> *is himself.*
>
> —PERSEUS IN THE WIND

hat I am, and why learning Arabic, is a mystery. If I say I do it for pleasure, there is a look of such incredulity that I begin to feel as self-conscious about it as if I were telling the most blatant lie," wrote Freya Stark to her mother as she shivered through the winter of 1927–28 in French-controlled Lebanon.[1]

Freya had arrived in the middle of December with a copy of Dante's *Inferno,* very little money, a revolver, and a fur coat. This last was to prove the most useful, for the weather was freezing. Immaculately polite and maintaining her good humor despite being wrapped from head to toe in woolens, she was just beginning to feel the throaty Arabic syllables slide more easily from her lips. She was thirty-four years old, stood scarcely five feet, one inch, in stocking feet, and was still extremely thin from a recent illness. Both the missionaries and the Arabs in the little mountain town where she had come to study agreed that she was perfectly charming. Few suspected that this appealing young person, so apparently unassuming, old-fashioned, even—they might have said—quaint, had a will of steel.

In November 1927, Freya had embarked on a cargo ship for Beirut, leaving behind what she had long concluded was an unacceptable life. "It is so wonderful to be away, really away; a new land opening out every morning," she exulted as the SS *Abbazia* tossed through the rough Mediterranean.[2] It did not matter that a cargo ship was all she could afford. She watched pigs, sugar, even once a Marconi telegraph machine being off-loaded between stops that grew more picturesque and unfamiliar with every passing day.

"We are now among islands in the Ionian Sea. Is not the very name an enchantment? The sea is quiet, the twilight falling. I asked the name of an island on the right. 'Ithaca,' says the Captain, as if the name were mere geography."[3]

She had sat in her deck chair, the relentless sirocco whipping the pages of her writing tablet, and felt that, at last, all the years of lonely study on her own, her determined efforts to make up for the schooling she had begged to have, which had been interrupted by the terrible Great War, no longer needed to be regretted so bitterly. It had been wrenching to slip out from under the attachments of family and embark on this journey. But if she had not gone when she did, she feared that she would never have got away, just as her sister Vera never did. Both had been prisoners to responsibilities they abhorred, but unlike Vera, Freya had refused to succumb. Instead, Freya had consoled herself by reading dazzling accounts of European explorers in the lands of the Arabs. One day, she had resolved, the world would hear of her "in the deserts of Arabia discovering buried cities."[4]

In 1920 Freya sensed a path quietly open. In April of that year everyone on the Italian Riviera was riveted by the events taking place at San Remo, only a few miles from Freya's home. The victorious Allies were gathering in that coastal town, and anyone who could tried to get a glimpse of the British prime minister, David Lloyd George, as he hurried back from and forth to meetings with Premier Georges Clemenceau of France. The purpose of the conference was to dispose of the sprawling territories of the defeated enemy, the Ottoman Empire. Because the United States refused to sign on to the League of Nations, the British and French were free to slice up the Middle East to their own imperial satisfaction. The Arab lands governed for over 467 years by the Grand Turk were to be "mandates" until such time as they "could stand on their own." Great Britain would supervise Mesopotamia, Transjordan, Palestine, and Egypt, while France would look after Greater Syria, including Lebanon. As for Persia, long the target of foreign influence, postwar turmoil would spark a coup against the old Qajar regime in 1921 and bring to prominence a Cossack Brigade commander, Reza Khan, who four years later would crown himself shah of a new Pahlavi dynasty.

Freya's heart had soared at the thought of visiting these regions. Like everyone else who had been revolted and depressed by the seemingly hopeless bloody trench warfare in Europe, she had raptly followed the successes of Colonel T. E. Lawrence in spearheading an Arab revolt against the Turks. It had been thrilling to imagine this young intelligence officer racing through the desert on camel-back in the company of hawk-eyed Bedouin warriors. But Lawrence was only the latest hero in the history of brilliant Eastern adventures, and Freya plunged avidly into its literature.

She began to consume all she could find about the early-nineteenth-century travelers. There was Johann Burckhardt, who disguised himself as a holy man and found the great Nabataean city of Petra before dying of plague in Cairo. Ulrich Seetzen located the lost ruins of Roman Jerash, mapped the Dead Sea, and was murdered by the imam of Yemen for being a spy for the czar. She read what she could get of the works of the great Orientalist Sir Richard Burton, famed for his search for the Nile and secret ventures into Mecca and Medina. Recently Freya had finished the vast and ponderous *Travels in Arabia Deserta* by Charles Montagu Doughty, who had died just one year before she herself sailed East. The lives of these explorers and the many others were filled with bold and daring deeds, and Freya read them with shining eyes. Since she was a child she had loved Kipling's tales of British imperial grandeur, and the story of Kim and the Red Lama had been her favorite book. That many of these Europeans had doubled as intelligence agents in the "great game" between their rival governments only intrigued her more. To Freya, the East seemed the most exotic place left on earth.

Many years later, when Freya herself was famous, she would insist that she had been drawn to the Orient because of "oil."[5] Certainly it was clear that modern industrialized nations would require limitless supplies of the substance. By 1908 large reserves had been discovered in southern Persia, and British interests had quickly formed the Anglo-Persian Oil Company. In 1913, as first lord of the admiralty, Winston Churchill had paid 2.2 million pounds for a controlling interest in the company to ensure a steady supply of fuel for the British Navy. Large quantities of oil were believed to lie beneath the deserts of Iraq and especially the independent peninsula of Arabia.

But whether it was oil or the sheer magnetism of the region that beckoned, it was clear that Europeans could travel more easily through the former Ottoman provinces now that the Great Powers had taken charge. Since 1920 Freya had sensed the lure of opportunity. Now a new zeal would be brought to the search for archaeological treasures, more surveys would be done and maps made, foreign customs studied, and the mandate governments would require administrators conversant with the languages of the region. Freya was an Englishwoman, despite a youth spent mostly in Italy, and she believed profoundly in the British Empire. The British more than any other colonial power, she was convinced, should be the messengers of enlightened governance, just as she believed peace and security along the routes to India were best guarded by a firm British hand. These were fluid times, with exciting changes in the wind, and surely there was a role for her.

So Freya had begun to study Arabic. Her family and friends had called it a "lunatic obsession" as she arranged for lessons with an old Capuchin monk who had lived for thirty years in Beirut before retiring to a monastery in San Remo. It was very inconvenient and cost her time from her farm duties, but Freya had been dedicated, walking an hour to the station several times a week to board a train to San Remo. "I studied Arabic with the hope that at some time it might lead me out of the endless Martha lane," she recalled many years later, referring to the biblical parable of Martha and Mary, "into some sort of fairyland of my own. But it was such a fragile hope, and so dear to me, that I never mentioned it to anyone."[6]

For seven years Freya bent over her Arabic verbs. At the beginning it was only a dream and an intellectual exercise that kept her mind alive in the stultifying existence she had endured with her overbearing mother. But she was unwavering, traveling up to London in 1926 to be tutored by an Egyptian. Then, in the spring of 1927, she had returned for classes at the London School of Oriental Studies. When some lucky investments paid off, she bought her ticket for Lebanon.

· · ·

The little village of Brummana was perched high in the hills over Beirut's graceful harbor, and Freya quickly learned it was pulsing with missionary zeal. Several Protestant groups had chosen it as an ideal spot in which to settle while they spread the gospel to the heathen. As had been arranged, Freya settled in with a Lebanese spinster, Mlle. Rose Audi, who fluttered about in high heels, the second-to-latest fashions from Paris, and wore her hair in a shingled bob. She was kind and attentive to her paying guest, although she seemed unable to do anything about the drafts that gusted through her icy house and kept the marble floors as cold as a tomb. On seeing that Freya was weak, and hearing that she had just recovered from a long bout of ulcers and an operation, Mlle. Audi did all she could to please, inviting to dinner some of the missionaries, whom she clearly felt were the appropriate companions for a young European.

The missionaries welcomed Freya. She asked good questions, listened intently to their answers, and explained herself, rather oddly, by saying that she had come to learn Arabic for pleasure. If her purpose struck them as whimsical, the new arrival was a lively participant in all discussions, especially those on local politics. When she joined eagerly in their favorite topic, speculation on the Hereafter, the missionaries' hearts grew even warmer. Her face was more intelligent than pretty, but her complexion was milky smooth, and her bright eyes seemed to miss nothing. Her smile was open and generous, breaking quickly into a grin that revealed two slightly crossed front teeth. She had a habit of arranging her hair rather peculiarly over one ear, and there were tiny scars around her right eye and temple. The kindly missionaries were too polite to ask questions, and a certain reserve in Freya's demeanor discouraged personal inquiries. Acutely aware of her status as a single woman, without money or important connections, Freya was at pains to be circumspect.

Initially, Freya was disposed to view the missionaries' work in a heroic light and relished all the theological talk. Soon, however, their earnest proselytizing grew tiresome, and she quickly realized that she must get on with her purpose for coming and not be swept up in a social whirl centering on the YWCA, Bible classes, and Meetings for Improving One's Mind. She engaged a young Syrian teacher named Salehmy, who fixed her with fiery eyes and, she said, spouted Arabic grammar "as if a cat were spitting."[7] Neither the missionaries and Mlle. Audi nor the Muslims in the little town could understand this curious passion for Arabic, and rumors circulated, to Freya's delight, that possibly Miss Stark was a spy.

Every day Freya went off by herself for a walk after her lessons, politely declining to attend prayers. After all, she had come to meet Arabs, not missionaries, and was touched by the patience the villagers showed her stumbling efforts to talk with them in Arabic. She was also eager to build up her strength; after her last operation her doctor in Italy had warned her that she probably would never be able to walk more than a mile or so. But Freya had always loved exercise, and the riskier and more strenuous, the better. Ever since her father carried her over the Dolomites in a basket when she was a baby, Freya had loved the great heights; when she was older she had climbed in the Alps. The chance to explore the rough cliffs behind Brummana delighted her, and it was also an opportunity to use the compass she had brought, in case someday, she thought dreamily, she needed to draw maps.

The shepherd boys, as astonished as everyone else at the sight of an Englishwoman hiking alone and jotting compass readings, stopped playing their pipes and stared until Freya hailed them with one of the fifteen or so ways of saying "Hello!" in the classical Arabic that she was trying to master. She marveled at cyclamen growing wild, the woods slippery with pine needles, the twisted and thorny limbs of terrabinth trees, and she was undeterred by the news that hyenas, jackals, and even panthers roamed the countryside. She wrote home that she had been cautioned against showing "too much sympathy" to hyenas, lest one "lure you into his cave and tickle you to death."[8]

Noticing that many of the stone houses were deserted, Freya listened sympathetically to stories of the famine that had decimated Greater Syria toward the end of the war. More than three hundred thousand souls had starved to death while survivors fought over garbage pails. When people died, friends removed their front doors and turned them into coffins. Freya was moved to see so many houses yawning open and empty.

If Brummana was merely poor, overlaid with a European veneer, and not the true East she was determined one day to find, Freya found it quite exotic enough as she wandered along its stone streets, noting pointed arches and stone columns from the days of the Crusades. There were new tastes like leban, hummus, and tahini to be enjoyed, and she loved the native costumes—fezzes, robes, striped pajamas, boots or pointed red leather shoes—and was impressed by the splendid mustaches, old baggy pants, and white turbans worn by the Druze men, members of a curious religious sect that intrigued her very much. The Druze women veiled their faces entirely in white, while the Maronite women merely tied black scarves over their hair. Both groups of women, she was assured, were in constant mourning for their menfolk killed in religious clashes.

Freya was fascinated by the ancient hatreds among Syria's many sects—religious, ethnic, and political fragmentations that the Ottoman pashas had ignored but that the new French colonial administration kept deliberately inflamed. The Muslim Sunnis enjoyed a time-honored tradition of persecuting the Muslim Shi'a, whom they regarded as heretics. Both Sunnis and Shi'a loathed the independent-minded Druze, while all three scorned the Alawites as underclass apostates.

The Christians were no better, Freya was learning. There was a long history of rivalry among the Eastern Orthodox, Greek, and Latin churches that in the past had provoked strong words among their protectors, Russia, Greece, and Rome. Much as these Christians despised one another, however, they loathed their fellow Christian Maronites more. The Maronites, arrogant in their claims of descent from the Phoenicians and having led the Crusaders to Jerusalem, were being championed by the newly arrived French. The Druze, who otherwise kept to themselves, viewed the Maronites as their most ancient enemies. As for the Protestants, like the Brummana missionaries, they were more or less seen as irrelevant except, perhaps, for the handful of American Protestants who, recognizing that it was better to inform than to convert, had founded the American University of Beirut, whose lights twinkled far below Brummana on the coast.

The rancor and immediacy with which ancient slights between religious groups were remembered—as if they had happened yesterday—were a revelation to Freya. Pulling her fur coat more tightly around her, she concluded that merely being cold was insignificant compared with living with murder and mayhem in one's heart. She was spurred to work even harder at the language so she could make an impartial way through this minefield.

"What I find trying," she wrote home, "in a country which you do not understand and where you cannot speak, is that you can never be *yourself*. You are English, or Christian, or Protestant, or anything but your individual you: and whatever you say or do is fitted to the label and burdened with whatever misdeeds (or good deeds) your predecessors may have committed. And then of course your sentences, intended with just the shade of meaning you desire, come out shorn of all accessories, quite useless for anything except the mere procuring of bread and butter."[9] How glad, she concluded, she would be when she could command Arabic so completely that she became a person and not a category.

In the meantime, Freya wrote another friend, "the East is getting a firm grip. What it is I don't know: not beauty, not poetry, none of the usual things . . . and yet I feel I want to spend years at it—not here, but further inland, where I hope to go as soon as I get enough Arabic for the absolutely necessary amount of conversation."[10]

· · ·

Now it was spring. The almond trees had bloomed, the days were longer, and the night cries of the jackals were replaced with the sound of villagers chatting as they gathered to enjoy blazing sunsets and warmer evenings. Over the winter Freya had established the pleasant pattern of afternoon saunters with a young English schoolmaster named Francis Edmunds. They had been introduced early on, and he had quickly taken to seeking her out. It was clear that he enjoyed her company as well as her trenchant responses to his embrace of the theories of Rudolf Steiner, founder of an educational movement that called itself anthroposophy. She wrote home, knowing how badly her mother wanted her to be married, that Mr. Edmunds was "a delightful young man with the merit of a nice profile and just about as incongruous here as I am." She added that she approved "his taste for ideas. . . . I do like people who have not yet made up their minds about everything, who in fact are still receiving."[11]

Mlle. Audi became positively giddy when Mr. Edmunds came for dinner and took to chastising Freya for having an insufficiently "tender heart" toward her guest. But privately Freya could feel her interest in the schoolmaster warming quickly. Often during her Arabic lessons her thoughts strayed back to some conversation they had enjoyed on a recent stroll. It was so stimulating, she thought, to be able to talk comfortably with a man on so many subjects. She confided that she was planning to go to Damascus, and he told her that he too wished to visit this great city, whose glorious past, as the former capital of the mighty Umayyad Empire, was the pride of the Arab people. Freya had already arranged to rent a room there with an Arab Christian family who lived by the Bab Tuma, or Thomas Gate, and now that the days were pleasant and her Arabic was sturdy enough to hold her, the time for her departure rapidly approached. She could have no idea how squalid her circumstances would turn out to be, nor especially could she know that her visit to Damascus would be the first step on the way to an astonishing career.

Damascus, Freya and Mr. Edmunds agreed, was essential to visit. Eight years previously Emir Faisal, the young Hashemite prince who had led the Arab Revolt, had attempted to set up his free Arab state in Damascus, which had long been the emotional center for Arab intellectuals looking for a grand national revival. During the war the British had promised his father, the sherif of Mecca, that they would back his claims to the title of caliph, or spiritual leader of Islam, if he would raise a Bedouin army against the Turks. The sherif, Hussein ibn Ali, a lineal descendant of the Prophet through the Hashemite clan, had been encouraged by the promises of British guns, gold, and expertise in support of the Arabs' cherished desire to be free from Ottoman rule. In 1916 the sherif sent two of his sons, Ali and Faisal, to the tomb of the Prophet's uncle Hamza, outside Medina, where they proclaimed Arab independence to fifteen thousand Arab recruits. Five days later the sherif himself stood beside another son, Abdullah, to announce that Mecca too was free. Constantly reassured by British officials and advised by Colonel Lawrence, who rode in their midst and taught them the use of explosives to blow up the Turkish railroad, the Arab irregulars swept north to join the British invasion forces led by General Edmund Allenby. Two years later they were pressing against the gates of Damascus, which surrendered on October 1, 1918. For the Arabs, reclaiming Damascus, the living symbol of past Arab greatness, was the triumphant first step in attaining their dream.

Those days after the war, when Arab nationalists, ex–Ottoman officials, and Bedouin soldiers had streamed into Damascus to help the young emir build his new Arab state, had seemed thrilling when Freya read the press accounts of them during the long hours of toil on her Italian flower farm. She had been stunned, as everyone else was, when a bare three months after the 1920 San Remo conference, the French general Henri Gouraud marched on Damascus, drove out Faisal's small Arab army, forced him into exile, and scattered the officials of the infant nation. It had seemed a shocking thing that the British government, after all their promises, stood by and did nothing. The press had reported at length on Lawrence's disillusionment, and later Freya would understand the extent of guilt experienced by a generation of talented British Arabists, who would spend their professional lives trying to reconcile British imperial interests with those of the Arabs whom their politicians at home had betrayed. But this knowledge, and so much else about the Arabs, was still in Freya's future.

For the moment Freya worked diligently to learn about Middle Eastern colonial politics. Through the winter months of 1928, she had listened intently to what people were saying about French policy in their new mandate. What she heard, she disapproved of heartily. And as she listened an idea began to form in her mind, one, she thought deliciously, that might even involve some personal risk. The French had established themselves at gunpoint, slicing off Lebanon from the rest of Syria and creating Alawite and Druze states to the north and south, on the theory of divide and rule. Scarcely two years before she had arrived, Druze chieftains, fed up with French discrimination in favor of their Maronite clients, had sparked a revolt against French rule that raced like brushfire through the country. The French had put it down ruthlessly. The Druze were now cordoned off in their mountain villages, and no one was allowed to enter. Why not, thought Freya to herself, slip through the cordon and interview these fiercely secretive people?

Freya's ambitions were somewhat inchoate, but she burned with the desire to know the region better. She had always wanted to write. Now could be her chance, if what she produced were good enough for publication. Heaven knew, Europe was intensely interested in what was happening in the mandated territories. Indeed the whole Middle East was going through major changes. The Fertile Crescent was a fertile subject.

When Freya whispered to Francis Edmunds that she thought it was possible to get past the French military into Druze country, he was horrified. It was a mad idea, he said, looking alarmed, which pleased her. It was much too dangerous, he insisted, not just because it was forbidden by the French but because the Druze themselves were well known to be hostile to outsiders.

Freya thought about it. But she packed her books, her clothes, and her revolver, and on March 14, 1928, boarded a ramshackle train for a ride that would take nine and a half hours, even though Damascus was less than one hundred miles from Beirut. Mr. Edmunds had promised that he would join her soon for a visit. Even so, she felt plenty of misgivings. It was not fear of the Druze that worried Freya, however. It was the awful thought that eventually, unless she could devise some alternative, she would have to return to Italy, to her domineering mother and that appalling life that had trapped her for so long.

CHAPTER TWO

A Nomadic Youth

> *The vision of death gives life and beauty to this world. . . .*
> *those are fortunate who see it early so that they may enjoy a*
> *sense of proportion for the remainder of their days.*
>
> —PERSEUS IN THE WIND

or years the person most admired, most heeded in Freya's life, whom she most yearned to imitate if she could not actually *be* her, was her mother, Flora Stark. Freya adored her tall, strikingly handsome, erratic parent. From her very earliest years she had looked up to her mother as the apotheosis of all that was virtuous and dazzling—to whom absolute submission had always been the price of safety. In this Freya was not alone. Flora exacted obedience from the people around her. She did not brook dissent. She was a born leader who could not resist an impulse to take charge, yet she led in such a way that those who followed often admired her greatly.

Everyone who met Flora Stark sensed her strength and vitality, and was caught in its magnetic pull. Nearly five feet, ten inches tall, with bold black eyebrows arching above flashing eyes and auburn curls encircling her lovely face, Freya's mother towered at the center of any company. She didn't need to be impatient, strongly creative, as talented a pianist as she was a painter, to attract attention. But she was those things, as well as imperious and unpredictable, and Robert Stark lost his heart from the moment he laid eyes on her.

Freya's father was quiet, slight of build, really no taller than his wife, and his enthrallment to his dynamic bride lasted for years. Small wonder that their first child, Freya, would also be captured by her mother's spell.

. . .

The story of the Starks began in 1878, when twenty-five-year-old Robert Stark knocked on the door of his uncle's villa in the Bellosguardo hills above Florence. This would be the first time he had ever met his aunt and uncle. His own family lived in Torquay, on the southwest coast of England, but Robert had been studying painting in Rome, and a summer break finally gave him the opportunity to visit his late father's brother, William Stark, a painter himself, and his four female cousins, who had all been reared in Italy. He must have been shocked to discover that Uncle William had recently died of rabies after being bitten by a mad dog. Robert found his German-born aunt, Madeleine Stark, and his cousins struggling with serious debts.

To Flora, however, the arrival of this well-to-do stranger must have seemed a stroke of immense good luck. She was probably as intrigued as he that they were first cousins; more important, however, he had money. She was only seventeen and did not relish an impoverished future. She married him that year and followed him north to his favorite part of the world, the solitary moors around Chagford, a little town on the edges of Dartmoor in Devon, England.

It was an unhappy match. Considering how temperamentally unsuited the two cousins were, as different as Latin sun and Saxon mist, it is curious that they shared anything so immediate as grandparents. The first Robert Stark, the father of their fathers, had been a leading figure in Torquay. This Robert Stark was a successful merchant who took issue with some of the tenets of the Church of England in the early 1800s and preached his dissenting theories to a loyal congregation in what is now the Torquay School of Art and Science. Perhaps the preacher had an overbearing personality, because both his sons, Robert and William, departed for a grand tour of Italy when they were young men, and William, who wanted to be a painter, never went back. Instead he spied a pretty girl riding in an open carriage on the Corso in Rome and fell in love.

The name of the girl, eventually Freya's grandmother, was Madeleine von Schmid. She was the daughter of a court artist from Aix-la-Chapelle whose family had fled the French Revolution. Although von Schmid was evidently talented, his income was small, and he had to send his intellectually inclined daughter to Rome to work as governess to an aristocratic

Roman family, the Rospigliosi, in whose grand palazzo Madeleine and William Stark were married.

This was the time of the Risorgimento, when the Hapsburgs' rule over northern Italy was ending, and in 1865, Florence, as the first capital of a united Kingdom of Italy, was attracting English, American, and German expatriates. Young William and Madeleine Stark joined a swelling throng of poets, artists, and writers like the Brownings, Trollopes, Thackerays, and Landors seeking a life in the vibrant city. The Starks decided to settle and begin a family in this lively crowd, many of whom they apparently knew. Even Franz Liszt came once as a guest and, seeing their daughter Flora at the piano, slipped onto the bench beside the little girl and accompanied her.

When Freya herself was a child, her grandmother Madeleine told her stories about those dazzling days before her husband's death brought poverty to the family and forced her into tutoring at a girls' school in Genoa. Freya remembered her grandmother always with a book in her hand, and she must have been a good teacher, for when Freya used to climb on her lap and nestle her head against her lacy bosom, Madeleine recounted the great classical tales that remained, Freya said, forever associated with her grandmother's warm person and the scent of her cologne. "The book of Genesis," Freya wrote in her autobiography, "myths of Greece, the Siegfried Sagas, the Seven Kings of Rome, Tasso, Dante, Goethe, came to me in this good way . . . modulated with the inflections of a voice that meant safety and kindness."[1]

Her grandmother, whom Freya called Grassig or Fatty, did not have the same warm relationship with her oldest daughter, Flora, who was not in the least intellectual, preferring bustle to solitary reading. The day would come when Flora Stark would admit to Freya that she did not like her mother, though tears flooded her eyes when she spoke of her dead painter father. Perhaps it was Madeleine's tendency to be mulish in doing what she liked rather than what her daughters advised, or the fact that Flora could never get her mother to hurry, or worse, that Madeleine had paid too little attention to her daughters when they were young. Whatever the cause, mother and daughter were not close. Yet by the time Flora and her sisters were all securely married, it was clear Madeleine was dependent on them. So the old lady was shuttled back and forth among the sisters on prolonged visits, unruffled by reproaches and unhurried no matter how late she was for a departing train. At the age of ninety-eight her eyesight finally failed and, no longer able to enjoy her books, she died.

Flora felt the same impatience with Robert's mother, but since she held the purse strings, Flora had no choice but to chafe in silence. Once, soon after arriving at the home of her mother-in-law, who was also her aunt, and whose house in Torquay was large, dark, and formal, Flora accidentally spilled a glass of red wine on the white tablecloth. The looks and silence that ensued were chilling, she told Freya years later. It was a hard introduction to an atmosphere very different from that of lighthearted Italy. Flora quickly decided that her English relatives were bourgeois, provincial, and uninteresting in the extreme. She could hardly wait to leave Torquay and, not much liking country life either, never adjusted to the lonely moors of Dartmoor that made Robert so happy. She prodded her husband to take her back to Italy or France, which he did frequently, as well as to various artists' colonies. "My parents treated Europe with extreme nonchalance as a place to move about in" was the way Freya put it,[2] but the truth seems more that they traveled to avoid confronting their differences.

At the beginning Flora and Robert, who were both talented, evidently thought of themselves as artists and were attracted to people who were similarly creative and slightly nonconformist. Hardly radicals, they might have been said to have been genteel bohemians. Flora occasionally smoked a cigarette, and she bought a bicycle and put on bloomers in order to ride it. Robert was well enough regarded to be invited to teach at the Kensington Art School in London, and his art was of such a quality that the Tate Gallery still possesses his sculpture of a rhinoceros. For a time they had a little house in St. John's Wood, London, where academics, artists, and intellectuals bonded against a philistine world. Flora flourished, at last in company she found congenial. She played the piano at the home of the English painter Sir Lawrence Alma-Tadema, and Edwin Bale, president of the Society of Watercolorists, painted her portrait, for she was widely admired for her beauty and flair. Later in her life a friend told Freya that Flora had once made such an entrance at a party, by wrapping peacock feathers around her emerald evening gown, that it was discussed for years.[3]

Robert, sadly, was not as easy in this vibrant social milieu as his wife. In fact, he was so reticent "you might forget he was there," according to friends.[4] He loved the outdoors and knew enough about trees and plants to be an excellent amateur horticulturalist. While Flora could never tell an oak from a maple, Robert lived surrounded by piles of seed catalogs and was forever planting specimen trees on the various properties he enjoyed developing in and around Chagford. He also had a passion for designing and building houses. Freya recalled that one of her earliest memories was being taken in her father's bicycle basket to the site of the latest house intended as their ultimate home, whose completion, she ruefully observed,

Flora Stark, Freya's mother, at age nineteen, a year after her marriage to her first cousin Robert Stark. This portrait was painted by Edwin Bale, a family friend and the president of the Society of Watercolorists, London.

Robert Stark at thirty-four, painted by Flora. Their common interest in art was not enough to bind their marriage.

Freya, right, was eager to please, while her sister, Vera, was often stubborn. Living an itinerant life, the girls were extremely close.

Robert Stark loved the soggy moors of Dartmoor and instilled in his daughters his pleasure in the outdoors.

Freya at age nine, her nose in a book, in a photograph taken at Asolo, probably by her godfather, Herbert Young, whom the girls often invited to join their games.

Ford Park, the last house built near Chagford by Robert Stark, and Freya's favorite home. An amateur botanist, Robert filled the grounds with rare plants, which flourish today.

Dronero, the northern Italian mountain town where Flora Stark brought her children when she left their father. A medieval bridge spans the river; nearby, the factory wheels that caused the accident still spin, producing rugs and carpets.

was "always yesterday or tomorrow" while the family waited in some dingy lodging for it to be made ready.[5]

In 1887, after nine years of roaming to satisfy Flora's yearning for something better than soggy Dartmoor, Robert and Flora settled in Paris to devote themselves seriously to painting at an atelier on the Left Bank. It must have been a fairly happy period, because Flora became pregnant. The child, a son, died before he was a year old. This loss, however, was quickly followed by another pregnancy. Perhaps the death of their first baby was the reason that Flora was so unprepared for Freya Madeleine Stark's premature arrival on January 31, 1893.[6] Perhaps she did not want to tempt fate by counting too much on a safe birth, but it would have been equally in character if Flora were simply too distracted to keep track of a baby's arrival. An enthusiast for projects rather than children, Flora would never be good at anticipating consequences, particularly the consequences of her own actions or their effects on those around her.

In any event Freya took everyone by surprise. There was no food, clothes, or equipment for the baby. Two bachelor friends and fellow artists—Herbert Young, an Australian, and Herbert Olivier, an Englishman—both of whom would play continuing roles in Freya's life, tramped through the snowy Paris streets to the Galeries Lafayette. They asked the help of a somewhat disapproving salesgirl to assemble a layette for a newborn that, they blushingly insisted, did not belong to them.[7]

Freya heard this story repeated many times by Mr. Young and Mr. Olivier while she was growing up. She also heard them describe how her mother was often late and how an anxious crowd would gather helplessly to watch the hungry baby howl for supper. Finally Flora would appear, tripping up the stairs, utterly indifferent to the concern she had generated. It seems that from the beginning Freya had to shout for her mother's attention, learning at the earliest stage of her life that the security of an attentive parent could not be taken for granted and that love, like nourishment and safety, was not necessarily easy to come by. Merely to survive, she evidently realized, she would have to make her wishes emphatically known.

· · ·

By the time Freya's sister, Vera, was born a little over a year later, the Starks had left Paris for Italy to live in a pretty medieval hilltown, Asolo, just ninety miles northwest of Venice. Asolo had been a favorite place for Robert, ever since he had been a student in Rome and Robert Browning's son Pen, who owned several houses there, showed him the town. Herbert Young was so taken with Asolo's special magic, he bought a villa, and

Flora loved being there because it meant she was not in Dartmoor. As for Freya, all her life Asolo would be the safe anchorage to which she knew she could return.

To the new parents, Asolo was as fine a place for babies as it was for artists, with its clean, pleasant breezes and a glorious view on a clear day all the way to the distant campanile of San Marco in Venice. Perched between snowcapped Monte Grappa and the Euganean Hills, wrapped by an ancient Roman wall, Asolo had twisting cobblestone streets, arcaded passages, and flower-decked balconies that had not changed since the Renaissance, except to take on a patina of age.

Although Asolo was extraordinarily peaceful and the Starks enjoyed the painting and picnics and badminton on Herbert Young's lawn, and although more friends came to enrich the growing colony, the young family inexplicably picked up once more and moved on after a year or so. Robert returned to supervise his building projects in Chagford, Flora took the children to her mother in Genoa, they all went to St. Ives on the English coast for the Starks to play golf, reconvened on Dartmoor, and then were off again to try some other place. Their nomadic pattern never changed.

If much of Freya's childhood seems to have been spent watching adults pack and unpack or being hoisted in and out of railway cars, at least her parents' presence guaranteed some sort of stability. Yet she obviously feared that one day she might lose her grip on the adult hand pulling her along. Once the family was visiting Robert's mother, a rather vague figure in Freya's memoirs, "a faded little flame" in muffled black taffeta surrounded by Victorian bric-a-brac whom she never knew very well. Freya was about four at the time. She asked the nurse putting her to bed if her mother would live forever.

"No," said the nurse. "Not forever; but for a long time."

"How long?" Freya wanted to know. "A thousand years?"

"No," said the nurse. "Not a thousand years."

That night when her parents went up to bed, they found Freya on the landing, half asleep and still sobbing, where she had curled up to be closer to those precious anchors who might die at any moment and certainly before they had seen a thousand years.[8]

Later in her long career the twin subjects of fear and death often emerged as themes in Freya's writing. And perhaps by trying to face them as she did, through her courageous travel, she succeeded in vanquishing them. As she once wrote in an essay, death was really "Separation," and the fear of death was nothing more than a "reluctance . . . to depart from familiar things."[9]

. . .

"Our wandering life made us precocious and pretty tough," admitted Freya in her memoirs, describing the kinds of naughtiness children might get into when left to their own devices. At the age of four, perhaps to get attention, or because she was already feeling the traveler's call, Freya flung a mackintosh over her arm one morning, lifted the gate latch, and strode out from the house near Chagford, headed for a life at sea. With her toothbrush and a penny in her pocket, she walked down the road toward Plymouth. She recalled in *Traveller's Prelude* that as she drew farther from home the road seemed very long and the course on which she had embarked rather lonely. It was a relief that the postman saw her and took her hand to return her to a rather surprised group on the lawn. Even so, she wrote, that first "moment of emancipation still holds that delight, of the whole world coming to meet you like a wave."[10]

In time her mother engaged a succession of governesses to follow the family on their peregrinations, but none of them could offer much more than a smattering of mathematics and instruction in various languages—so probably their companionship was more important than their pedagogy. Freya, with her quick intelligence and ardent curiosity, thirsted for a proper schooling all through her childhood but mostly had to teach herself. She and Vera began reading very early and loved to dress up as the heroines in the stories of Ivanhoe or King Arthur's Round Table. Freya usually initiated the games and wanted to lead them, which occasionally provoked rebellious refusal on her sister's part. Nevertheless the girls were devoted and extremely loyal to each other. Vera did not lose her temper or argue as Freya did but simply dug in stubbornly and endured. Once, Freya said, Vera sat in her chair for twelve hours rather than apologize for some infraction for which she felt she had been unjustly punished.[11]

Freya, by contrast, yearned for approval, a craving she never lost and one that doubtless added fuel to her extraordinary charm. She was deeply unhappy when her parents or their generally indulgent friends withdrew their smiles, and she worked hard to get reinstated in their favor. One time she was sent to the corner for pulling an inviting bit of torn wallpaper off the wall. Instead of staying in the corner and sulking, as Vera would have done, Freya kept drifting away ("People are always remaining in unnecessary corners," she observed later) until finally her father could not resist her winsome manner and brought his painting stool to keep her company. Freya remembered thinking with delight that now they were *both* in the corner.[12]

Even so, the young Freya could boil over in quick rages. When she was quite little and her father beat her at chess, she buried his red queen in the garden. One of the rare times she was whipped with a birch switch was for trying to poke her mother with an umbrella. A letter from her father written in 1931 from Canada makes an affectionate reference to her once having hurled an inkpot. "I'm glad I'm 7,000 miles away," he wrote, adding that if his dog Betty had been around, she would have learned, as had others in the family, "what it was like to have books thrown at them."[13] One suspects that all her life Freya carried some degree of rage, having internalized the tension in her parents' house and always possessing a fear that she might be lost or abandoned in the terrible fire of their disagreements.

• • •

In the Stark household Flora ruled over domestic affairs with absolute authority. Her children, like the maids, and probably also her husband, coming from outdoors or the warm kitchen, crossed into Flora's living room with diffidence. Freya recalled, "To us she was remote, but still came like a vision in the evening to lie on our bed and tell us a story before she went to dine. In the daytime we saw her always with a background of groups of people sitting on chairs, drinking tea on the beach, with flounced parasols and immense hats; and we tried to slink by unperceived so as to escape the social duty of shaking hands with strangers."[14]

All through Freya's childhood and youth, she regarded Flora as an exalted paragon, and the prospect of entering her mother's realm gave her, she remembered, "a sort of temple feeling."[15] Vera, however, did not share these exaggerated feelings and later became estranged from their mother. Yet Flora seems to have remained utterly unconscious of the admiration she stirred in her older daughter's heart and of the child's desire to protect her. Instead, Flora exploited Freya's willingness to do her bidding, oblivious of her emotional needs, taking for granted that she would be obeyed.

Their shy father was more relaxing company. Robert Stark clearly wanted his daughters to love nature, especially Dartmoor, "the oldest rock in England," as he did. He taught them to identify birds, listen to the songs of crickets and tree frogs, and not be repelled by slimy things like salamanders. Freya's gift for capturing in her prose a sense of nature and landscape obviously derived from this early training. From her father, who in some ways treated her like a son, she acquired a traditionally masculine sense of land contours and geology as well as an alert eye for different kinds of vegetation—talents that later surprised the men at the Royal Geographical Society and the generals with whom she talked strategy in the Second World War. Robert also encouraged his daughters not to cry when they were hurt, unlike Italian children, who, Freya ruefully noted, would be scooped up immediately and petted. Robert wanted his girls to be brave; indeed both parents placed a strong emphasis on stoicism. Freya later wrote,

> He bribed us with double pocket money (twopence a week instead of a penny) if we walked across the pine wood to the far fence and back in the dusk alone. The wood was full of brambly hollows into which the evening slid. At the fence, before turning, I looked out into the bishop's part, and saw the deer grazing in open security and peace in the last yellow rays of the sun, and pulled myself together to return through the gathering darkness of the pines. The shadows seemed to settle between my shoulders. I dared not look round, or even walk quickly, for panic was ready there to pounce. I went very carefully and stiffly, till safety and the little gate in the fence were close in sight, and then I ran with all the Eumenides behind me, and clicked the latch upon the outer world of Fear.[16]

In due course Freya's courage and endurance would be cruelly tested.

Freya always regarded this brief period of relatively normal childhood—normal despite its vagabond aspects—with gratitude and affection for her father. Later, during years of suffering, she idealized him, turning him into a figure quite different from the absent phantom he was. She persuaded herself that she resembled him, not only physically in being short but also temperamentally, in his love of nature and athleticism; in fact, there was much more of the imperious and mercurial of her mother in Freya than she ever acknowledged. Of her father, she said, whenever she and her sister were tired, "there was always a big, very gentle hand—the veins knotted all over its outer surface and brown with constant living out of doors." Recalling those sweet days and the man who soon faded from their lives, Freya wrote, "All the feeling which my father could not put into words was in his hand—any dog, child or horse would recognize the kindness in it."[17]

Unhappily, however, Robert Stark had a serious shortcoming. He was stingy. Not about such things as the necessity of a pair of stout boots or a horse's bridle but about delights that meant nothing to him, such as a new dress, or hat, or pretty set of china. Freya learned her lessons well and in the future was always very careful with money herself, although she never abandoned her delight in clothes or pretty china, or especially hats. As a child, however, she could not have guessed that her parents' altercations would set off a disastrous train of events.

. . .

In the summer of 1948, Freya sat at her desk in Asolo. "My mother," she scribbled, was "so improbable. If I don't explain, it looks very louche, and if I do it is rather brutal."[18]

Freya was famous then and had begun to write her autobiography. She was wrestling with the problem of how to explain the extraordinary decision her mother took, when she was ten and Vera nine, to leave her husband and go into business with an Italian count. Flora, she was insisting to her readers, was both sexually ignorant and unaware in the way of so many women of that very Victorian era. Freya was positive that her mother was "extremely un-sexual," despite the scandal she was to create. "Men admired," said Freya, "but I never saw them fall in love with her."[19]

Be that as it may, when Flora Stark abruptly left her husband to join Count Mario di Roascio in Dronero, Italy, most people believed the liaison was sexual. Even the tolerant artists of St. John's Wood were shocked. Most found it impossible to believe that stunning Flora would have undertaken such a radical step had she not been under the influence of sexual passion. Only her girls had witnessed the freezing exchanges between their parents or caught their mother attacking a piece of sewing afterward with a face darkened in fury and understood they had been fighting again.

The twenty-three-year-old Italian nobleman who sparked the disaster was introduced to the Starks when he was on a visit to London. His arrival seemed innocent enough, and Robert apparently liked him, although the children, showing singular clairvoyance, did not. The young count was blunt in manner and boastingly self-confident, the exact opposite of their father. He hummed with ideas for providing employment to the people of Dronero, the provincial seat of his family. He must have been able to impress his listeners, for later Lucy Beach, an American who bought a house in Asolo and knew him slightly, said that she too was struck by what a clearheaded businessman he appeared to be and appreciated his sensible suggestions for widening the distribution of locally made silks from an atelier she was funding.[20]

When they first met, Robert invited di Roascio to Chagford and took him on walks over the moor, while in the evening Flora listened with rapt attention to his plans for converting a factory run by Catholic priests into a large-scale coir rug and basket operation. The order had started the factory to give employment to the local handicapped; the count envisioned a profitable as well as philanthropic enterprise. Listening to Mario's thrilling rhetoric of noblesse oblige and his vision of bringing prosperity to his region, Flora was magnetized. And so evidently was the count.

Robert, whatever his differences with Flora, had apparently been faithful to her, and now he must have sensed the seductive pull of the Italian on his wife. He must have been at least a little jealous. Freya never commented on this, but she did mention that her father offered to teach Mario how to box. One is left to imagine the two men squaring off, their jackets thrown on the grass as they circled and sparred. Perhaps Robert succeeded in landing a punch or two on Mario's bleeding nose, but it was Robert, ultimately, who lost the fight for his wife and children.

When Flora took an apartment for herself and the girls in the Dolomites, at Belluno, the following summer, Mario took rooms nearby for several weeks. It was probably there that she made her secret bargain. Without telling her husband, Flora lent Mario sixteen hundred pounds to buy the factory. It was not clear where she obtained this money. Possibly it was household funds that Robert had given her to pay for the holiday or money she had secretly saved. In any event, she and the count agreed that she would have one-third ownership of the new business, would work with Mario at least six months out of the year, and in due course, when the factory was making a profit, he was to repay her.[21] When Robert discovered that she had put his money into the factory, he was enraged. But by that time it was too late.

Sometime in the late winter or early spring of 1903, depositing her daughters with Robert's mother in Torquay, Flora left England. It is not clear if she meant the move to be permanent, but it was. She rented an old villa in Dronero rather incredibly named La Mal Pensa or "The Ill-Thought-Of," which exactly described the local townspeople's attitude toward this eccentric Englishwoman. Mario's own family also made it plain they wanted nothing to do with her.

In late spring Flora sent for the girls. Believing it to be just another Italian holiday, they said good-bye to their ponies, the dogs and ducks, and their Manx cat, and traveled down with their governess to this remote, poor, snowbound Italian town. It would be sixteen years, after the First World War, before Freya escaped, but Dronero would be Vera's prison for the remainder of her tragically short life.

It is easy to see how Flora might have been swept away by dreams of earning money of her own. Her marriage was unhappy and unfulfilling; her husband had given up art for country squireship. He disliked the city life that she enjoyed, and she had long resented her dependency on his tightfisted control of money. Ironically, although Flora despised his complacent, conventional-minded relatives, the year after the breakup Robert's mother died and left him a tidy inheritance, which might have eased the couple's financial situation had it come in time.

In Dronero the children felt their ostracism from the first. Freya wrote,

The worst things were said about [my mother] and they filled our growing years with a shame, discomfort and agony which no one who has not been a child, dimly suffering and only half understanding, can ever realize. My mother, however, went on serenely, devoting herself with extraordinary contentment to those mats of woven or brush coco fibre which are, incidentally, among the most ugly carpets in the world. Filled with affection and happiness herself, she never noticed that all our lives were heaping themselves in little ruins about her.[22]

· · ·

For a time Flora kept a cook and a maidservant, but eventually they had to be let go, along with the children's governess, to whom the girls were devoted. Their lives had abruptly changed for the worse. Every morning the girls were required to clean the oil lamps and dust the house, while Flora left early for the factory and did not reappear until evening. Every night Mario joined them for dinner, and he and Flora talked endlessly of new designs and dyes while the girls simmered with resentment that this strutting foreigner took almost all their mother's time. When the last underpaid maid quit, the girls had to work even harder. They had no friends. They were snubbed by the town, although the French nuns, in the convent school where they went for a few hours each day, were kind. Freya happily devoured Racine and diligently worked on French grammar.

Even today Dronero is a rather grim town in the Piedmont, shadowed by mountains, clinging to its site over the gorge carved by the Maira Torrente as it thunders down out of the Alpi Marittime. When Freya was a girl there was only one bridge, a crenellated arch built during the long-vanished prosperity of the fifteenth century and called il Ponte del Diavolo, or "Devil's Bridge." A tributary from the river snakes off to the opposite bank, and in this churning stream turbines still power the factory where Flora was to work for twenty-five years.

Heedless of the loneliness of her daughters, Flora was energized by her new project. In Dronero she could dispense well-bred compassion on simple mountain people who, she wrote in a memoir during World War II, were "not handsome, rather short and thickset, with disfiguring cases of goitre," but who gave her their respect while she gave them employment. Providing local work for young people who previously had gone as far as Nice and Monte Carlo to be a kitchen maid or plate washer, "and too often returned depraved in morals and diseased in body," said Flora,[23] was the outlet for an idealistic streak in her nature as well as for her enormous energy. She was apparently almost indifferent to having her money returned, even after it ultimately became a bitterly contentious issue between Freya and Mario that dragged on for years. Although Flora made barely enough salary to survive, it was as if the experience of working and not the factory's potential for profit was what excited her. Possibly also, in her own way, Flora was in love with the count and did not want to jeopardize his enterprise by insisting on being repaid.

At least once Robert came down to Dronero, which he surely would not have done if Flora were openly having an affair with another man, a man nineteen years younger than his wife. But the tension between the Starks was electric. One afternoon, turning the corner, Freya saw her parents in intense conversation. Suddenly Flora picked up a flowerpot and threw it violently. There was no talk of divorce, but Robert would have nothing to do with the factory and returned home. After this, no money came from England to help them out until much later.

The girls gave secret names to the factory. Behind Flora's back, Vera whispered they should call it the Pedestal because "Mama worships it." Freya, more intellectual, called it Moloch after the Semitic god who required the sacrifice of children.[24] Both girls, who had their mother to themselves only on Sunday mornings, swore they would avoid all philanthropic activities when they grew up.

The winters were freezing, and they could scarcely pay for fuel. They could afford a fire and a hot bath only once a week. From a life of servants, pets, and visitors, they had fallen into living on a weekly budget of ten pounds. Their maternal grandmother and one or two friends came to help out, but Mario quickly drove them away with his overbearing personality, which Freya described as "short, bouncy and dictatorial." She came to loathe him, blaming Mario for all the catastrophes that befell her sister and herself, and in her memoirs dismissed him savagely as "a cock on a dung heap," crowing incessantly about himself.[25]

The loyal family friend Herbert Young evidently agreed, a discovery that pleased the girls greatly when he came over from Asolo for a visit. Touched by their plight and realizing how lonely they were, he sat with them for hours reading aloud Sir Walter Scott's novels, which Freya adored. The more romantic the book, the more she loved it. Mr. Young also gave Freya a copy of Shakespeare's works, which she pronounced "very well written," and the grown-ups laughed. Starved for proper schooling, Freya fell eagerly on the occasional books sent by friends: the stories of Kipling, Edward FitzGerald's *Rubaiyat of Omar Khayyam,* poetry by Keats, Wordsworth, Shelley, and Byron, long passages of which she committed to memory and astonished friends years later by reciting at length. In this strange exile Freya imagined Ozymandian ruins, where "the lone and level sands stretch far away," or Sennacherib coming "down like the wolf on the fold, his cohorts . . . gleaming in purple and gold." Young as she was, she was deeply affected by these Orientalist glamorizations, and they became a part of her forever. Someday, somehow, she wanted to find herself on the Golden Road to Samarkand.

Despite the fact that Flora never once suggested that she was sorry for having jerked the girls away from their father and their pleasant life in Devon, Freya continued to adore her mother. As far as Freya was concerned, Flora was still a vibrant, beautiful, profoundly admired if distant figure, who now stood as their sole bulwark and protector. Freya resolved to do all she could to help make her hardworking, exhausted mother's life easier—even if in some secret part of herself she could not forgive her.

. . .

One day in 1905, shortly before Freya's thirteenth birthday, the girls were taken to see new machinery that had just been installed in the factory. Mario and their mother had been discussing the renovation of the works for months, and now at last Freya and Vera were to see how it looked.

At this time both sisters had thick chestnut locks that fell almost to their knees. They were proud of their hair and took turns arranging it, sometimes twisting it up in a bun, adorning it with ribbons, or just letting it flow down their backs. On this particular day, Freya's hair was loose.

Mario, dressed as usual in a dark suit, led the way to the back of the factory, where the gleaming steel hummed and spun, generating a current of air that lifted the women's skirts and blew their scarves against their faces. Impatient to see how the system worked, Freya stepped too close. A sudden gust of wind blew her hair against one of the great steel wheels. She was caught and yanked violently toward the ceiling. Her body whipped out horizontally, and her feet struck a pillar at each revolution of the wheel. Probably it was only seconds, but Freya remembered feeling as if it had been hours before Mario wrenched her free. Someone ran to pull the switch, but Mario did not wait. Instead he grabbed her legs and literally tore her out, leaving a long shank of hair dangling from the wheel.

They laid her on a mattress. She was bleeding profusely and in dreadful pain. Half her scalp was ripped off, including her right ear; the right eyelid was pulled away; and all the tissue around her temple exposed. A doctor was sent for, but Freya was only dimly aware of the shouts and confusion. Her clearest memory was the look of panic in her mother's eyes.

. . .

In the days that followed Freya nearly died. She was taken to Turin, the nearest major city, and placed in the care of a specialist who attempted grafts using a donor's skin. Her body rejected the graft, and, since this was before antibiotics or blood transfusions were available, she grew rapidly weaker. By good luck, however, a young doctor from Dronero heard of her case and suggested a novel approach. He managed to have her transferred to the main hospital in Turin, where in an operation without anesthetic he removed the skin from her thighs and grafted it to her head. A net was laid over the newly applied tissue so that the wounds could be dressed without disturbing the graft. Although the agony of her flayed thighs was almost unbearable, Freya gradually began to heal.

Her ordeal in the hospital lasted four months. Again and again she would awaken from fitful slumber and, as if it were a miracle, she would find her mother waiting at her bedside. Vera came, solemn and quiet, although it was two months before Freya saw her father. Could it be that Flora did not tell him what had happened? Was she too afraid of what he would say when he heard? Whatever the explanation for his long delay, when Robert Stark did arrive he sat wordlessly for hours at a time. Freya remembered him patting her on her shoulder until the spot became sore, but she knew it was out of affection and said nothing.

Friends sent gifts and cheering letters. One of the gifts was an atlas that Freya pored over, staring at the brightly colored maps: England pink, Italy blue, and great empty patches as yet uncharted. She closed her eyes and dreamed of distant possibilities. She felt, she later said, a certain detachment from all the emotion surrounding her, as if she were merely an observer of events somehow outside herself. She tried hard to be true to the stoic ethic that her parents had stressed, saying when people later asked why she undertook her difficult journeys that she sought the mastery obtained by "the disregard of hardships. The essence is whether they are voluntary or involuntary. To be given a cold bath is not a merit in itself; to take one voluntarily is quite a different matter."[26]

. . .

A magnificent and surprising reward followed the accident. For the first time in her life, Freya found herself the absolute center of her mother's attention. Flora was at her daughter's side constantly—absenting herself only when Robert visited. Freya's beautiful, idealized, distracted, and unpredictable mother, whose affection meant so much but who had so seldom been available, now suddenly belonged—or so it seemed—

exclusively to her. "I can still feel the warmth and delight of my mother's presence," she wrote in her memoirs. "She now devoted herself to me and I *discovered* her as it were. Her love, which now became greater for me than for Vera, probably dates from this time when I was nearly lost."[27]

It was almost a love affair, the near worship of Freya for Flora, who made lacy caps to hide her daughter's scarred head and hurried to bring her soothing drinks. Ultimately Freya would need to break free from that primary bond, but for many years her mother was the person for whom she was prepared to do anything.

Vera, left, and Freya on a 1913 picnic in Chagford, shortly before Vera married Count Mario di Roascio. This photograph was taken by Dorothy Waller, whose family lived near Ford Park. Freya stayed close to the Wallers and visited frequently over the years after Robert Stark left for Canada.

William Paton Ker, Freya's adored professor, who made her an honorary godchild and helped with expenses so that she could escape her labors at La Mortola and go mountaineering.

CHAPTER THREE

A Long Siege

> *The whole human endeavour is to keep intact at least the*
> *outward adornments of that first visitation [of love]:*
> *like the riderless horse, or the empty armour,*
> *they are borne through the slow funeral procession*
> *of the life that follows Love when it departs.*
>
> —PERSEUS IN THE WIND

f in 1914 talk in the cafés was about the tangle
of antagonisms in the Balkans or the recent defeat of the Bulgarians
in that region's second ugly war in two years, or about jingoist excess
and intractable ethnic divisions, still no one had the faintest notion
of the magnitude of the disaster waiting to happen. No one knew
that a young Bosnian revolutionary acting for Serbia's clandestine
Black Hand Society would assassinate the Austrian archduke and
plunge the world into war. Indeed, at this time when the tiny Balkan
states were doing their death dance and the imperial powers emitted
Olympian growls, Freya was preoccupied with other thoughts.

In the spring of 1911 she had succeeded in matriculating at Bedford College, London, a real school at last after the grim years in
Dronero. She had been mired there, working as the factory's book-
keeper, but she agitated tirelessly for a chance for proper schooling.
She had wanted to attend the University of Grenoble, but her father,
declaring her "too foreign" already, was willing to pay tuition only

at an English school. Now she had been enrolled for a year and a half, and it was her twenty-first birthday. Her mother sent her a dressing case of Moroccan leather, and her mother's friend Viva Jeyes, with whom she was living in St. John's Wood, gave her a party.

"How can I tell you my own mother how I think of you?" she wrote to Flora in Dronero. "I love you—only that you are like the blue air I live by—all to me that is best and sweetest, so that when I see a lovely sky, or picture, or flower, or anything beautiful and good I think of my dear one. . . . I think my soul came to me quite suddenly, when I was about eleven years old," she wrote, referring, possibly unconsciously, to the attention she was given by her mother after the accident. "And all at once I realized how precious you were to me—since then have we not been growing nearer and nearer? When we go to the next world I hope St. Peter will not know which is which."[1]

Freya's effusive loyalty to her mother was still unwavering. Even so, in the last few years a tiny crack had appeared in her childhood conviction that her mother was perfect. Some irrevocable decisions had been made that shattered any lingering hopes her family might be reunited. In 1912 her father had left England to begin a new life as a commercial flower farmer in Creston, British Columbia. More incredible, the previous year Vera had married Mario di Roascio.

. . .

In 1910 Flora had moved herself and the girls into Mario's house. Freya was seventeen, and although a bit self-conscious about her damaged looks, she had learned to pull her hair over her brow and secure it with a ribbon or pretty bandeau. Destined to be small like her father, she had exceptionally beautiful skin and a narrow, quizzical face given to quick changes of mood. An unusual, melodious, almost singsong quality in her voice, much remarked on in later years, was already evident. As a friend would say, Freya possessed the gift of "a voice for poetry, a voice that understood the beauty of words."[2] It was pleasant to listen to its mellifluous rise and fall, and clearly her voice, together with her laughter and intelligence, brought Mario suddenly to find young Freya very appealing. Because she also had at this time a dutiful attitude to housework and bookkeeping, Mario's interest grew keen.

Although Freya never suggested that there was anything more sinister in Mario's behavior than his possessiveness and egotism, the household must have been fraught with sexual possibility as the girls matured. Mario, then thirty, chased away not only any occasional young man attempting to call but female friends as well. As the reigning male authority in their lives, he had an extraordinary advantage, and in due course Freya realized that Mario was behaving toward her as a suitor. At first she believed that Mario's attentions had been sanctioned, even possibly suggested, by her mother.

Terribly innocent, her only education in sex having come by whispered comments from the girls in the convent and her efforts to extrapolate from close readings of Darwin's *On the Origin of Species,* Freya did her best to see the only man on their lonely horizon as a lover. She accepted a gold ring from Mario, but, anxious to know her mother's views, she sought and finally found an opportunity to bring the subject up. To Freya's amazement, Flora protested that she knew nothing of Mario's intentions. It seems that Flora had been as blind to the romance taking place under her nose as she had been to all other emotional subtleties in her family. Having discovered that her mother did not care one way or the other if she married him, Freya turned Mario down as politely as possible, thus slipping away from a potentially explosive role as her mother's rival. Soon thereafter she left for London.

Vera was not so fortunate. Lacking her sister's determination to get what she wanted, and denied the sculpture lessons she desperately begged for because neither her father nor Mario would pay for them, Vera stayed at home. Turning eighteen, she found it was her turn to receive Mario's attentions. Eventually he proposed, and she accepted with resignation. "I hope that I shall be a good friend to him," she wrote Freya of her news. "I hope I shall grow bright enough never to let him get bored with me."[3]

At least, Freya thought, her sister would find a measure of happiness as the wife of a nobleman, but she could not help sorrowing that Vera had been caught in the trap Freya herself had escaped. Sure enough, in 1911, when she went to Dronero at Easter time, just before the wedding, Freya found her sister sunk in misery. Vera had been disappointed that the family's last house in Devon, Ford Park, had been sold so she could not have her dream of a wedding in England and instead would be married in the austere Dronero cathedral. Herbert Young had refused Flora's request to use his Asolo villa, so appalled was he at the thought of the marriage; Flora would be angry with him for years.

Far worse from Freya's point of view, Vera confided that Flora was conspiring with Mario to force her to convert to Catholicism. In addition, they had refused to allow Vera to register in her own name a parting gift of two thousand pounds that Robert Stark had given each of the girls. Knowing that the money would become Mario's under Italian law, Freya argued—to no avail—that this was against Vera's best interest. "There were things my mother did that were hard to forgive," Freya said in her autobiography.

Vera, already overwhelmed by the scale of the wedding Mario and her mother were planning, suddenly realized that Flora had no intention of moving to a house of her own. For the next seven years—even after Vera's babies were born—Flora continued to preside over the household as Mario's chief companion and business partner, relegating Vera to second-class status in her own home and the beginning of a brooding despondency.

The night before her wedding, Vera wept in her sister's arms. "I think this was the last time that I arrived in Dronero with an easy mind," Freya later wrote. "Always, from now on, a numb feeling of trouble to come would settle on me as I drew near. . . . I never had the same faith in my mother again. What happened to my father had, I suppose, never really penetrated, but nothing could make me forget Vera's misery."[4]

. . .

Safe in London, Freya gave in to a rejuvenating feeling of expectancy; the future could bring anything. She was grateful to Viva Jeyes, one of the few people from the St. John's Wood crowd who had remained loyal to Flora, and who had put the girls up a number of times on the visits they were able to make to their father in Devon. Freya was impressed by her mother's elegant friend, an American whose husband, Harry Jeyes, had been an assistant editor of the *London Standard* before his recent death. Viva, who was blond and very pretty, always beautifully dressed, and had no children of her own, had taken a special interest in Freya, whom she called her "budding genius."

When Freya first encountered it, the Jeyes household had been a revelation. It was not only the exciting talk at dinner of books and politics, but for the first time Freya had witnessed a couple being openly demonstrative. Harry Jeyes had pulled Viva onto his lap and kissed her publicly. After Harry's death Viva was a sought-after widow, living at 11 Grove End Road with her stepfather, Edwin Bale, president of the Society of Watercolorists. "Small, neat and pink," according to Freya, Mr. Bale took the eager girl under his wing and helped her invest her father's gift of two thousand pounds. At one point, when she most needed to hear it, he told her: "My dear, your mother talks like an angel and acts like a fool."[5]

Viva took her to tea parties and dinners and introduced a dazzled Freya to towering literary figures like H. G. Wells and W. B. Yeats. As the honorary secretary of the Women's Anti-Suffrage League, Viva also invited her to canvas for the cause, so Freya met the redoubtable opponent of women's right to vote, Mrs. Humphry Ward. To Freya, she looked like "a dictator in skirts."[6] Nevertheless, she was impressed. Freya approved of

Mrs. Ward's insistence that there was only one way for a lady to behave and listened attentively as she offered majestic injunctions to her audiences. Ladies must never speak of "Propaganda," she counseled sternly, only of "Persuasion." It was a message that Freya did not forget. Years later, when she was organizing women for her own project in Egypt, she echoed this view. Curiously, Gertrude Bell, a distinguished Arabist with whom Freya would often be compared as she began making her mark in Middle Eastern affairs, happened to be a cofounder of this movement. The two women were destined never to meet, but Bell would always be a shadow figure in Freya's life. Neither of them showed the slightest interest in women's issues; both always regarded the intellectual capacities of their gender with ill-concealed contempt. It is likely that the league's staunchly pro-imperial bias and insistence that public policy should be kept firmly in male hands strongly influenced Freya's thinking in the years to come.

Although Freya felt dowdy and "podgy" and desperately wished she could afford beautiful clothes, she made a good impression on the lively friends of the St. John's Wood circle. At a time when superb conversation was regarded as one of the highest arts and the well-turned phrase as seductive as a well-turned ankle, Freya jumped into the exchanges with a shy but genuine relish. Not only did her youthful appetite for ideas appeal to Viva's mostly male guests but she quickly saw that a little well-placed flattery was very helpful in gaining information and approval.

At this time the "scramble for Africa" was a hunt in full-throated cry. There was furious rivalry among the European states over what colonial spoils remained. France and Germany had come close to blows over who would dominate the Congo and Morocco, while Italy, greedy for a belated share and stimulated by the extremist nationalist rhetoric of Gabriele D'Annunzio, had launched a force to annex Tripoli, the last toehold of the Ottoman sultan in Africa. But it was the pugilistic behavior of Germany that most preoccupied the journalists and academics at Viva's table. The British were alarmed by Berlin's aggression on many counts, including their fear that Germany's projected Baghdad railway would threaten their own control over Mesopotamia. The kaiser was pushing hard to gain influence at the Ottoman court and had sent one of his generals to train Ottoman troops in Istanbul, and Viva's guests knew Britain would never acquiesce to German dominance in the Middle East. It was beginning to look as if war might be unavoidable.

Listening, fascinated, to these discussions, Freya felt the British were invincible. Surrounded by these articulate men of the world, she ached to polish her own Englishness, sorely neglected during the Dronero years. She loved everything about England, the manner, style, and especially the language, with all its elegance and richness, which she was all too aware she spoke with a foreigner's accent. There was a grandeur, she felt, in being a British citizen, a member of the great empire on which the sun never set. Holding an English passport made her feel wonderfully legitimate, less like an outsider pressing her nose to the glass. As a British citizen, she was no longer an exile from Italy but a certified member of the greatest civilization on earth.

. . .

As for school, Freya had taken her precious opportunity seriously. Even though she was disappointed in her fellow students, whom she found on the whole a rather "dull lot," interested only in jobs and exams, she wanted to be liked and wrote home a bit despairingly about her drab clothes and too big nose. Her professors, however, approved of the industrious little student from Italy and began to include her at teas for the brightest students. She plunged earnestly into the most English of courses available—signing up for Anglo-Saxon, history, and Shakespeare—and excelled in everything including Latin, except for mathematics, which she thoroughly loathed.

In particular, Freya was riveted by the lectures given by William Paton Ker, a charismatic professor and chairman of Scandinavian studies at the University of London. When he came over to teach at Bedford College, he was greeted by such enthusiasm that the classroom floor trembled with the thump of his students' welcoming feet. A fellow of All Souls, Oxford, Professor Ker was a towering figure in academic circles who read in fifteen languages, including Icelandic and Provençal. He was an authority on the Celtic and Norse gods, the Vikings, and medieval epics. His colleagues called him an Olympian, and Freya was his instant worshiper.

The lanky, athletic bachelor, who wore a pince-nez and fancied good wine, regularly took his students and a collection of deferential godchildren on strenuous hikes through the countryside. They gathered at his house on Gower Street, near the British Museum, and competed fiercely to show off their command of literary niceties. It was not long before Freya was included in this adoring crowd and won a place as an honorary goddaughter. For the first time in her life she was exposed to a world-class intellect and responded with all her heart and soul. "He taught me all I knew of English literature," she would always tell friends later. Professor Ker would become the father figure that Freya sorely needed in the absence of her own father and her refusal to assign the role to Mario, and the professor's influence on her was enormous. When she published her first successful book, *The Valleys of the Assassins,* she dedicated it to Professor Ker.

When war was declared in August 1914, and school was forced to close, Freya sadly packed to return to Italy. A single bright note at this anxious time was the professor's promise to stay in touch.

. . .

If the war deprived Freya of the rest of her education, it offered a compensation. She got a chance to become a nurse. Flora was guardedly willing to let Freya train at a small hospital in Bologna, called the Clinic of St. Ursula, but came along to make sure she was installed in properly chaperoned lodgings. No sooner had her mother departed, however, than Freya realized that many of the "nurses" working by day were actually ladies of the night, fired by patriotic zeal and the hope of a more regular income. As the doctors seemed to be delighted to have any help they could get, Freya decided she would simply omit this detail in her reports home.

Anything was better than being in Dronero, but Freya actually enjoyed her duties. She was instructed to administer anesthesia to patients during surgical operations, which she managed with the help of a small bottle of smelling salts kept handy in her apron pocket. One day she gave a patient so much chloroform that the woman nearly died, and after the crisis had passed, Freya fainted. A young surgeon picked her up and said consolingly: "You must not get so agitated, Signorina; we have all killed somebody."[7]

Not long afterward Freya met Quirino Ruata. A doctor and professor of bacteriology, he was tall, bearded, and thirty-eight, and spoke eloquently of music and books. Almost immediately Freya fell deeply in love. She called him Guido and waited for him to arrive in the evenings—always properly, in the presence of a chaperone. "When I heard him walk up the stairs . . . my heart felt as if it were being drawn out of its socket—one could not tell whether it was pleasure or pain," she said of this intensely romantic period.[8] Back over the Christmas holidays in Dronero—where at last Vera had emerged from her depression following the birth of a baby girl, Leonarda—Freya slept with Guido's picture under her pillow.

In the early winter of 1915 Freya accepted Guido's proposal of marriage. She was wonderfully happy. They visited Umbria together to meet Guido's family, whom Freya liked enormously. Dronero, however, was not so pleasant. Mario's territorial instincts were instantly aroused, while Flora rushed to take over the wedding preparations. Before long she had selected a house for the couple and was ordering their furniture. Freya saw Guido's jaw set and knew he was offended. Even so, when spring arrived Freya quit the hospital and returned to Dronero with love in her heart and a wedding to plan. She was unaware that she had picked up a serious infection.

Whatever the illness was—possibly mononucleosis—she was soon left so depleted that she could barely lift a glass of water to her lips. She lay in bed for days, which turned into weeks, vaguely aware of her mother's irritation with her weakness. Worse, Guido's letters began to trail off. Eventually, stronger but still unwell and acutely uneasy, Freya roused herself and persuaded Flora to come with her for a brief visit to Guido in Bologna. Flora, insensitive as ever, would not let the couple alone. Instead, they exchanged formal trivialities that left Freya burning with questions she could not ask. She went home to Dronero, a gathering dread in her heart.

From friends Freya learned that Guido was to be sent with other military doctors to the front. More alarming, Vera's little Leonarda fell sick. The sisters took the infant to the hospital in Turin, where they nursed her night and day—but she died in Vera's arms. Now it was Freya's turn to be gravely ill. Physically vulnerable, she contracted typhoid, which was raging through northern Italy during the war. Even Flora became genuinely frightened as new and dreadful fevers shook one daughter and the other wept unconsolably over her baby's death. Always attracted to the Roman Catholic faith, Flora now converted secretly and spent long hours with the local priest. Guido visited once, but after he left his letters ceased altogether.

Only later did Freya learn about a passionate attachment Guido had had to a musician who had left him to go to America. When the lady learned of his engagement to the English nurse, and of the excellent director's post that Guido had recently been assigned, she abruptly returned to Italy. In the late spring, when Viva Jeyes came down from London to take a barely recovered Freya for a spirit-lifting sojourn by the sea at Alassio, Guido's letter breaking off the engagement arrived.

Freya was shattered. She begged Viva to come with her to Bologna. As she later recounted, "Guido did not wish even to see us, but Viva insisted and went along to see him while I sat at my window and looked at the orange sky with swallows flying dark against it—and the sight of such a sky always brings back an ache of pain."[9]

Her hotel room happened to look out on a brothel. Freya, not understanding at first what she was witnessing, watched as naked women sauntered below, throwing flimsy robes about themselves as they leaned out from the windows to banter with young men in the street. Stirred by many conflicting emotions, she watched the sexual pageant unfold, dimly realizing that these women who made love for commerce had the chance for a fulfillment that she might be denied.

That evening Guido reluctantly agreed to have dinner with Freya. It was an agonizing meal, although Viva, with more sensitivity than Flora had shown, let them talk alone. Freya offered to give herself without marriage. Guido, looking tortured but still offering no explanation for his behavior, turned her down. Once more she stumbled back to Dronero, feeling as if "a corpse" was in her heart.[10]

. . .

If it was hard enough for Freya to endure her own unhappiness, it was salt in the wound to suffer Flora's. Like an enraged lioness protecting her cub, Flora let fly a fusillade of letters, demanding Guido return furniture and other gifts. Worse, she tore off to Perugia to confront his parents and insisted on explanations and apologies. Mortified, distraught, at a loss to know what had suddenly repelled him—could it have been her looks?—Freya pleaded with her mother to let Guido alone. Instead, Flora cabled Robert in Canada to drop everything and come back to take his daughter to Egypt, the mountains, anywhere, as long as it was away from her unspeakable disgrace.[11] Although in June Freya had received a loving note from him telling her he did not think it "feasible"—despite his longing to do so—to come over for the wedding, when he got Flora's news Robert rushed to Ottawa to book passage.[12] A letter from Freya assuring him that she was coping reached him just as he was ready to embark.

At the beginning of August 1916, Freya fled to Viva's soothing house in London. The Battle of the Somme had opened in July. On one day during that summer of carnage, the British lost over sixty thousand men. Londoners tried to encourage themselves with the reported advances of the Allies while volunteers flocked to recruiting posts. Freya, still thin and weak, hoped to put her recently certified nursing skills to use in work that was not too strenuous. On August 9 she wrote Flora to ask for her certificate and references from St. Ursula's, explaining she had stored them in the bottom drawer of her bedroom cabinet.

"Please," she begged, "they are mostly private things and will you shut it up afterwards?" She also pleaded with Flora to cease writing Viva invective about Guido. "It only makes me unhappy, takes away the possibility of her helping me and does no good to anyone. It is better you shouldn't write about this business at all because it really does harm. . . . Don't write to *anyone* about Quirino, at least not to say more than that circumstances are difficult for us both. If things come right as I hope and believe, it will do no good for all my English friends to think ill of him, and what you tell Viva is not even fair!"[13]

On September 6, nearly a month later, Freya asked again: "Are you sending my certificate?"[14] She was keeping herself busy helping Viva once a week at an all-night canteen set up to serve coffee and sandwiches to sol-diers going through Paddington Station. One night a Zeppelin was shot down in the center of London. By day soldiers could be seen everywhere dressed in the blue fatigues of the recuperating wounded. Every morning whole pages of the newspapers were filled with lists in small print of the names of the dead; as many as a thousand officers were killed each week. On everyone's lips were questions about the fate of loved ones. Freya waited for her certificate, accompanied Vera on errands, composed son-nets to show Professor Ker, and thought of Guido.

In the meantime, no certificate came from Dronero. "Did you look in the right place for the certificate?" wrote Freya on September 13 in mounting frustration.[15] She made repeated requests over the next few weeks until finally, on October 13, nearly ten weeks after she first asked for it: "I think I shall wire you for that certificate: I *must* have it, and am just getting more and more miserable with nothing to do: if you knew what it is to me!"[16]

But Flora saw no reason for her daughter to return to nursing and risk her health again. "I think we have paid our Scot to the war," she finally wrote in a letter that didn't reach Freya until the end of the month. Reluc-tantly, however, she mailed the long-sought certificate, conceding snap-pishly that Freya was "a free agent."[17]

Deeply depressed, Freya took an interim job so as not to continue bur-dening Viva. She accepted a salary of thirty-five shillings a week in the War Censor's Office, where she put her good German, Italian, and French to work. It is possible Professor Ker helped her, as he was doing "confi-dential work" for the government himself. Freya stayed until March of the following year, remembering years later that she had learned how to spot covert messages in seemingly harmless mail, a skill she said stood her in good stead as a propagandist in the Second World War.

At the end of November friends passed on the news that Dr. Quirino Ruata had married his musician-lover. Stunned, Freya tried to accept the blow with a forgiving heart. Not so Flora. "He was merely a cold-hearted egotist," she railed to her grief-stricken daughter. "Nothing can regenerate this radical vice of heart . . . the living amongst corrupt creatures, may have made his heart really arid. . . . no woman can undo that scar—this mean view of woman will persist and come up through everything. . . . God has saved you from a dreadful fate."[18] To Freya's horror, Flora then instituted legal proceedings against Guido.

Unable to prevent her mother from escalating her guerrilla actions against Guido into full-blown war, Freya wrote furiously, "I need not—should not need to say—what I feel about this news." Flora was demanding payment for Freya's trousseau, for the cost of mailing back presents and furniture, for a little portrait of Freya that, in fact, had been returned earlier. Imploring Flora to respect matters that are "too personal and sacred for anyone to tamper with," Freya was in anguish. "If you could know the misery this action of yours is causing me, you would care more for my happiness than for your point of pride."[19] Not until mid-January, however, could Freya get her mother to withdraw the legal action.

Freya never recovered from the pain inflicted by her mother's rage. Although she tried to behave with dignity herself, dutifully returning wedding presents and informing friends of her canceled wedding plans, Flora had shown no such restraint. As far as she was concerned, there was nothing good to be said about the man her daughter loved. It was as if Flora were determined to make Freya hate him. Preoccupied with avenging her own injured pride, Flora seemed incapable of consoling her daughter. Freya could only conclude that she was responsible for bringing pain and humiliation to the parent on whom she depended and whom she loved deeply. Clearly the only thing that would make her mother happy, and the only thing that mattered if one wished to think of oneself as a successful woman, was to find a husband. And Freya hadn't done it.

All the time Freya had been studying in London, Flora had hinted that she ought to be out looking for eligible bachelors. The fact that Flora had left her children's father to live an unorthodox life in another man's house evidently did not matter. Flora was conservative and traditional in her expectations for her daughters but not when it came to her own actions. In a way this contradiction would be liberating for Freya—she could go against convention when she needed to—but as the future would show, her mother's Victorian notions stuck with her. Freya would always hate to be perceived as "improper," and most of all she hated not being married.

Flora's extremism was nothing new. She had been fierce and unyielding about so many things. As a child Freya had seen her mother burst into rages and had cowered miserably. When Freya was only fifteen Flora had sent her up to Devon to extract furnishings from Robert Stark's house because Flora had learned that his new sister-in-law had moved in with her husband. There followed an extraordinarily painful scene, but Freya, ever her mother's obedient vassal, had succeeded in driving the woman from her father's house and packing up the belongings that Flora insisted were hers. Flora's greed and need to dominate became an unfortunate model, which Freya might have wished to disavow but which nevertheless surfaced periodically in her own behavior. Her mother's rage against her failure to marry, however, was worse than anything Freya had endured before, fueling her grow-

Freya and her family on a climbing holiday in Switzerland with William Paton Ker. Standing, left to right: Count Mario di Roascio, Dorothy Waller, Vera, an unidentified friend, Professor Ker, Freya, and, as chaperone, Flora, who was fully a head taller than her older daughter. The two young men were friends of Freya's.

Freya succeeded in climbing Monte Rosa from the Italian side, an arduous twelve-hour ascent up a solid ice wall. It was a feat previously achieved by only one other woman.

L'Arma, the farmhouse on the Italian Riviera, just over the border from France and below the railroad tracks, overlooking the Ligurian Sea. Robert Stark helped Freya buy it, and here she struggled to make a living for herself and her mother at flower farming.

Casa Freia, in the picturesque Italian hill town of Asolo, in the Veneto. Given to Freya and named after her by her godfather, Herbert Young, the villa is shown in this recent photograph connected by an ancient Roman arch to the opposite house, La Mura, rented before the war by the Californians Lucy and John Beach. It was through Mrs. Beach's efforts that the tessoria was revived in Asolo.

ing anxiety that she might never be desirable enough for a man's love. It left her with a hunger that lasted all her life.

Many years later Freya composed a poetic essay in which she included a caution against the forces that can interfere with love's hope and rapture. "No crime short of murder," she wrote, "can be comparable to the crime of destroying in another the capacity to love: and this happens sometimes through the rashness of parents, or the sight of misery in adolescence, but more often through some bitterness of experience when youth is still defenseless . . . and wounds leave a scar difficult to heal."[20]

And so that dreadful chapter of romance and rejection closed. In the meantime Italy, already fighting Austria-Hungary, had declared war against Germany as well. Freya hoped she might heal her own heart by binding the wounds of others.

. . .

At five-thirty in the morning on October 29, 1917, ladened down with her coat, an overcoat and mackintosh, and carrying her knapsack, Freya crossed the wide Tagliamento River in darkness. This was the Italian front, on the extreme northeastern border, thirty miles from Slovenia. In a matter of hours the bridge over the swollen flood would be blown up by its Italian defenders. For days, as the hills thundered with the muffled sound of cannon, villages burned, and roads were a sea of desperate refugees, rain had fallen remorselessly. Mud grabbed at her shoes; she had not bathed in a month. She was mortally tired from the long hours and heartbreaking work of tending men with shattered or amputated limbs, of changing dressings covering wounds that didn't heal, from which little rubber hoses carried toxic pus.

Two days earlier they had been told to close Villa Trento, the English ambulance unit near the town of Gorizia, a bridgehead held by the Austrians north of Trieste. During the first two years of the war the Italians had tried to force a passage into Austria-Hungary, but after eleven bloody battles, and without the men and supplies promised by the English and French, they had managed to creep forward a bare few miles. Now the effort was collapsing. Beginning on October 24 in a dense fog, the Austrians had attacked at Caporetto, a border town in the foothills, and were advancing quickly south. Freya and the other nurses had been mesmerized by the artillery fire dancing over the hills; occasional shells even landed in the villa garden, while exhausted ambulance drivers struggled back from the front with more wounded. Suddenly the demoralized Italian troops broke ranks, and with shouts of "*Tutto e perduto*—all is lost," the retreat became a rout.

The Caporetto Retreat is a famous chapter in the history of World War I.[21] Almost too late British and French troops were rushed to the breach and a new defense line was drawn at the Piave River, just miles above Venice and Verona. For months people feared that the area from Venice northwest to Milan would be lost. Ultimately the Austrians were driven out, but in the meantime nearly three hundred thousand Italian troops were taken prisoner; even more deserted. As far as the people in Northern Italy, especially the Piedmontese were concerned, the behavior of their own army was no better than that of the British and French and equally scorned. No wonder the charismatic voice of the young Benito Mussolini, preaching against the decadence of the current European establishment, fell upon ready ears.

Freya became part of the long, weary stream of cars, animals, and humans gutting the road and moving south at a snail's pace to safety. After sixty-four hours without rest and very little food—mostly offered by looting troops—Freya caught up with her colleagues in Padua. There the hospital unit briefly regrouped. They had been luckier than their patients; most of the doctors and nurses had made it through. Freya was amazed to discover herself at last in a town with ordinary shops selling normal merchandise—and she promptly bought a chiffon blouse, the most frivolous and unwarlike thing to catch her eye.

. . .

It had not been easy to arrange this post at the front, but after quitting the Censor's Office in London, Freya had finally obtained work at a hospital in Highgate to get certification from the British. Viva was enthusiastically behind the decision, but other friends had expressed concern that Freya "looked much too frail a person to stand the racket of nursing," as her friend Margaret Jourdain had told her, adding that she was sorry to see someone with so many "brains" wanting to take on such a job.[22]

Highgate turned out to be every bit as grueling as everyone had predicted, but with her usual determination Freya kept at it and was assigned to the unit in Italy just two months before the disaster of Caporetto. Freya was so well versed in the arts of endurance that she made a tough, compassionate, and hardworking nurse. She kept a diary of her experiences, and if she could be eloquent, spare, and precise describing the beauty of a red sunset, the look of leaves camouflaging double-barreled howitzers, or the extraction of a piece of shrapnel as big as a hazelnut from a boy's hip, she was economical with her own emotions. "I think something must be the matter with me," she noted in her diary a week or so before the retreat. "I weep so easily now."[23]

Eventually the English medical unit was disbanded, but her war experience gave Freya a taste of danger and excitement that she would never forget. She had seen young men dying with screams on their lips and others whisper piteously for their mothers as they sank into unconsciousness. But she had witnessed gallantry too, and the awesome nature of war touched deep chords that moved her profoundly.

The experience left Freya with an urgent need to write. For a while before the war ended, nurses were still in demand. The pandemic of influenza that began that year would ultimately kill 20 million people throughout the world. Typhoid set loose by polluted water was also taking a terrible toll. Freya began work in a Turin hospital, where despite the long hours she managed to write at least two finished stories on her occasional days off. But either because she believed they were not sufficiently polished for publication—which was not the case—or because they said too much, she laid them away in a trunk for fifty years. Not until 1968, when her good friend Lord David Cecil, Oxford professor of literature, was visiting her in Asolo and helped her select essays for a collection coming out that year as *The Zodiac Arch,* did she show them to anyone. He was obviously struck by their power, for he suggested they be included even though they were fiction.

When she was twenty-six, Freya's talent was already unmistakable. These stories are beautifully crafted, evoking not only the impact of the war but also the powerful physical feelings and passionate disappointment she felt over her lover's rejection. Yet in the end Freya moved away from fiction, as if she had concluded that travel writing and essays were a safer medium. In these two surviving pieces there is such an intensity of feeling that one is left to wonder if it was too dangerous for her to explore those deeply personal regions from which a writer of fiction must necessarily draw.

. . .

Once more Freya headed back to Dronero and the company of a work-drugged Flora, Mario absorbed in local politics, and her deeply depressed sister—who by this time had lost another baby. Painfully distant, Vera attended her surviving child, Angela. At one point during the war, Vera had slipped out of the house and wandered off into the hills until a search party found her. "She both felt and made life unbearable," wrote Freya in her memoirs, "and told me that she was so wretched that it pleased her to make everyone else so too."[24] It was clear that Dronero was no place to settle if Freya herself wished to be happy.

. . .

On November 8, 1918, Kaiser Wilhelm II abdicated in Berlin. The war was over; people poured into the streets, disbelieving and hilarious. In Paris the idealistic former professor from Princeton, President Woodrow Wilson, arrived to a tumultuous welcome, carrying his famous Fourteen Points and their magic recipe for a lasting peace. In Turin they white-washed street signs and wrote his name in huge letters. Not long after-ward, in history's capricious fashion, these same people would turn on Wilson for opposing their grandiose plans for annexing the Southern Tyrol as well as territories around the Adriatic. Those who had just sung the American president's praises now asked their butchers for a pig's head and called it the Wilson cut.

In the meantime it was time to count the war's losses. Ten million had perished, 20 million were wounded, and untold numbers of non-combatants were crippled, displaced, and impoverished. Four empires—the Hohenzollern, Hapsburg, Romanov, and Ottoman—had collapsed. Not only was Europe in bankruptcy but the reformist theo-ries that had boiled out of Germany and ignited a revolution in Russia were spreading everywhere—no less in the Piedmont, cradle of Italian nationalism and fledgling industry, and home to growing ranks of dis-contented urban workers. To add to the chaos, prices were skyrocket-ing, and soon the Socialist party dominated Parliament in Rome. Turin saw some of the worst agitation: armed radicals seized a number of factories while peasants and workers fought gun battles. In Dronero, Mario's factory was safe—at least for the time being—but it was no longer turning a profit.

In this atmosphere of social tension and invidious class divisions, Freya persuaded her father to help her buy a house on the Ligurian coast near Ven-timiglia, ninety miles south of Dronero. She insisted that Flora come with her. It was time, she said, that Vera and Mario be left alone. Reluctantly, Flora agreed, or at least said she would come until Freya had "settled in."

The region Freya chose was beautiful, sun-dappled and covered with jewel-colored fields of flowers dotting cliffs that fell precipitously to the blue sea. This was a flower-farming area, and Freya believed that she could make a living as her father had in Canada, raising flowers commer-cially. She had seen enough of nursing to decide it was not the career for her. With high hopes and new enthusiasm, Freya moved her mother into L'Arma, a small, four-room villa perched on two and a half acres in the lit-tle town of La Mortola, just over the French border from Menton. All

A portrait of Freya's godfather, Herbert Young, painted by his friend Herbert Olivier.

A youthful portrait of Flora Stark's friend Viva Jeyes, painted by Viva's stepfather, Edwin Bale. When Flora sent Freya up to London, she usually stayed with Viva, who was married then and living in St. John's Wood. The childless Viva called Freya "Budding Genius" and helped her both financially and by performing her errands— until her criticisms and jealousy over Freya's growing success spoiled the friendship.

around her were the grand villas of the rich, while on the riverbank village women pounded their laundry with stones.

Showing the flair for renovating that later amazed her friends, Freya drew up plans for adding rooms. She ventured for miles by train or bicycle to locate cheap sand or gravel or concrete, enjoying the good, hard exercise, returning through the mimosa-scented air by moonlight like "a bat at dusk."[25] Flora, in her customarily robust way, created murals and painted furniture but never ceased talking about returning to Dronero— just as soon as she found her daughter a husband.

They were, to put it bluntly, dirt poor. In those days, however, that didn't mean that one couldn't pay a lira or two to hire a pair of hands even poorer, so they did have help. There was a peasant woman who came in to do housework; later they had a gardener. At this point Freya received barely ninety pounds annually from stock that Mr. Bale had invested in for her. Without her father's departure gift, they would have been even more straitened, because Flora's money was still tied up in the Dronero factory. Mario made no effort to return it, so Freya, with Robert's support, finally brought a suit against him, with Flora as an unwilling participant. Whenever a document required her signature, Flora balked, precipitating another argument and dragging the case on for years.

They were living on the edge, but only Freya seemed to recognize it. Sugar and butter were no longer staples in the larder. They subsisted on homegrown beans and potatoes, and bought a goat to provide milk. Freya spent sleepless nights conjuring ways to cut costs. Kind friends gave them secondhand clothes, which Freya bit her lip and accepted. She slipped across the border to Menton because it was cheaper to buy coffee in France. To earn a hundred pounds, she even concealed a priceless old Sienese painting under some blankets in her cart and took it over the border for a collector who wanted to avoid Italian export laws. It was the sort of risky act that thrilled her and reminded her, she felt, that she was still alive.

Being poor was a grueling struggle. Freya hated the constant watchfulness, the sense of obligation to generous friends, the sacrifice, the sheer hard work. With no proper water system, they had to carry hundreds of buckets of water daily down the hill when it didn't rain. And during this epic effort the knowledge gnawed at her that she was not doing anything that she wanted to be doing or thought was significant. She realized that her father might love farming, but it was not the right course for her. She wanted to write. And in the evenings she was too weary to pick up a pencil.

As a sign of how badly this young woman yearned to join the feast of knowledge, how intellectually thirsty she was—and how determined she was not to be defeated—an image stands out from a letter to her father: Freya was stirring a pot of stew on the stove and reading Virgil at the same time. Always trying to make up for her lack of a formal education, in one week she managed to cover the *Aeneid,* Horace, and a new book on economics by John Maynard Keynes. A ferocious hope, a buoyant conviction that the future *would* be better, sustained her. In 1921 she wrote her father thanks for "a lovely fat bundle of Literary Supplements, enough to last me for weeks and weeks and make me feel that I still belong to the living and thinking world."[26] But she was clinging to that world by her fingertips and mostly felt like "a miserable failure."[27]

It helped that the Italian Riviera was a beautiful place and friends from London enjoyed coming down—even if they had to bring their own food. Mr. Bale and Viva Jeyes came and introduced Freya and her mother to a widening group of vacationing British. Flora still talked about returning to Dronero, but her social instincts were stimulated by the company of the rich occupants of surrounding villas. Herbert Olivier and his wife, Margaret, bought a neighboring house, and finally Herbert Young and Flora patched their rift so he too could visit.

In the summer of Freya's thirtieth year, Viva Jeyes introduced the Stark women to the Buddicom family, who owned a villa and a yacht in Bordighera, not far from La Mortola. They had a daughter, Venetia, whom Freya liked instantly; the two quickly became close friends. They were a study in contrasts, with Venetia as tall as Freya was short, her eyes tranquil and blue as Freya's were light brown and inquisitive. Reserved, intellectual, a sympathetic listener to Freya's storytelling and dreams, Venetia brought out all Freya's stifled ebullience and laughter. They weren't sure, they would giggle, what to commiserate about most: the too-few available bachelors since the war or their mothers' efforts to marry them off. Before long they had gone together to Spain and got along beautifully. Freya could not help feeling a bit envious that Venetia was prettier than she, but Venetia's admiration made up for it.

Freya also looked forward to annual visits from Professor Ker. She adored the erudite sage and outdoorsman, hanging on his every word, and was secretly delighted that he was the only person before whom her mother lapsed into "shyness." The well-off son of a Glasgow merchant, Ker had a delicate way of being generous to the Stark women without offending. At one low point he gave Freya a badly needed gift of three hundred pounds, insisting over her protestations that it had already been designated in his will. He included her on much-appreciated holidays in the mountains, sometimes with some of his godchildren, and a number of times he sent tickets for trips to London. When they accompanied him on mountaineering trips, he quietly paid for guides and often the hotel. They tried not to let him give too much, and once Freya and her mother left early rather than let him accept the cost for everything. Under his tutelage, Freya climbed in Courmayeur, where the professor suffered a minor heart fibrillation, a warning of the condition that later killed him. On several occasions he took her across high passes beneath Monte Rosa, and once they climbed the Breithorn together on a hike that took fifteen exhausting hours through soft snow.

It was a great shock and terrible loss when at nine thousand feet, climbing Pizzo Bianco near Macugnaga on the Italian side of Monte Rosa, Professor Ker had a fatal heart attack on July 17, 1923. Along with one of his goddaughters, Freya waited a sorrowful afternoon for a rescue team to bring the professor's body down.[28] She was now bereft of all three of the men to whom she had given her love: her father, absent for years; her lover who had rejected her; and now her revered teacher. The world seemed very lonely, and very cruel.

. . .

As a tribute to Professor Ker, Freya climbed the Matterhorn, and Monte Rosa from its Italian side, with its daunting wall of sheer ice and risk of avalanches. Only one woman before her had managed this ascent, and not long before her climb three alpinists had been swept to their deaths on the same route. Freya and her guides left at midnight, when the ice had a hard crust. It turned out to be a twelve-hour effort up an icy face to the summit. Of the climb she wrote, "When I shut my eyes and think of it I can still hear the swish of ice crumbs slipping past us as the guide cut steps above."[29] These were not feats for the faint-hearted; they belonged to a high level of mountaineering with experienced guides and ice equipment and stand as examples of her courage and athletic prowess.

Perhaps Ker's most significant contribution to Freya's life course was to suggest that she test herself against the discipline of a non-European language. Knowing Freya was fluent in English, French, Italian, and German, and had started to study Spanish, the linguist asked why she didn't take up one of his favorite languages, Icelandic, which he had been teaching for years at University College. After all, wasn't her name that of a Norse goddess? By this time, however, Freya's thoughts were on the exciting news that had emerged from San Remo that spring. The diplomats had departed, but talk of mandates in the Middle East still filled the air. She thought it over and chose Arabic instead.

. . .

Flora had no more understanding of why her daughter wanted to study Arabic than of why she persisted in something so arduous and unrewarding as flower farming. That Freya's efforts kept a roof over their heads seemed not to have penetrated. All Flora could think of was the sixteen years she had devoted to building up the Dronero factory. It had been the greatest fulfillment she had ever known. She missed it. She would not stop talking about going back—and all the while her daughter seethed.

"I felt an immense bitterness towards my mother. . . . she was making great weather over the loss of her own life and caring very little for the waste of mine." Worse, Flora could and would not do housework. She was, said Freya, "psychologically unable to attend to things that bored her . . . full of affection, but not a concrete burden, even to the ordering of food, was ever lifted from me."[30] At the same time Freya felt she could never let down her guard; it was up to her to keep prodding Flora to face their realities, to make their flower business successful, to take the necessary steps to get back her unpaid salary and share of factory profits. Freya remembered that this continual hounding made her literally nauseous. Small wonder then that she became seriously ill.

The first symptoms appeared in April 1922 and were noted in her diary. Not until 1924, however, when she was in nearly constant pain, were gastric ulcers diagnosed. She was put on a regimen of milk, raw eggs, boiled macaroni, and ham—and required to spend at least half her day lying down. "That charming doctor of mine recommends great laziness in the morning: so I have the luxury of being late and also feeling virtuous!" she wrote.[31] Freya was delighted to be sick and fall back from duties. It was a pattern she later followed whenever she was under great stress—obviously an unconscious bid to return to that distant time when her mother had devoted herself to her wounded daughter. As far as Flora was concerned, however, her daughter was there to serve her, so despite her own evident administrative skill, she either could not or would not run the farm and release Freya to her books. Later, even as Freya's name began to be recognized, Flora had difficulty allowing her the peace in which to write.

In the meantime the prescribed diet did little to heal the ulcers. By the end of 1924, surgery was called for, and Freya was carried prostrate by train to a hospital in Aosta. The operation was deemed a success; she began her recovery, and at least for the first week had the comfort of her mother by her side. But when Freya reluctantly dispatched Flora back to L'Arma to see to the farm, she heard almost immediately that instead of looking after their flower operation, Flora was off in Bordighera nursing a friend.

"I felt that everything was going to rack and ruin," said Freya, "and it was." To add to her despair, her surgeon was delayed in Turin with a case of the flu so lethal that his assistant died of it. With no physician in atten-dance Freya's incision became septic, her temperature soared, and she was in agony. "I knew enough about nursing to realize that my wound *must* be opened again, and got the nun to bring the little silver probe and tried to hold her hand steady while she did it; the other nun was in tears at the foot of the bed; the wound had healed too much for anything but a knife, and after an attempt at which both their resolution and mine failed, they gave it up and begged me to offer up my sufferings to the Lord."[32] Freya was unwilling to consign her soul so easily. She summoned the strength to shriek at the top of her lungs until hospital personnel were dispatched to rouse the surgeon from his sickbed. He got to the hospital and let out a pint of pus just in time.

At last Freya was put on a train for Asolo and Herbert Young's to recu-perate. Flora was to join her but, true to form, forgot where they were to meet and neglected to pick her up at the station. Freya, alone on the empty platform, sank down on her suitcase and gave in to bitter tears.

A slow rebellion was growing. She had to get out of this appalling rut. By the fall of 1925 she was sufficiently recovered to go to London. Although for a bleak moment her doctors discussed the necessity of a sec-ond operation, a Harley Street specialist pronounced that another six months flat on her back would serve just as well. For Freya the period was a time to rest and resume her studies. She took Arabic lessons with an Egyptian and began reading in earnest the history of the Middle East. She even undertook to learn a bit about cartography and how to use a com-pass. Quietly she made inquiries with London friends about employment opportunities in the East, but the only jobs that turned up were with fam-ilies of colonial officers moving to Iraq or Egypt or Iran who needed a gov-erness. Freya was not enthusiastic.

In the spring, vastly improved, Freya returned to Italy to stay again with Herbert Young. It was there that she heard about Vera.

• • •

In the spring of 1926 Vera had taken her children for a holiday by the seashore at Varazze. There she had a miscarriage and immediately devel-oped septicemia, a virulent form of blood poisoning. Flora and Freya stayed with her for two agonizing months as Vera gradually weakened. Full-time nurses bathed her, and Freya watched with sadness as the decision was made to cut off her sister's shining chestnut hair, so like her own had once been. Gaunt and pale, shaken by chills, Vera could no longer rise from her bed, and it was clear the end was near.

"She accepted it all with the same quiet detachment with which she had faced her life. We had long heartfelt talks at that time and she thanked me for the years of happiness she had with Mario since we had gone from Dronero; if she had not been left alone there, she would have run away and got divorced she told me"[33]—and, Freya could not help adding silently, might have had a chance at old age. She also might have lived if penicillin had been available, but that revolutionary discovery was still a decade off. Vera died on September 23, 1926. She was thirty-three.

"I have known two great sorrows," Freya wrote in her autobiography. "The loss of Guido and of Vera; but the one has long since healed and is ordinarily forgotten, and Vera's death is still as harsh as ever and will be as long as I can feel. I cannot help believing that if she had wanted life more, she could have held it: but she was not interested, and accepted death as she had accepted her marriage and her baptism, and no one outside her could help. In her last years she was happy in a quiet way, but never knew the radiance which alone makes life worth living, even if it comes for only a short gleam and disappears."[34]

From that moment on Freya knew that she would never allow herself to be passive and heel to an unacceptable fate. Her sister had died from bowing to the agendas of others. For herself, somehow, some way, she would snatch a life of quality from the drab choices she had thus far been presented—and it would be radiant.

PART TWO

THE ROMANTIC NOMAD

*There is a certain madness comes over one
at the mere sight of a good map.*

—LETTERS FROM SYRIA

The Mysterious Druze

> *I am in Damascus. It is a*
> *wonderful fact—but I really am.*
>
> —LETTERS FROM SYRIA

*F*or a brief, terrible moment toward the end of 1927, Freya thought she would have to cancel her carefully laid plans to go East. She had thought about nothing else for years; she had arranged for her mother to stay with Herbert Young in Asolo; an American lady there had offered Flora a job running a small weaving atelier that provided employment for local women and made Flora happy because it was much like the work she had so enjoyed in Dronero. Freya had also made some good investments and rented the flower farm so they could count on a small but steady income. Then suddenly, from Canada, came the shattering news that her father had suffered a stroke. Desperately torn but sure that he needed her, she prepared to undo her arrangements. At the last moment her father wrote urging her to go on. He was recovering, he assured her. She could visit him later, after her trip to Syria. It was a reprieve that left Freya weak with gratitude. By the beginning of December she had disembarked in Beirut.

The lovely months spent in Brummana practicing Arabic and enjoying the company of the young schoolmaster Francis Edmunds seemed to have passed in a dream. It was spring now. She was rocking along on the slowest imaginable train, gazing out the window at fields and orchards in the high Beqaa Valley on her way for a month's stay in Damascus. Mr. Edmunds had promised to visit, and so had Venetia Buddicom, her dearest friend from home. Freya was glad to know she would have some company because just before leaving, and despite the exciting plans she was making for Venetia's visit, she had suddenly felt overwhelmed by panic at the thought of tearing herself away from her pleasant new acquaintances and her familiar lodgings in Brummana. She wrote home that she felt like "a waif starting off into the unknown again."[1]

By March 15, 1928, unable to afford a hotel, Freya was installed in a rented room in the house of an Arab Christian family named Khalil who had been recommended by the Brummana missionaries. "Imagine," she wrote her mother,

> *one of those little backyards in Venice as the entrance to my home. You climb up rather rickety stairs, through the lower litter of garments, saucepans, old shoes, and flower-pots to a pleasant room with seven windows; where, unless you are extremely careful, everyone can see you while you dress. I really think the bed is all right: I didn't at first, but have come to the conclusion it is only the greyness of home washing. I have found nothing alive anyway: in fact what I complain of is that everything smells as if it were dead. The children's clothes were bundled out of my room, and various necessities like jugs, towels, mirror, rug, brought in at intervals while I sat rather dismal on the bed. That has a lovely yellow quilt and two long hard bolsters. I do manage to get hot water in the morning. But there are so many smells.*[2]

· · ·

For as long as Freya could remember, Damascus had conjured all that was beautiful and alluring on the Eastern horizon. A graceful oasis on the edge of the Syrian desert, filled with sparkling fountains and delicate minarets, it was surrounded by orchards of figs, pomegranates, almonds, and apricots. It was the oldest continuously inhabited city in the world. From the time of the Assyrians, Damascus had enjoyed a rich history. Alexander the Great had seized it from Darius the Persian, and when he died his Macedonian generals, Ptolemy and Seleucus, had fought over it. Later Pompey conquered it for Rome. It was on the way to Damascus that Saul was overwhelmed by visions and converted to the new Christian faith to become Saint Paul, and it was here that the head of Saint John the Baptist was said to be buried.

In 635, after a six-month siege, the Byzantines surrendered Damascus to the armies of Umar, founder of the Umayyad Empire, which would ultimately put more territory in the Islamic embrace than Rome had ever encompassed and bequeath to the city such a reputation for glory that even today it is considered the beating heart of the Arab world. After the last Umayyad caliph fled his Abbasid assassins in 750, after the Crusaders failed to take it from Saladin, after the conquering Mongols, Hulegu Khan, and Tamerlane each savaged it in turn, Damascus passed quietly into the hands of the Ottoman sultan in 1516. Thereafter it had remained undisturbed and prosperous, a gathering point for pilgrims on their way to Mecca, until the devastations of the recent Great War. After the Ottoman Turks surrendered, and the cheering Bedouin warriors poured into the city, waving swords and shouting their desert war cries, the fate of Damascus and the entire Middle East had been altered forever.

By 1928 Damascus was a shabby vestige of its former glory. Sanitation was poor, public transportation was minimal, and half the city was still in rubble. During the recent rebellion sparked by a Druze revolt and quickly joined by a majority of tribes and religious groups, all of Syria was aflame. The French, Syria's new masters under the League of Nations mandate, were pitiless in their response. Flying low over crowded rooftops, they had loosed thousands of pounds of bombs on Damascus and reduced other Syrian cities to cinders. Acres of houses, market stalls, orchards, and gardens were destroyed. Civilians and students were rounded up and shot without a trial, and the bodies of insurgents were dumped into Martyr's Square, where at night mothers and sisters came to see if they recognized a loved one. The French had won because they had the strength, but the city remained alive with hatred and distrust, while uniformed French soldiers marched through the streets. Freya watched the robed and turbaned inhabitants avert their faces, knowing that the embers of the rebellion still glowed.

· · ·

In the house by the Bab Tuma that cold March, appalled by the stench, with family members drifting in and out all day, Freya noted grimly that the inside temperature was 17 degrees Fahrenheit. Snow dusted the lemon trees outside, and despite her determined efforts to be optimistic, almost immediately she was down with a severe case of dysentery.

A doctor was called and to her relief ordered that she be provided eggs ("I tried to anchor my mind on the fact that nothing much besides old age can happen to the inside of a boiled egg," she wrote to her mother),[3] but she was sick for two long weeks. Writing to Venetia Buddicom, she reported that she knew she had sunk to the nadir of debasement when, awakened by an itching sensation over her body, she inspected herself with a flashlight. Realizing that it was merely fleas biting her flesh and not the first signs of measles or some other illness, she sighed, shrugged, turned over, and went back to sleep. "I am trying to think I don't mind about cleanliness; if one could make oneself independent of these physical things, how easy it would be to travel. . . . I try to read Dante and not look at my meals as I eat them."[4]

Freya's stoic childhood training stood her in good stead, and when she felt stronger she began daily excursions around the city and into the covered *souk,* or market, edging past panniered donkeys and the occasional horse in splendid red and gold trappings, inhaling the pungent smell of spices, fragrant breads fresh from the oven, and succulent fruits laid out in decorative rows. Thrilled by the color and energy about her, she threaded her way through throngs of women pulling their veils aside to bargain, the din of potters and tinsmiths, basket weavers and leather workers. An occasional notable billowed past in flowing robes, and she watched more than one erect Bedouin from the desert stride several paces ahead of his tattooed wives. It surprised her to see so many blue eyes, and she wondered if they were not the legacy of some Crusader ancestor. Listening to the muezzins' summons to the faithful wafting through the air, she wandered along one of the main thoroughfares known as the Street Called Straight, admired the remains of thirteenth-century walls, the old Citadel, and the vast and glorious Umayyad mosque—once a Roman temple, then a Christian cathedral, and now the oldest surviving Muslim place of worship and fourth holiest sanctuary in Islam, after Mecca, Medina, and the Dome of the Rock in Jerusalem. She saw for herself the tattered evidence of the French bombardment and ugly lengths of barbed wire still scattered about. It made her feel increasing sympathy for the Arabs, who yearned to be free from foreign rule. It must be extremely unpleasant, she thought, to have one's city occupied by foreign troops.

She discovered how safe it was for a woman to wander alone in an Islamic land, for despite what the missionary ladies told her, she had learned that Islamic tradition treats women with exquisite respect. Nor was there street crime, despite the numbers of small urchins who often clamored at her knees. Only once did she feel threatened. An old fellow approached her as she was photographing ruins, salaamed, and suggested, "oh lady," she should follow him to see something even more interesting. He led her down dark and twisting streets to one of the city's *hammams,* or public baths. As he ushered her into its dim interior, she was suddenly surrounded by nearly naked men in towels. With great aplomb, murmuring something polite, she thrust her camera before her face as if to take their picture, thanked them profusely, backed to the heavy door, and fled.

Her solitary wanderings provoked comment among the Syrian missionaries, who had been alerted to her arrival by their Brummana confreres. Soon Freya's desire to avoid missionaries became an article of faith. "I do find those ladies too suffocating. Even the young ones seem to have all natural interest in life and buoyancy taken out of them and think of nothing but their own narrow little . . . path of self righteousness. I have to use so much self-control not to say wrong things all the time, and even so they look on me as world and flesh if not actually the devil." Expressing her own passionate originality, Freya continued indignantly: "They suffer from stagnation of the brain, and that surely produces stagnation of the soul in time. To feel, and think, and learn—learn always: surely that is being alive and young in the real sense. And most people seem to *want* to stagnate when they reach middle age. I hope I shall not become so, resenting ideas that are not my ideas, and seeing the world with all its changes and growth as a series of congealed formulas."[5]

It was going to be hard, she was learning, not to be crushed or diverted by the criticism of strangers. She would have to be tough and look to herself for confidence. She remembered noticing as a child, when she had shuttled so often back and forth between her intellectual German grandmother in Italy and the silk-gowned and bourgeois grandmother in England, that people had very different attitudes about what was right and what was wrong, and were generally inclined to believe that only their own way was correct. Freya resolved to keep her mind open.

. . .

During this Damascus sojourn Freya had her first memorable encounter with the desert. She had been introduced to members of the El Azm tribe, one of Syria's great feudal families, who measured their wealth in villages and agricultural properties.[6] The young sheikh, dramatic in his flowing gold and brown robes, and his sister, Amatallatif (whose name, Freya noted delightedly, meant Handmaid of Allah), were both patrician and modern-minded Arabs. Although Amatallatif wore a veil in public, she was educated and a year or two later, while still in her twenties, founded a school for girls that survived through World War II. Her brother, with whom Freya plunged exuberantly into the relative merits of the Bible and the Koran, had been funding health clinics throughout the city for several years. Their kindness encouraged Freya's growing conviction that the most aristocratic people in the East were the Muslims, and that Christian converts were in the main shopkeepers or lower-class clerks, and not interesting. Moreover, she decided, it was the people of nomadic Bedouin stock, whose ancient tribal connections were their primary identity, who were the "true Arabs" of the East, the authentic nobility, and not the settled townsfolk.

This was by no means a new conclusion for a European to come to. A host of nineteenth-century travelers awash in mid-Victorian romanticism had hurried East to escape what in their view was the West's soulless commercialism. They usually returned to compose paeans to the desert tribesman as the last repository of chivalry and honor. The poet Wilfrid Blunt and his wife, Lady Anne, granddaughter of Lord Byron, felt such a strong kinship with the nomads and were so taken by the "purity" of the desert that they later bought an estate in eastern Egypt, close by the Red Sea. There, as Blunt put it, they could give in to their compulsion to "cast off the slough of Europe, to have done with the ugliness and noise, to bathe one's sick soul in the pure healing of the East. The mere act of passing from one's graceless London clothes into the white draperies of Arabia is a new birth."[7]

Freya, a romantic herself, fell eagerly in step with this thinking, and when the El Azms took her far out into the countryside toward the desert's edge, famously described by the eleventh-century Persian poet Omar Khayyam as the region between "the desert and the sown," and she caught her first glimpse of Bedouin tents and grazing flocks, she was deeply moved. There on the rim of the savanna she saw that great vista of sandy desolation that has both attracted and repelled man since time immemorial. Staring out as the car churned over hard sand and the road seemed to melt into the horizon, she witnessed something magnificent:

> *Camels appeared on our left hand: first a few here and there, then more and more, till the whole herd came browsing along, five hundred or more. I got out and went among them to photograph. The two Beduin* leaders, dressed gorgeously, perched high up and swinging slowly with the movement of their beasts, shouted out to me, but Beduin Arabic is beyond me. I can't tell you what a wonderful sight it was: as if one were suddenly in the very morning of the world among the people of Abraham and Jacob. The great gentle creatures came browsing and moving and pausing, rolling gently over the landscape like a brown wave just a little browner than the desert that carried it. Their huge legs rose up all around me like columns; the foals were frisking about: the herdsmen rode*

---

* Freya chose to spell the word without the o.

*here and there. I stood in a kind of ecstasy among them. It seemed
as if they were not so much moving as flowing along, with something indescribably fresh and peaceful and free about it all, as if
the struggle of all these thousands of years had never been, since
first they started wandering. I never imagined that my first sight of
the desert would come with such a shock of beauty and enslave
me right away. But I left it feeling that somehow, some time, I
must see more of the great spaces.*[8]

It was more than a wish; it was a private vow. Freya would spend a lifetime confronting fear, loneliness, illness, intense discomfort, and danger in
order to see more of the great spaces. If she were still uncertain about how
she would realize the dream, it was clear to her now that the East was her
calling.

. . .

Venetia Buddicom, who had been traveling for several months in India,
was due to arrive shortly. Freya had promised to meet her in Brummana,
but because Francis Edmunds had said he would come to Damascus for a
visit, she waited impatiently, frustrated that he had not told her the exact
date of his arrival.

Recovered from dysentery, she now caught a cold and fretted in a letter to her mother that her face would be swollen and unattractive just as
Mr. Edmunds showed up. Although Freya was all too aware of her
mother's anxiety that she was doing nothing about getting married, she
was enjoying this new freedom to roam. She had recently written a friend:
"I have just come to the conclusion that I simply can't bear to part with
my own charming and amusing life while I am still well to enjoy it."[9] Still,
she knew it would please her mother to hear about a nice bachelor in the
wings, so from the moment she met Francis Edmunds, she had been
reporting on him at length. Furthermore, she quite liked him.

She was napping in her room when she heard his voice outside. Almost
at the same moment, however, another bachelor friend, a Frenchman
whom she had met in Beirut, turned up as well. The men were gratifyingly
horrified by her digs, and the Frenchman went to a hotel, but Francis
gamely opted to share the pain and spend the night on the roof. In a gesture of true sacrifice, Freya gave him her bug sprayer, amused to think
how much fodder for gossip this rooming arrangement would give the
missionaries. For several days the three enjoyed sightseeing, although
Freya would have preferred having Francis to herself. Together in the
Frenchman's car they raced back to Brummana, where Freya stroked

Freya Stark in Arab dress, 1928, after her first trip to the East and venture into the forbidden territory of the rebellious Druze.

Venetia Buddicom, whose family owned a villa near the Stark women's home on the Italian Riviera as well as a large estate in Flintshire. Venetia became Freya's closest friend, and the two traveled together in Spain and the Levant before Venetia hurt her back in a riding accident.

Mlle. Audi's starched white curtains, relieved to see cleanliness again. They had shared a pleasant interlude, the sort to encourage warm feelings. So before she left Brummana, Freya invited Francis to visit her in Italy during his summer vacation. Because they shared a great admiration for the poet, she suggested that they make a pilgrimage to the places Dante had lived. It must have hurt and surprised her when he turned her down.

Twenty-five years later, however, when Freya wrote her autobiography, she lightly dismissed her friendship with the young schoolmaster who had brightened the cold evenings in Lebanon. She credited him with bringing to her attention the stimulating ideas of Rudolf Steiner but remarked: "When I returned to Brum[m]ana in 1929 and saw him again, he was absorbed in a new and promising pupil; she was younger than I was, and much prettier, and a visible proof, I felt, of how difficult it is to keep to the abstract in this world."[10]

Actually, however, Francis's pupil was the teenage daughter of the head of the Quaker mission school and was far too young to interest him romantically. Reading Freya's book those many years later, he admitted to feeling injured that he had been so "slightingly dismissed." He confessed that he had not accepted Freya's invitation because he had not wanted "to arouse expectations which would not be fulfilled."[11] But those who came to know Freya best understood that she always found a way to tailor unpleasant facts to her liking, and it was much more agreeable to look back on a romantic rejection by remembering that someone who had interested her had been captured by another than to think he had not been interested at all.

Freya was finally learning how not to be hurt. She was carefully crafting a skill that would sustain her all her life. If people made Freya unhappy, were unkind or indifferent to her, they simply receded from view, curling beneath the waves like discarded pages from her notebook as her ship sailed boldly on.

In the meantime Venetia Buddicom had finally arrived, eager to be shown the sights. Freya could hardly wait to tell her the latest details of the travel scheme she had concocted.

· · ·

Freya's friendship with Venetia had been a joy from the moment they met. In the company of this gentle and intelligent person, just a year or so younger than herself, Freya unclasped the protective sheath she wore in her mother's company. She had visited Venetia several times at Penbedw, the Buddicoms' sprawling mansion on a four-thousand-acre estate in northern Wales, and was invariably reluctant to return to her own hard labors after enjoying riding, hiking, and good talk in Penbedw's peaceful glens. The two women corresponded constantly, and Venetia's letters were always full of admiration at Freya's cleverness. Best of all, Venetia never seemed to mind when Freya took the lead.

Now they were setting off again, and Freya as usual had a plan firmly in mind. She had decided they should "penetrate" the region known as the Jebel Druze, or Mountain of the Druze, although it had been under French martial law ever since the recent Druze rebellion. Security would be tight, a thought that only made Freya's heart beat faster, especially because everyone had assured her the trip was impossible. When Venetia had written from India to ask if they weren't dreaming to think they could get past the cordon, Freya had cheerfully dismissed her doubts. Quoting one of the Arab proverbs she was forever scribbling into her notebook, she answered airily: "The wise man sits by the river, but the fool gets across barefoot." That, she added, "is what *we* are going to do."[12]

. . .

In early May, jiggling along on their wooden saddles, listening to the rhythmic tinkle of cockleshells and blue beads on the harnesses of their donkeys, Freya and Venetia rode through the barren landscape leading into Druze country. They had provisioned in Damascus and crept out five days before during the cool of daybreak so as not to arouse attention. Now they were beginning to feel the sun's heat and to be newly annoyed that Najm, their guide, had forgotten their large waterskin in his haste to get them away. But he was a Druze, Freya assured Venetia, and ought to know where safe water could be found in this forbidden territory. Keeping to a steady southern course through cornfields withering from a prolonged drought, they had put the majestic sight of Mount Hermon, blue-flanked and crested with snow, behind them. On their left stretched the brown Syrian desert. It was wild country, Freya thought, where nothing seemed to grow that did not have spikes, and a fiery wind was hot on their faces. Occasionally they passed rubble that had once been a town, perhaps built by Phoenicians or Romans, or maybe once an Umayyad stronghold or Crusader fortress.

Najm, cautious for all his dashing yellow boots, was reluctant to let them rest very long by the watering holes during the day for fear of bandits or Bedouin raiders. He told them that some travelers he'd guided a few years back had been robbed and murdered on this road and that he would be sorry to repeat the experience. So they pressed on toward the blue hills that were their goal. During the first days they had passed people and their animals, and once four French armored cars had raced by but did not notice them. The previous day a police car had actually stopped, and three agitated officers began bawling at Najm for directions. Freya could not resist the temptation to nudge her donkey forward to see what it was all about, and though the officers stared at her strangely, they were clearly in too much of a hurry to ask questions.

The day before they had ridden along the Leja, a great volcanic shelf from which rock villages had been cut that were as black as night. They rarely passed other travelers now, and when they did Najm took care that it was a restrained meeting with little conversation. At night they asked for lodging in the black villages. Najm would inquire for the "most comfortable" house, and they would be taken in and fed, the villagers always refusing compensation despite the war and drought. Freya was struck by how sturdy, big-boned, and dignified the Druze men were, despite looking like pirates, with their wild locks plaited into pigtails and their shining, kohl-rimmed eyes. The women too were big, swinging layers of skirts under close velvet bodices and festooning their hair with gold dowry coins under long veils. Many of the men wore ragged European or Turkish uniforms obviously acquired during the war. Freya was touched to see how many jackets still had regimental buttons attached.

Few of these people had ever before talked with a foreigner, certainly not two Englishwomen asking to bunk down by their hearth—or preferably, because Venetia loathed fleas, in their bean gardens outside—but they were unfailingly courteous, and Freya was kept busy to the point of exhaustion answering their questions and translating for Venetia.

At the start of their trip, they had passed through villages that belonged to Circassians, a people descended from the Christian slaves of Georgia who had served the Ottomans for centuries. Many Circassian men had volunteered to fight on the French side during the revolt, and the Druze had retaliated viciously. The memories of those massacres were very fresh; in one town equally populated by both groups, Freya felt palpable tension. However, she found the Circassians far less attractive, "pouring out of their low doors like rabbits," and could make no sense of their odd language.[13] It was to the Druze and their reputation as fierce fighters that she was drawn.

She could hardly wait to get into the rugged, high reaches that these secretive and rebellious people had occupied for nearly a millennium. A homogeneous group dominated by their aristocratic ruling families, the Druze were a closed community, which frowned on intermarriage and kept to their mountain strongholds. Their tightly held beliefs, obscure to outsiders, were not revealed even to the uninitiated within the sect but known only to their sages, who wore distinctive tightly wound white turbans. They were said to possess a canon including 111 sacred letters and a scripture called the Book of Wisdom. In a country where every religious group seemed to be a nation unto itself, the Druze were known to be reservedly polite, disciplined, and extremely wary of strangers venturing into their midst.

The Druze were a heretical branch of a previous heretical Islamic off-shoot, the Isma'ilis, who had broken from the main branch of Shi'ism in 760 in a succession struggle. At the death of the Sixth Imam, so called because the Shi'a regard him as the sixth in the line of the Prophet's legitimate successors, his eldest son, Ismail, was passed over; his younger son was made the Seventh Imam instead. But Ismail's supporters never abandoned his claim as the Prophet's rightful heir. By the last quarter of the tenth century, the Isma'ilis' radical faith had engulfed North Africa; they had conquered Egypt, founded Cairo, and established themselves as the Fatimids, an Isma'ili dynasty. A Fatimid caliph, al-Hakim, whose cruel and bizarre behavior suggested he was deranged, made himself the center of a cult worshiping him as God Incarnate. The reign of terror he imposed on Cairo ended in 1021, when he vanished without a trace—murdered, it was suspected, by his sister.* Nonetheless, some loyalists remained convinced of al-Hakim's divinity and were forced to flee Cairo for their lives. These missionaries scattered throughout the East, each developing unique interpretations and followings, until today the largest community of Isma'ilis can be found in Bombay. One cultist, Muhammed ibn Isma'il al-Darazi, although assassinated in Cairo in 1019 (probably with the blessing of al-Hakim, who considered him too powerful), had been responsible for the cult's penetrating Syria; it was from al-Darazi, therefore, that the disciples of the new movement gained their name, Druze.[14]

Freya sensed in the Druze a subject worthy of study. In her budding efforts to explore the world of Islamic beliefs, the Druze appeared to belong to one of the most intriguing of the many heterodoxies that had plagued the faith from its beginning. At this point she had no way of knowing that her interest in the Druze would lead her to another cult, whose hold on her imagination would have thrilling consequences and launch her career as a traveler and explorer.

In the meantime the notion of observing a people whose rites were carefully obscured, who had no public places of worship and ignored the

---

* Until al-Hakim's reign the Christian holy places had been respected by the Muslim caliphs. However, Hakim broke that tradition, persecuted the Christians, and ordered the destruction of thirty thousand churches in Egypt, Palestine, and Syria. When word reached Europe that he had desecrated the Church of the Holy Sepulcher in Jerusalem, it became one of the motivating provocations for the First Crusade in 1096.

five daily Islamic prayers, was enormously seductive. Freya understood that the Druze were not supposed to discuss their religious beliefs, but she couldn't help hoping she might get a chance to do so. So far she had been with simple villagers, and because the Druze carefully separated those who were allowed to share occult secrets and those who merely obeyed, she knew she would have to wait until she was in the heart of their domain. She had a letter in her kit that she counted on to open the door to one of the chieftains; then perhaps she'd have some luck. The letter had been given her by Salehmy, the young man who'd taught her Arabic grammar in Brummana; his childhood nurse happened to be a servant in a Druze chieftain's camp.

. . .

They had left the larger town of Sawara el Kebir before light, skirting a lonelier outpost, Khul Khuly, when they saw in the distance French flags waving over a French garrison. Lest they be spotted, they stepped off the easy "Sultan's Way" and guided their donkeys along a rough mule track. Venetia was not feeling well, perhaps from breathing the fumes of her Keating bug sprayer, which she had used liberally in close quarters, or possibly from the brackish water they had reluctantly been drinking. Both were drenched with perspiration, but Freya was pleasantly surprised to find that her own body seemed to be holding up well. By afternoon Najm had brought them into the foothills of the Jebel Druze, and they were climbing toward Shabha, a village strung high along a black ridge. This, at last, was the center of Druze territory. As the light failed, and the sweet smell of white dianthus perfumed the cool twilight, they clattered through an old Roman gate, their donkeys' hooves striking loudly against the ancient marble pavers. Through the gloom Freya made out the gleaming headdresses of Druze men squatting on doorsteps and thought to herself that "the centuries were whispering behind them."[15] Najm knocked on a door. Two veiled women admitted them. Venetia and Freya, weary and grateful, were invited to wash their hands and faces. They had just settled into the embrace of soft sheepskins on the floor when the French military police arrived.

. . .

As they were conducted into the garrison, Freya whispered to Venetia that they must try to look "jaunty." Venetia, observing that the iron grilles they had just passed were the front of a jail, said she wasn't sure she was feeling terribly "jaunty." The next thing they knew, they were being ushered into what was apparently an officers' mess. A group of men stared in open astonishment, their forks suspended in midair, as an officer in a white uniform came forward. The "desmoiselles" were to be "guests" of the garrison, he said. They would not be returning to the Druze village, he added, and he identified himself as the *mustashar,* or senior intelligence officer. They need not try to retrieve their baggage; it would be brought to the post and kept until further decisions could be made.

When the mustashar indicated they were to join the table for dinner, Freya and Venetia asked to be allowed to wash up first. Once they could talk privately, they wondered what on earth they should say was their reason for wandering in Druze country. Giggling nervously at their predicament, they agreed they would put the blame on inaccuracies in their Thomas Cook guidebook. Also, although there was clearly nothing she could do about it, the knowledge that Freya's little notebook, with her unflattering comments about the French jotted in the margins, might be found if they searched her baggage added even more spice to the situation. Venetia looked apprehensively at Freya. It was, as Freya later said, "an uncomfortable meal."[16]

With narrowed eyes and distant courtesy, the officers began to grill the two women. Venetia's schoolgirl French was no match for Freya's, so Freya did most of the talking, getting the distinct impression that it was she, not Venetia, on whom suspicions were settling. She quite liked the feeling. Indeed, that they had been apprehended by the French seemed almost too good to be true; *here* was a story to write—and she was sure they were in no real danger. Although she had not meant to reveal that she spoke Arabic, thinking she might learn something interesting by keeping the fact secret, when Najm was hauled in and questioned, Freya encouraged him in his native tongue, giving herself away.

How, the officers asked them, had the desmoiselles managed to drive into the country without being noticed? They hadn't driven, the ladies answered truthfully. They had come on donkeys.

"Donkeys? From where?"

"We came from Damascus."

"Damascus?" Their interrogators exchanged glances. Did the desmoiselles not realize that Damascus was almost sixty miles away? Where had they slept?

"In the villages," purred Freya. "We were very well treated."

"These people appear to be better than they are," murmured the mustashar, and Freya knew he meant the Druze.

When the officers then asked why they were *riding* in the Jebel Druze, Freya and Venetia simultaneously chorused that they were amazed to have discovered there were *roads,* protesting that no such convenience had been mentioned in their guidebook. "You really should get it brought up-to-date," Freya added reproachfully. "It is very *pénible* to go about on donkeys, and you would have *lots* of tourists if they only knew what an *easy* country it is."

The assumption that the French army wished to encourage tourism through a rock-strewn wasteland recently torn by bloodshed appeared momentarily to throw their interrogators offstride. One, looking hard at Freya, said he thought it very strange that "the Agence Cook should send you."

They hadn't exactly been sent, Freya and Venetia hurried to explain. They were traveling for pleasure. A third officer then drawled in an especially unfriendly tone: "Some of your compatriots travelled here . . . just before the rebellion," alluding to whispers that had been floating through Syria that English spies had helped to incite and supply the insurrection. Ignoring the insinuation, Freya inquired if the officers had had many visitors.

"Mesdemoiselles," responded the mustashar, "you may say you are the first. When your coming was reported, we dismissed it as a quite impossible rumor." When several officers added that such travel as they had been doing was dangerous, Freya, wondering if she had found her story, pounced: "What danger? Is it not all quiet now?" The French could only answer: "Perfectly quiet."

"We knew that it was quite safe since you have taken it over," she said agreeably, delighted to annoy them.

• • •

When, eventually, they were taken to a room at the garrison and left alone, Venetia confided to Freya that she was worried they might cause an "international incident." She reminded Freya that her cousin had only recently stepped down as the British governor of Bombay and she had just come from traveling in India with him. That could easily strike French officialdom as odd. At worst they might assume she was spying for the British and at least wonder why someone with as many Foreign Office family connections as Venetia would want to be deep inside a French military zone.

Much as the prospect of being imprisoned as a spy titillated Freya, she feared the greater probability was that they would be forcibly removed from the area. Even if the mustashar let them continue but assigned them a police escort, it would mean the end of any further conversations with Druze. Through a thin partition separating their room from his office, Freya could hear the intelligence officer talking with his men, and she

pressed her ear to the wall to listen. They must not under any circumstances, she whispered to Venetia, accept "a French Guided Tour." Suddenly they could not stop giggling, holding each other and gasping.
Maybe the mustashar would decide the whole incident was as ridiculous
as it seemed to them and would let them go.

That night, after making a great fuss about the guard outside their
room, whom Freya insisted was affronting their modesty, she scribbled a
note to her mother: "We felt that as we had no choice about remaining, it
was better to do so as guests, and have been very careful to keep the matter on this footing, which is making it much more difficult for our poor
jailors to do anything about us. Whatever they suggest in the way of
detainment, we thank them for effusively, and tell them how charming it
is to find such unexpected hospitality, how delightful to have a bed with
nothing in it besides, and water to wash in, with a policeman to bring it to
you."[17]

It was a jousting match that Freya loved. Venetia was less sanguine,
continuing to worry about possible unpleasant fallout for her family or
the British government. Freya urged her to keep laughing and flirting.
They demanded pajamas—"You've taken our luggage!"—and eventually
some were produced from a soldier's gear. "The feminine element has
obviously not been known in Shahba before," Freya noted archly.[18]

The next morning she was allowed to see her baggage just long enough
to get her own nightclothes. Najm, who had been questioned at length and
wore an expression of absolute blankness, was standing nearby. Freya
stooped, ruffled through the suitcase, snatched out the inflammatory notebook, and thrust it into the alarmed guide's ample waistcloth. The poor
man began perspiring nervously, and when they went back to their room,
Freya and Venetia laughed wildly.

For the next two days, while the two women continued behaving as if
they were guests at a garden party and the garrison discussed what should
be done about them, the mustashar obliged them to accompany him as he
toured his district. Freya had begged him to let them ride his horses, so
each morning they set off in the company of six guards. He showed them
new roads, water supplies, and schools—all projects, Freya noted to herself, that the French were forcing the villagers to construct.

The previously cordial Druze now cast them black looks. Trotting
along, the mustashar admitted that, as far as he was concerned, the Druze
were "barbarians who cannot understand that France is Civilization and
Civilization is good." If it is forced upon them, Freya later recalled him
declaring, "they will come to understand it, and accept it gratefully in time.
A strong regime is necessary while they are becoming accustomed to what

Left: Druze elders, called a'kil ("One who can be trusted with the secrets of the Order"), traditionally wear white turbans, mustaches, and baggy trousers secured at the waist with wide cummerbunds.

Sheikh Mut'ib el Atrash of the powerful Atrash clan, leader of the Druze Revolt in 1925, an insurrection that ignited a countrywide rebellion against French rule in Syria, and which the French put down ruthlessly.

Bedouin unloading camels outside the Damascus Gate, Jerusalem, 1920s.

they themselves will wish for when once they are sufficiently educated to judge. They will then be happy to find themselves under French rule."[19]

Freya smiled encouragingly but inwardly seethed. As far as she could see, the mustashar's views were identical to those of every other Frenchman she had met in Syria. She privately compared the French methods with the "looser" system the British were establishing in their neighboring mandates of Palestine and Transjordan. So far as she could tell there was no evidence that the French were doing anything to support private business initiatives, or to rebuild agriculture, and nothing to get the devastated economy back into the hands of the people. "It is ridiculous to call this a mandate," she fulminated, "for I believe there is not a Frenchman in this country who intends to let these people ever govern themselves." Beyond that, she said, "it is their bad manners [to the natives] that annoy me so. They talk of them and to them as if they were scarce to be considered as human beings. If the Druzes ever get a chance, they will not leave a man alive in the whole district."[20]

. . .

Confident that her mix of coquetry and interest had disarmed his suspicions, Freya now admitted to the mustashar that she carried a letter to one of the rebel chieftains. The French officer, who had already discovered Salehmy's letter when he searched her bags, was impressed by her candor. By then they had overheard him tell one of his subordinates that they were "ladies erudite and distinguished."[21] It looked as if he would let them go. Emboldened, Freya asked if he knew other Druze chieftains they might meet. On the third day she knew he had decided to release them when he gave them a note to Sheikh Ahmed el Hajari, whom Freya otherwise could not have imagined getting in to see. Sheikh Ahmed was the high priest of all the Druze, and evidently the mustashar had come to believe their travels were harmless and nonincendiary. Freya, who had relished every minute of their detainment, told the mustashar that they couldn't *wait* to get home and tell their mothers about having been regarded by a French intelligence officer as *"agentes politiques!"*

. . .

There was one brief moment of anxiety as they bade the mustashar goodbye. He told them that he was sending them the rest of the way in a government car. At once Freya and Venetia rose in protest. He simply couldn't, they chorused, looking aggrieved, disappointed, flirtatious. They *must* have their darling donkeys. Slyly, they even suggested he should come and protect them on the third beast, which was so absurd he laughed and his resistance collapsed entirely.

Najm caroled with relief as their little party put the garrison out of sight and cantered along in a holiday mood through countryside that was more cool and green than the dry Leja plain. As they reached higher ground they saw pomegranates, figs, and walnuts flourishing on the hillsides, and eventually they arrived in the small village of Kanawat, the home of the Druze supreme spiritual leader. A dignified old man with a fine aquiline profile and neat white beard, he was none too pleased at their arrival, peering nearsightedly at the surprising letter of introduction they presented from his people's enemy, the French mustashar. When he was informed, however, that his callers were English, not French, he softened slightly and welcomed them politely. If he was amazed by the appearance of two European ladies, his conduct was formal and correct—although Freya and Venetia could not help noticing that he and the gowned elders attending him avoided getting close or touching them. Later they learned that infidels were expected to keep their polluted Christian hands out of harm's way by crossing them against their breasts when being greeted.

"I think we disappointed the High Priest," Freya wrote her mother about the interview.

> When he learned that V. came from India, he and all the evening gathering became suddenly very eager and wanted her to explain the secret religions of the country. Unfortunately she is not at all up in these. I explained Buddhism as well as I could, and we then told them a little about Thibet [sic] and the Devil Worship of Central India: this was what they wanted and they were intensely interested and asked many questions of which V. could not answer many. This was very disappointing, and I made matters worse by translating Devil Worship literally, and was surprised to hear a sort of groan of horror go round the room. I then remembered vaguely that the Druses do not believe themselves to be unique in the world, but hold that somewhere in the Far East there is another people of Druses who are coming as conquerors westward in the last days of the earth, to join their brothers in the Jebel. We were on delicate ground. I believe Sheikh Ahmed had hoped that we came to give him a message. He gave us up as inadequate and gathered with the Elders round the table at the far end of the room where they read in low voices out of little green books.[22]

They had better luck with less august Druze, who were delighted to hear them tell their tale of incarceration at the hands of the French military. Soon the villagers were recounting their own searing experiences during the uprising, the desperate barricades they had put up against French tanks, the terrible bombing raids by French planes, which left them no shelter, and the bravery of their families, so many of whom had been killed.

"The water of this land has madness in it," a young man observed sadly. "Every ten years we have a war." He offered to show them his wounds, immodestly whipping up his long striped gown to reveal arms and legs pockmarked by scars. He thrust at them a scrap of paper that turned out to be a receipt for one rifle and a revolver. "I got the guns from killing a French soldier. Now we are disarmed, and all I have are these," he said, waving the receipts. "And when the Bedouin come to take away our sheep we have no means of driving them away."[23]

Moving on, Freya and Venetia passed through Suweida, a center of battle where the French had been blockaded for five months and their relieving forces slaughtered by Druze warriors in acts of suicidal bravery. Eventually, eager to present their letter from Salehmy, Freya and Venetia arrived in the small village of Resas, on the edge of the fertile Hauran plain. The letter opened the way to Sheikh Mut'ib el Atrash, one of the powerful Atrash clan, who had only recently been allowed back from exile. Many Druze leaders had been executed or permanently banished, but Mut'ib had received a cautionary pardon. He proved an imposing figure, with a drooping black mustache and heavy gray cloak riddled with bullet holes. He told them that its dusty color made him difficult to hit and its folds caught bullets. Warm and courtly to his visitors, he invited them to stay, apologizing for living in a nomad tent; the French, he explained, had dynamited his house. That night, as she would later do many times in the future, Freya settled under a great haircloth canopy, listening to the snorting of camels tethered outside, and heard women talk of their prized possessions—clothes and china and rugs—things women everywhere like to discuss. Only in this case they spoke sadly, because these precious things had been broken or destroyed during the rebellion—lost to the grand ambitions of French colonial rule.

"The League of Nations is a long way away," Mut'ib remarked that evening, "and it is not we who write the newspapers. But we shall succeed in the end. The Druze does not change. We know how to keep in touch with each other under any government. And we know how to wait. The English do not help us, but they allow their nations some freedom, and all that surrounds us is on our side."[24]

It was probably then, watching the superb old chieftain wave a hand toward the darkness outside, feeling transported to an ancient world of traditions more powerful and imperative than any she had experienced before, that Freya conceived the image of the genie summoned by Aladdin's magic lamp. Are we not all slaves of the Lamp, she wondered— the mysterious consciousness of race and culture that binds men and keeps them separate? The shining object must be handled carefully, she thought. A careless stroke could bring the genie springing to life in the service of Arab nationalism. "Who," she later wrote, referring to the heavy responsibility of the mandate powers, "would not tremble to be among the Guardians of the Lamp?"[25]

For Freya the British were the better guardians, infinitely better than the French. But she desired to bring a warning home, and wanted to be listened to. She had learned a great deal and felt a profound sympathy for the Arab people, whose aspirations for liberty, she sensed, were poised to spring as commandingly to life as the genie and threaten Europe's colonial schemes. She would try to get an article written about all she had seen, she resolved. And then she would come back to write more.

· · ·

Their trip was nearly over, and the two friends had got "along in pleasant harmony," which, said Freya, was "remarkable considering the strain of extreme discomfort." They had not had a real bath since they left. At times Freya had felt "broken to bits," exhausted by the effort of constantly interpreting, and sometimes had just enjoyed an Arabic conversation by herself without Venetia. She had been relieved, however, to learn that "when V. is meditative with downcast eyes, I now know that she is merely localizing a flea," and not resentful.[26] As for herself, Freya had proved that it was quite feasible to travel with the utmost simplicity, a muleteer or two and light gear, deep in the country away from tourist facilities, relying on the kindness of locals. It was also a cheap way to go, she noted with satisfaction. Later in the course of her wandering life, Freya would continue to take advantage of native hospitality and be sparing with her tips, persuading herself that she shouldn't exceed local norms and "spoil" those who helped her. In this view she was by no means the first; past European travelers had made such conduct a standard practice in remote lands. Because their disappointed guides, or hosts, or provisioners usually had no authority except Allah* to which they could protest, they generally

---

* Allah is the Arabic term for God, or Jehovah, the same all-powerful deity worshiped by the other two great monotheist religions, Christianity and Judaism, and not a word referring to some kind of Oriental deity.

accepted whatever was paid, concluding simply that Europeans in general and British in particular were terrible "scroungers."[27]

When Freya and Venetia emerged from the country of the Druze, first passing through Basra, with its great basalt amphitheater built by the Romans, they had been away more than two weeks.* Bidding farewell to Najm—Freya's first guide to be undertipped—and their donkeys in Salkhad, they hired a car to take them through the Roman ruins of Jerash and in due course crossed the Allenby Bridge over the Jordan River into Palestine. The Holy Land brought a new set of excitements, including their first visit to Jerusalem. From there they went on to Cairo and panted up the giant steps of the pyramids, happy at having reached the two great goals of any visitor to the East. It had been a merry journey that Freya would always remember, although nothing could quite match the high drama of those days in the Shabha garrison, where they might so easily have touched off an international incident.

Weeks later Francis Edmunds wrote Freya from Brummana that her travels in Syria had left "a trail of surmises and not a little dust." He said that the Brummana community was still perplexed about

> why you should choose to live and perhaps die in the slums of Damascus merely because you wish to learn Arabic. Neither can they see why you should choose to stay in a native household, rather than at a public hotel of known repute in the company of a wide circle of English, French, and German-speaking people. As for the venture in the Desert, that indeed is difficult to understand! Is it likely that you would wish to risk your skin merely to see a pile of ugly old ruins, and is it likely that your friend would wish to risk her skin merely to keep you company? And why should you be so friendly with the Druses? And anyway why are you so specially interested in people who must still be regarded as something of a menace to the existing government? and how did you manage to get such valuable introductions?

He ended: "I merely repeat the sort of rumours that have been floating about. If you should ever come out here again before you are completely forgotten, you will be a character crusted over with quite a

---

* At the time of Freya's adventure, little of the Syrian Hauran, including Basra's ancient town, had been excavated. Freya's letters, therefore, often neglect to mention ruins built with the distinctive black blocks that a modern visitor invariably finds, after Palmyra, among the most remarkable in Syria.

mythology: people will knit their troubled brows in obvious perplexity."[28]

Freya quite liked that. She wouldn't at all mind becoming a myth.

. . .

For all the curiosity generated back in isolated Brummana by the odd behavior of Miss Stark, in more sophisticated circles there was a well-known precedent for a woman traveling in the Jebel Druze—a very illustrious woman, in fact, the distinguished Arabist Gertrude Bell. In 1905 Bell had published her account, *The Desert and the Sown,* to considerable acclaim. Freya had read the book carefully and probably even planned her trip using its material because there was not much else, other than her much-maligned Thomas Cook's guidebook. Bell had been the first European woman to venture into the Jebel Druze since the eccentric Lady Hester Stanhope had sought out the Prince of the Mountain in 1812 and reported seeing Druze devour sheep raw, their wives wearing horned crowns on their heads, and anyone who dared ask a religious question murdered on the spot.[29]

From the beginning it seems Freya felt a keen rivalry with Gertrude Bell and may have seen herself as the successor to the spinster diplomat who became the first female Oriental secretary and who helped draw the boundaries of present-day Iraq at the end of World War I. Just a little over a year before Freya arrived in Lebanon, a few days before her fifty-eighth birthday, Bell had committed suicide with an overdose of sleeping pills at her house in Baghdad.

Freya might well have seen a challenge in matching the prewar account of traveling through Syria in which Bell made it clear that the Ottoman authority was hopelessly shattered. Freya could demonstrate that Syria was now under the autocratic thumb of the French. Although both women shared the view, as Bell had put it, that "few such moments of exhilaration can come as that which stands at the threshold of wild travel,"[30] Freya never gave Bell credit for being an inspiration for her own traveling. In fact, it was just the opposite. When a publisher asked Freya just before the Second World War if she would write Bell's biography, Freya instantly rejected the offer, saying she was "not very fascinated" by Bell's life.[31]

Yet Bell *was* fascinating. And Freya knew it. Besides being beautiful and aristocratic, Bell had been a brilliant scholar and was physically courageous—attributes that Freya admired. The daughter of a wealthy, well-connected, and intellectual father, Bell had begun traveling—as Freya had—in a quest for personal freedom and hoping to gain stature beyond what was ordinarily accorded a single woman. As Freya would, Bell found the East a congenial venue that provided scope for her intellect. She put her linguistic skills and stunning understanding of Arab tribal society at the service of the British Empire, penetrating the all-male bastion of the Foreign Office, where, thanks in part to her influence, the British chose Emir Faisal over other Hashemite princes to be crowned king of Iraq.

There were many similarities between the two women. Both were accomplished Alpine climbers, both gifted writers, and Freya, like Bell, became fascinated with archaeology. Yet if Freya's Druze trip paralleled Bell's twenty-three years earlier, this was never mentioned when the letters Freya wrote home about it were published during the Second World War under the title *Letters from Syria*. Perhaps she cannot be held entirely responsible, since the book was edited by a friend. Still, it was evident that Freya was keeping score.

"I am re-reading Gertrude Bell's *Syria* and comparing her route with ours," she wrote a friend in 1929. "She, however, travelled with three baggage mules, two tents, and three servants: so I consider we were the more adventurous. She also says that the water in the J. Druse is 'undrinkable by European standards,' so I suppose our standard cannot be European: or perhaps an Italian education has hardened us?"[32]

Comparisons between the two women were inevitable from the moment Freya was recognized in scientific circles, yet she never acknowledged any debt or conceded that Bell had been a trailblazer in the East. Indeed, the comparisons that Freya felt dogged by all her life seemed actually threatening to her. "My Siamese twin," she would complain irritably to friends of some new reference in the press to herself and Bell.[33] It was as if every success that Freya had, and she would have many, was so precious to her and filled such a bottomless need that she could not be generous about her deceased rival. Freya was a fighter; it is fair to say that in part her mother had made her so. She had needed to be fierce to survive. And just as her mother was unforgiving to those who opposed her will, Freya learned to give no quarter to anyone or anything that stood in her way or threatened her fragile self-esteem. Her competitiveness became her strength.

Yet in important ways Freya and Bell were conspicuously different. Freya started out without rank or money or an Oxford education as Bell had enjoyed. She was mostly self-taught. Although statecraft came to interest her intensely later on and she deserved her reputation as a foremost expert on the Middle East, primarily she was a gifted writer with an ethnologist's instincts—and far, far too free a spirit to play the constrained game required of diplomats. Unlike Bell, Freya started out poor, an outsider, and a maverick—willing to trust her life to simple native guides instead of the retinues that accompanied Bell. And in the end she roamed much farther.

. . .

"I am longing for badminton," Freya wrote dreamily as her ship steamed homeward.[34] The friends had parted in Cairo; now Venetia was on her way back to England and Freya to Italy. It would be wonderful to see her mother and godfather in Asolo, where no one was "spitting" or "eating with their fingers" and the bug sprayer could safely be put away in favor of games on the lawn with friends. The thought of a day's pause to shop in Venice—perhaps for a hat, or a parasol, and definitely she needed new shoes—was very alluring. She had been gone seven months and spent only two hundred pounds. She had asked her mother to keep her letters and was confident that the fat pile bearing exotic stamps was waiting in her mother's desk. For the rest of her life Freya preferred this way of maintaining a record, rather than keeping a regular diary.

Freya felt enormously pleased with all she had learned. In the future, she decided, it was better "to stay longer in one place," unlike Gertrude Bell, who had constantly moved from one campsite to the next and who also, Freya believed, "didn't have enough adventures: perhaps because she went with her own tents." Freya was now thinking she would like to "dig in" in order to "get to the heart of things." In a letter she said, "If I live and I am free, I should like to have a little shop for a time somewhere in an eastern town. Say Hama or Aleppo? Great possibilities for observation—in fact the ideal for a meditative life."[35]

At this point Freya wasn't sure just what her next move would be. But her Arabic was good now, and she yearned to return. She had no desire to banish the "dim but insistent" feeling that "the whole of my future must be rearranged."[36] Moreover, her exposure to the fascinating and inscrutable Druze had sparked a desire to know more. In addition to the Indian connection about which the high priest in Kanawat had queried Venetia, she had learned that they were somehow connected to a weird and diabolical sect in Persia who had terrorized the East during the eleventh and twelfth centuries. The Crusaders had known about them, known they were called the Assassins, and carried back to Europe fantastical and horrifying tales. What was the connection? Did any Assassins survive? Could she get to Persia to find out? Her skin prickled with excitement and a sense of danger. She must go to London and look up what was available on this strange cult.

· · ·

Freya was not home a month before she was hard at work on her first article discussing the French "imperium" in Syria. She described her trip and the policies of the French that she had found so repugnant. "Troops are there in force and the people unarmed. If the regime can last for some time, and succeeds in educating a 'French' population in its schools, it may become permanent; the old independent social structure will at any rate be destroyed. Whether what takes its place will have any principle of life in it is more doubtful."[37] Hoping to stir her British readership to action, she concluded her article by invoking the image of Aladdin's lamp as the burning spirit of Arab nationalism. "The French are not going to like it much," she wrote her father, because "it is far too truthful for publication."[38] Nevertheless, it was immediately accepted by *Cornhill Magazine* and came out in November 1928.

Eager to return to Syria without incurring opposition from French officialdom, Freya chose not to reveal her authorship. She signed the piece "Tharaya," the Arab name for the dazzling star at the center of the constellation Pleiades. When the angel Gabriel brought the Revelations to the Prophet, so the story goes, Tharaya had risen in the dawn sky and sweet rains had watered Arabia, bringing *tharwa*, "a time of plenty." Arabs love the Pleiades, a guide and reassurance in the desert sky, and they often call their daughters Tharaya because it means "She Who Illuminates the World." It was a name to reckon with, Freya reflected.[39]

Perhaps it was a bit grandiose to imagine herself able to illuminate the world. But anything was possible, Freya was now allowing herself to believe, if she could only detach herself from the tender shackles that had kept her bound to home for so long.

CHAPTER FIVE

Ah, Baghdad

> *The beckoning counts, and not*
> *the clicking latch behind you.*
>
> —TRAVELLER'S PRELUDE

*N*o sooner had Freya returned to Europe than she was immersed in plans for getting back to the East. When her article on the Druze was accepted by *Cornhill Magazine,* she was overjoyed. She had to establish some credentials in the region if she were to find a role there. After all, Gertrude Bell's route to government service had been through published expertise, so it is easy to imagine that Freya hoped a similar avenue might open up for her. In any event, her article impressed *Cornhill's* editor, Dr. Leonard Huxley, who was willing to honor Freya's reluctance to reveal her real name.[1] He evidently agreed that it might jeopardize future travel for her in Syria if the French authorities knew the identity of their English critic. He accepted Tharaya as her nom de plume and invited her to submit more stories, while pointing out the new talent to his young assistant, Arnaud Robin Grey, who was working at the magazine between terms at Magdalen College, Oxford. In due course Grey, adopting the name John Murray, would assume the leadership of a distinguished family publishing firm by that name and share a singularly close working relationship with Freya that would bring great dividends to them both. But this was still a few years off.

In addition to the good news about *Cornhill,* Freya was enjoying for the first time a tentative confidence that her finances were in some state of order. Even before she had gone off to Lebanon, she had been receiving about three hundred pounds a year from investments—beyond what she needed to support her mother. She figured it was enough to get along, though barely. The endless suit against Mario looked close to settlement, and a wild gamble on the stock market had paid off. On a tip Freya had bought shares in the Canadian Grand Trunk Railway, which, to her amazement, had soared. When she went to the bank to collect, a beaming manager told her that she had shown such confidence in the stock that the entire staff had invested.

Better than that, the year before, Herbert Young had offered Freya his house. "I have had you, my dearest, in mind for sometime," he had written her in 1926. "I propose to make a will in your favor, leaving all my Asolo properties to you: the house and garden and furniture, etc. etc. Of course, I don't want to tie you down. . . . Don't I go away myself pretty often? But I want you to have it and keep it as a home. . . . People have called this earthly paradise—and I know you love the place."[2]

With this generous act Herbert had solved many problems, especially providing Freya's mother a place to stay in Asolo while she worked as manager and chief designer of the small silk-weaving atelier owned by an American lady, Lucy Beach. Herbert seemed pleased to have Flora's company despite their past rift and rechristened his house Casa Freia. For Freya it would always be a sanctuary to which she could return after some adventure far away.

If Freya could only have known how close she now was to a fascinating life she might have been less depressed by the family responsibilities that again crashed down upon her. Instead she felt herself stumbling from one problem to the next. She had to go to Dronero ("so dreadfully lonely") to check on Vera's children.[3] There, Mario asked her to stay. Despite her hearty dislike of her brother-in-law, she was torn. She sympathized with his grief and was genuinely fond of her niece, Angela, twelve, and her nephews, Paolo, nine, and Roberto, six. Even as she battled with her conscience, Canada also called. Since his stroke her father's letters were revealing a visibly shaking hand, and Freya both wanted and knew it was her duty to see him as soon as possible.

She loved these people—her father, Vera's children, her mother—but with all her heart she pined to do something beyond looking after others. It was both a cri de coeur and a promise to herself, therefore, when Freya wrote Flora from Dronero: "I shall not reach my own work until I am about forty. I do however hope to reach it eventually if there is anything of me left."[4]

The famous arch of Ctesiphon, soaring intact from the ruins of the ancient capital of the Sassanian Persians in the Iraqi desert. That Freya was able to scale the arch caused much comment in Baghdad's colonial circles.

Right: A scene of ordinary street life in Baghdad when Iraq was being administered by the British under a League of Nations mandate.

Captain Vyvyan Holt, center, stands with fellow officers in full dress uniform. They are attending a 1930 conference with King Saud of Arabia and King Faisal of Iraq.

There were troubles at L'Arma, too. Freya discovered that the "charming scamp" to whom she had rented the farm had mismanaged it. Flora had done nothing, leaving all the problems for Freya to take care of when she returned from Lebanon. It was as if a hydra's head of tasks always loomed in her path. She felt exhausted, the glorious energy of her recent travels vanishing like smoke. Thoroughly sorry for herself, frustrated and resentful, she began to feel "a bit sickish" as the old ulcerated colon flared. Her doctor told her she should start planning for an operation in the spring and confined her to bed. The thought of being an invalid again made her desperate, but when Herbert Young, ever sensitive to his young favorite's needs, suggested a spell of invigorating climbing in the Dolomites, which he would pay for, she accepted with alacrity, fled to the bracing mountain air, and was soon strong enough to embark for south-western Canada.

· · ·

Outside the small town of Creston, she found her seventy-five-year-old father living in a four-room log cabin, possessing a view of the 7,650-foot Smith Peak across the border in Idaho. Clearly diminished by his recent stroke, he still struggled to maintain a commercial business raising cherries, plums, pears, and especially apples. He claimed to be happy with his rustic life, boasting that the soil was as rich as that of the Nile Valley, and confided that he hoped to win another prize for his apples, as he had some years before at the Crystal Palace Fair. Freya was grateful that his manager, or bailiff, as Robert called him, had accompanied him from Devon. The bailiff and his wife lived in an even smaller cabin down by the stables and barns.

Freya stayed four months. How many more times, she wondered, would she and her father be able to be together? Her father had not relinquished his companionable pipe, and she feared it would kill him. He encouraged her to go to skating parties and a few local dances, but despite enjoying the rawboned, optimistic New World, she could not get over the angry feeling "of all these chunks of life taken away from what my own life is," as she wrote her mother in February 1929.[5]

So she sat at the kitchen table and applied herself to a trove of information on Iraq and Persia that she had hauled across the Atlantic to study. She managed to dash off another story for *Cornhill*—a cheerful, uncontroversial piece this time, about the Canadians she had met, to which Dr. Huxley soon gave a favorable reception. Huxley also saw no objection to Freya's continuing to use the pseudonym Tharaya. After all, as she told her father, she did not want their friends in Creston "to feel they are turning into copy when they come to call."[6] She quite relished keeping her name a secret. She was entertained by her private drama and could choose whomever and whenever she wished to let friends in on the secret. And should she investigate some of those mysterious cults in the East that had so sparked her interest, wasn't it just as well to keep a low profile?

After she bade her father good-bye, boarded the train to cross the snowy Canadian prairie to Halifax, and thence took the steamer for Southampton, Freya decided she would stop in London en route to Italy for a bit of study at the British Museum. There she looked up travelers who had crept secretly into Mecca and checked out as well the ancient network of Roman forts in Transjordan. But what persisted, she felt, as the most "promising" subject was the story of the Assassins. Perhaps, she wrote her father, she could combine "a sort of history with travel notes" about this monstrous cult. "I am very vague about it all," she admitted, "but am trying to find out some more before going out"—if, she finished ruefully, it hadn't "been done by some thoroughgoing German already."[7]

In any case, it was clear to her that Baghdad must be her next objective.

CHAPTER SIX

The Assassins and the Lurs

> *One life is an absurdly small allowance.*
>
> —LETTER TO A FRIEND,
> NOVEMBER 18, 1929

*A*t the end of October 1929, Freya finally succeeded in reaching Baghdad, the fabled capital of Iraq. Scheherazade, the princess storyteller of the Arabian Nights, neglected to mention anything about the summer temperatures of 120 degrees, the mud and muck that oozed in the spring, the wearying dust that blew through every season. In the broad, muddy waters of the Tigris, one was likely to see a body floating along in the busy river traffic—maybe human, or perhaps that of a donkey or a drowned sheep.

Even so, the name alone—Baghdad!—was enough to stir a romantic heart. Surrounding this flat, sun-baked city were scattered ruins that told a glorious history. To the north lay the once great Assyrian cities of Nineveh, Khorsabad, and Ashur, whose temples had gleamed with treasures captured by Sennacherib's plundering horsemen. To the south, near the banks of the Euphrates, were the ruins of Uruk of the Sumerians and Ur, where Abraham was born. Babylon was only eight miles west of Baghdad, and a few miles farther lay Kish, the Mesopotamian city that flourished before the biblical Deluge. Over the desert a great Third Dynasty ziggurat still towered at Borsippa. Close by as well soared the famous arch of Ctesiphon, capital of the Sassanian Persians captured by the Prophet Mohammed's warriors only ten years after his death. And the point where the twisting Tigris and Euphrates joined was Basra, now the land of the Marsh Arabs but, according to legend, the Garden of Eden from which God banished Adam and Eve.

For untold centuries camel caravans shuffled through Baghdad carrying silks and spices bound for Damascus and the Mediterranean coast, or wound their perilous way east over impossible mountains and the vast Taklimakan Desert to Peking. While Europe struggled in medieval backwardness, the black flag of the Abbasids waved over Baghdad. The Abbasids, having murdered their rivals the Umayyads, transferred the Muslim capital from Damascus to Baghdad and made it a city so glorious that even Constantinople trembled before Abbasid power. From the moment the caliph al-Mansur laid the first brick in 762, Baghdad became the center of an extraordinary intellectual and artistic flowering. Harun al-Rashid, or Aaron the Upright, sent emissaries to Charlemagne and the Chinese emperor and ruled over virtually all the Middle East and Northern Africa. Many a tale in the *Arabian Nights* celebrates the brilliance of the great caliph under whom Baghdad reached its apogee.

Eventually, however, corruption set in. While the court dined on fish tongues and drank from gem-encrusted goblets, the sweet scent of decay drifted through its gardens. In 1258 the Mongols thundered up to Baghdad's gates and battered the walls with their mangonels. They swarmed over the ramparts and destroyed every palace, mosque, library, and school, butchering the inhabitants until the streets ran with blood. The caliphal family, together with three hundred officials, were hacked to death. For the next seven hundred years Baghdad crumbled into a ruin of mud-brick buildings and dusty streets, a neglected province of the Ottomans, until it became, as Lady Anne Blunt remarked passing through in 1878, "uninteresting . . . a colorless Eastern town, and nothing more."[1]

But in 1921 a momentous change occurred. The British arrived with the Hashemite emir, Faisal, whom the French had ejected from Syria, and crowned him king of Iraq. His claims to legitimacy were impeccable, for he traced his ancestry back to the Prophet, while his family basked in their inherited role as Keepers of the Keys to the sacred Kaaba in Mecca.* Faisal quickly showed that he could be a diplomat as well as a Bedouin

---

* The late King Hussein of Jordan was the grandnephew of Faisal I of Iraq and the grandson of Faisal's brother Abdullah, installed by the British as king of Jordan.

warrior. It would take all his skill, Freya was soon to see, to manage the mix of races and religions in his arbitrarily created kingdom—whose borders had been drawn in great part thanks to the efforts of Gertrude Bell.

Freya arrived in Baghdad shortly after the stock market crash of 1929 sent shock waves around the world and felt triumphant that she had managed to get there on a total expenditure of forty-five pounds, with ten pounds still in her pocket. The Depression settling over the United States and Europe, which guaranteed a war with Germany ten years later, would affect her and everyone else in short order. But for the moment Freya was more interested in finding a cheap native place to stay—without exciting the negative notice of the starchy British colony, which kept to itself in comfortable bungalows among the date palms in the suburb of Alwiyah.

An Arab friend in Damascus had put Freya in touch with a local member of the Baha'i movement, an enlightened and rationalist religious reform sect from Persia, who helped her find three rooms up a steep staircase and behind a stout door that had to be opened with a foot-long latchkey. To make sure no uninvited guests descended from the roof, she parked an open pot of paint on the steps into her bedroom ("If a cat comes along and overturns it in the middle of the night I shall get a most awful fright," she wrote her father)[2] and was free to get the hang of the city—the narrow streets, the picturesque bridge of boats that spanned the Tigris, Gertrude Bell's little museum of antiquities. There was still an echo of Turkish rule in the fine old wooden houses that Turkish pashas had built along the Tigris, with galleried courtyards and terraces commanding a river view. A single boulevard called the Shari-el-Rashid ran through the huddle of houses and shops.

Freya was immediately fascinated by the marvelous array of ethnic types and sects: rugged Kurds from the north, Armenians, Assyrians, Jews, Chaldeans, Yezidi, Christians, Greeks, Turks, Persians, and Arabs from the desert. She was struck, too, by the enormous numbers of Shi'a, whose battles with their Sunni brethren at the beginning of Islam had occurred near Baghdad. She wanted to see their holy cities, where the great dramas of schism had been enacted, like Al Kufa, where the Prophet's cousin and son-in-law Ali, according to the Shi'a—Ali's "partisans"—the rightful inheritor of the Prophet's mantle, was murdered in 661. She wanted to see the mosque at Karbala built to honor Hussein, Ali's son, who was revered as the next "Rightly Guided One." In 680 Hussein had been chased, caught, and slaughtered along with his family and little party of followers by the Umayyad army, the standard-bearers of what would become Sunni Islam, whose adherents subscribe to the rightness of election over blood line in choosing a *khalifa* or successor.* Revulsion against the massacre of the Prophet's family had spawned the Shi'a doctrine, central to which is a strain of unexpiated grief over the world's injustice as well as an implacable hostility to the Sunni "usurpers." People told Freya that the atmosphere radiating from the Shi'a shrines was "sinister, obscurantist, and anti-government."³ What was more, the Shi'a were "fanatical." Infidels were not allowed so much as to touch the threshold of a Shi'a mosque, let alone enter it. They would be torn to pieces by the faithful if they did, she was assured. In fact, not long before, an inquisitive infidel had recently met just such a fate. Freya found the prospect of a secret visit very tempting.

She engaged her native friends in talk of politics and heard their complaints about the snobbery and arrogance of the British. All too many, she decided, of the so-called Christian colonialists she was meeting were far from acting as they preached. "If Christ were living now and were proposed for the Alwiyah club, say—not only would He not be elected, but the proposal would be generally considered absolutely bad from every point of view," she wrote her father indignantly. "Muhammadans may neglect their religion, but there would be none of this fundamental *antagonism* to Muhammad if he were to appear today."⁴ She was convinced by all that she had witnessed that religion was far more deeply integrated in the habits of everyday life in the East than it was in the West.

This was a time when the artificial lines laid down by the partitioning European powers had swept together some uncomfortable bedfellows in the new nation of Iraq. The Kurds and the Assyrian Christians wanted their own independent states—while the Sunni and Shi'a were even more mutually hostile than Freya had found them in Lebanon and Syria. Although the mandate granted by the League of Nations was due to expire in 1932 and the British had promised to withdraw their "advisers" and give Iraq true independence, many British colonials doubted the wisdom of withdrawal. Not only was it a matter of the old imperial hubris that "Britain knew best," but given the volatility of the differing parties, the state could go badly wrong. What was more, at this time the British had their hands full. Egypt chafed under the British Empire's "veiled protectorate," while in British-mandated Palestine the Arabs had launched a full-scale campaign of violence against Jews pouring in to buy Arab olive groves in order to create a Jewish homeland. The last thing the British

* The great majority of the world's Muslims, perhaps 85 percent, are "people of the Sunna," who look for guidance in discerning God's will both through the Holy Koran and the Sunna— the habits and practices of the Prophet and the first community of Followers who gathered with him in Medina.

needed now, it was hotly argued, was to wish even more disturbances on themselves in Iraq; its oil reserves and strategic position on the Persian Gulf were simply too important. The key here was to keep things on an even keel—even if it meant deferring independence.

Suddenly, Freya noticed that her house stank. Even her Armenian maid, essential to decent living and paid scant wages, found the mysterious foul humors wafting up from an ancient cistern insupportable. Whether it was garbage or the rotting corpse of some long-dead Assyrian, she never learned, but Freya was all too aware that the British wives were looking askance at her choice of a place to live. One evening a British lady came up to her at a party. Was Freya aware, she inquired, that the way she was living was "lowering the prestige of British womanhood"?[5] Freya smiled her way through the incident but resolved to be defiant. She liked her "slum,"[6] she insisted to friends, and wrote home zestful accounts of nights pierced with police whistles, a morning discovery of a murder next door, a visit by a crisply uniformed Iraqi policeman to collect cash to "protect" her. Finally a health officer arrived and begged her to leave. When he promised to help her find another place, Freya reluctantly assented. She was as amused as everyone else when she learned that she had been living in the prostitute quarter.

Soon she was resettled, this time with a balcony and a lovely view of the Tigris, with its exotic water traffic, including barges crammed with chanting Shi'a pilgrims on their way to the shining domes and four golden minarets of the nearby holy city of Al Kazimiyah. Her landlords were a Syrian Christian shoemaker and his tiny, quiet wife. They were kind to her, and she liked them and their friends.

Immediately, she plunged into language lessons, including Persian, and arranged to attend a girls' school for Arabic grammar. She seized every chance to see and do whatever she could inside or outside the city and, despite a tight budget of two rupees a day, managed to collect carpets, Assyrian cylinder seals, old bronzes, and glass beads—always preferring to go a little hungry rather than give up a nice antique. Slowly but surely Freya made the acquaintance of Baghdad, eventually even getting to meet some of the Iraqi royals. She also visited as many of the great archaeological sites as she could, once scaling the tremendous stone arch of Ctesiphon. It was a much-talked-about escapade, and when the Belgian king arrived a few years later, he could not imagine how she had done it.

One evening, longing to see for herself what it was like inside a Shi'a sanctuary, Freya persuaded a Muslim friend into taking her to the mosque at Al Kazimiyah, where the Seventh and Ninth Imams were entombed. Nervously covering herself from head to foot in black veils, she and his wife trailed behind "in true female Eastern fashion" as he and a servant led the way under the stars to the mosque's vast courtyard. At the sanctuary door they removed their shoes—Freya had taken the precaution of wearing the most "un-English" pair she could find—which were lifted to a shelf by a man with a stick to prevent contact with impure things. "It was a weird feeling to know that really one's life depended on not being recognized; and still weirder to see people looking straight at one and to remind oneself that they couldn't possibly see through the black veil," Freya reflected as she entered the shrine and passed through a heavy curtain into the innermost sanctum. Engulfed by perspiring penitents circling the tombs, moaning, sobbing, wailing, and beating their breasts in religious frenzy, Freya felt helpless. Perspiring now herself, the hot breath of the pilgrims on her back, she finished her circumambulation as full of emotions as everyone else and did not again smuggle herself into a Shi'a mosque.[7]

Some of the friends Freya made here she would keep for her lifetime. Stefana Drower was the wife of the British legal adviser to the Iraqi government and had written a number of novels with Eastern themes. Unlike most colonial wives, Mrs. Drower was passionately interested in the Arabs, spoke their language fluently—better even than Freya—and was documenting the religious beliefs and rites of some of the more obscure sects, like the so-called Devil Worshipers, or Yezidi, who believed that at the end of the world Hadudmadud would come and gulp down all the seas and all the rivers.[8] Mrs. Drower also studied the Mandaeans, or Sabaeans, a cult revering John the Baptist that was given to frequent and enthusiastic baptismal ceremonies.

Another whom Freya liked immediately was Lionel Smith, a lanky individualist at the Ministry of Education, who kept his socks up with red tape and astonished everyone by turning down the headmastership of Eton. They shared an instant rapport when Freya learned that Lionel had been a godson of her hero, Professor Ker. It happened also that he had been the last Englishman to see Gertrude Bell alive; they had had lunch the very day Bell took an overdose of sleeping pills. Lionel lost no time in telling Freya that she should admit she was "eccentric," and she endeared herself to him by agreeing that she would, if he would admit he was "eccentric" too.

It was Lionel who introduced her soon after her arrival to Captain Vyvyan Holt, a tall, capable officer, extremely reserved and so ascetic in his habits that one acquaintance called him a "yogi soldier."[9] Freya was seated beside him at one of Lionel's dinner parties. For the first several courses Holt hardly said a word. Then at coffee he suddenly turned to her

Above: Stefana Drower, left, was an authority on some of the more obscure cults of the region. Here she is shown lunching at an outdoor café in Tekrit with her daughter Peggy.

Above: Veronica Bamfield, the statuesque wife of a British army officer in Baghdad, admired Freya, who introduced her to native Arab life and culture. Most colonial wives, however, remained ignorant of the people among whom they lived, preferring bridge parties and gossip at the British club.

Freya with the Shammar chieftain Sheikh Ajil, one of his sons, and a pet bustard. The visit Freya and Stefana Drower paid to the Bedouin encampment in the desert caused a flap with the colonial authorities.

and remarked that he'd sacked his houseboy that morning for pursuing the cook with a knife under the dining room table.

Captain Holt had been appointed to fill Gertrude Bell's position as Oriental secretary and was now quietly monitoring the behavior of the outlying tribes, mostly by playing one off against another. Like the rest of British intelligence, he was also keeping a vigilant eye out for Bolshevik agents working their way south to foment anticolonial agitation. Well-suited to his job, Holt was an accomplished linguist who spoke ten languages, including fluent Arabic. However, he was also a snob, utterly convinced of British superiority, who strictly confined his interactions with Iraqis to the office—unless they happened to be good at polo.

He was also handsome, bronzed by sun and wind. As one woman said, Holt wore "the aroma of the desert" and "strode" into a room.[10] Struck by his stern, rather mysterious aura, Freya began to seek him out, while he, like Lionel Smith, clearly viewed Freya as "eccentric." When she confided a special plan she was developing to explore in Persia, he told her about a political officer who had been tied to a tree for a year by wild people. "He told me I should get to know him because he is as mad as me."

Because Holt was an important figure in the small community, privy to inner government politics, Freya had another reason to cultivate him. In due course they established the habit of riding together in the cool hours before daybreak. Freya found Holt's extreme self-control very appealing. His taciturn manner reminded her of her father's; it was a quality she admired, believing it to be the essence of Britishness. Even though she personally sympathized with the native peoples, she was impressed by Holt's brilliant exposition of the imperial position and ultimately adopted many of his views. Anxious to understand the nuances of foreign policy, she listened attentively as he stressed the importance of protecting the routes to India, the jewel in the imperial crown, the cornerstone of all British actions abroad. To Holt, Freya's intelligence and teasing gaiety were refreshing. She openly admired him, something hard for anyone to resist, so he was soon responding with a grudging interest that expressed itself more often than not in disapproval. Freya wrote Viva Jeyes that Holt took "it as a matter of course that I am to reappear among his archives where all the troublesome characters are docketed."[11]

Freya chose to interpret his disdainful remarks as signs of interest and, convinced she could break through his reserve, enjoyed twitting him. Once when he had arranged a party for the high commissioner's wife and mistakenly invited a lady who had been dead for a year, Freya told him that their friends had been "much disappointed" that the lady didn't show up. On a much later occasion, when a well-known Palestinian nationalist was expected for lunch and kept the table waiting, Holt answered the telephone. When he was told that the missing guest had been murdered on the way over, he responded: "I suppose we need not wait lunch any longer."

Freya considered this magnificently understated and composed the following ditty:

We needn't wait lunch any longer.
Our guest has been murdered en route:
To divulge it we'll wait till we're stronger,
Perhaps with the brandy and fruit.[12]

There were some old colonial hands who wondered if Holt might be homosexual[13]—he never married and could easily have been attracted, like Lawrence, to Arab bisexuality. Yet there is no available confirmation of this, and it is possible his extreme discipline extended to sex. In any event, Captain Holt came to consider Freya a close friend, caring enough to worry about the dangers she insistently plunged into and inviting her to visit him when he learned that Russia would be his next assignment.

Although Freya had tried to be resigned to being a spinster, she felt herself falling in love again. The thought that Holt might not be attracted to women never occurred to her—but then she was very naive, even obstinately so, as friends later remarked, about homosexuality. She allowed herself to believe that he must love her too and thought about him constantly.

• • •

Despite, or perhaps because of, her passionate youthful attachment to her mother—who, after all, was extremely masculine in her aggressiveness—as Freya matured she found she preferred men's company. Men, she seems to have concluded, were not only more reliable but far more interesting. For her seventieth birthday she was given a party to which only men were invited, and Freya thought it was wonderful—exactly what a party ought to be. Certainly her encounters with the disapproving colonial wives of Baghdad helped confirm her suspicion that most women were small-minded and lacked the intellectual ability of men. She had provided the gossips with plenty of ammunition from the moment of her arrival, making friends with natives who would never have been invited to the British club, taking Persian lessons from a gnarled old sayyid, and, most shocking of all, traveling into the forbidden outlying countryside, where if she had got into trouble it would have gravely inconvenienced the authorities. So it was not only the ladies who criticized, it was also their husbands.

On one much-talked-about occasion her men friends, even Lionel Smith, were irate to discover Freya had accepted an invitation to a falcon hunt with the Shammar tribe. It was special to be invited to the desert encampment of the enormously tall Sheikh Ajil al Yawer, a dashing chieftain well known as a great warrior. The Shammar Bedouin had dominated the Syrian desert for untold centuries, wandering with their flocks through changing seasons, a fluid and self-contained community beyond the reach of central governments and tax collectors. Despite the efforts of the British to put a stop to their activities, they continued to plunder trade routes and pilgrims as their traditional right.

Neither the Ottoman Turks nor the British had found reforming the fiercely independent tribesmen an easy task. They ignored the new boundaries and pursued their age-old rivalries with the more southern tribes of the Nejd, ruled by King Saud of Arabia. Because the Colonial Office backed Hashemite claims against the Saudis, Sheikh Ajil was happy to ally himself with the British. Just a few years earlier the British had sent a squadron of armored cars to help Ajil with a major border skirmish and then watched helplessly as his forces pursued his fleeing rivals over the newly drawn border and stole their flocks. It was hard enough to enjoin this independent nomad to obey British law without having British ladies stirring up trouble by nonsanctioned visits.

Freya was understandably excited at the prospect of seeing Ajil's encampment and talked it up to numerous ladies as well as to Stefana Drower, urging them to come along—no doubt puckishly aware of the implications if they accepted. Most wanted to and scuttled home to ask permission of their husbands. To a man, with the exception of Mr. Drower, who respected his wife's scholarly leanings, the husbands forbade the excursion, and the ladies dropped out. Freya and Stefana went anyway and were deeply moved by the peace and grave dignity of nomadic life. The nomads treated the British women as if they were a third sex, welcoming them into the main tent to be waited on by black slaves, to lounge against silken cushions in the company of keen-eyed tribal chieftains, then sent them back to the women's tent to sleep among the ladies of the tribe. The two returned home safe and sound to tell rich tales of ancient customs witnessed firsthand in the desert.

As there had been in Brummana, there was talk in Baghdad that Freya was a spy—which only annoyed her ("If I were a spy I'd be playing bridge all day long and living at the club," she wrote).[14] But the general criticism and frosty attitudes got under her skin, leaving her periodically depressed by the effort to keep a foot in both East and West. "It makes me feel like a kind of pariah from my own kind, and awfully disgusted, because after all I really have done nothing . . . beyond wishing to talk as much Arabic as I can, and regretting that we [the British] can't be less superior and more polite," she wrote her mother.[15] And while protesting that she was "as much an imperialist as anybody"—in those days it not being politically incorrect to do so—Freya did encourage others by her actions to adopt more open views.[16]

One such friend was Veronica Bamfield, the statuesque wife of an army officer. She was intimidated by Captain Holt, whom she found "saturnine and clever," but delighted and set at ease by Freya, fourteen years older, with whom she "felt no age difference." "Nobody," she remembered more than sixty years later, "could chuckle like Freya." Baghdad's colonial life was great fun and very gay with "hunting and pig roasts by day and dances and cabarets in the evening." Visits to the Souk would have been all she knew of real Iraqi life had she not allowed Freya to drag her off to take tea in Iraqi ladies' harems, where such intriguing subjects as the "difficulties" of living with second and third wives were intimately discussed, Arab women not being as repressed as their European sisters on the subject of sex. Freya "opened the doors of the world to me," said Mrs. Bamfield, remembering how one evening Freya invited her to dine with the famous explorer Sir Aurel Stein, who had discovered the eighth-century Diamond Sutra, the oldest printed document ever found, in western China's Taklimakan Desert.

One night when her husband was traveling in Kurdistan, Mrs. Bamfield stayed at Freya's house. She said that she will always remember how touched she was when after dinner they prepared to retire for the evening and Freya said softly: "What I should *really* have liked, is to be very pretty."[17]

· · ·

The moments Freya let down her guard were rare. Only to her intimates did she confess her true longings. "I feel I have wasted so many years just in learning how to live," she wrote Venetia Buddicom at a dispirited moment when Captain Holt was again avoiding her. "And now the machinery is all a bit worn and creaky and all the beautiful gloss gone off it."[18]

Yet Freya, now thirty-seven, was feeling her earlier despair give way to an expanding hope. She *could* change her life; she had watched herself do it—although precisely to what purpose remained as much a mystery to her as the question of what Miss Stark was doing in their midst intrigued the Baghdad community. Freya enjoyed being directionless, learning purely for learning's sake—and adjusting, if that was her fate, to a spinster's life. Yet she had absorbed too much of her mother's work ethic to be content to remain unfocused. Learning, observing, taking notes was the best answer for the moment, but she was alert to opportunity.

If there were low spots, she now admitted she was mostly happy. There were full days, interesting lessons, and rewarding friends. Against the advice of "the experts," who said it didn't matter, she had decided to study the Koran on the theory that it was the best possible way to communicate with strangers in the Muslim world. "If I had not known the Koran and been able to talk to the old man from his own standpoint," she said, referring to the wizened old mullah with whom she was studying Persian, "he would never have started all these tales."[19] Sitting cross-legged on the old sayyid's floor, she listened for hours as he solemnly recounted folktales whose whimsy she found irresistible. She had discovered, she announced in a letter to Venetia, the way to make herself "bullet-proof." All she had to do was boil a hoopoe bird at night by the Talisman Gate. "You must never turn round though the Jinns come and pluck at your clothes, but when the breast bone of the hoopoe has boiled so long that it floats to the surface, you take it and tie it on your arm, and you are bullet-proof while you wear it!"[20]

. . .

Now Freya concentrated on the Muslim scriptures. Well before alighting in Baghdad, she had learned that the Koran (*Al-qur'an*, meaning "reading" or "recitation"), dictated to the Prophet by the messenger angel Gabriel, was the embodiment of Islam's theology, law, science, and wisdom. The Koran, together with the Sunna, or traditions of the Prophet's life, and hadiith, the Prophet's nonprophetic utterances, was the standard for the faithful in a belief system where there is no separation between religion and politics and no concept of a secular state. In Islam, Shi'a or Sunni, schismatic or orthodox, rich sheikh or poor nomad alike, draw on this extraordinary work of sublimely inspired poetry to overcome differences, explain problems, and share mutual pleasures. Whether the issue was simple theft, or adultery, or a crime like murder, or even great matters of state, such as jihad, or holy war, one turned to this sacred text, which was also the basis of the curriculum in the *madrassas*, or Islamic schools, as well as in the great Islamic universities. By studying it Freya knew she would be able to get closer to the heart of people she was determined to understand. "The thing about the literature of any country is that it is a sort of climate that one breathes," she later said.[21]

She was deeply satisfied to discover how saturated the Koran was with references to the Old Testament as well as to Jesus (Isa), Mary and Joseph, and Saint John the Baptist in the New Testament. At least thirty chapters invoked Moses, while the stories of the Creation, the Fall of Man, and the Flood were mentioned again and again to convey moral lessons. Abraham himself appeared as the founder of the Kaaba, the ideal predecessor in a faith that the Prophet had seen as a grand continuum and expansion of the earlier Judeo-Christian beliefs, to which he had been exposed as a young man.[22] Although Mohammed had been the illiterate son of a caravanner, his travels as a trader had exposed him to the views of Jews and Christians as far away as Jerusalem, and he was inspired by their theologies, incorporating from them many elements for his reforming vision.

Freya could use the Koran to venture delicately into such intimate subjects as polygamy or concubinage and especially the lively topic of the veil, a custom dating back to Hammurabi's code and traditionally the mark of a virtuous woman. The farther she traveled, the more Freya would hear traditionalists among the ladies of the harems insist that the veil gave them freedom. Not only did it confer dignity but, concealed in the anonymous veil, they could go about their business in privacy.

To find a link between Islamic ideas and her own culture was a stimulating exercise. Freya began rereading the Bible and discovered that Rebecca had veiled herself in Isaac's presence and St. Paul had insisted that women cover their heads when they prayed. The custom of the veil began to seem less alien, even as the Ramadan fast echoed Jesus' own fasting in the wilderness and the weekly Friday congregational prayer began to appear much like the Christian Sunday sermon. Freya was coming to understand how Mohammed had viewed himself as one in a long line of God's messengers—after such great prophets as Moses and Jesus—and his followers thought of him not as divine but rather as the last, or the "seal" of the prophets, completing and perfecting the two other great religions. Yearning to travel through the Islamic world, she now saw herself as one of "the People of the Book," the Bible, which Islam respects as a holy document, and thus she prepared herself to be welcomed by her Muslim friends in an important commonality.*

Freya showed wisdom and sensitivity in attending to this essential and exciting literature with its traditions and beliefs. "One is surer to get nearer to them *really* if one comes at them from behind as it were, through the things they knew as children, or that their parents and nurses knew. . . . When I take the old Mullah's standpoint, I know where I am

---

* What "the People of the Book" means to Muslims is somewhat complicated: The heavenly book, or Kitaab, which expresses God's will, was partially revealed over a long period of time by various prophets whose messages are contained in the Old and New Testaments. However, these incomplete revelations have been corrupted by erroneous Jewish and Christian interpretations and practices, Muslims believe; only Mohammed received God's complete message.

and what to expect: when I take a European standpoint with a 'civilized' Oriental, I can never know where I am, for I have no means of judging what 'European' means to him; it is certainly not what it means to us."[23]

Again and again Freya would discover how important her knowledge of the Muslim holy book was in gaining the respect and confidence of the people she met—most notably during World War II, when she was invited to talk with distinguished Muslim clerics, including the scholars of the venerable Al-Azhar University in Cairo. The notion of calling herself an ethnographer, as reviewers later did, did not occur to her: at this time her quest was simply for knowledge and personal satisfaction. Perhaps her exposure to the grand similarities was ultimately responsible for keeping her from committing to any specific set of religious beliefs, other than an amorphous faith that God existed. Instead, she would say: "I wait at the gate."

Although the shape of what she was trying to achieve by her study and travel remained as nebulous as her religious convictions, Freya's ambition was as steady as an unblinking beacon. There was no question in her mind that at last she was getting somewhere. In a happy letter to Flora, she wrote: "I feel that I really may end by doing something; only it is not a thing that can be hurried. But in three years' time I could know enough Persian, Turkish, Kurdish, and Arabic to get about, and I believe I would be the only English woman in the Near East to do so: and then something amusing is bound to turn up."[24]

. . .

"Something amusing" was indeed about to turn up. By this time everything was in order for Freya's long-planned venture alone into a remote area of Persia. Ever since encountering the priests of the Druze she had wanted to locate the ruins of the fortress castles of the ancient Assassins, bizarrely connected to the Druze, who had been the most effective terrorist group in history. For nearly two hundred years—until the great Mamluk sultan Baybars flushed the last devotees from their castles in Syria in 1273—this sinister sect had held the East in a reign of terror. Determined to destroy the Abbasid Empire, to punish mainstream Sunnism and its "false" caliphate in Baghdad, the Assassins infiltrated palaces, garrisons, and stableyards from Persia to Syria. By dint of trickery and deceit, they won access to and often the trust of their intended victims, then plunged a consecrated dagger into their hearts. No prince, vizier, cleric, or military leader associated with Sunnism dared venture abroad without a coat of mail beneath his robe. Notables did not feel safe even in their homes, so great had been the fear of these cunning fanatics.

The Fatimids of Cairo were no more safe from the Assassins' daggers.

Like the Druze who had split with Cairo, the Assassins saw the Fatimids as archenemies and plotted against them. The Crusaders, descending in waves from Europe to reclaim the Holy Land, soon recounted to an alarmed and fascinated West extraordinary tales of Assassin treachery. A new term, *assassination,* suddenly appeared in the language. Troubadours sprang to the theme and composed lurid songs about the Assassins to entertain feudal courts. A German priest, advising King Philip VI of France against the hazards of an Eastern expedition, said: "They sell themselves, are thirsty for human blood, kill the innocent for a price, and care nothing for either life or salvation. Like the devil, they transfigure themselves into angels of light, by imitating the gestures, garments, languages, customs and acts of various nations and peoples; thus hidden in sheep's clothing, they [are put to] death as soon as they are recognized."[25]

It was said that the monk-warrior Knights Templar, with their secret rituals and dedication to political interference, modeled their order on the Assassins, who wore—when not disguised—white gowns with red turbans and boots, "the hues of innocence and blood."[26] The Templars adopted a similar costume, a white mantle with a large red cross stitched to the breast. Some said the Masons also borrowed the idea of binding their fraternity together with esoteric ceremonies because they were so intrigued by the fanatic loyalty of the Assassins to their order.*

Freya knew enough about the Assassins' history to know their name derived from the Arabic word *hashish.* A mysterious leader, the Old Man of the Mountain, was supposed to have administered the hallucinogen to young recruits, the *hashishiyyin,* who swore absolute fealty to him. The Old Man's impregnable fortress in Alamut was described by Marco Polo at length in his *Travels.* On the theory that Heinrich Schliemann had discovered Troy by reading Homer's *Iliad,* Freya was taking her copy of Marco Polo's *Travels* with her to see if she could find the famous garden of delights where the Grand Master's *fida'i,* or initiates, woke up from their drugged sleep to believe they were in Paradise. In William of Tyre she read the story of how Count Henry of Champagne, returning from Armenia, had gone to Persia and been entertained by the Old Man, or Lord of Alamut, who demonstrated the obedience of his fida'is by ordering one to jump over the battlements to his death—then offered to command the

---

* In part the cult's dedication to secrecy grew out of a Shi'a tradition known as *taqiyya,* or concealment, which was adopted from the very earliest days of Islam's division as a way to survive persecution by the Sunni: one is given moral dispensation to hide one's beliefs if they are likely to provoke hostility. Thus the Isma'ilis, Druze, Alawite, and other offshoot sects often keep their beliefs secret. Among the Assassins, however, the principle of taqiyya became a fiendish tool. There are probably modern parallels with the members of such sects as the military wing of Hamas in Israel or Osama bin-Laden's terrorists in Afghanistan.

same from another if the horrified knight needed further proof of Assassin loyalty.

From an 1835 study by a German Orientalist, Joseph Von Hammer-Purgstall, Freya knew the name of the founder of the line of Grand Masters to be Hasan-e Sabbah, and it was to the ruins of his castle, in a hidden valley in Alamut, that she headed. The sketchy maps that Captain Holt had obtained for her from intelligence did not precisely locate Hasan's mountain, called the Rock of Alamut, but she was determined to find it—and perhaps some of the other equally inaccessible castles in the Persian mountains below the Caspian that the Assassins had controlled.

In April 1930 Freya set off from Baghdad with Captain Holt's maps, typhoid and plague inoculations, mosquito netting, and quinine—for there was a lot of malaria where she was going. Stopping in Hamadan, in the foothills of the northern tier of the Zagros Mountains, she discovered that due to some hitch between the banks and the mail, she had only two pounds to pay for a trip that would require at least two weeks of travel in very remote mountain valleys. Possibly she was becoming more Eastern than even she realized, for with a cheery "Allah will provide!" she started off. It was a plucky—foolhardy, really—thing to do, but Freya would not be deterred.

By begging a seat in a native car and sharing her lunch with fellow passengers, she managed to get to Qasvin, where Allah did in fact come through nicely. A wealthy doctor, whose family had owned vast properties in the region for generations, warmed by an introduction she produced from a friend, turned out actually to own Alamut mountain and the rock itself. Getting to it, however, promised more difficulty. The doctor was helpful, loaning her his *charvadar,* a muleteer named 'Aziz, who brought along two other wild-haired, bearded subcharvadars, Ismail and the Refuge of Allah. In this villainous-looking company, Freya set out to climb over rough terrain to the nearly inaccessible, poverty-stricken valley in the folds of the snowcapped Elburz Mountains where the Assassins had once reigned supreme. Her charvadars looked after her as if they were "her mothers," gathering around her cot when they spent the night.[27] She felt she might never adjust to the sight of the Refuge of Allah's greasy head just beneath her, resting on her saddlebags, exhaling fumes of garlic with his snores.

For ten days she dragged her unwilling guides up rocky precipices, happily recalling the old tales of murder and mayhem and wondering exactly where were the supposed fifty other castles on which Hulegu the Tartar "fell like a thunderbolt" in 1256.[28] Without seeing another European face, she forded swollen streams, gloried in the displays of wild tulips and hyacinths, drank unboiled water, and was not offended when her unclean Christian hand proffering a bag of infidel chocolates was refused. Sometimes she was hard-pressed to win over hostile mountain folk, but mostly she was received with the respect and extreme courtesy she found so moving about the peoples of the East.

Amazed and curious at the spectacle of this small Englishwoman traveling alone, poor villagers who fed her along the way—her two pounds stretched rather far as a result—either took her into their huts at night or let her spread her blankets out in the open under the stars. More than once she turned a flashlight on in the darkness to eye a scorpion sidling up to her mattress. Privacy was almost nonexistent, although she would always be given the best, or sometimes only room if taken to someone's house; she often found herself washing surrounded by a group of giggling women and young children watching intently. She did her best to administer advice and such medicines as she had to the sick—all the while gathering folktales and stories of djinns or discussing the finer points of Koranic hadiith.

When a Persian policeman challenged her lack of proper permits, demanding to know what she was doing in this remote part of the world with a camera and mapmaking materials, Freya boldly retorted that she had no permit because she had been told that he was the ultimate authority. He was immediately placated, as she had anticipated, although it was a barefaced lie. "Persia is not good for one's morals," she mused.[29]

Freya had two specific goals, and she achieved them. One was to locate the Rock of Alamut, more correctly named Qasir Khan, a grim and shadowed place high in the mountains behind a rock defile, impossible to have located without a guide. Stirred by its sinister associations, she carefully explored, measured, and recorded its position and attributes. Aware that other Europeans had reached the famous terrorist hideout—a Russian explorer had actually been there only a year before, and even T. E. Lawrence had scrambled up its rocky flanks before the war—Freya took particular care to be the most meticulous in her observations and later, when she wrote about it for the Royal Geographical Society, the most compelling and vivid in her descriptions. Thus it was that Freya refreshed the story of the Assassins for a public that had kept the name but long lost the connection to its source.

More important as a contribution to science, she filled the empty spaces on His Majesty's Government's maps and corrected mistakes, locating half a dozen new mountains and at least two hitherto unmarked villages. North of the Caspian Gates, through which the fabled Silk Route once passed, east of the Caucasus, through which mounted archers,

Scythians and Cimmerians, had once burst over the Iranian Plain, these mountains had lain virtually undisturbed in modern times—and Freya was delighted to have an opportunity to expand geographic knowledge. Climbing to 10,250 feet, she could see the sweep of the entire mountain range to the Caspian mists. Wrestling with her compass in the icy wind, she identified numbers of cartographic errors, including the fact that the officially designated mountain range was placed on the wrong side of the valley. She also heard about another castle, which the locals called Lami-aser, supposedly surrounded by a ruined garden, just as Marco Polo had described, at about 11,000 feet and still covered with snow. Freya resolved to come back.

It was not, she told herself, that she enjoyed being cold and dirty or having her face and hands chapped raw. But if that was the price of getting to where she wanted to go and seeing the marvelous things she had seen, it wasn't exorbitant. Beyond that, unlike in her previous life, when how pretty she was or whether she had money or social position counted so much, here in the East none of these things seemed to matter. Here, among simple mountain people, she was a personage, a traveler bringing tales of other lands, accorded all the respect due a representative of a distant European power. In this truly wild place, as never before in her life, Freya experienced a sense of freedom and command that infused her with a joy almost mystical in its power.

At last, triumphant, weary, and longing for a soak in a proper tub, Freya hitchhiked out of the hills to Resht and thence to Hamadan, where she was vastly relieved to find her money waiting. From there she continued on to Baghdad and watched delightedly as surprised intelligence officials reviewed her corrections to the government's maps. When Captain Holt and his colleagues pronounced that she had done brave work, Freya preened inwardly, though she took care to appear modest and grateful. When she departed for Italy at the end of June 1930, word went out that Miss Stark was a "competent" explorer, and people talked about her with new respect.

· · ·

It was good to be back in Asolo again and to see her mother and Herbert Young. She told them laughingly that she was relieved to no longer be "viewed as a Phenomenon."[30] They caught her up on a dozen bits of local news, and Freya realized that Flora, sixty-nine by now, had flourished in her absence. Her mother, she was relieved to see, was utterly absorbed by the silk-weaving factory, or tessoria, which she was managing for Lucy Beach. She had introduced innovative new designs, improved the way the silks were dyed, and was hard at work training a staff of young women to increase the tessoria's production. And, as she had in Dronero, Flora enlisted the support of the rich villa owners in helping local peasant women find jobs. Poor, patient Herbert was finding his house a center of social life and was doing his best not to grouse about all the commotion. At seventy-nine he enjoyed driving about in the new Rolls-Royce he had bought just before the Crash and pottering among his antiquarian books and manuscripts. The Depression had reduced his stock holdings, so when Flora insisted they needed the extra income, he reluctantly agreed to take in a paying guest.

Happy as it made Freya to see the old people in such good shape, she did not want to linger with them long. She had exciting plans now. That "something interesting" was definitely taking shape, and she had work to do in London.

• • •

In her autobiography Freya would write that her old life, the spinster's existence of drudgery in Dronero and the arduous farming at La Mortola, faded away "like Eurydice." She was Orpheus now, emerging from the depths, looking over her shoulder as old hopes, like marriage, dimmed, but eager for a different, sun-blessed, freer future—if she could make it happen. Pondering that it had taken so long to find a direction, she tried to explain:

> *This was not due to timidity, for I was morally brave by nature, and physically by will—nor did it happen through a lack of interest in the unknown. It came I think from a feeling which influences me greatly, whose beginning I cannot remember and whose origin I cannot trace—a feeling for the value of affection in itself, and a reluctance to waste any of it that happened to come my way. This has little to do with one's own capacity for affection; my mother, the most exuberantly expansive of human beings, never hesitated to toss by the wayside what seemed to me the most precious and delicate possessions. Perhaps it was the sight of her recklessness, and the knowledge that I had no such command of riches; perhaps, and I think more probably, it was merely pity, the sight of something beautiful wasted, which made me feel towards love in general as one might towards a piece of porcelain forgotten in the middle of the road: one would go out of one's way to find it a safer place. It is a niggardly feeling, for the wealth and variety of love can be counted upon to overflow all loss: the general richness*

will compensate those who cross hither and thither on our path,
while we make straight for the targets of our heart. But I cannot
do so even now. The friendliness of a tramp will make me pause
on my way, and I am happy to rub a donkey's ears in the sun. To
be asked, and not to have it in me to give affection, is a pain; and
only the brevity and tread of Time force me to renounce anything
of the varieties of human friendship. My mother and Asolo, my
father in Canada, the four children, the opening East—for as long
as I could I tried to keep them all.[31]

Freya was learning a painful truth: one has to choose in this world. If
you do one thing, you can't do the other. Her fear of separation, fueled by
too many partings in her young life, initially inhibited her from taking
dramatic risks to develop her talents as a writer. She had stayed close to
home for a variety of reasons, among them trying to find a husband and
imagining that her mother needed her.

But now a sense that the clock of her allotted time was running ever
faster, and that her mother was safe and happy without her, accelerated
her determination to do *her* work. Herbert assured her that he supported
her "eccentric wanderings,"[32] so Freya at last resolved to absent herself for
considerable periods of time—although each leave-taking still required an
effort. Even so, she could not help but recognize that when she was away
from these dear people, her spirits lifted in excitement. Those early midnight dreams of finding "buried cities in the sand" were beginning to
assume a compelling reality.

CHAPTER SEVEN

The Importance of Friends

> *One is so apt to think of people's affection as a fixed quantity, instead of a sort of moving sea with the tide always going out or coming in but still fundamentally there: and I believe this difficulty in making allowance for the tide is the reason for half the broken friendships.*
>
> —LETTER TO VENETIA BUDDICOM, MAY 20, 1934

*F*reya would be exceptionally lucky in her friends. Presently she would have some very powerful supporters happy to pull levers on her behalf and grease the wheels for subsequent achievements.

Growing up as she had in Dronero's isolation, without the chance to giggle with other girls over boys, or share with them her dreams and secrets, Freya learned to hide her exuberance behind a quiet, modest, and formal facade. Yet those who really knew her—Venetia, Professor Ker, teachers and others met in London through Viva Jeyes—recognized her talent, enjoyed the charm of her company, and put themselves out to help her. Now she had new friends in Syria and Iraq too, and that knowledge boosted her confidence. She began to loosen the tight reins she imposed on herself, increasingly saying what she wanted, laughing aloud at what she thought was funny, and charting without so much agony the course she felt was right.

Freya had a natural drawing power. Although she remembered herself at this time as shy and self-conscious, others saw an incandescent combination of animation and wit, coupled with a spellbinding gift for narrative. She was never beautiful or possessed of a graceful body, yet she had an enchanting quality that brought admirers clustering to her flame. "She was never boring," remembered a goddaughter. "She was full of unexpected remarks, the amazing joining of ideas that could completely change your view of things." Another said: "She created magic kingdoms when you were with her."[1]

Freya did not take her widening circle for granted. She worked as hard as a devoted gardener, cultivating new relationships with letters and invitations until they bloomed into friendships. As the years went on, seldom did she prune a friendship—as the staggering piles of letters from friends and acquaintances at the University of Texas at Austin make clear— although it could happen on occasion. Later, when she was famous, the truly close, the designated intimates, would come to understand how intense she was about her friends, treating those she cared for "as if they were lovers, rejecting those who had not measured up, or who had let her down somehow, spurning them exactly as if they had been lovers," as one recollected.[2] In Freya's view one was either *for* her or against her.

It is interesting to hear from someone who admired Freya long before she became a sought-after personality. An old friend, who was to remain so for more than sixty years, tried to recapture what it was about Freya that attracted him when he first met her in Asolo in 1929, when she was thirty-six. Sheridan Russell was a concert cellist who had come to spend the winter in Italy, ostensibly to practice but actually to recover from a devastating broken romance. Given an introduction to Flora Stark, he was invited to Casa Freia for tea. It turned out to be a large gathering dominated by Flora, still tall and striking. Freya sat in a corner, saying nothing amid the chattering guests. "She wore a rather silly bandage around her head. At least I thought it looked rather silly. I didn't realize at the time why she had this thing on her hair. She didn't say a word. Everyone else spoke. I didn't terribly like her looks. When I left, she came out with me to the gate and said, 'If you are staying in Asolo for a time, perhaps you'd walk with me tomorrow at five o'clock.' So I smiled as graciously as I could and said, 'Thank you, I'd love to.' How could I say I wouldn't? I was doing nothing in Asolo except practicing. So with bad grace I came the following day at five o'clock to fetch her."

Mr. Russell, now bent and in his nineties, paused and shook his head.

"I wasn't out a quarter of a minute with her when I said to myself: 'What's this?' This intelligent, charming person was saying something interesting immediately as we started off, was noticing everything. Within half a minute I was hooked."

On that first walk with Freya, Russell, a man who clearly preferred straight talk to sentimental effusions, discovered her remarkable knowledge of flora and fauna, her pleasure in exploring the secrets of the physical environment, her appreciation of quaint and easily overlooked details about the town and its Piedmont setting. Her curiosity seemed comprehensive—she conjectured equally well on what a shift in the direction of the wind might portend or the methods a mason used to cast his bricks. The way her mind worked, the surprises of her thoughts, delighted him. Creative himself, he immediately recognized her as an original.

Before he had the chance to experience more than sixty years of her generosity, he believed this originality and intelligence were her most engaging aspect. He never had much money—he became a social worker later—so several times Freya paid for a rail ticket so he could make a summer visit to L'Arma. When he married she welcomed his wife both to L'Arma and to Asolo despite a tendency Freya later exhibited to treat wives—especially those who were younger and prettier—quite harshly. What Sheridan Russell thought was most significant about her unswerving kindness to him, however, was that "I couldn't be useful *ever*. I was not an important person. Simply she was good to me."[3] This testimony is at odds with later detractors, who accused Freya of cultivating only the great, the famous, or the useful.

Evelyn Lambert, who owned a villa near Asolo, considered herself a close friend and went with Freya on many trips in her later life. She described her as a "dextrous avoider."[4] Said Mrs. Lambert, smiling, Freya simply did not do what she didn't want to do, adding that she herself didn't much like to do so either. Mrs. Lambert surmised that Freya had had quite enough of answering her mother's bidding in her youth and had resolved never to be taken advantage of again. Anything that smacked of getting involved in other people's troubles sent Freya gliding smoothly to the sidelines.

Some who had been good to her and expected a favor in return were unpleasantly surprised by this trait, which was not so apparent at the start of Freya's career. But as she evolved into a petted favorite, it was an aspect of her personality that hardened. There would be those who would see her as grossly selfish, but others wrote off her lapses as the behavior of an artist. She gave her company, they said, and that was gift enough.

A godson, Malise Ruthven, who was so influenced by Freya that he became a teacher of Islamic studies, wrote in a charming memoir of his famous godmother:

> *If there was an element of calculation and ruthlessness in her treatment of people—and there were people who, in the course of her long career, felt they had been ill-used by her—this was never from motives of petty selfishness. Artists are like Robin Hood: they may take from the rich who possess wealth, opportunities or knowledge, to distribute their own talents as gifts for the rest of us, to alleviate the humdrum burden of our lives by entertaining us or opening our minds to perceptions of truth we could never achieve unaided. Most of those, including her wealthier friends who provided her with loans, or gifts, or who otherwise helped in her travels, considered it a privilege, knowing her egotism was magnanimous, her selfishness disinterested. Those—like myself— with nothing more than time and affection to offer have been lavishly repaid with both.*[5]

In part Freya's willingness to exploit favors sprang from the culture of her youth as well as observing her mother's example. At the turn of the twentieth century, when necessities were frequently difficult to come by, the intervention of friends was often the only way to send or receive things. Clothes and food were made and grown at home rather than store-bought. Neither the need for privacy nor the press of tight schedules was felt so acutely as both are now. Friends thought nothing of staying for several weeks at a time when they visited, and when they went home their access to a needed item and willingness to send it were part of the way things were done. Flora and her friends helped one another in countless ways—whether it was getting an Italian maid for someone's London house or sending to Asolo materials unobtainable in Italy. That Freya constantly found herself in distant parts of the world and counted on centrally located friends to run errands for her—and in turn thanked them with exotic gifts or, better yet, the pleasure of her company, was simply an extension of her mother's modus operandi, which Freya adopted. One might even say she perfected it.

As Freya put distance between herself and her mother's long shadow and her name began to count, Flora at last discovered that she was proud of her daughter—almost too much so. She intervened in countless ways with her well-positioned friends to help Freya's career. In fact, her primary task ultimately became facilitating her daughter's traveling—having clothes made and sent, holding on to her letters, entertaining her friends in Asolo. Once she saw purpose in it, Freya later wrote, her mother

> *concentrated on me all the affection which her nature was bound to bestow, selfless and overwhelming; other objectives disappeared, and I sometimes felt—with regret for my ingratitude—that the amount of this affection was more than I could manage.*
>
> *If I happened to dine out, she would lie awake till I came in to say goodnight; and however late I might sit after dinner, would never go to bed before me. These silly things oppressed me. I felt like a small raft—inadequate to be alone to support a human soul on the deep sea where it swims. It also made me be egotistical, for I knew that the greatest pleasure I could procure my mother was to let her give—her time, her thoughts, her love: my letters in these years are full of vanities and make me, in fact, less modest than I am and far more snobbish, for I told her everything about myself that I thought would please her. And when now some unexpected flattery comes upon me, a sense of loss comes with it, for there is no one left to whom it can give that innocent satisfaction.*[6]

The effect on Freya, however, was not innocent. Flora was "overwhelming," and even if she did not intend harm, harm was done. The mother's expectations, her furious energy concentrated on this surviving child whose talents she was belatedly recognizing, her implicit demand that Freya succeed—as if to fulfill Flora's own need for success—these things took their toll. Always lurking underneath was an assumption: Freya must not fail.

Freya would have loved to have married, if for no other reason than to relieve her mother of anxiety. The constant emphasis Flora put on marriage kept Freya from ever feeling whole in the eyes of the world. From childhood she had striven to protect her idealized mother from life's wicked pressures—and she had failed. She had taken Flora's side against her father, she had tried to protect her from Mario, and she had done what she could to support her through the awful hardships of Dronero—but Freya had been helpless against an unfeeling adult world. That is why much later Xandra Hardie, former wife of one of Freya's godsons, said: "Freya had a sorrow in her voice when she talked about her mother. She spoke of her in a way that suggested their family life had been quite formal—as if the learned demeanor of her youth had been formal. But because the family had fallen on hard times, she had seen her mother reveal emotions, worries about money and, indeed, *work* harder than she ever expected to. It was as if she had witnessed her mother in a kind of 'fall from grace' that must have been very shattering to a child." Mrs. Hardie paused thoughtfully and added: "If you imagine your mother as a rather beautiful, slightly distant, elegant, cared for, servanted person—and what you see when you've grown up a little bit is this exhausted person trying to fix the loo in the tessoria—well, you would carry that with you all your life."

Mrs. Hardie, recalling meeting Freya about 1963, when she was introduced by Freya's godson Grey Gowrie, said that the celebrated writer had a reputation among her friends of being "fanatically selfish" as well as jealous of pretty young women. Mrs. Hardie, known then as Bingo Bingley, was in her early twenties, blond, and very pretty—so she was more than a little apprehensive. To her surprise, she and Freya hit it off instantly.

I'm not—I'm very, very seldom frightened of people. So she didn't scare me in the sense that I wasn't trying to occupy some ground that might belong to her. If she wanted to have close chats with Grey, that was fine by me. But also, I adored her. She was very clever, which I loved. I hadn't at that point known very many clever people in my life, and that was wonderful. She was highly focused, which I liked also. She was interested in me and I was curious about her and I'm sure I flattered her. I hadn't met anyone like her before. And I loved her humor, and she liked mine. It was quite clear, I suspect, to both of us early on that we didn't mind— we were neither of us afraid of a spat. She said to me once, with a look of relish: "I love a fight. Especially about money!" But we never fought,

said Mrs. Hardie, who later loaned Freya money, which Freya completely repaid, to build a house. "We always got along very well." [7]

Mrs. Hardie met Freya when she was firmly established and in her seventies, but H. C. ("Nick") Bailey, an American, became acquainted with her before World War II, when he was only sixteen and his parents had rented a house for the summer in Asolo. She was "very slight and rather fey," he remembered, and people in town spoke curiously about her traveling "by herself in remote places." Freya's mother had bustled over to the Baileys' house on the first day of their arrival with an invitation to play badminton, and Nick had been struck by how Freya seemed to "stay in the wings" when her imposing mother was around. He and his brother, however, liked Freya, finding her "funny, cheerful, and gay," and became

*Flora Stark in her sixties. She stood ramrod
straight, but a hard life had begun to tell.*

a little defensive when his parents referred scornfully to the "oddness" of a household where two elderly people lived together unmarried and a spinster entertained a colonial officer from Baghdad for weeks at a time.[8]

. . .

Late in the fall of 1930 Freya returned briefly to Canada to see her father, who by then was having difficulty walking and had to lean heavily on his stick. Although later she looked back gratefully on the companionable silences they shared during that last visit together, her heart and soul were now dedicated to getting back to Baghdad—she thought of nothing else, even as she feared that she might have to cancel everything to look after her father. Terribly torn, she passed anxious days in his cabin rereading Marco Polo. "I think I have located the two hills [Marco Polo] mentions near Alamut and this ought to be quite important," Freya wrote to her mother. "I am going to try to go east anyway, even if I have to sell capital at this time of crisis. I think I shall have to come and stay with Pips very soon. So I shall strain every nerve to go before, even if it means travelling third class."[9]

In a letter the following month she begged for relief from Flora's constant peppering of concerns over finances, which were affecting everyone in 1930. She exploded: "You must try to take the *whole* of Italian worries off me, so I can . . . *rest* and not feel the weight always hanging over. . . . if I could just get a breather now and then."[10]

. . .

It was positively joyous for Freya to find herself in England a month later and to know that—for the moment—she was free to do what she pleased. Gleefully, she tore off for a holiday with Venetia Buddicom, waltzing up to Flintshire to be coddled and encouraged by the friend she had not seen in a year. Venetia's father had died in the meantime and left her Penbedw, the four-thousand-acre estate whose idyllic peace Freya loved. Venetia could be counted on to be good to her.

At the time of Freya's sister's death, Venetia had written: "I know the bleak country you are going through and how long the road seems. Yet companions there are and I would be one if you'll let me."[11] For years Freya and Venetia had regarded each other as closest friends. "Not to see you for two whole years!" Venetia had exclaimed when Freya confided that she meant to go East for an extended stay. "It seems to me almost a disaster!" She told Freya that they must make "most special efforts" to write often. It was hard enough that Freya was "wrapt in Eastern shrouds absorbing the philosophy of the Orient" and herself "in a background of petty business."[12] They mustn't let themselves grow any farther apart, Venetia cautioned.

But despite the differences and distance, the friendship flourished with shared books, ideas, and their mutual concern over the lack of romance in their lives. Venetia had also suffered an unhappy love affair, and periodically Freya would write dolefully that perhaps they should think of spending their old age together—if fate persisted in leaving them spinsters. After their Jebel Druze adventure, they had discussed plans to meet in Baghdad, but sometime in 1929 Venetia's neck or back was broken or seriously injured in a hunting accident at Penbedw.[13] She eventually recovered enough to supervise her large holdings, but it would be a long and painful convalescence, and all travel plans had to be scrapped. Freya did her best to cheer her friend with lively letters about what she was doing and who she was seeing, while Venetia returned the kindness with occasional gifts of money or books, excellent advice on investments, and, best of all, a number of extremely valuable introductions.

The most important was to the man who had married Venetia's cousin, Sir Henry Lawrence, formerly the commissioner to Sind and acting governor of Bombay in 1926. In 1928, before joining Freya in Beirut, Venetia had accompanied the Lawrences on a six-month tour of India and for some time had been suggesting to Freya that she and Sir Henry should meet. Now that Freya was in England, she invited both to dinner, confident they would enjoy each other.

They did. Freya found Sir Henry a "charming little ugly man"[14] who was every bit as fascinated as she was by the history of the Isma'ilis, the schismatic group that ultimately spawned both the Druze and the Assassins. In turn, Sir Henry was much taken with Venetia's small, lively, and obviously very intelligent friend, so keen to hear all he could tell her about Bombay, home to the largest Isma'ili community in the world. He suggested that she meet the religious and secular leader of the Isma'ilis, the corpulent old Aga Khan. The khan cut quite an urbane figure in London society; indeed, one of his prize racehorses had recently won the derby. To Freya it seemed extraordinary that he was the lineal descendant of the ancient Assassins or that his followers annually paid him his weight in diamonds. Sir Henry explained that the khan's legitimacy had been confirmed by British law after a much-publicized trial in Bombay in 1866. In addition, the khan and Gertrude Bell had been friends, so Freya was disappointed that fall when Sir Henry was unable to arrange a meeting. Nevertheless, he assured the Isma'ili leader that Miss Stark merited his help. In due course the Aga Khan's letters on her behalf would open a number of important doors.

In the meantime Freya hied herself off to the British Museum to refresh herself on the history of the Isma'ili, Druze, and Assassin cults. Buried in the silence of the vast reading room, she was crestfallen to learn that accounts by nearly fifty travelers on the Jebel Druze already existed. "I wonder if there is anything left not written about," she mused. "The only thing not over done is *thinking.*"[15] She decided to abandon further investigation of the Druze and devote herself to the history of the Assassins.

An even more important favor of Sir Henry's was to introduce Freya to the Royal Geographical Society. No other organization so attracted her admiration. Its membership reflected the establishment's finest minds and most accomplished diplomats, explorers, archaeologists, and military officers. Since Freya had first stayed with the Jeyeses at St. John's Wood and Viva had taken her to hear RGS lectures on the many conquests in this great age of exploration, she had nursed the hope that one day she too might be deemed worthy of membership. So it was thrilling to meet the man who guarded the gate of such an august bastion of male power. Lionel Smith, back from Baghdad and on his way to his new academic post in Scotland, also put in a good word for her—so Freya was brought to the attention of Arthur Hinks, the society's stout and rather humorless secretary, through two impeccable connections.

The Royal Geographical Society did not take easily to women. In 1892 it had suffered a momentary lapse, admitting a number of accomplished female explorers, but the decision caused ferocious opposition. "Their sex and training render them equally unfitted for exploration," railed Lord Curzon, just back from serving as viceroy of India, "and the genus of professional female globe-trotters with which America has lately familiarized us is one of the horrors of the latter end of the nineteenth century."[16] The doors clanged shut again; the policy was reversed and remained so until 1913, when a few women were reluctantly admitted—although not until 1933 was a female council member elected.

Freya could hardly believe the warm reception she received when she arrived at the imposing, dark stone building on Kensington Gore. Sir Henry and Lionel Smith had brought her articles to Mr. Hinks's attention—she had recently been published in *The Spectator* and *The Contemporary Review* as well as earlier in *Cornhill*—and particularly emphasized her cartographic discoveries. Mr. Hinks professed himself deeply impressed and told her he not only approved of her interest in the Assassins but would provide her with help if she were to do more exploring in Persia. He offered to publish in *The Geographical Journal* a paper she proposed to write on the cult and introduced her to the society's mapping expert, who initiated her in the secrets of aneroids, prismatic compasses, and the Abney level.[17] Soon Freya was happily measuring her paces and timing her walking speed in St. James's Park. To her father she crowed that she was proving every bit "as promising a student as Gertrude Bell."[18]

Freya's introduction to the Royal Geographical Society was a turning point. Her mentors had given her an invaluable entrée. From that moment she never ceased keeping Mr. Hinks abreast of her exploration plans, purring to him in charming letters, to which he responded with unqualified admiration, both for whatever she might currently be attempting and for the delightful way she described it.

. . .

By June 1931 Freya was once more Baghdad-bound, this time with "a feeling I was beginning to know . . . a feeling as if the body were pulling itself away, safe but lacerated, from numerous tentacles: if there had only been one it would probably have anchored me."[19] She meant a husband, of course. But she still hadn't found one. Not yet anyway. She could, however, have a life of her own—*if* she were willing to seize the day.

CHAPTER EIGHT

A Treasure Hunt
in Luristan

> *I have found that one can nearly*
> *always do what one sets out for,*
> *if it is only one thing at a time.*
>
> —BEYOND EUPHRATES

In Baghdad, Freya found a rather nice red carpet awaiting her. Secretary Hinks had written that little Miss Stark was "a serious student who avoids publicity" and that in the eyes of the Royal Geographical Society she was engaged in work "worthy of help."[1] Barely had she stepped off the mail truck and been enveloped by Baghdad's familiar dust than a series of invitations from the high commissioner were delivered—dinner if she would like, perhaps a ride, would she join him for breakfast? Freya basked gratefully in this unfamiliar sunshine. Unfortunately it was mid-July, and an all too literal sun roasted the city. People arose in the middle of the night to do their work in order to avoid the stifling daytime hours. Soon a typhoid epidemic broke out, and Captain Holt rushed to organize a quarantine. If Freya didn't leave immediately, he told her, they would have to keep her in Baghdad like everybody else. Chafing to get off to Persia, Freya caught a plane for Hamadan without saying goodbye. But once there, staying as a guest of the British consul, she mooned over her last dinner with Vyvyan. "Capt. Holt was so cross and snubby the last evening," she wrote her mother. "I feel if only I were a *little* prettier and younger it would make all the difference with him."[2] She would have liked to have been at his side, helping the attractive Oriental secretary with the emergency. Instead, she was on her way to the rough heights of the Elburz and very different company.

Ismail, one of the subcharvadars, or muleteers, from her trip the year before, now presented himself as her guide. He looked like a convict, she thought, reeked of stale cheese, kept his ragged trousers tied with a string, and sported an outlandish peaked hat on his filthy head. The year before she had decided he was terribly stupid, but, having no choice this time, she mounted her mule. Prodding their sweating donkeys across rice fields and salt marshes, they stumbled through blistering heat toward the high passes. It was quickly apparent that archaeology held no charms for Ismail, who had been forced to escort her by 'Aziz, her previous guide—himself detained, or so his message said, by a "family illness." Ismail stalled at every detour or unbeaten path that an enthusiastic Freya wanted to investigate because he knew malaria infected the valleys at this time of year and he was terrified of getting sick. Instead, it was Freya who got malaria.

Her first goal was the Shah Rud Valley and the castle called Lamiaser, which she had not been able to reach the year before because it had been covered with snow. Subsequently she had read the works of Arabic scholars and learned that it was one of two that had resisted the Mongol invasion long after the other Assassin fortresses had surrendered. If she could get to it and properly identify it, she knew it would be a major coup. There was no previous record of a European exploring Lamiaser.

Days of lonely travel followed, livened by meeting some Kurdish peasants who were astonished to hear that Arabic was not the language of the British. Another night she slept on a kindly peasant's roof, only to be awakened by what sounded like pigs grunting beneath her mattress. There were no pigs; it was her host and hostess, who had crept in to sleep beside her. When at last she spied the desolate, windswept precipice of blackish rock high over the malarial plain that was Lamiaser, she had to force Ismail to scramble with her to its slanting shelf, where she was elated to find the remains of watch towers, gates, and buildings scattered over the ramparts. Here, in 1258, the wife of the last Grand Master of the Assassins, dressed in all her jewels, had hurled herself to death rather than be captured by the Mongols.

Freya prowled the desolate rooms, sorting through shards that looked as if they had remained untouched since the awful moment of the castle's destruction. Confident of her triumph, she set about to photograph and document the site, mindful that a properly scientific report for the Royal Geographical Society should include extensive data on such things as the fortress's ingenious water conduits and system of cisterns. As the arduous day ended and darkness threatened their descent, she took a last look at the meadows far below, where shepherds rounded up their flocks, and reflected on the contrast between such a peaceful scene and the hallucinogenic passions that had burned here seven hundred years before.

The valley was still hot, and mosquitoes buzzed around them day and night. The Shah Rud was engorged by spring rains, and Ismail had difficulty swatting his mules over the narrow track, "telling them the most distressing things about their parentage."[3] Before long Freya felt unwell. Very quickly she was so sick that she begged to stop outside a remote village, slipping weakly to the ground by a little whitewashed shrine. Under the shade of a pear tree, intermittently delirious, she gave in to the shuddering fevers of malaria complicated by acute dysentery. Was this her moment to die—alone in this strange, wild place that she had insisted on coming to against the advice of so many? An image of her father, so vulnerable himself, rose before her and, frightened that she might never see him again, she told herself that it would be outrageous, absolutely unacceptable, to die before he did.

She forced herself to root through her bags for quinine and medications but was so weak she couldn't find them and sank back exhausted. Ismail, probably roused by the thought of a *francesi,* or maybe the lady was an *englesi*—infidels were all the same to him—dying in his care, went back over the mountains to find help, while women emerged from nearby mud huts and squatted silently around her cot. A village headman strolled up self-importantly to deliver the condolences of the tribe, turning his back on her as he spoke out of politeness. Finally Ismail returned, leading a young doctor on vacation whom he had fortuitously come upon in a village five hours away by mule. For six days the doctor stayed with her. Now and then he would inquire softly, why did she wander this way alone through Persia? When she only groaned, he administered injections of quinine, camphor, and emetine until the fevers abated and she felt up to risking the trip by mule back to Qasvin, where she could get a car to the hospital in Teheran. Swaying dizzily, she let Ismail and the doctor hoist her into her saddle, where she suddenly changed her mind. The good mountain air would heal her, she decided. She was going to be all right if she could just get into the mountains.

Freya followed the doctor back up to his tiny village and stayed a month. Slowly she recovered, gazing at the snowy summit of Takht-i-

Sulaiman, the second highest mountain in Persia, soaring above the Elburz Range. She estimated its peak to be about 15,000 feet (it is actually 14,730) and decided she badly wanted to climb it. What a feat that would be—as far as she knew no European had previously conquered it. The name of the mountain meant "the Throne of Solomon," the villagers explained, because, it being the coldest place on earth, Solomon had brought the beautiful queen of Sheba there to lie with her. He was old and she was young and only in such a freezing place as this could he lure her into his warm tent.

As it turned out, the prize of conquering Takht-i-Sulaiman would belong to a young officer from the British Legation in Teheran the following year. Ismail, apparently not so stupid after all, deliberately took her to the wrong starting point for ascent, and by the time Freya realized it, it was too late. Even so, scrambling up scree to a lofty ridge, she paused to contemplate the peaks of the Elburz glittering under the sun, pierced by the white cone of Mount Damavand, Persia's tallest summit. Coming down through tiny hamlets called Shutur Khan or Kalar Dasht, Dohtar Qal'a or Delir—where the children burst into tears and fled at the sight of her—she spent good evenings by the fire with village elders talking of Alexander and Darius, the expected yield of local crops, why she wasn't married, whether she ate pork, and was she really a woman? And all this in Persian only recently learned. Up in the heights she would awaken to a spectacular sunrise painting the morning sky and watch it sleepily as she picked stray lice from her clothes.

As she roved through wild valleys, carefully marking and measuring for the government's maps, Freya jotted notes with a delighted and appreciative eye: "The mist still hung on our flanks like Cossacks round a retreating army," she later wrote, capturing a transient moment in her much-admired account, *The Valleys of the Assassins*.

> *Out of its softness, as we rode up along the banks of the Halis stream which waters Bijeno, came a sound of drums. It was a column of pilgrims, some fifty souls, as it might have been in the days of Chaucer, setting out on their way to Meshed in Khorasan. Most of them were old people, some few on donkeys, others walking along with staffs; a good many women among them, and no one apparently with more luggage than would be tied up in a striped handkerchief. The two large shallow drums that made the noise were carried by a couple of young men in the rear. They all greeted us. "God give you strength," we said as we passed, which is the correct thing to say; and they were lost again in the mist.*[4]

In another scene from *The Valleys of the Assassins,* she described the villagers of Shahristan, who

> *might have been South Sea islanders before the days of Captain Cook so little were they influenced by . . . contacts with civilization. They rushed to me as if I were a circus. Twenty times or more I was asked to stand up on a roof to show myself full length to new audiences. Only the Elders, ardent Shi'as with a Dervish among them, withdrew and cast self-conscious glances from a distance, ashamed to show interest in so negligible an object.*
>
> *It is a remarkable thing, when one comes to consider it, that indifference should be so generally considered a sign of superiority the world over; dignity or age, it is implied, so fill the mind with matter that other people's indiscriminate affairs glide unperceived off that profound abstraction: that at any rate is the impression given not only by village mullahs, but by ministers, bishops, dowagers and well-bred people all over the world, and the village of Shahristan was no exception, except that the assembled dignitaries found it more difficult to conceal the strain which a total absence of curiosity entails.[5]*

Finally Freya meandered back to Teheran, where the sad news awaited her that Robert Stark had died. The telegram from Canada had arrived as she lay delirious on the Persian hillside. Freya regretted that she had not stayed longer when she had last been in Creston. "I cannot feel sad for him," she wrote Charles Ker, "for we so feared long illness and incapacity for him, but sad for myself, for he was a most dear friend and companion and I feel I ought to have been there."[6] She pondered whether she should rush to Canada, but it seemed beside the point now. Instead, she handed her maps to the British Legation's military attaché, who passed them on to the War Office for evaluation ("good and thorough work"), took a deep breath, and headed back to Hamadan, bound for Baghdad.

But on the way she was distracted by art from Luristan graves.

• • •

Freya kept running into bronzes, offered on the sly or even in respectable shops, and couldn't resist them any more than the lovely bits of jewelry or pottery or beads offered along the way for incredibly low sums. Why not a little detour to see if she might not find the source of these treasures? Since 1929 the international art market had taken a great interest in the powerfully designed Neolithic works—vessels, jewelry, horse trappings—

often bearing cuneiform inscriptions from twelve to nineteen centuries before Christ. They were found in graves in one of the most remote parts of Western Persia, called Luristan, "probably the least known of the provinces of Persia," as a Royal Geographical Society review of Freya's adventure later said.[7] These aboriginal Persian peoples, with their drop of Arab blood and hennaed beards, were known as bandits and untamed ruffians. Travelers had been loath to enter the mountainous region once ruled by independent Lurish princes called *atabegs*. Even the police of Reza Shah, the peasant-soldier now ruling Persia, were afraid of enforcing law in such a lawless land and patrolled with trepidation.

Not so Freya. She was eager to go. She wanted both to find bronzes and to bring back a properly scientific description of the graves. If looting wasn't moral, she reflected, the shah himself wasn't preventing it, and at least she would steal with archaeological integrity—measuring and photographing the treasures in situ. She doubted she'd be murdered, although it was an energizing thought. The real problem would be the police who stopped unauthorized wanderers.

With a charvadar named Hajji (an honorific for one who has made a pilgrimage to Mecca) and another guide who was so sodden with opium he could barely stand, Freya plunged into deep country—as usual without credentials. After barely two days of crossing ten-thousand-foot passes, however, she was spotted by an officer who galloped over to arrest her. It turned out to be none other than the chief of police, accompanied by some constables—all resplendent with curved swords and brass buttons—on their way to Alishtar. Trapped, she smiled. She was to come with them, said the officer, so with a great show of elaborate courtesy all around, she gracefully capitulated.

Having by this time concluded that the Khava Plain was not where the bronzes were, Freya allowed herself to be conducted to Alishtar and the shabby office where the provincial governor was lounging in the midst of his advisers. Inspecting her curiously, he announced that she should take his photograph and summoned one of the soldiers to bring a pair of trousers. Freya studied a fly on the ceiling as two valets assisted him in removing the pair he had on and donning a pair that was grander. But he also assigned her a police escort, which prompted Freya to note regretfully that she had probably made herself "too important." Still, better this, she thought, than being clapped into a Persian jail as a vagrant.[8]

Slightly daunted but determined to make the best of it, Freya rode on with a *sardar* as escort, which "was like disturbing an ant hill so great was the dislocation and agitation our arrival always caused; it was as if our appearance made the Lurs wonder which of their crimes had found them

*Freya picnicking in "Devonshire," her name
for a pleasant glade on the Tigris not far from
Baghdad that belonged to an Arab friend.*

*An unpaved
street, typical of
towns in Iraq
before World
War II, leading
to the great
domed mosque
in Samarra.*

out."[9] She alternately charmed, cajoled, and tricked the sardar into areas where there might be gravesites and struggled to pry information from the Lurs, one of whom attempted to steal her bags and most of whom looked thoroughly murderous. On one frightening evening they stumbled wearily into a Lur camp only to have her guide recognize a man with whom he was having a blood feud. A tense, sleepless night ensued, with the guide and sardar ready at the tent flap with their guns across their knees, followed by a stealthy departure at dawn.

More than once, stopping in some roadless wilderness while Freya inquired about graves, her sardar leapt from his horse to snatch off the Lurs' felt hats and demand they throw away their tight-waisted, pointed-sleeved coats, which made them look like medieval pages. The Lurs hung their heads in shame. As this traditional clothing was far more practical than the Western dress Reza Shah was insisting they adopt, Freya twitted the police about playing such a sorry role in "modernizing" their new nation.

But police or no, Freya enjoyed the adventure enormously. She had gone hoping to find graves holding skeletons of humans and horses, which might have shed light on how the horse culture came to Persia. Instead, she discovered that the horse graves were mostly in the southern region of the Ittivend Lurs, a tough and menacing people. She pushed as far in that direction as she could, but the soldier refused to go farther. Instead, she gathered useful knowledge on where various types of graves were located and what their typical characteristics were, such as how a skeleton might be arranged or what sorts of artifacts were commonly interred with it. Unfortunately, many areas with cemeteries that she located had already been looted, so Freya asked the natives to show her their treasures and did her best to learn the circumstances surrounding the discovery of each piece. She bought as much as she dared—but was cautious about revealing that she had money. Traveling in such an area with even a small amount of baggage was hazardous.

One morning, in the valley of Gatchenah among the Nurali Lurs, Freya was alerted by shouts and hurried out of her tent to see men racing down the crest of a hill. A grave had been discovered in a cornfield. She arrived just in time to prevent the Lurs from hacking the skeleton to pieces. It was a poor grave, containing crude bits of pottery and some flints, but she photographed the crouching skeletal figure diligently, bought a pot or two, and went away with the skull wrapped in a handkerchief.

Freya had been the first European woman to venture through Luristan, and she could return home with a report for the archaeologists and an enlarged and annotated map to submit to the War Office. She had succeeded in adding a number of hitherto unnamed valleys and passes, which constituted "a valuable addition to our geographical knowledge of these parts of Persia," as *The Geographical Journal* later reported. Moreover, it was added, because she had put herself "beyond the last [police] outpost," she had been "at serious risk; to have ventured there at all argues great physical courage."[10]

By the end of October, Freya was back in Baghdad, warmly greeted by British and Arabs alike. But from the unpredictable Captain Holt she did not hear a word. He had spent two months as her guest that past summer in Asolo, but she had to call on him personally before he acknowledged her return.

. . .

The time from Freya's return to Baghdad in October 1931 until her packing up in March 1933 was an exceptionally happy and memorable period—despite a nagging hurt and perplexity over the officer whose affection and approval she so craved. She persisted in assuming that the problem was her lack of beauty—it simply did not occur to her that Holt might not be interested in women. Otherwise, Freya no longer lacked for admiring attentions. She was a dinner guest who rewarded her hosts with vivacious warmth and lively stories. Although she was still considered unconventional, most now forgave her. The high commissioner's wife came over at a party and pressed her hand. "I'm so glad we are rescuing you from going native," she said, beamingly conferring absolution on the community's prodigal who so dangerously consorted with "wogs."[11]

Freya's escapades provided marvelous grist for table talk. People enjoyed reporting the latest Freya news. Did you hear, they would whisper, that Miss Stark went to the Muharram procession—in disguise? A Shi'a Muslim ritual that reenacted the martyrdom of the Prophet's grandson Hussein, Muharram was a time of religious frenzy and violent mourning, with thousands of keening penitents beating themselves with chains and whips, and throwing mud on their faces as they paraded to the mosques. It was definitely something foreigners should avoid if they didn't want to get hurt. An American in Teheran a few years before had been torn into pieces when he was caught pretending to be part of the wailing crowd. Freya, undeterred, with a camera hidden under her *'abba*, took photographs and sent them to the *Illustrated London News*.

From the military there was admiring talk about her maps, which the Royal Air Force was having printed up, while a large crowd attended a lecture Freya was invited to give. A scholar in Paris had contacted her, declaring himself impressed with her detailed travel accounts in *The Geographical Journal* and stating his belief that she had discovered the location of an ancient Persian city.[12] She was learning Russian ("a brute of a language"),[13] attempting to learn golf, and entertaining regularly. She had instructed her servant, hired for a few pennies a week, to buy enough at the market every Friday to provide dinner for five and thought herself rather clever not to fret about when best to throw a party, just plan to have one once a week.

If it hadn't been for the dismayingly peckish note that was beginning to creep into letters from her old protectress, Viva Jeyes, Freya would have felt her cup was overflowing. Viva had been a great help in many ways, serving as a London mail drop, acting as a liaison with the Royal Geographical Society, and overseeing Freya's small investment portfolio. But lately she had seemed jealous of Freya's successes. Freya decided to pay no heed. Nothing should spoil her recent pleasure in life. Even spinsterhood was seeming less disastrous.

"I used to feel," she wrote Venetia,

> *that I had missed the real reason of life by not marrying, and was out of the stream in a backwater as it were. But now I feel this is not so. I think the human being is just coming to that point where sex is no longer the only means of progress—as it has been so far: we are just stepping along into a wider world, and need not feel lonely, except in the way that pioneers are lonely. Life is easier for married people: but I think it ought to be if anything richer for us, so long as we take it with full hands and not with the inferiority sense which has often ruined the lives of spinsters. Don't you think this is so? Anyway it is a comfort to know that all the greatest thinkers are with us; I think there is not one who considers marriage as a necessity to the fullness of life—though personally I would like to be married.[14]*

Still, Captain Holt continued to blow hot and cold; she was never certain how she stood with him. One day he would ask her to ride, another he would lose his temper and stay angry for days over a small thing like Freya speaking to him when he was teeing off on the golf course. Yet just when she was feeling most miserable about him, he would surprise her with an act of warmth and concern that erased all the previous neglect. One such moment came when Freya, whose income had been plummeting as a result of the worldwide financial depression, started to panic. When she mentioned her problem to Captain Holt, he introduced her to the editor of the *Baghdad Times,* and in no time she had been offered work at twenty pounds a month to put Reuters dispatches into more readable prose.

Freya was by no means sure that she wanted to be a run-of-the-mill wage earner, even if the job *were* in journalism. She was, however, quite clear about how she expected to be treated. On her very first day, when none of her male co-workers glanced up as she entered the newsroom, she cast a steely look over the array of desks and announced to their occupants that henceforth when she arrived they must stand up. "Office women are to be thought of as queens," she declared grandly. Astonished, her colleagues complied.[15]

This rather extraordinary incident revealed an emerging element in Freya's character: a tendency to act imperiously when she felt her social status questioned. Doubtless she felt vulnerable because she lacked the protection of a husband, but also she was determined never again to be treated as a nobody to whom people could "turn up their noses" just because she lacked "the padding of worldly possessions."[16] In this Freya merely followed her mother's example, for although Flora had been earning her own living for many years, somehow she always made it seem as if she were handing largesse to her employees, with a hauteur that commanded respect.

As it happened Freya's new colleagues at the paper not only stood for her from then on but quickly realized the new "office lady" was a serious talent. Her delightful pieces, often gently tweaking the pomposities of the colonial establishment, were received with considerable amusement and before long compiled and published locally as "Baghdad Sketches."

It was with Holt's help that Freya made some important journalistic coups that added to her growing reputation. At this time, when their League of Nations mandate had expired, the British were preparing to hand over Iraq to the Iraqis. The question was: who exactly were the Iraqis? The same bitter divisions between ethnic and religious minorities that assail the region today were tearing at the artificial boundaries of the new state. Besides the Shi'a, who had no wish to be governed by a hated Sunni minority, there were the Chaldeans, the Assyrians, and especially the Kurds. This huge subgroup, reaching from Turkey through northern Syria and from Iraq into Iran, were in rebellion. They had asked for and been denied a nation of their own. Now the British were trying to bomb them into quiescence, and two RAF pilots had been shot down and captured. Captain Holt, who spoke Kurdish, secretly went up to the camp of the Kurdish chieftain and negotiated their release.

London clamored for news while Parliament debated the wisdom of the bombing policy—and Freya got the story. What's more, she got it into *The Times* of London. Her well-placed friend had seen to it that she was provided with all the dispatches, background briefings, and maps necessary. It was truly her hour of glory, presented by Holt on a silver platter.

Increasingly, the Baghdad community was giving Freya credit for being a player in their midst. Even though she still quavered periodically to her mother over her lack of beauty ("I always find it takes people about a month to overcome their first impression of my plainness"),[17] she somehow managed to be thick with the most attractive bachelors, many of them intelligence officers keeping an eye on the dangers of Bolshevik infiltration from Soviet Russia and willing to educate her and involve her in policy discussions. If some of them turned out to be homosexual, she didn't seem to know it. Such things were just not discussed in polite society; England, after all, saw homosexuality as a criminal offense as late as 1967.[18]

In her male circle was the dashing Captain Gerald de Gaury, reputedly the illegitimate son of Lord Kitchener, who became resident in Kuwait. There was also Evan Guest, who was to write a comprehensive work on Iraqi flora and later joined Freya in seeing that an Islamic room was added to Gertrude Bell's museum, hitherto overly weighted, they felt, in favor of early Mesopotamian history. When Evan once spent the night at Freya's as a convenience, he left his tie and cuff links on the downstairs table, causing Freya great consternation. She feared the servants would leap to the wrong conclusions.

It was not easy, after all, for a single woman to protect her reputation and live as Freya did. One way to make sure she was treated with appropriate respect was never to let down her vigilance. Her dignity remained a subject about which she seldom joked. It was another reason why she liked Holt. Besides being demonstrably brave and a gifted linguist, he was correct in the very reassuringly starchy and emotionally throttled English way that Freya admired enormously. Nobody was ever as tenaciously British as Freya. She determinedly adopted as many British mannerisms as she could—as a counter to being seen, as Harold Nicolson described her on their first meeting the following year, as "a funny foreign little thing." Like all converts, Freya sang a little louder in church.[19]

Thus the behavior of a man like Eric Maxwell deeply offended her. Maxwell was a judge working in Baghdad without his wife. Freya had met them both several years earlier in Ventimiglia, knew they were having marital problems, and was enjoying Maxwell's company. He had offered to teach her to drive his car, which she, always interested in new challenges—especially those connected with physical danger—made especially terrifying because she could never remember how to use the brake. But they had a good time together, although she allowed in her droll way that it was really "barbarous to have to rush along with one's eye on the road all the time."[20]

Soon they were off on a week's jaunt to visit the Chaldean bishop in Persian Kurdistan. Almost immediately Maxwell, who doubtless assumed that a free spirit like Freya was equally available with her favors, made it apparent that he expected her to sleep with him. He did not do this very gracefully, and Freya was stung. Furious, deeply unsettled, and anxious, she turned on him indignantly, which seemed only to stimulate Maxwell's ardor. Back in Baghdad he persisted, suggesting they go together to Bokara and Samarkand. "He says," Freya wrote her mother, "he has never met anyone so virtuous as me."[21]

Maxwell continued to press his suit until Freya was writing again to her mother: "and all this Eric fuss is so fatiguing—I believe he has never had to go without anything: he is like a woman over it, incapable of holding himself in hand, and really very selfish—for I have told him I care for someone else. . . . I find myself with mid-Victorian ideas of morality, and no one to share them with except C.H. [Captain Holt] who persists in thinking me fast and modern."[22]

Eventually Freya dismissed him in no uncertain terms, and Maxwell was evidently devastated—so was Freya. Three times the lovelorn judge called on her asking for forgiveness, which she granted, but she refused to go out driving with him anymore. "He is going all to bits: a dreadful result of never disciplining himself. . . . I feel absolutely *defiled,* not because Eric is a married man, but because it is not love, just a sort of delirium which has seized him."[23]

Judge Maxwell's passion for Freya was the only time the record is absolutely unambiguous about her being the object of a man's ardent sexual desire. But Freya, no Hester Prynne, was not about to sacrifice her hard-earned approval in society by a fling with a married man. What was more, she was truly shaken by Maxwell's clumsy assault on her physical person and deeply inculcated sense of decorum. Coping alone in desolate Kurdistan with a man's sexual urgency had caused strong feelings of revulsion. Whether this means Freya was frigid, or unbendingly Victorian, or simply in love with another man is hard to say. Certainly Maxwell's suit had been poorly presented, and she would not be the first woman to turn down a man because she just didn't want him.

• • •

It was time to go home. The aggrieved note in Viva Jeyes's letters was escalating; she had begun chiding Freya for "abandoning" her responsibilities to the old people in Asolo. And while Flora was not exactly demanding

Freya's return, she mentioned in a letter to "Dearest Girlie" that every night after dinner she would go to sit in Freya's room so that she would seem "less far away."[24] Then in January 1933 came the sad news that Vera's daughter, Angela, had died of peritonitis—a particularly painful way to go. Over a thousand mourners from all over the province had attended her funeral, Flora wrote from Dronero; even the crown prince had telegraphed.[25] The loss of her beloved fifteen-year-old niece was very hard on Freya. She worried about the effect Angela's death would have on the other children. As she had said when her father died: "There are too many partings in this world."[26] To his credit, Captain Holt was gentle to Freya while she grieved.

But it would never do to leave Baghdad without one more madcap escapade—especially if it dropped into her lap. An eighteen-year-old Lur arrived on Freya's doorstep with a fantastic tale. His father was a tribal chieftain in a small tribe in Kebir Kuh, a part of Persia still unmapped. A number of years earlier, the boy told her, he had been shown some daggers and jewels by a tribesman who said he had found them when he had been caught in a storm and taken refuge in a cave. The man, noticing a sparkle in the blackness, investigated and found twenty chests of gold ornaments, daggers, idols, and coins. The boy finished this dramatic yarn by warning that he had rivals who were also after the treasure and might not stop at anything—including murder.

Needless to say, Freya was fascinated. Furthermore, it had been an officer from intelligence who had sent the lad to her, so her adventure seemed to have a semiofficial—if secret—countenance. Only recently *The Manchester Guardian* had reported on the alarming degree of tribal unrest in Iraq's interior and urged the government to forbid women to travel outside the four major cities. But either because British intelligence privately disagreed with this assessment or because they had become convinced Freya was up to the job and could be useful doing more quiet mapping for them, she was given a green light. It was as if she were one of the "pundits" made famous in Kipling's *Kim* who traveled anonymously through the subcontinent surveying for the Geographical Survey of India.[27]

"Don't mention this to *anyone*," she wrote breathlessly to Flora as she set out in September 1932.[28] She reentered Luristan on a donkey, draped in native clothing, three Lurs at her side as guides. She bluffed her way past the border guards ("The great and almost only comfort about being a woman," she said, "is that one can always pretend to be more stupid than one is and no one is surprised").[29] She climbed over from Bedrah into Pusht Kuh and reached the Saidmarreh River, untouched country except for occasional tents roofed in oak leaves and lonely shepherds wearing long velvet coats with daggers stuffed in their sashes. Enduring hunger, gale winds, nights on rocky terrain, and a guide who appropriated her Burberry coat and fell to praying when dinner had to be got, Freya encountered dervishes, idol worshipers, and armed tribesmen; attended both weddings and dyings; and attempted to scamper with ibex on the side of a nine-thousand-foot-high mountain.

The long and the short of the adventure, however, was a touch anticlimactic. Although she evaded the authorities for a time, the Persian police finally caught up with Freya. She was interrogated politely about antiquities and, her innocent disclaimers notwithstanding, escorted by heavily armed constables to the border. She had not been able to get close enough to the mountain cave that allegedly held the treasure, although at one point she was able to slip away from her keepers for a few hours, concealing an empty bag and flashlight beneath her skirt. She hoped the Lurish youth would find her as she waited under a tree. He never showed up, but her police escorts did.

If there were no treasure, once again Freya had mapped and measured and once again was returning from a remote land with hard new information for the War Office's maps. Best of all, as far as she was concerned, ten men were rumored to have been sent by the rival treasure hunters to kill her, and the Baghdad community, having got wind of the story, was full of concern for her.

It could not have been a better note on which to leave. In March 1933 Captain Holt waited with her one cold, windy evening for the mail truck that would take her away. It arrived stinking of fish, but the ticket to Amman cost only two pounds, ten shillings—and Freya was broke. When Holt said irritably, "You enjoy being uncomfortable,"[30] she searched his face and assured herself it was his way of showing affection. They bade good-bye; he promised to visit again in Asolo, and she was off. It had been a remarkable three and a half years.

Recognition

> *It has been a mixed time in many ways . . . the real difficulty is*
> *not the eccentricity of my being here but the fact that I do seem*
> *to be a foreigner and a stranger. . . . If you had brought me up*
> *in a proper English way, I would have known that so long as*
> *one says and does like everyone else (and that is so impossible*
> *to guess!) one can think what one likes.*
>
> —LETTER TO HER MOTHER, FEBRUARY 20, 1930

*T*he small, slender, forty-year-old woman who returned to Italy in 1933 had now attained an authoritative command
of the Levant, Syria, Iraq, and Persia. She had admired the landscape, tasted the food, and acquired a sympathetic understanding of
the East's many peoples. She had broken bread with villagers and
peasants and been welcomed by European officials, pashas, emirs,
and sheikhs. She had met the men digging out the East's great treasures, from Sir Leonard Woolley, who excavated Carchemish and Ur,
to Sir Aurel Stein. She was familiar with the myriad sects and faiths
of the region, having visited their humble shrines as well as their
great mosques. In the shadow of mountains she had walked with
shepherds, and in the desert, slept in nomads' tents.

All the while Freya thought long and hard about whether colonial
peoples should be allowed to govern themselves and concluded that

most people would rather take their lives into their own hands, even if doing so meant going without bridges, paved roads, and modern hospitals. She was certain that while the British did it better than anyone, it was better not to be doing good for people who didn't want to be done for. She was beginning to formulate for herself a definition for a "new imperialism," which kept a benign eye on former protégés but no longer actively governed.

In the last seven years she had endured all kinds of physical discomfort, from hunger and thirst to being crawled over by fleas and flies, and there had been more than one occasion to agree with Baudelaire that "the Orient without sun is nothing but a heap of filth." She had suffered dengue fever, sandfly fever, boils, quinsy, malaria, influenza, dysentery. Considering herself an observer, she had been deeply moved by sweeping vistas in uncharted territory, awed by the fading footprints of history on ruined cities, and especially impressed by the wisdom she found in cultures vastly different from her own. She had often been very happy; she had also been depressed.

In 1930, at the age of thirty-seven, before going off to the Caspian mountains, Freya had written her mother that she was "feeling so old . . . as if my whole life were wasted and now it [was] too late to do anything with it." It was all such uphill work, she continued in profound discouragement. "As if what I *do* do were not worth doing: no one seems to think it is, but just wonder at me and are sorry for me if they are nice, and disapprove if they are not. To be just middle-aged," she lamented, "with no particular charm or beauty and no position is a dreary business." She said that she felt as if her efforts had taken her "nowhere in particular" and that she was "most dreadfully lonely, envying all these women with their nice clean husbands whose tradition is their tradition, and their nice flaxen children who will carry it on in the same simple and steady way. And," she continued bitterly, "though it *is* my tradition too, no one thinks it is, because of a silly difference of form and speech and fashion—so that I feel as if I *had* no people of my own. If only I could eventually find some work that would make me feel settled and interested . . . but no one seems to want women very much."[1]

It was an anguished wail, a familiar cry that has echoed down the ages, repeated by women whose sense of pride and desire for respect has been injured by a society generally indifferent to any talent or capacity they might have except that of breeder or caretaker or servant or pretty tool to enhance domestic life. Today, though women are often torn between their desire for home and professional accomplishment, they can at least make a choice. Before the Second World War they had more limited options.

Not to be married, not to be running a household, was failure, pure and simple. But in Freya's case it was somehow more piteous, not just because she knew she wasn't pretty, or because under the hats and hairpieces lurked the terrible scars of the factory accident, but because at bottom she would always feel she was an outsider. She could never entirely overcome that odd, lonely upbringing in Dronero, the unconventional, quarreling parents who loved her but lived apart, her foreign accent and manner, which she felt undercut her ever having a truly secure place with that flaxen British tribe she so admired. If these things were the goads that spurred her to high performance and ultimately gave her strength, she did not always see it that way. *She* knew that she had courage and imagination; she wanted others to acknowledge her abilities. She wanted to be taken seriously, to be respected for herself, to be justified, and, yes, to be admired.

The Baghdad years, 1929 to 1933, had affirmed a lot for Freya. She had found that she could, in fact, make a life as a single woman away from Vera's motherless babies, Mario's selfishness, her mother's bossy dependence—even Viva Jeyes's possessive jealousy. She had stood on her own two feet, felt the warmth of approval from a community whose good opinion she coveted, discovered that she could differ and not be cast into outer darkness, and live, if it came to that, on the earnings from her writings.

She allowed herself to take a real satisfaction in those things she had managed to accomplish during this time; after all, were they not fairly considerable? She had acquired Arabic and Persian, studied the Koran and other Islamic literature, written a book, undertaken several explorations that had broken new ground and added to the British Geographical Survey; she could boast a number of well-received articles in respected journals and the beginning of a solid professional reputation. When she walked into the Royal Geographical Society, people knew who she was. Despite the occasional periods of despondency, surely this was a good beginning.

Yet nothing could prepare her for the astonishing turn of fate that lay just ahead.

. . .

Herbert Young and Flora met Freya's train at Castelfranco. Nearly the same height, with similar heads of snow white hair, they finally showed their age. Herbert, now over eighty, was thin and stooped. Flora, at seventy-two, in a lace-collared shirtwaist and pearl choker, was still statuesque, but her handsome face was lined.[2] Indifferent to the occasionally raised eyebrows of outsiders to Asolo's small community, they had long since slipped into the easy comradeship of husband and wife—Flora running the house, Herbert reading, painting, and occasionally fussing about her inclination to embroil them in too much social activity.

While Freya was away, they had kept a constant, sustaining stream of letters flowing to her, and now they came to bring her home. As they drove through the familiar pastures dotted with dark cypress trees and hedgerows of Normandy poplars, Flora, unable to contain her excitement any longer, burst out with extraordinary news. Freya had received a letter from the Royal Geographical Society, and she had opened it. It contained an announcement that the RGS was awarding Freya the Back Memorial Prize for her travels in Luristan and for her cartographic contributions. It was an honor that this most prestigious of societies had been extending since 1882 to stimulate geographic discovery and promote the work of geographers and explorers. Freya would be the third woman to receive it.

It was a thrilling moment. As she walked through the gate of Casa Freia, the home that had been Herbert's gift, and at last crossed the threshold of her own front door, Freya was overwhelmed with happiness. She tried to be modest about the prize. This, just for walking by herself in the Persian hills? Although the stipend was not great—amounting to only fourteen pounds, worth much more then than now—the honor was all she could have hoped for and more than she had dared dream. It opened no end of possibilities. Suddenly she was being embraced by the fraternity she most admired—the world of soldiers, diplomats, and explorers who were the hub of England's intellectual establishment.

The reading public's appetite for news of discoveries—archaeological, geographic, geologic, oceanographic—was voracious. Almost every day announcements were made of extraordinary finds, and the press covered them with rapt attention. Explorers and archaeologists were heroes and their discoveries hot news. Bertram Thomas and Harry St. John Philby had both crossed the trackless waste of Arabia's Empty Quarter, and Charles Lindbergh had flown solo across the Atlantic. Only eleven years before, Howard Carter had found the fabled riches of Tutankhamen's tomb buried in Egypt's Valley of the Kings, igniting a mad Egyptomania on four continents. Eleven years before that, the world was captivated by the race to the South Pole, won by Roald Amundsen, who had eaten his sled dogs to survive, and tragically lost by Robert Falcon Scott, whose frozen body and haunting diary were found months afterward. The assaults on the Himalayas had begun, producing many heroic stories, although the conquest of Mount Everest would have to wait until 1953. The ocean depths—the very last frontier—were also being explored; in 1932 two Americans had descended to the unprecedented depth of three thousand feet in a new machine called a bathysphere. Archaeological teams from many nations were busy digging at ancient sites in out-of-the-way places, exhibiting the same fevered competitiveness as the explorers, while an eager public waited breathlessly for their reports.

It was to this community of visionaries and risk takers that Freya felt summoned. No longer an object of suspicion, she was Miss Freya Stark, Explorer. She had arrived—and she intended to make good use of the opportunity.

PART THREE

THE TRIUMPHANT NOMAD

*Some day I must make a list of the reasons
for which I have been thought mad and
by whom: it would make such
an amusing medley.*

—LETTER TO HER MOTHER,
MAY 16, 1930

CHAPTER TEN

A London Whirl

> *The great thing about being a*
> *Traveller is that everyone tells*
> *you the amusing things*
> *they* have *done!*
>
> —LETTER TO HER MOTHER,
> NOVEMBER 6, 1933

Neither Flora nor Herbert Young was able to accompany Freya to London to receive her prize. "I am being literally rushed off my feet!" she wrote home breathlessly.[1] There were interviews with the BBC and newspaper reporters, photograph sessions were requested, a cartoon of her even appeared in the *Daily Sketch*, giving her, she complained, "terrible ankles." *Who's Who* sent her forms to fill out, over which she laughed nervously. "And where, if anywhere, was I Educated? And what is my Career?" she puzzled, all too aware that her "career" was still a bit fuzzy even in her own mind and her self-acquired "education" far from orthodox.[2] A well-known artist offered to paint her portrait, and from all over London came invitations to dinner with society figures and the men who called themselves Arabists. Best of all, from Baghdad came enthusiastic congratulations from Captain Holt.

In the late afternoon of June 19, 1933, looking smart in a tailored dress and matching narrow-brimmed hat, Freya arrived at the portals of the Royal Geographical Society. Fifty years earlier, in this vast hall incised in gold with the names of the great explorers, Sir Richard Burton and John Speke had railed at each other over which of them had discovered the correct source of the Nile. Now a crowd of over one hundred, including the dean of Westminster Abbey, the first lord of the admiralty, and the astronomer royal, gathered to hear Sir William Goodenough, the society's outgoing president, present the awards. As Freya awaited her turn, five heroes of exploration stood to be honored: J. M. Wordie and Erich von Drygalski, who had survived dangerous expeditions in Antarctica; Noel Humphreys, who had conquered Africa's highest peaks; Khan Sahib Afraz Gul Khan, who had mapped much of Central Asia; and L. S. B. Leakey, the paleogeographer who was working on climate change in East Africa and would later discover the remains of earliest man.

Finally Sir William turned to Freya. "To you, Miss Stark," said the silver-haired president, "is awarded the Back Grant. . . . We recognize that you travel alone with no great regard for your own safety, and without troubling officials too much on that account. We have profited greatly by your literary talent and the attention you have paid to getting accurate transcript of the names along your routes, contributing to the correctness of our maps. Although you may not have completely solved the problems of the famous Luristan bronzes you have, at any rate, found one of the sources, and we hope that you will continue to prosecute your researches."[3]

Thus the official blessing of the Royal Geographical Society was bestowed upon Freya, and forever afterward her adventures would enjoy the favor and often the financial support of this illustrious body. Giddy inside and composed without, she accepted her diploma and shook Sir William's hand. Turning to the audience, praying that her voice would not betray her nervousness, she thanked the society for "this great honor." However, only she knew how deeply she meant it when she added, "I am sure many have felt as I did, that when one is still a little doubtful and rather discouraged, sometimes, by one's friends, it is most encouraging to receive the sympathy and understanding of the Society."[4] It was a very sly wink at all those in Baghdad who had criticized, scorned, or obstructed her. Now they would have to think twice before laughing at her plans.

The next day King Faisal of Iraq, who had been escorted to England by four British destroyers and nine airplanes, arrived in London on a state visit. Crowds thronged the route to Buckingham Palace as the Arab sovereign rode with King George in an open carriage followed by one hundred mounted Scots Guards. But pictured just as prominently in the newspapers was the new celebrity Miss Freya Stark.

. . .

Partly bemused, partly amazed, and very, very pleased, Freya accepted the attention. The BBC invited her to lecture, and four publishers asked if she would be interested in writing a book. Minnie Granville, a neighbor with a summer home in La Mortola who had long been a close friend of Flora's, now wrote Flora and Herbert that Freya was being "lionized" and said she worried that Freya was rushing away too soon for a visit to Venetia Buddicom "when the world is at her feet at the height of the London season."[5] At the same time Bernard Granville, Minnie's husband, who admired Freya's ability and had been a witness to Flora and her friends' efforts to marry her off, delivered himself of an astonishing and prophetic pronouncement: in a marriage, "she would be clipped and spoiled."[6]

In the fall Freya gave her first lecture. The venue was the packed auditorium of the Royal Asiatic Society. Freya looked slender and girlish in a white dress. There was a polite hush as she stepped up and Sir Denison Ross, head of the School of Oriental Studies, cataloged her accomplishments. The audience clapped loudly, touched at the sight of this slight creature so much in the news, who had evidently shown such courage in the face of unknown perils. Quietly, artfully, with consummate poise Freya commenced a carefully crafted speech in a voice that at first revealed a disarming feminine quaver but gradually found exactly the right pitch, so that even those in the very farthest rows could hear every word. Diffident, ladylike, and masterly, she recounted tales of her adventures in Luristan. The crowd roared with pleasure.[7]

"The lecture was a triumph," Minnie Granville gushed to Freya's mother in a letter a few days later. "Everyone so interested and pleased. She has a very pretty delivery. Her voice so soft and nice and very distinct. I knew she was nervous. It is a great ordeal—and I never saw her sit with her eyes cast down before. Ha! But when she got up it didn't show a bit in voice or manner. . . . She is a little puss. You have no idea how nice she is looking."[8]

The talent that Freya showed from that first important appearance onstage developed into a mesmerizing gift for public speaking. Although she always maintained that her stomach was in knots when she had to give a talk, her slightly foreign, almost singsong voice delighted her listeners almost as much as the exotic content of her speeches. In this pretelevision age lectures drew large crowds, as eager for entertainment as they were for information. Freya's performances soon were invariably packed. "Fascinating little thing," sighed a friend of Minnie's. "She sort of lifts one into another world."[9]

At one lecture a Saudi Arabian official showed up in flowing white robes, and Freya showered him with attention. Ever in excited attendance, Mrs. Granville again wrote Flora: "Lord and Lady Allenby were in front and His Highness, a dark somebody. I thought he was Persian, but he was Arabian, and seems to have given her an invitation to Arabia—just what she wanted. She flirted all tea time with him in Arabic. He looked very stodgy and safe but likely to be very useful."[10]

Just ten years earlier Abdul Aziz Ibn Saud, the leader of a puritanical sect called the Wahhabis from central Arabia, had done what no tribal chieftain before him had been able to do. In superb control of his fierce horsemen, Saud had overrun the Hejaz, home to the holy cities of Mecca and Medina. The British-supported Hashemite sherif, the Hereditary Keeper of the Keys to Mecca, was driven into embittered exile, his dream of being named caliph shattered. Saud had united Arabia for the first time, and it was clear to the competing oil companies that there would be no prospecting without the favor of the newly crowned king. Not only was he in control of the sacred places of Islam but with the cessation of a British subsidy of sixty thousand pounds annually, he owed Britain nothing and was making a point of remaining neutral. If Freya wanted to go there—and she very much did—she would be entirely dependent on the king's goodwill.

Freya also thought it would be helpful to cultivate Lord Allenby, the tall, lean hero of World War I, whose victorious armies had defeated the Ottoman Empire and who knew all the Middle Eastern heads of state. Lord and Lady Allenby had attended at least two of Freya's lectures. During one of them she was horrified to see the old general's great domed head droop in slumber but was reassured to learn that he was almost totally deaf and frequently nodded off during lectures. She fared better seated next to him at a dinner party, where she shouted into his ear that she would love him to describe his famous entry into Jerusalem in December 1917. Winningly she attended as the legendary soldier, known as the Bull, explained how he had realized that he must get off his horse and walk into the sacred city as a sign of respect. She remarked that he was only following the precedent of Umar, the great Umayyad caliph, who had done the same thirteen hundred years earlier.

At one party after the next Freya found herself in the company of the very explorers, diplomats, and soldiers she had admired since she began her studies of the East and whose names seemed almost mythic to her. One by one she was meeting the men whose choices, right or wrong, had shaped the present Middle East. There were the "kingmakers" who promoted the ambitions of the Hashemites of Mecca. Sir Percy Cox, former high commissioner of Iraq, Gertrude Bell's superior officer, was spare, crook-nosed, and blue-eyed, looking every inch the soldier-conqueror equally at ease on horse or camel. He was a consummate listener, and she told him he looked like pictures she had seen of the duke of Wellington.[11] There was Sir Ronald Storrs, former British resident in Cairo, the man who had introduced T. E. Lawrence to the sherif of Mecca. He was clever, coolly self-confident, a witty conversationalist, linguist, and piano player. She enjoyed him and felt he liked her. She met Sir Kinahan Cornwallis, tall and lanky, who had worked in the Sudan before serving in Syria with Emir Faisal, whose personal adviser he had become when the emir assumed Iraq's throne. Freya wondered if the rumors were true that Gertrude Bell had been passionately in love with Cornwallis, twenty years her junior.

The cynical explorer-genius Harry St. John Philby—friend and confidant of King Saud—was introduced. People didn't suspect it then, but Philby's tirades against British imperialism were clearly affecting his son Kim, who would become a spy for the Russians. There was Bertram Thomas, Philby's protégé, who had beaten him at being first to cross the Rub al Khali, Arabia's Empty Quarter, and there was General Lord Allenby's fellow soldier General John Shea, who had accepted the surrender of Jerusalem from its Ottoman governors.* Sir Denison Ross—and countless others—also helped Freya with Arab introductions.

To all these men Freya gave her attention, listening, admiring, entertaining them with droll little stories, which she mixed with well-aimed flattery. She wanted them to become her friends and to be there with help when the time came. But two in particular entered her life who would count even more.

Sydney Cockerell, director of the Fitzwilliam Museum of Cambridge

---

* The true story of the Ottoman surrender to the British was slightly more offhand. Before General Shea arrived at the city gates, two British advance scouts were met by the mayor of Jerusalem holding a white bedsheet attached to a broom pole and carrying the documents of surrender. The mayor was accompanied by a young photographer named Larsson, whose job was to record the ceremony and who had supplied the white sheet. The surprised soldiers, being NCOs, refused to accept the papers, as did several more arriving troops. It began to look to the Jerusalemites as if nobody would let them surrender. Finally Brigadier General Watson entered the town, the documents were accepted, and Larsson could photograph the event. Commander in Chief Shea had got stuck in mud en route and appeared long after the excited crowds had dispersed. When Shea learned that young Larsson had captured on film the real moment of surrender, and not the moment when he stood on the steps of David's Tower to proclaim martial law, he demanded that Larsson destroy the negatives and all copies of the picture. He sent an officer to see that his order was executed. Fortunately, however, a copy of this historic moment has survived and is in the possession of Larsson's son Theo, a resident of London who has written a delightful book about his youth in Jerusalem titled *Seven Passports for Palestine*. It happens that Theo Larsson is the husband of Herbert Olivier's granddaughter, Barclay Sanders Larsson, whose family knew Flora and Freya Stark as well as or better than anyone this author was able to interview.

University, had met Freya in 1931 at Viva Jeyes's house in St. John's Wood. He found her smart and interesting on the subject of the Arabs, but as an infrequent visitor to England she was not a person he would likely bump into again in the normal course of events. When, however, the news of her Back Grant award appeared in 1933, he decided to attend the ceremony. From that point on he concluded that Freya Stark was somebody whose career was worth following. Clearly she was now on her way to stardom—and if any man gravitated to talent it was this diminutive sixty-seven-year-old scholar. Cockerell looked somewhat like Sigmund Freud, with his neatly clipped beard and piercing eye. He had proved himself such an innovative director that the museum world still invokes his name; he had made the Fitzwilliam into "one of the finest museums existing," Bernard Berenson pronounced. Not only did he present the collection in a fresh and more coherent way but, recognizing the importance of continual acquisition—of both money and new works—he earned the sobriquet "scrounger of genius."[12]

Over his lifetime Cockerell had amassed an important personal collection of medieval and Renaissance manuscripts. But he also collected people. As a young man he had brazenly cultivated the acquaintances of John Ruskin, the critic, and William Morris, one of the founders of the Arts and Crafts Movement, ultimately becoming the latter's literary executor. He also made himself essential—and executor—to both Thomas Hardy and the poet and anti-imperialist Wilfrid Scawen Blunt. It wasn't that Cockerell was a toady. On the contrary, he had a fine eye and literary ear for ability. Disclaiming any talent of his own for originality, he admired it in others and made himself useful to many leading lights in the world of art and literature of his time.

The list was long and altogether remarkable, and Cockerell assiduously nurtured it by constant and prompt letters written in a precise and infinitesimal hand: to Henry James, James Barrie, Samuel Butler, Rudyard Kipling and his first cousin Edward Burne-Jones, Algernon Swinburne, Charles Doughty, Leo Tolstoy, Ezra Pound, W. M. Rossetti, Hilaire Belloc, George Bernard Shaw, T. E. Lawrence—to name only a few. He also succumbed to the temptation to cull from the letters of his esteemed friends material for two anthologies, *Such Good Friends,* published when he was seventy, and *Friends of a Lifetime,* which came out in his ninetieth year. The volumes raised a few eyebrows among critics, who could not help pointing out that Cockerell surely also corresponded with people who were not so famous—and that some of the letters were not intrinsically very interesting. They agreed that among the best were those written by Bernard Shaw, T. H. White, and Freya Stark.

The correspondence was initiated by Freya, but as they were both to prove world-class letter writers it hardly matters. On January 22, 1934, she wrote to congratulate Cockerell on being given a knighthood, and he wrote back to thank her. It was not long before he offered to show her Doughty's notebooks at the Fitzwilliam. In the meantime the daily notations in his diary changed from having met "a nice Miss Stark who has travelled alone in Persia" to "marvellous little Freya Stark, who is off again in a fortnight or so for a perilous journey across Arabia . . . one wonders whether she has sufficient stamina for such a journey."[13]

Cockerell supported, petted, and encouraged Freya for over thirty years—almost completely by letter. He was fascinated and impressed by her rapidly composed sketches, which so beautifully caught the flavor of people and landscape; he told her—and others, because he was certain it was true—that Freya Stark was one of the most gifted letter writers of the age. It was as a result of Cockerell's urging that Freya undertook to write her autobiography during World War II, and she dedicated it to him. Its publisher was John Murray VI, latest in the long line of John Murrays whose publishing company had been selecting winners since before the Battle of Waterloo.

Jock Murray, as he liked to be called, tweedy and trim with a long, narrow face, high forehead, courtly manners, and a preference for bow ties, was only twenty-four when he came into Freya's life. Eager to make his own mark in the family publishing dynasty, he had been a restless scout for suitable new material since working at the family-owned *Cornhill Magazine* between terms at Oxford. As the assistant to Dr. Leonard Huxley, the *Cornhill*'s editor, he had been given the task of cleaning out Dr. Huxley's desk when the editor died shortly before Freya returned from Baghdad. Jock found one of her articles in a drawer. He had been impressed by the piece she had written in 1928 on her journey into the Jebel Druze. Discovering this latest, a discussion of British policy toward the rebellious Assyrians, he promptly wrote her to say he would like to publish it. In addition, he wondered, might she be interested in writing a book for the house of John Murray? Freya responded immediately. She was enclosing "Baghdad Sketches," she said, noting that her publisher in Baghdad thought it could use a British edition.

Murray's interest in her therefore predated and, from Freya's point of view, was more compelling than what the other publishers now blandishing her could offer. Jock recognized the talent in "Baghdad Sketches," which was considerably more lighthearted than the rather serious articles she had previously given to the *Cornhill*. But like another British publisher, Methuen & Co., which had turned the book down, he feared that

Sir Sydney Cockerell, former director of the Fitzwilliam Museum, Cambridge University, antiquarian book collector, friend and confidant to the famous. He thought that Freya was one of the most gifted letter-writers of the age.

Jock Murray in his fifties. The head of the John Murray publishing house, he was Freya's loyal friend and editor, who bent over backward to support Freya's needs. Even the task of getting a tin bathtub sent to remotest Yemen did not daunt Jock.

the public for it was not large enough.[14] He wanted an altogether new book—and decided that he must not miss her lecture. As soon as he could push his way through the press of admirers, Jock invited Freya to 50 Albemarle Street, the handsome mansion just off Piccadilly where his forebears had lived and run their thriving book business since 1812.

. . .

The spacious drawing room into which Jock ushered Freya was hung with the same gold paper, somewhat age-darkened, that had dazzled guests when it was put up in the 1830s by John Murray III. Freya instantly responded to an atmosphere saturated with faded Regency splendor and literary genius. Charles Darwin had brought *On the Origin of Species* to these hallowed rooms. Beneath a coffered ceiling, marble busts stared down from tall bookcases. The walls were adorned with portraits of the firm's immortals: Sir Walter Scott, Washington Irving, David Livingstone, Charles Darwin, George Gordon, Lord Byron, curly-haired and full-lipped, looking dreamily out of his golden frame above the mantelpiece. In the grate below, Byron's private memoirs had been burned as his friend and publisher, Jock's great-great-grandfather, looked on in the company of three other devoted friends of the poet, and in these very chairs the famous French belletrist Mme. de Staël had traded witticisms with England's men of letters.

If Freya had any reservations about putting her budding literary career into the hands of this young man, they now vanished. Jock, steeped in the family business since he was a boy, had an earnest, anxious-to-please air that both appealed to and reassured her. His practiced solicitousness proved seductive to all his authors—to Freya it became positively addictive. Throughout his life Jock demonstrated a flair for flattery and conciliation that kept his writers nicely disinclined to take their work elsewhere: "Always look after your authors" became his dictum. That way, he told his son John Murray VII, who eventually inherited the business, "they will always remain loyal to you."

Jock looked after his writers' needs with the combined devotion of a broody hen and a shrewd merchant who recognized a mutually advantageous relationship when he saw one—and he gave unstintingly of his time. When Jock married—a development that caught Freya rather unpleasantly by surprise—his wife and later his children quickly learned they would have to share him. "My mother used to feel that when he left their house to go to [the office at] Albemarle Street, he thought he was going home. I didn't see him a lot when I was growing up," said John Murray VII. "I once met one of his authors who said: 'You *can't* be Jock's son! He never was married!' "[15]

While stories abound of his writers' eccentricities—endured gallantly by Jock—he did the most for Freya. As the years went on she became something of a tyrant in her requests for errands and odd chores, yet he never flinched from the challenge and always tried to help her. While she was abroad he received her mail and answered her invitations, and when she came to London he arranged her dinners, got her tickets for the theater, and, as often as not, put her up in his house in Hampstead Heath. A telegram from Freya requesting that a tin bath be shipped into the interior of Yemen was not unusual. It was as if they both understood that these attentions were a way of reassuring Freya that he cared—and she desperately needed caring—so he performed his duties with an apparently forgiving heart.

Jock was amply rewarded for his interest in this talented author who had so abruptly appeared on the scene. In May 1934 he published *The Valleys of the Assassins*. The book was a huge success, coming as it did on the heels of its author's celebrity. Where she had traveled and what she had seen were lively enough, but her tale was told in an idiosyncratic and original voice, rich in imagery and verve. C. J. Edmonds, reviewing it for *The Geographical Journal,* called it "a gem" and lauded her courage. "In this framework of geographical, archeological, and historical research Miss Stark, who combines acute powers of observation and a delicate sense of humour with the fundamental qualification of a knowledge of the language, religion, and social practice of the country, has constructed a delightful narrative. Few authors have caught so happily the atmosphere of travel in the remoter parts of Persia, whether on the road or in the village, or in the nomad camp. A most interesting and charmingly written book."[16]

Within six months Murray's had reprinted it three times—indeed it is still in print today. It was the book that established Freya as a significant figure in literary and exploration circles, the first broadside from a pen that would ultimately contribute thirty books, and the start of a reputation that would place her as England's preeminent travel writer. The critics raved, declaring it "a travel classic." *The Evening Standard* said its "destiny" was "inclusion in the aristocracy of letters." Even Lawrence of Arabia, in self-imposed exile at Cloud's Hill, his cottage at Moreton, called Freya "a gallant creature." To Sydney Cockerell, who had sent him her book, Lawrence wrote: "She unfolds herself as a remarkable person. It is astonishing how the book takes life."[17]

· · ·

Suddenly, Freya *was* the Tharaya of her innermost dreams, glittering in a Pleiadic cluster of England's most brilliant scientists, thinkers, and doers.

With the publication of her evocative descriptions of her travels, people she esteemed had listened to her views with interest and respect. She had won a chance to sit at the table of knowledge and influence, and if she partook intelligently, diligently, and productively, she felt that she could, in fact, "illuminate the world."

Not all the consequences, however, of her new status were what she sought. Unable to suppress her elation over the publicity attending her award, Freya told Viva that the attention made her feel "shrinking," while Viva acidly rejoined that she was being falsely modest.[18] Whether because she had not been invited or because she did not care to, Freya now ceased automatically staying with Viva when she was in London, telling herself that Viva's company made her feel like "a sea-anemone poked at with a stick [until it] closed up altogether."[19]

Although her mother urged Freya to hang on to the relationship, even Flora recognized Viva's shortcomings. But knowing that her daughter benefited from Viva's social and literary connections, not to mention Viva having promised to leave Freya her diamonds and silver, she begged her daughter to be indulgent. "She has never really had a chance," Flora wrote anxiously. "From a baby [Viva] was flattered. . . . Harry Jeyes spoilt her— and she has never had to meet realities."[20]

In the end, however, despite all Viva's past help, despite her mother's pleas and reminders, gratitude gave way to resentment. As far as Freya was concerned, Viva's friendship came at too high a price. She wrote, "She spent most of the time we were together reminding me of anything that might depress me."[21] For Freya, it was far less painful to spend the time with Venetia Buddicom.

Viva retaliated by reassigning her treasures in her will to their mutual friend, the Starks' neighbor in La Mortola, Margaret Olivier, wife of their old painter-friend Herbert Olivier. When Viva died of cancer in 1937 and Flora discovered the betrayal, she stormed off to the Oliviers and demanded the jewelry and silverware. "They are Freya's!" she trumpeted like an affronted Valkyrie. Mrs. Olivier wilted before the onslaught. "Freya," recalled Margaret Olivier's granddaughter, "was a candle next to Flora's blowtorch."[22]

Thus Viva became the first of Freya's intimates to be gently set aside as she began her ascent into a new and more rewarding world. Freya would remain a loyal friend to many of her old comrades, but she was learning to discriminate between those who were worth her while and those who were not. And once a relationship became unprofitable, uninteresting, or both, she showed little compunction about stepping smartly on.

. . .

In the meantime the heady times continued. Captain Holt and several of the handsome young officers from Baghdad visited Freya in Asolo, where they painted, played badminton on the lawn, and endlessly discussed British policy in the East. Freya and Holt, chaperoned by Minnie Granville—because it would never do to go together alone—attended a League of Nations meeting in Geneva dedicated to the problems of the Assyrians in Iraq, a humanitarian issue watched closely by all their colleagues. The Christian Assyrians were agitating for autonomy while the British stood by without making any particular moves to repress them—a policy greatly resented by the Iraqi Muslims, who looked on it as favoring Christians. The situation represented a particular thorn for Captain Holt as the chief intelligence officer on the spot.

Tragically, the growing anti-Assyrian hostility sparked a riot in August 1933 in which a large number of unarmed Assyrian villagers seeking protection with the police were massacred by the Iraqi Army. The incident shocked the international community, putting into question the new state's ability to deal with its minority peoples, including the vast Shi'a population in the south as well as the Kurds to the north. More alarming, it was an early and sinister signal of the growing power of the Iraqi Army, which would later rise against the Hashemite monarchy and murder their young king in 1958.

Captain Holt and Freya watched these developments closely, and Freya leapt at opportunities to contribute her opinions in official circles. That winter in London, when she delivered lectures at the Royal Central Asian Society, the Royal Asiatic Society, the Forum, and the BBC, she commented at length on British policy in Iraq. In 1934 the Royal Asiatic Society presented her with the Burton Memorial Medal, making her the fourth person and first woman to be so honored. She brought an impressive familiarity and wisdom to her observations about a region whose history, politics, and especially now whose oil seemed almost daily to acquire more importance for the future prosperity of the British Empire.

. . .

During this exhilarating period Freya decided to go forward with something very important to her. If she were to be a public figure, she wanted to look the part. Telling no one but her mother, Venetia, and a few friends like Minnie Granville—and especially not Viva Jeyes—Freya checked herself into the public ward of St. Andrew's Hospital on Dollis Hill, deliberately chosen because it was a distance from London. Ever since the accident that had ripped the hair and skin off one side of her head, Freya had longed for cosmetic surgery—both to alleviate pain from damaged nerves and to do something about the scars around her temple and eye. Loaded with books on Arabia, she settled in to have her head shaved as bald "as one of the worst Roman Emperors."[23]

"I like being in a ward and having all the other people to study," she wrote her mother about the eleven working-class women who were treating her very respectfully and calling her a "lady."[24] The process was long, painful, and exhausting. Two days after her friend's forty-first birthday Freya wrote Venetia that, although "every sudden movement still makes my heart feel like a bird trying to escape, the head is mending all over and the eyebrow I hope will be elegant."[25] Unable to read, she whiled away the hours reciting to herself all the poems she could recall. Then an acute infection prolonged the ordeal. Almost no one visited because few knew about the operation, and Freya was adamant that it stay that way. "It is my affair and I know what to decide about it and the one thing I do not want is that it should be told to people secretly," she wrote angrily to her mother on hearing that Flora was telling friends in Asolo.[26] Always private about very personal matters, Freya was galled that Flora persisted in showing so little sensitivity. Freya wanted to emerge like a butterfly from its chrysalis for a beautiful new life.

Then her friend Stefana Drower in Baghdad wrote her that Captain Holt was gravely ill with pneumonia. Freya went into agonies. Should she fly to his side? She could do nothing until her head was healed, but she could send him money. Breathlessly, she waited for his few terse notes. "Such a pathetic letter," she happily reported to Flora, "saying he had been thinking of me during his long sleepless nights."[27] She discussed with Flora bringing him to Asolo to recuperate. How she would have loved it if only Holt would have proposed marriage. No one, possibly, could be more suitable. He was an Arabist, interested in all the things she cared about; by now they had so many friends in common—and surely, surely he cared for her. Why else would he have spent so much time with her in Asolo?

. . .

The year following Freya's recovery, Holt again visited Asolo, where they evidently had a painful exchange, referred to flickeringly in her autobiography. She indicated that she had finally broached the subject of her love and been brusquely rejected. Except to say that she had squandered years "walking down a one-way lane with only a blank wall at its end,"[28] she did not elaborate, nor are there letters illuminating this encounter, although the two maintained an intermittent, polite, and unrevealing correspondence until Holt's death.*

For Freya, the encounter in Asolo could only have been a humiliating reprise of the rejection by her earlier lover, Guido Ruata. Ever tender about her plainness, Freya had again been found wanting by a man she loved and hoped to marry. Yet why, one wonders, did she allow herself to be so blind to the clues that Holt gave her about his lack of interest?

Since first coming to Baghdad Freya had been attracted to the kinds of bachelor officers who were a prominent part of life in the colonial community. She would always be drawn to lean, clever men in uniform who risked their lives, cloaked their intimate thoughts in a cool, superior British manner, were nonchalant about their bravery, and disdained to complain if they were hurt. These were Britain's guardians, who fit her romantic notion of the male ideal. She hero-worshiped them secretly and was thrilled when admitted to their circle. Vyvyan Holt epitomized the type, and his lack of ardor meant Freya could enjoy a close camaraderie and still feel safe. She sought respect; being viewed as a libertine would have been even more devastating to Freya's self-esteem than the fact that she wasn't pretty.

Freya would cheerfully have had her body completely reconstructed if she could have done so, because she was acutely appreciative of beauty in others and felt its absence keenly in herself. Her defense was flight into the imagination, a kind of dream safety that had sustained her as a girl in books, romantic poetry, and tales of heroic deeds. She wrapped herself in these romances and became the star of her own adventure story. When things went beyond the control of her forceful personality, inventiveness, or charm, if the problem was something she could not alter or manipulate, she didn't pine or remonstrate, she merely buried what was threatening or damaging to her sense of worth.

Veronica Bamfield, her friend from Baghdad, told of joining Freya in Paris in the 1950s. When Mrs. Bamfield's purse was stolen, Freya comforted her and lent her money to get home, saying revealingly: "The only thing to do, I have discovered, when something unpleasant happens, is to pretend it didn't."[29]

Freya would make an art of pretending, and such self-deception often blinded her to how others really felt. After seven years of pinning her hopes on Vyvyan Holt, she abruptly brushed them aside. "Suddenly, the thing that had been part of me and had hurt so much was outside of me,

* When he died in 1958, the British government praised him for his bravery as a captive in North Korea during the Korean War, an experience that evidently ruined his health.

like a dead puppy which the mother can turn over and sniff at and know that it is dead."[30]

. . .

Eventually Freya's head healed. Enormously pleased with the results of the surgery, which had substantially reduced the tightness and scarring around her eye and given her an eyebrow, she left the hospital in mid-February. Her bald head wrapped in a chic velvet turban, she immediately plunged into a frenetic social schedule. She stayed two weeks with Venetia, then hurried to Scotland, back to Devon for a stay with her friends the Varwells at Thornworthy, trotted off to Stirlingshire to visit Professor Ker's family, saw a cousin of Charles Doughty in Charmouth, checked in with her former professors at the School of Oriental Studies and Mr. Hinks at the Royal Geographical Society, and in the evenings hurled herself into one party after the next with a crowd that included such talented lights as Peter Fleming, Ruth Draper, Rose Macaulay, Virginia Woolf, and the Julian Huxleys, as well as assorted social lions, including Lady Ottoline Morrell and the mistress of Petworth, the countess of Egremont. And all the while more good reviews of *The Valleys of the Assassins* appeared in the press.

But the need to pin down another journey loomed over the gaiety. The moment she got back to Asolo, the black moods caught up with Freya. She tried to work. "Everyone tells me that I *must* travel now that I feel quite inclined to stay still," she confided gloomily to a friend.[31] But she knew she had no choice. Flora was bustling about town, boasting about her daughter's plans, distracting her from her research by constantly urging her attendance at lunches and dinners or little soirees. At the same time a stream of inquiries from associates, admirers, and the London press added to the pressure. Where did Miss Stark intend to go next? There was no alternative but to bend doggedly to the task.

The place that beckoned was Yemen, the ancient land from which the queen of Sheba had departed to visit Solomon. What if she were to explore the legendary capitals that had flourished along the incense route? Their wealth had fascinated classical writers who listed the treasures carried north through the Arabian desert to the Mediterranean. Beside frankincense and myrrh, beside the all-important spices, caravans had carried ebony, ivory, gold, cinnamon, apes' skins, and peacocks. Both the Old Testament and the Koran referred to Bilqis, queen of Sheba, who stunned King Solomon's court with her splendid gifts. The hoopoe bird, Freya read delightedly in an Arabic tale, was sent to summon this powerful queen. Solomon, told that the queen had the hairy legs of a goat, ordered his courtyard paved with glass so that when Sheba arrived she would lift her skirts believing it was a stream to cross. When the great queen arrived and lifted her robe, she revealed legs that were as shapely and beautiful as her face. The king was smitten; he took Bilqis to bed, and from their union was born a son who founded Ethiopia.

The Egyptians called this region the Land of Punt. To the Hebrews it was Ophir. To the Arabs it was al-Yaman, the southernmost band of the Arabian peninsula—a land of rugged mountains and deep gorges, sandy wastes, volcanic spills, and verdant oases. To Freya, it was sheer romance. That Yemen was also an enormous tract of unexplored ruins added to its allure. Might she actually discover treasure? Excitement spurred her.

Bilqis's Sheba—or Saba—was perhaps the best known but by no means the only powerful kingdom in Yemen. Through the centuries many other cities also grew rich supplying, taxing, and exploiting the trade route through their territory. Of all the exotic goods transported, by far the most valuable was frankincense. From Nineveh to Thebes, Jerusalem, and Rome, this greenish resin from native trees was burned on altars, painted on courtesans, applied to wounds, and used to mummify the dead. The workers harvested it under sacred rules, and, like diamond miners today, they were subjected to body searches to ensure that no precious scrap escaped. The Roman historian Pliny observed that it was no wonder a land producing something so costly should be called Arabia Felix, "Happy Arabia." So extremely rich was Southern Arabia that would-be conquerors from the Assyrians in the eighth century B.C.E., the Romans in the first century C.E., and the Ottoman Turks in the sixteenth century tried to acquire it.

In the north the Nabataeans of Petra had probably grown the richest on this traffic. But, to the south, over a period of fifteen hundred years before the birth of Christ, numbers of other kingdoms had risen and fallen, their fates tied to the trade. When a Greek sailor sometime in the first century C.E. discovered the secret of the shifting monsoon winds, the monopoly on overland passage gave way to trade by sea, and the great southern kingdoms, deprived of the tax revenues, slowly expired. By the end of the seventh century C.E., all Arabia had succumbed to Islam— submitted, that is, for the word *Islam* in Arabic means "submission." As the religious rites of Islam did not require incense, and Christian worship used it either not at all or in far smaller quantities than had earlier pagan rituals, overland trade gradually tapered off and the peninsula settled into obscure poverty.

By 1934 the latest of a long line of imam Yahyas was still ruling Yemen's northern territories. Extremely xenophobic, the imam had dropped a thick curtain over his dominions, shrouding them in back-wardness, protected from any hint of the infidel European influence that was corrupting the rest of the Arab world. Large areas of Yemen to the south, however, had come under a watchful British eye since the British seized the coastal city of Aden in 1839, steadily expanding their authority until the area become Great Britain's South Arabian Protectorate. The Colonial Office regarded Aden as a key post on the way to India and was attempting to end age-old rivalries between warring tribes in the interest of stability. A vaguely defined zone between the imam's lands and those of the protectorate was referred to by the British as the Violet Line.

As Freya pored over the sketchy maps that were all that was available on this area, she realized with growing disappointment that it might be difficult, even impossible, to get very far into the imam's cloistered territory, and especially hard to make it as far as Marib, the legendary capital of Sheba's kingdom. Marib lay too deep on the imam's side of the Violet Line. But with a shiver of excitement, she realized there was another potentially thrilling prize. Snaking farther to the east over desert, the old frankincense route had once connected Marib to Shabwa, capital of the kingdom of Hadhramaut, referred to in Genesis as the Hazarmaveth or "Enclosure of Death." Pliny called the city Sabota and reported it had sixty temples and wealth beyond description. No European explorer had ever reached this now buried city; Freya reasoned that if she started through the area patrolled by the British, she could slip over the Violet Line from the east and be the first to find it.

Of late the thought of danger had come to occupy her rather more than usual, for in June she had had a brush with death while mountain climbing, and the memory of the incident continued to surface. She and a friend, Lucy Selwyn, had gone mountaineering in Bavaria and the Dolomites. It was to have been a renewal after the trying winter in the hospital. As she, Lucy, and their guide, tied together with ropes, struggled up the Winkler Turm near Vajolet, Freya slipped. The others were already out of sight. With the rope tight beneath her armpits, she swung in an excruciatingly slow circle over the Alpine meadow far below. As the arc brought her back to the cliff wall, she was just able to grasp a handhold and pull herself painfully up and over the rock, to where her friends waited. Although Lucy noticed that Freya was ashen-faced, Freya said nothing, simply sucked on some sugar lumps. Yet the experience, so dreadfully akin to one long ago, affected her for years. The peace she'd felt in those minutes when she floated out of control remained a strangely comforting memory. If this was all there was to death, then death had lost its terror—and she could handle anything. Emboldened, Freya once more set her face to the East. This time, to Arabia.

CHAPTER ELEVEN

At Last, Arabia

> *I cannot put the whole of life
> into writing: it seems to me so
> very subsidiary to living.*
>
> —LETTER TO VENETIA
> BUDDICOM, MAY 31, 1933

In November 1934 the ship bearing Freya down the Red Sea passed through the Gate of Lament, or Bab al-Mandab, the narrow strait that separates Arabia from Africa, and anchored among the dhows in the Aden harbor. The weather was pleasant and reasonably cool, not like the summer, when temperatures can go as high as 120 degrees Fahrenheit, accompanied by such wilting humidity that people unused to it can develop boils and funguses in vulnerable places. She had a touch of dysentery, either from a brief stop in Cairo or perhaps from the ship's galley, but otherwise she felt ready to step out of the "modern age of bustle and chicanery into an era of elemental conditions; where faithful friendship is jostled by the blackest treachery and the crude facts of a semi-barbaric life are encountered at every turn."[1] This was an English traveler's view of the area in 1911; Freya had every expectation that nothing would be terribly different twenty years later, and she relished the prospect.

She had prepared carefully. Ever the student, always stern with herself about self-improvement, Freya was elated to find a subject that required reading Herodotus, Strabo, *The Periplus of the Erythrean Sea,* by an anonymous author, as well as Pliny, Claudius

Ptolemy, Diodorus Siculus, the Koran, and the Bible. For months she had studied the Sabean script, the written language of the kingdom of Sheba. She had done research in London and traveled to Germany to find out what there was at the Munich Institute about Saba and the other ancient cities that had been its rivals: Najran, Ma'an, Awsan, Qataban, Hadhramaut, and Himyar, a kingdom that dominated the ports in southwestern Arabia in the first two centuries C.E. She had found that both the Sabeans and the Himyari had been prolix writers in stone; their temples and buildings were reputed to be covered with inscriptions. Eager to be ready should any epigraphic opportunities present themselves, Freya also familiarized herself with Himyaritic hieroglyphics.

During the summer in Asolo, Freya had labored over an elaborate map that collated nearly five hundred ancient place names. She hoped that she could trace the main trade route using whatever landmarks and ruins still existed. Unfortunately most of the names were located in northern Yemen. She knew that a European man would have difficulty getting into the imam's kingdom; an unveiled European female would find it impossible. Somehow, though, she *must,* because on just one side or the other of that unmarked fluid border, the Violet Line, lay Shabwa, her designated trophy.

Assumed to have been a trading station from the beginning of time, Shabwa lay deep in the desert that began at the western extremity of the Wadi Hadhramaut. A 350-mile-long valley embraced by massive plateaus and filled with verdant fields of date palms and alfalfa, the wadi was the longest and most fertile valley in Arabia, dividing the Indian Ocean from the barren wastes of Arabia's Empty Quarter. Wild frankincense dotted its rocky eastern hillsides, and ancient irrigation systems captured water from the seasonal monsoons. The towns of the Hadhramaut were now dominated by two tribes, the Qu'aiti and Kathiri, whose keen rivalry, Freya would discover, kept the small number of British officers posted in Aden busy maintaining peace.

If she could get to Shabwa, Freya wondered if she might find evidence of the vast treasure said to be buried in its ruins. The site had been the secret object of every explorer ever to penetrate southern Arabia.[2] Bedouin reports confirmed the city's existence, drifted over with sand and fiercely guarded by a tribe whose only livelihood was the salt mines nearby—and Freya wanted desperately to be the first to reach it. Excitedly, she wrote Venetia: "If I *do* succeed, it will lift the veil off quite a big little corner of historical geography."[3]

Having settled on her target, she had a new worry, she told Venetia: "If *only* the British authorities will keep gentle and quiet and not interfere. No one has been anywhere *near* where I want to get, as far as I

know, and there must be masses of old ruins strewn all over the countryside."⁴

In addition to all her other careful preparations, Freya had obtained an
impressive array of introductions from important people. The old Aga
Khan helped her, as did her mother's new friend Lady Gwendolen Iveagh,
whose enormously wealthy husband was head of the Guinness Brewing
Firm and who had recently purchased a villa in Asolo. More to the point,
Lady Iveagh was the sister-in-law of the colonial secretary and former
viceroy to India Lord Edward Halifax, who was persuaded to see to it that
the good offices of the nizam of Hyderabad were engaged. Before long the
nizam's prime minister, Sir Akbar Hydar, was in touch with the sultan of
Mukalla, who provided six letters, gorgeously embossed with crimson
coats of arms, to various other sultans and important personages in the
interior. "They say that I am a Lady of the Aristocracy and must be given
two servants and two sepoys: this will have to be toned down to be useful:
I shall take up poverty as a religious principle; there is nothing like making a virtue of necessity," Freya wrote Venetia.⁵

She did not add that Sir Akbar had also told the sultans that "Lord
Halifax assures me in his letters that Miss Stark may be trusted not to take
undue advantage of any letters that you may give her."⁶ Armed with her
open sesames, as she called them, Freya believed she could count on a
month and a half in the Hadhramaut with virtually no expenses except the
cost of guides, a few odd provisions, and an occasional tip to someone
particularly helpful. Her money was tight, but if she were careful and
lucky, she should expect to pick up at least a medieval manuscript or two,
perhaps a bit of interesting jewelry, and always, of course, some indigenous dresses to add to her growing collection of native costumes.

Most useful of all were the two introductions Freya carried to a
remarkable Frenchman in Aden, Antonin Besse. One had been given her
by her La Mortola neighbors the Herbert Oliviers. The other, to Freya's
delight, had come from Lady Allenby herself. In all the region of the
Indian Ocean, there was no one more influential than this tycoon, who
had built a trading empire that stretched from Abyssinia to East Asia.
Volatile, cunning, an aesthete, devoted to physical exercise, demanding of
his family and European employees to the same degree that he was sympathetic to and supportive of his native workers, he dominated the community of Aden and anything and everyone he came into contact with.

Besse was fifty-seven and married for a second time in 1934, when he
and Freya met. She was forty-one. Having made a fortune in part through
his first wife's money, Besse had divorced in 1921 and married his children's governess, Hilda Crowther, a Scotswoman, who was away when

Antonin Besse of Aden, the Indian Ocean tycoon who later endowed St. Antony's College, Oxford. This picture was taken between 1919 and 1921, about the time that Evelyn Waugh visited the Aden Protectorate and captured Besse's forceful personality in his amusing account, When the Going Was Good.

The amazing high-rises of Shibam, the malodorous town in the Hadhramaut where Freya fell seriously ill with measles. Today Shibam, constructed of mud bricks and jammed on an escarpment with streets barely wide enough for a donkey to pass, is a World Heritage site. A pile of typical mud bricks is in the foreground.

Freya arrived in Aden in December. Half a head taller than her husband, Hilda quickly became the linchpin in his life—as Freya would learn to recognize. Hilda understood Besse's genius, his voracious desire to be loved, and his need to dominate. She blinked at his minor affairs with secretaries and helped the company steer through the upheavals caused when Besse dazzled the young male executives with his charm and personality, then invariably grew disenchanted and fired them. He was subject to fits of depression but also a vast generosity that created medical clinics for his workers, schools for Arab children, and ultimately St. Antony's College at Oxford University. Besse was enormously admired by the Arabs; when he died in 1951, the shops of Aden closed spontaneously.

Like many others of his generation, Besse was attracted to the Nietzschean ideals—to be hard, to act heroically, to live dangerously. Before these precepts were forever tainted by the Nazis, whom Besse despised and consistently opposed, they reflected his view of life as a self-made man. Any new friend who came into his orbit, whom he thought was interesting and teachable, was invariably presented with a copy of *Thus Spake Zarathustra* and Kipling's poem "If." Freya would more than qualify.

Besse was powerfully built, shortish, with slightly receding, thick gray hair and a mustache. He served excellent wine at dinner, wore a very thin gold watch, and was always meticulously groomed.[7] The English novelist Evelyn Waugh, traveling to Aden in 1931, enjoyed his keen sarcasm as well as the contrasts he found in such a complex personality. "They said of him that he thrived on risk and had made and lost more than one considerable fortune in his time," Waugh wrote. When Waugh accepted an invitation for a "little walk on the rocks," he was unprepared for the test Besse would put him to and wrote an amusing account of it, disguising Besse as Mr. Leblanc. Said Waugh: he looked "magnificent. He wore newly creased white shorts, a silk openwork vest, and white espadrilles laced like a ballet dancer's round his ankles. He held a tuberose, sniffing it delicately."

But if Besse's costume suggested a dandy, the so-called walk proved otherwise. "He went right up to the face of the cliff, gaily but purposefully as Moses may have approached the rocks from which he was about to strike water. There was a little crack running like fork-lightning down the blank wall of stone. Mr. Leblanc stood below it, gave one little skip, and suddenly, with great rapidity and no apparent effort, proceeded to ascend the precipice. He did not climb; he rose." Waugh, by then incredulous as well as exhausted, had barely survived the climb when Besse proposed they take a swim in the shark-infested sea. "We always bathe here, not at the club," he quoted Besse saying gleefully. "They have a screen there to keep out the sharks—while in this bay, only last month, two boys were devoured."[8] Waugh took a deep breath and swam.

. . .

When Freya and Besse were introduced on the day of her arrival, they immediately liked each other. In the absence of his wife and younger children, Besse and his pretty daughter Meryem, by then in her twenties, entertained the much-commended English lady writer in their massive stone house in the Arab Quarter. Freya, like all his visitors, was impressed by the good Persian carpets, books, pictures, and art objects, which all breathed a marvelously Mediciesque atmosphere into such an impoverished part of the world. In addition, there was a piano and a vast collection of classical records to satisfy Besse's love of music.

"He has a passion for everything beautiful. He is indeed a charming person, so impulsive and kind, but not with just words, for he always follows out his proposals. He is very much what Mario might have been if he carried out what he said," she wrote her mother, stressing admiringly Besse's quality of "exacting *everything* from those he cares for, the absolute domination." Reflectively, she added, "It makes him no doubt difficult to live with."[9]

Besse disliked conventions and conventional people and pointedly never joined the British club in Aden, which was the hub of all the main social activities. Instead, instinctively drawn to originals, he did what he could to help the interesting new arrival. He found Freya a small flat nearby complete with houseboy and had food sent over when she was not dining with him. While she recaptured her fluency in Arabic with a young Yemeni teacher, and was treated for what had proved to be chronic dysentery, he sent word to his contacts in the interior that Freya would be coming and should be helped. It would not take her long to discover that "his name is like gold in this country."[10]

Freya spent an ecstatic month in her little flat, enormously enjoying the benefits of being a woman in a town full of bachelor officers. Furthermore, because her arrival had been preceded by wildly exaggerated stories—she had her own airplane; she would arrive with a train of camels—she was accorded immediate and fascinated attention in this little backwater. "I am notorious and treated like an Author,"[11] she reported gaily to Flora as she sallied out to be entertained by the tiny but enthusiastically sociable community who despite the heat kept up a brisk schedule of tennis and dancing parties. Officialdom sprang to her cause with gratifying alacrity, advising her on the safest route, sending messages to the imam's *wazir,* and discussing what should be done when she reached the imam's border.

By now she had worked out the outlines of a journey through the Wadi Hadhramaut. It seemed sensible to start at Mukalla on the coast of the Gulf of Aden, go north by donkey or camel, and finally get a car and driver when she reached the high plateau, where a limited road descending into the wadi connected some of the bigger towns. There could be some danger too, as the Hadhramaut had long been the scene of active warfare. The tribes had wrecked their irrigation systems, poisoned their date palm groves, and brought farming pretty much to a standstill. Although there seemed to be peace at last, the prospect of new violence at any moment made safety concerns paramount.

A young political officer was eager to offer Freya advice. Harold Ingrams, whose fluency in Arabic, personal bravery, and sympathy with the tribes was credited with achieving "the English Peace" that year, had just returned from a journey north with his wife, Doreen, who had the honor of being the fifth European civilian and second woman to have traveled any distance into the interior.[12] Those few who had gone before had all encountered serious problems with the tribesmen, and one man had barely got out with his life.

Harold Ingrams's business was to pursue Britain's policy of tribal pacification and not to write colorful accounts to attract the admiration of learned societies. Understandably, he was concerned that Freya might unwittingly stir up the dust he had worked so hard to settle. Still, he and Doreen were intrigued by her, although Doreen remembered feeling a bit uncomfortable with what she saw as Freya's rather "mannered" style. The talked-about author was obviously clever, knowledgeable, and quite entertaining, but not, as Doreen put it, "relaxing company"—nor was she much interested in what women had to say when there were men around. Doreen concluded that the visitor was "flamboyant" but not someone with whom she could feel intimate very easily.[13] It was an acute perception. Freya was burnishing her new persona, burying the shy girl of her youth and creating a self-sufficiency to match her growing reputation as a person of fearless, even heroic, deeds.

• • •

When the Ingrams showed her some shards and other archaeological bits they had found in the interior, Freya was excited and encouraged. However, they told her they couldn't imagine that it would take less than seven fifteen-hour days, with no water sources and plenty of hostile tribesmen en route, to reach Shabwa, whose exact location could only be guessed. Freya began to realize that her journey might be far more difficult than she had anticipated. At least she could draw comfort from the news that the mythical city remained unconquered by any European explorer.

In Aden she fell into a delightful daily pattern of study in the morning and afternoons with Besse in his office. There she read, wrote, and watched admiringly as he ran his empire—making decisions about the transport of oil, hides and skins, coffee, mother-of-pearl, incense, gums, nuts, and ambergris. It seemed to Freya that he dealt on an epic scale, and she was awed and fascinated as she observed him trading in goods such as apes and peacocks and sandalwood that evoked the ancient traffic of the East.[14] On other days she visited the busy port of Aden, its streets filled with richly robed sheikhs and Arab clerks with spectacles and umbrellas, mahogany-skinned men from the desert, oiled with indigo and naked except for their *futahs,* or loincloths; women with blue lips and yellow daubs of turmeric behind their veils. She was followed by noisy little boys and their shy sisters, whose hands were like lacy mittens of henna-painted patterns.

On Christmas Day, Meryem Besse gave a dinner party for sixteen hard-working young men from her father's company and four ladies, including Freya. She recounted that Besse, who dreaded social duties of this nature, descended "into gloom as the hour [for the party] drew near. I found him all ready dressed like a sacrificial victim and a lovely table laid on the roof: all the young clerks, very shy and naturally not at their best."[15] They played games for a bit, but when dancing began, Besse turned to Freya and murmured: "I cannot *bear* it: are you coming?" Sweeping up a pile of blankets to keep her warm, he crept down the stairs, bidding her to follow. Under a rising moon they drove to his launch.

> We passed by all the lights of Aden—people dancing in bunga-
> lows, sailors feasting on the ships. . . . we made for the entrance
> point; the sea and wind freshened, we were round the corner
> under the black hills and rocks, Orion above, and Taurus and the
> Pleiades. Then no lights at all, except three yellow and a green
> from some travelling ship at sea; the spray in a light rain on our
> faces: Monsieur Besse and I lying in great comfort on cushions,
> while he kept the tiller with one hand—the Somali [captain], with
> his big turban sticking up in a little tuft, looking to sea ahead of
> us. "It cleans the soul," said Monsieur Besse, and made a little
> gesture of horror every time I mentioned the party. We went on

and on. "I know a cave, we could sleep on the sand . . . ," said
Monsieur Besse, ". . . but Meryem would be anxious."
    I thought this quite as well,

Freya noted coyly to her mother, "as I may just as well keep some shred of reputation."

With the eerie light from a small lighthouse flashing, Besse deliberately brought them through a boiling riptide that tossed the boat violently in the dark sea; for a while it seemed they might capsize.

I had not the faintest idea where we were, what time or what
world we were in. We made for a cleft between mainland and an
island; shot through with great skill; saw a little sleeping beach
and tall houses. I couldn't think where we were. Monsieur Besse
refused to say; he suggested it might be the moon; he went
through some tortuous little ways by a small white mosque, by a
few sleeping goats who looked familiar, and landed at his own
door: we had come right round the Aden volcano, which is
attached to the land by only a very narrow neck. I don't believe I
have ever enjoyed a Christmas evening quite so much.

Besse had enjoyed it as much as Freya. Her cleverness had appealed to him—and now she had shown an attractive streak of recklessness. In the weeks that followed he took her almost daily on his favorite scrambles over the volcanic cliffs. As Evelyn Waugh had discovered, these little exercises were not for the fainthearted, but if Waugh had been disconcerted by Besse's challenges, Freya was only too pleased to go along with this fascinating, driven man with whom she shared such intense rapport.

They were now spending evenings as well as days together. She was no longer Miss Stark, nor he Monsieur Besse. They were now Freya and Anton. Having demonstrated verbal prowess to their mutual satisfaction, and each responding to the other's strong romantic streak with garlands of quoted poetry, they moved on to discuss their philosophies and share more private thoughts. On his veranda at night under the stars, they spoke in heroic terms of their weariness with ordinary life, their disgust with mediocrity, their yearning for solitude. Freya told Anton that she craved *ataraxia*, a Greek concept meaning the attainment of perfect peace or transcendent calm. He responded that he wanted to be able to *feel* exquisitely, to be capable of experiencing all the most extreme emotions, from psychic pain to exultant happiness.[16]

The South Arabian people, like the Red Sea Arabs and those of the Maghreb, are proud of their decorative windows and doors, viewed as important architectural elements of an Islamic house. This window was photographed in Mukalla, a seaside town on the Indian Ocean from which Freya traveled into the interior.

Bedouin ladies from the Wadi Hadhramaut who live in rock caves and tend goats. The slitted masque veil worn by the lady on the right is a style seen only in this region.

The Wadi Hadhramaut, the great Arabian valley through which the frankincense caravans once wound their way to Mediterranean ports, is bounded on either side by the high jol over which Freya climbed by car and donkey from the coast. On the back side of the jol stretches the endless sandy wastes of the Empty Quarter.

A tattooed lady from South Arabia. For festive occasions, she will also have her hands and feet elaborately painted with henna. She wears a fine collection of the handsome silver bracelets much prized by collectors of ethnic jewelry. The very best examples were often the work of Yemeni Jews until the exodus for Israel after 1948.

Anton told Freya that he liked her sharpness, her quick assessments of people, and her "malicious eyes" that "shone glitteringly."[17] He applauded her daring—and her toughness—which he said perfectly fit his Nietzschean criterion of life lived with passion and creativity beyond conventional standards. Before long he had her reading *Thus Spake Zarathustra* and thinking about a mythic hero who could free civilization from its "slave morality." To her, listening to his stirring words as they talked under the stars, Anton himself seemed such a hero, the first overwhelming and magnetic man she had ever known, and she felt quite swept away.

She confessed her secret fear of not being strong enough to get to Shabwa, but he exhorted her to firm action and promised her all the help he could give. When she finally left he followed her with letters, encouraging her and willing her to overcome all obstacles: "If you think you are the only one to believe in your success, undeceive yourself because I am also sure of it. Your will is too supple, your obstinacy too big. . . . you are precious to many people, and to one more." And he concluded, "Very tenderly, I kiss your lips."[18]

. . .

After midnight on January 13, 1935, almost a month after her arrival in Arabia, Freya sailed for Mukalla as a gratis passenger on one of Anton's little steamers. Her next adventure had begun. Three days later, thanks to the efforts of both Besse and Lord Halifax, she was welcomed as a guest in the palace of the absent sultan of Mukalla. Although she liked to think that she was in the back of beyond, the only European for hundreds of miles, her circumstances were hardly primitive. She was comfortably ensconced in a room with a dressing table and furniture covered with pink chintz and roses. If there was a fine veil of dust over things, a few cigarette butts left by earlier visitors, no lock on the door, and bats flying in and out, her bathroom at least had European plumbing. She graciously accepted the car that the sultan's retainers had put at her disposal and went off to see the sights.

She visited markets where such valued provisions as indigo, sea slugs, and rotting shark meat were sold. The stinking fish, it turned out, became a diet staple on her trip. She looked in at the sultan's prison, where in an age-honored tradition he kept hostages to ensure tribal quiet. Repelled by the conditions, she sent around a small donation.

Freya had told Venetia that she intended to make a virtue of being poor—beginning with enduring the universal surprise and frequent disapproval that she traveled without servants. People these days, she sighed, seemed to have lost any relish for "independent poverty." Her two guides were "wild little men of some earlier world," slathered in indigo, which promptly transferred itself to white bedspreads or clothes or anything else their curious hands touched.[19] Later, shivering in the desert, she learned that this indigo coating somehow served the unlikely function of keeping their naked bodies warm. Their uniform was a scanty tattered loincloth, a silver armlet over the right elbow, a black wool ribbon around their uncombed locks, and a black cord around the neck—which could double, they assured her, as a tourniquet if one were wounded. To complete the costume each man carried a huge curved dagger jammed into his waistband, to which his fingers strayed nervously as he inspected her or surveyed his surroundings. These daggers were the famous *jambiyyas*, whose handles made of prized rhinoceros horn were thought to convey ferocious sexual powers. Freya was determined to have one for herself.

After winning a tough negotiation for four donkeys for the price of three to carry two saddlebags, five tin boxes, and food, Freya and her party were ready to start. She took a last long look at the beautiful Mukalla beaches, mused silently that if ever she *were* to marry and have a honeymoon it should be here, shook hands with an emir from the sultan's court (who, having just washed for prayers, covered his with his shawl), and headed for the interior.

· · ·

Soon Freya was riding north through a barren, stony landscape dotted with thornbushes and caves, where, she was told, "shy men" hid between robberies but were desisting at the moment thanks to the recent peace. There were no other signs of life, except for an occasional camel caravan winding down from the highlands. Climbing the high *jol*, or plateau, she reviewed with a practiced eye the geological formations that created this inhospitable expanse, read the pitch of the land, the watersheds and drainages, all the while taking photographs and scribbling notes. Never snobbish to native peoples as so many colonials were, Freya was curious about and interested in her blue companions and immediately established a pleasant camaraderie, struggling to understand their Arabic dialect. She accepted their meals of rotting fish and greasy rice, which pleased them mightily as they had heard that most *nasrani* (Christians) ate apart, which offended their ticklish Bedouin pride.

At night she asked that her bedding be moved a bit away from the fire as she had done in Persia and found once again that her guides' natural sensitivity and sense of dignity made it easy to get moments of necessary privacy. As Doreen Ingrams later wrote in her own account of travel in the Yemen, women had to follow "the principle of the ostrich." If a sanitary napkin needed disposing, it was best to just stick it under a stone cairn, while to relieve oneself one simply walked away from camp, turned one's back, and assumed that if one "could not see the Beduin they could not see [her]."[20]

If there were a single thorn in this otherwise tranquil march, it was a soldier who had been thrust on Freya at the eleventh hour by the Mukalla governor, who wanted no blame in the event of a mishap. The soldier, she decided, a large ebony-skinned slave, was both stupid and stubborn, clinging to whatever idea he had with "the tenacity of people to whom ideas are not an everyday occurrence."[21] That he was trying to protect her, however clumsily—like rushing over to push her down in the saddle with indigo hands when they were bumping over rough terrain—did nothing to appease her irritation. To her Bedouin, however, she gave dollops of face cream to polish their daggers.

This singular band—Freya, the huge black soldier, the two Bedouin, and a small nephew—arrived six days later in the palm-sheltered oasis of the Wadi Doan to the thunder of rifle fire rolling through the valley. The Bedouin were shooting into the sky to welcome them. Thanks again to her letters of recommendation, Freya was immediately escorted to the primitive mud castle of the governor of Masna'a and ushered into the harem. There she found herself in the middle of a measles epidemic.

For a time she scrambled over the rocky terrain looking for ruins and had one nearly fatal venture to a remote village where she was stoned by a hostile crowd of men and boys, but before long Freya too succumbed to the highly infectious disease. For a week she lay delirious on a pallet as a rash broke out over her body. The ladies of the harem and their children wandered in and out, chatting, arguing, and peering at her closely. Several squatted at her side to sternly warn her that it was dangerous to use scented soap. Others debated whether she should be cauterized on the back of the neck with a branding iron, evidently a time-honored curative. Roused from her stupor, Freya protested vehemently. However, there was not much she could do to avoid an old witch, who leaned over her prone body muttering incantations and spat juicily on Freya's head to vanquish the djinns.

"I am longing unspeakably for a wash. Nothing can persuade them to give me water till tomorrow—the seventh day. . . . I find that one doesn't get much dirtier after the first two days. Anyway I know all about life in the Middle Ages," Freya wrote miserably to Flora.[22]

At last able to rise, and determined to carry on, Freya gathered her patient Bedouin guides together with the slave soldier and shakily mounted her donkey to begin a grim two-day trip through hazardous country where infidels were considered unwelcome. Although they had four guns, better protection was found in a barefooted young sayyid, or holy man. The sultan had provided him in the belief that it was unsporting to shoot at a descendant of the Prophet. In this company she reached Hajarain. The trip was without incident except that her tiny donkey collapsed beneath her every few miles.

· · ·

Back in Aden, Antonin Besse was dealing with the mounting crisis in Ethiopia—or Abyssinia as his generation referred to it. Italy had long had its eye on this African nation, and it was now feared that the Fascists would move to annex it. At the beginning of 1935 Italy had mobilized fifty thousand troops, and they were marching north from Italian Somaliland. Anton, who did a lot of business there, saw the tragic specter of ill-clothed and underfed Abyssinians armed solely with sticks and sabers being butchered by modern Italian arms. The prospect sickened him, he said in a letter that reached Freya by Bedouin runner, and he envied her "pursuing an aim that brings you back to the past," a considerably more congenial place, he thought, than the present. He added that he was preparing to go to Abyssinia in a few days and probably would arrive just as war started.[23] Freya received the news with apprehension. Anton's letter stoked the fire that had been ignited during those midnight conversations on his veranda.

He was now talking to her of love with exquisite delicacy: "A love which asks for nothing, which on the contrary aspires to give all, cannot bring about any evil, and should not frighten," he wrote her soothingly in his native French. "Let yourself be caught by it, Freya, and be happy to know that you are loved." Freya found his words as seductive and exciting as he meant them to be. "My thoughts surround you incessantly, tenderly, suffering and rising up with your defeats and successes in that march forward that is surely difficult but which will be won," he rushed on. An "exceptional being," he told her, cannot be an "onlooker" to "the march of other men."[24]

It was the kind of message she wanted from him—to believe in her, knowing the frailty she had confided. "Open your heart," he exhorted her, "lest it should suffer, lest it should die. I am anxious to have news from you, tender friend, whose lips I kiss longingly."[25]

Ten days later another letter, written just before he left for Addis Ababa, came: "Since you left I have lived in solitude and at the moment I desire to see nobody. I relive our evenings together, during which ennui could never set in, and I feel that we do not know anything but the fringes of the carpet representing each human life. It will be delightful to find each other again, even richer through the experiences we have gone through. Very tenderly, I kiss your lips, AB."[26]

The fire in her heart roared into full flame.

· · ·

Still weak from the aftereffects of measles, but buoyed by Anton's verbal caresses, Freya pressed on. Having witnessed at first hand promising fields of shards scattered around Hajarain, Meshed, and Hureidha in the Wadi Doan, and collecting fragments that bore Himyaritic inscriptions, she correctly concluded that there were ruins beneath the sands worth investigating. A year later she would return with an archaeological team, who would make the first scientific excavation ever undertaken in Yemen. But now Shabwa was her goal. By mid-February she was in Seiyun, a medieval Arab town surrounded by corn and other crops tended by groups of peasant women who in their peaked hats and black cloaks looked like covens of witches. Freya's introductions saw her welcomed to one of the houses of the al-Kaf, a powerful family of merchants who traded in Java and wore gold coins to button their jackets and whose young sons each had a slave of his own. When Freya took a walk through the town, she was accompanied by two slaves, who used their rifle butts to sweep the crowd from her path.

Before she left the comforting green of the great valley and its well-tended fields to head for the rigors of the desert, Freya saw all she could of the Hadhramaut, traveling its length and staying in villages where the nizam of Hyderabad's introductions continued to stand her in good stead. In one harem after the next, her person, clothes, and undergarments were meticulously examined by curious ladies with turmeric-painted faces and spectacular dresses of silk and embroidery. Their menfolk scrutinized her views on religion and politics.

The extraordinary architecture of the Hadhramaut—unique towers built of harmonious local materials that rose to vertiginous heights—astonished Freya. It was as if the Yemeni had invented the skyscraper, she thought, as she photographed tapered ibex and oryx horns secured at the corners of building tops, curious water clocks, and a variety of unusual ornamental details derived from Southeast Asia, where Hadhrami tribesmen had sought work during hard times at home.

In Tarim, a famously holy center of the Shafi'i school of Sunni teaching, where the pious sayyids averted their eyes and drew their long, white gowns away from her polluting presence, the town fathers welcomed her as a woman of great learning. The first Western woman ever to come there alone, Freya puzzled her interlocutors with her interest in ancient archaeology and her inquiries about the pagan period that to them was "the Time of Ignorance," before the Prophet had restored truth and justice with his revelations. But they applauded her interest in medieval Islam. They allowed her to look at precious early Islamic manuscripts and engage in theological discussions with their most revered leaders. She wrote it all down with a lively eye and a sympathetic heart.

Always Freya used her quick wit and good humor to defuse trouble. One night she arrived at a house protected by bulletproof shutters on the very outskirts of the desert. Here she was questioned by a particularly truculent Bedouin, one of a group that had gathered to see for themselves this unlikely female from another planet. As the man's questions grew more hostile and her host seemed at a loss to calm him, she finally asked: "Are you then a prince? Is this *your* house that you thus treat me?"[27] Bested, the man fell into sullen silence and the indigo audience roared with appreciative laughter.

It was at about this time that Freya heard the unpleasant news that another explorer, a German, was also seeking Shabwa, and her competitive instincts flared. She had learned from the sultan of Qatn that because the imam of Yemen and King Ibn Saud of Nejd had lately resolved their differences, it would be safe to cross the desert to Shabwa—accompanied, of course, by appropriate tribal hostages.* The journey should take only three days, he told her, as she pressed him to help get her on her way. The Bedouin told her she was bound to see giraffes; they still roamed in that forgotten place. If only she were not so tired still from her bout with measles, and not so anxious to get there first, she would have been jubilant. She worried now whether she could make it, and aware that news traveled fast among the tribes, made a point of disparaging the German to those with whom she talked, saying he had written a book that contained inaccuracies and unkindnesses about the Yemeni people.

In Tarim, Freya had found a chemist who seemed to know what he was doing and who offered to give her medicine and injections to make her feel better. His prescriptions did make her feel more like her usual energetic self, and she managed to keep going for another ten days. Unfortunately, Freya had acquired a habit from previous travels of medicating herself with great gusto but utter ignorance. This time the results would be alarming. The dysentery had returned, and she had started to take large quanti-

---

* To cross desert territory regarded as the domain of a particular tribe, the immemorial Bedouin custom has been for the traveler to pay an agreed sum for a *rafik*, or hostage, offered from the tribe to guide the way. As long as a rafik is with the foreign party, his kinsmen will not attack. A desert journey of significant distance could require a series of rafiks.

ties of emetine. She also decided that malaria must be responsible for her postmeasles lethargy and fevers, so she added Atebrin to the mix. It was a nearly catastrophic combination. As she moved on to Shibam, her heart began racing furiously, accompanied by such severe chest pains that she gasped for breath. Suddenly she was so weak that a servant had to lift her head to give her milk. Afraid her heart would give out, she lay on a dirt floor, imagining herself dead and carted off for immediate burial, aware that in this land of extreme heat it was the custom to bury the dead on the day of death. At least, she remembered thinking ruefully, Muslim graves were inclined to be spacious, because "the dead body has to sit up soon after death and answer questions of the two angels."[28] But it was no laughing matter. She begged her host to get a message to Aden asking for rescue.

Luckily for Freya, the chemist from Tarim had been sent for and arrived in the nick of time. He recognized she was suffering an angina attack and injected her with loconol, which saved her life. Another ten days passed; then one morning as she rested on the terrace of the al-Kafs' bungalow, she heard the distant throb of engines. Out of the blue sky four Royal Air Force bombers descended with a doctor who declared she must be hospitalized at once; she could not possibly survive a journey overland on a litter. It was a black moment indeed, the end of her dream for Shabwa.

But it also added a thrilling dimension to Freya's growing fame. She was brought out of the Hadhramaut by the RAF to the British hospital in Aden. After weeks of rest and care, she was transferred by stretcher to the SS *Orontes,* bound for Italy, applauded by crowds of passengers and crew who had lined the decks to witness the dramatic evacuation of the courageous explorer. Antonin Besse, in Abyssinia, sent his daughter Meryem to nurse her on her journey, then hurried to Suez to see for himself how she was. Unable to stay, he insisted that Meryem continue with her all the way back to Asolo. The international news trumpeted the story; broadcasts dubbed Freya "one of our most daring young explorers"; telegrams flew between the Colonial Office, Aden, and Asolo, where an anxious Flora received a flood of reassuring letters from friends and officialdom. Lady Iveagh wrote Flora that she had been in touch with her brother Lord Halifax at the Colonial Office and that "everyone was talking about Freya."[29] Katharine Woolley, a friend and the wife of the renowned archaeologist, happened to be in Aden at the time of the rescue. Visiting Freya in hospital, she found her pale and thin but glowing in the midst of friends and hospital staff.[30]

From that day forward Freya was firmly established in the public's mind as an intrepid traveler, braving alone what few others would dare. Although it would be months before she was strong enough to travel again, the outpouring of concern, admiration, and affection was everything she could have wished—except for one thing, Anton's presence at her side.

By the end of April, he and Hilda were at their house at Le Paradou, near Cavalaire in Provence. "You know, my tender friend, my life does not belong to me anymore," said the longed-for letter in the tiny script. "Only a brutal break of which I am incapable under the present circumstances, would give it back to me. So I cannot hasten to you and stay with you as I would really like to. I feel that I would know, except for your time of prescribed rest, how to encompass you with tenderness, to"—here he used a word that could mean either "pamper" or "fondle"—"you. I would choose among my favorite books the best ones for your state of mind and I would read to you until the moment in which your heavy lids hid that keen gaze, and sleep invaded."[31] But he promised that he would come soon—with his wife—for a visit in Asolo. He would take Freya to Le Paradou so that together they could climb the Maures Mountains.

. . .

While Freya recuperated and enjoyed her fan mail, she fretted over her failure. To have come so close and then to have lost the prize of Shabwa rankled, and she was determined to get back to the Hadhramaut to score in another way. While she was sweating on her dirt floor in Shibam, the much despised German, a photographer named Hans Helfritz, had made it to the buried city's outskirts, staying just long enough to take pictures before being driven off by Bedouin. "I know it is vulgar to want just to be the first, but yet it is bitter when one has come so far," she wrote Venetia, adding: "*Damn* the German."[32]

. . .

Though Helfritz reached the perimeter of Shabwa, it was none other than the great Arabian authority Harry St. John Philby who finally made it inside—a year after Freya's attempt. When Freya heard the news she was profoundly vexed, noting that Philby "has gone and taken Shabwa on his way home from Najran—*and done it by car!*"[33] With the knowledge and linguistic skills to explore and record what he saw, and under the protection of his friend King Saud, Philby made his visit to the impressive fortress ruins, a serious and thorough inquiry that included sketches, epigraphic copies, and maps, which remain important references.

But the triumph was really Freya's. Although she never got there, her quest had dramatized Shabwa for the world; it was hers in spirit, and the name would always be connected with her. Philby would pay his respects to her effort in his 1940 report, *Daughters of Sheba*. Freya's own account, *The Southern Gates of Arabia*, published in 1936, became a bestseller for the firm of John Murray and caught the attention of Queen Elizabeth, the Queen Mother. To be sure, her triumph was not without its critics. The bureaucrats of the Colonial Office always took a dim view of private citizens roaming in uncharted territory, even when they had such distinguished backers as Lord Halifax. It was completely against regulations to use the Royal Air Force for private undertakings, and this raised the whole issue of the government's obligation to spend taxpayers' money to rescue private citizens from pickles they had got themselves into. Lieutenant Colonel Morice Lake, second in command at the secretariat in Aden, told Freya when he called on her in the hospital that it was unlikely she would be allowed to explore there again, prompting Freya to tell Flora: "I suppose I have dished women's chances of going alone for at least half a generation. This is the really sad part about it all—and I can hardly bear to think of it."[34]

In the tight little colonial community of Aden there were some who whispered that Freya had abused native hospitality while others hotly exclaimed outrage that Freya made no effort to compensate the government for the cost of her rescue. In fact, Freya was initially informed that she would have to pay the RAF and was terribly worried about it. Doreen Ingrams happened to be at the hospital when an Air Force vice marshal came in and heard Freya charmingly confide her problem. "Oh, my dear," Mrs. Ingrams recalled the vice marshal expostulating, "we won't *allow* it!" With one stroke the obligation was waived. It was an example of what her detractors later accused Freya of doing systematically, using people to her advantage. "She cultivated people if she thought they could be useful," agreed Mrs. Ingrams many years later. "But," she added kindly, "often people are prepared to be used—and after all, she didn't always use them against their will. Often they were delighted to be of service."[35]

CHAPTER TWELVE

A Passionate Attachment

How brittle in reality are all the things whose permanence is never questioned.

—TRAVELLER'S PRELUDE

*T*he Italy to which Freya returned was grim with military preparations and talk of war. The government was handing out material so people could sew uniforms. Walls were scrawled with Fascist graffiti. The evening *passeggiata* was no longer the carefree exercise in which young men and women strolled in the cobblestone streets and cast flirting glances at one another; the looks they exchanged were sober: the boys had donned black shirts and the girls covered their pretty dresses with black cloaks to show their party loyalty. The papers reported on the zeal of both British and French to placate first Hitler and now Mussolini, but their appeasements were only whetting Il Duce's appetite for colonial aggrandizement, just as they had encouraged Hitler's megalomania. In Britain in June 1935, Stanley Baldwin had become prime minister and appointed Sir Samuel Hoare his foreign secretary. Hoare had joined Pierre Laval of France in a secret agreement negotiated in Rome to concede to Mussolini an even greater portion of Abyssinia than he had originally hoped to obtain—a stupid and unnecessary concession that would stir a furor in England when the truth came out a few months later, shaking the government and resulting in Hoare's resignation.

"The Abyssinian business makes me sick," Freya fulminated to friends, echoing what she had learned from Antonin Besse. If the Italians succeeded, she declared, "I really don't think I can *bear* to live here: it is all very well to shut oneself away from politics, but if one feels that a real crime is being done, it does not seem right to just turn away and think of something else. However, I am doing my little bit by telling everyone who asks me that the Abyssinians always mutilate their prisoners, which rather damps enthusiasm."[1]

To her distress, Freya found her mother in sympathy with the Fascists, and the two argued heatedly. Flora approved of the trains finally running on time, the new road systems, the draining of the malarial swamps around Rome, the Lateran Treaty, which gave the Vatican autonomy, and especially Mussolini's efforts to suppress the Mafia in Sicily. When Mussolini ordered that only the Italian flag could fly on national holidays, Flora pulled down the Union Jack over their house, then Freya ran it up again. The fact that Mario was the local Fascist party chief in Dronero only made matters worse.

At almost daily odds with Flora, Freya turned to Venetia Buddicom, who was ever encouraging in her responses: "I think you had much better let your temper go and protect yourself from keeping it—there are few things so exhausting as keeping one's temper." She added: "I wish you could get to the peace of Penbedw."[2]

Their letters crossed once or twice a week, full of affection, opinions, news—such as the shocking motorcycle accident on a dusty road near Bovington that had killed Lawrence of Arabia. Legions mourned him, including the king, while such friends as Winston Churchill, Nancy Astor, Mrs. Thomas Hardy, Augustus John, and Siegfried Sassoon attended the funeral and gave thanks that he had not survived with a ruined brain. Already a translator of Homer and author of a novel, *The Mint,* Lawrence had recently completed *The Seven Pillars of Wisdom,* which was being privately circulated and which Venetia sent Freya. Freya wrote her condolences to Lawrence's friend Sir Sydney Cockerell. She did not mention that her Arab friends in Baghdad had called Lawrence *mal'un* or "accursed," a spy who had deliberately deceived his Arab comrades.*

But it was the letters from Antonin Besse, usually in French in his

---

* British Foreign Service officers were generally aware of the contempt in which Lawrence was held by the Arabs. Sir Laurence Grafftey-Smith remembered in his memoirs, *Bright Levant:* "One thing that surprised me in my conversations with King Hussein was that he never once mentioned the name of Lawrence. Nor, indeed, did I ever hear Lawrence spoken of, while I was in the Hejaz, by an Arab, except for the one Bedu who came claiming arrears of pay. I had come to the Hejaz expecting to find a legend, and there was only silence. Two years after his entry with Faisal into Damascus, Lawrence was not a subject for conversation" (p. 160).

minuscule hand, that Freya read most avidly as she sat embroidering in the garden. He and Hilda had just departed after a brief visit to Asolo, collecting Meryem before going on to their estate in the French Midi. Anton had been corresponding with Flora from the time Freya had vanished into the Hadhramaut, and he was interested in meeting her at last and seeing the two women at home together. Hilda Besse told friends later that they were struck that the mother seemed the stronger of the two personalities; certainly the one who ran the house and to whom the townspeople looked up. Like others, they could not help noticing that when she and Freya were together Freya took a backseat.

Now Anton was telling Freya that it was her turn to come see *him,* to discover *his* magic retreat, Le Paradou. Hilda, indulgent of her husband and apparently secure in her status as first in his affections, graciously seconded the invitation. After the Besses left, letters vibrating with concern for Freya's health and holding assurances of Anton's love arrived in a steady stream. He desperately needed to be refreshed, he said, and longed to be with her again, away from soul-corrupting commerce, preoccupations with diplomatic crises and the pusillanimous behavior of Europe's leaders toward the "sawdust caesars," and above all the constant fear that he and his family would end up in exile. He painted a delicious picture of the summer months they would share at his "blessed" Le Paradou and tantalized Freya with promises of climbs together in the nearby mountains. He missed her, he said, and was sustained by her love.

One after another the dangerous letters—admiring, affectionate, reminding her of shared moments and philosophical kinship in an unworthy world—came to Freya's door, an ever more exciting drumroll leading to Le Paradou, where all the things he wanted to tell could be said at last. "We are both at the point where words are unnecessary, I have felt, and this almost at all hours, surrounded and comforted by your thought. It envelops me like a shield and would have made me invincible had the weakness been exterior. For my part, I can testify that except for the hours where serious decisions have required the greatest concentration of thought, you have been with me, in me, like my breath or the rhythm of my heart. . . . How exquisite it [will] be to have you for two weeks all to myself in this lost and exquisite spot."[3]

These were thrilling words; Freya read them and smiled softly. Learning that Anton was planning a trip to England and eager for her friends to meet him, she wrote introductions to the people in England she cared for most: Professor Ker's nephew Charles Ker, the Arabist Rhuvon Guest, Lucy Selwyn, with whom she had suffered her near-fatal fall the year before. But the friend she most urgently wanted him

Antonin Besse of Aden in 1937.

to meet was Venetia. On June 2, 1935, Freya wrote her from Asolo: "I felt sure you would be pleased with the Besses and am so glad the meeting took place."[4] From England, Anton reported that he liked "the silent Venetia, this deep lake, Venetia."[5] Evidently Venetia reciprocated. Now they were all friends.

Content, Freya turned her attention to her book about southern Arabia. Expectations were high; Jock Murray and Sydney Cockerell were inquiring for news on an outline, and Jock came down for a short visit to discuss it—accelerating the pressure. With so much talk of war, Freya was also wondering if she shouldn't get her money out of Italy, yet she was concerned about her mother's financial situation and considered creating an annuity for her. It had been clear since Freya had been rescued from the Hadhramaut that she could actually die on one of her adventures and leave her mother in straitened circumstances. It was natural and very useful to turn to Anton for investment advice.

But it was hard to concentrate on much with her visit to Le Paradou fast approaching. At last, in the second week of July, Anton appeared in Asolo without Hilda. His arrival had been preceded by a spate of urgent and excited letters brimming with details on what Freya should pack and declaring that he was "at your command, my Queen, and your most obedient subject."[6] The long awaited hour had come. Chaperoned by Flora, they first drove west to Liguria to show Anton La Mortola. There they left Flora and set off over the western Alps to France. At Barcelonnette they spent the night. In her memoirs Freya remembered the trip ecstatically: "We lost our way among the lesser roads of the plain where dusty ox-carts with creaking axles are hidden in the maise . . . wound down among the lonely woods of ilex and mimosa, the hills where the Saracen pirates raided away the vestiges of Rome."[7] Their car kept breaking down, there were no garages in sight, but they were indifferent to inconvenience. In due course they arrived at Le Paradou, where Hilda awaited them.

Then, on July 22, just days after their arrival, came a cryptic message to Venetia: "I . . . have gone through a rather shattering crisis. I will tell you but not write."[8] Five days later another letter in a calmer tone arrived: "What can I have written to you? The crisis was not financial and I am sailing into more peaceful waters: it was just one of those Decisions which are apt to appear like sudden dragons in one's path—and when the time comes, there you are with the necessity for choice upon you, and nothing to substitute for it."[9]

The moment, feared and hoped for, clearly had come. Anton had made the inevitable advance, but had she turned him down?

. . .

Venetia Buddicom's eyes were beautiful, and her hands were lovely, with long, graceful, expressive fingers. Otherwise, her body was too thin, even bony. But it was her extreme quietness that struck acquaintances on first meeting her. She was not taciturn; she was quiet. To the people who surrounded her, to the tenants who farmed Penbedw and whose every child, animal, and woe Venetia knew and gave sympathy to, to the friends and cousins who gathered for long visits and pheasant shoots, Venetia's silences conveyed a sense of peace and ease. When much later, sometime in the 1960s, she suffered a stroke and partial paralysis of one side of her face, it was said that people hardly noticed the difference.[10]

The clothes she wore were the colors of the land—never bright or showy, never dashing and chic like the ones Freya loved. The books she read were travel, philosophy, science (she got her degree in forestry) rather than fiction, and she closely followed the publications on farming and husbandry; as often as not a guest looking for her through Penbedw's great rooms would finally find her upstairs in her sitting room, reading quietly by the fire. Her father, C. Harry Buddicom, heir to railroad money, had spent his life as a country squire, and when Venetia's brother died in the World War—in a terrible freak accident while cleaning his gun—the family was devastated. After Mr. Buddicom's death in 1930, Venetia inherited Penbedw, staying on quietly with her mother in the great house among the woods and meadows of the Welsh countryside that joined the vale of Clwyd.

The four-thousand-acre estate became Venetia's career and source of fulfillment—especially after a riding accident nearly invalided her. She had always been a superb horsewoman, but after falling and crushing her back, and enduring a long, painful convalescence, she never rode again, although she kept a full stable of horses and continued the tradition of house parties and hunts. She was cared for by a loyal nurse, and when Freya was convalescing after measles, Venetia offered to send her to Freya. "Nurse would adore to come out to you," she had written. "If you would like her to, I would love to pay for the journey as I cannot come out myself."[11]

The injury shaped Venetia's life. Although she walked for miles over her properties, she was never again fully free from discomfort. Her carriage was exceptionally erect, and while in later years her face became drawn in secret suffering, it was in neither her nature nor her training to complain. After the accident Venetia never strayed far from Penbedw—although she did visit Asolo several times and occasionally went down to London. Nor did she ever marry. Several early letters refer to an unhappy romance with a poet named Mervyn, whom Freya evidently also knew, and of whom Venetia said, his "remote, untouchable and terribly loving personality almost overwhelmed me. I never felt that he would like me if he really knew me—and I never felt I should ever really know him."[12] Instead, Venetia threw herself into the business of looking after her tenant farmers, who called her the Miss.

The friendship between Venetia and Freya became a strength and consolation to them both. Freya wrote Venetia weekly, sometimes more often, and reserved the most amusing of her anecdotes for her friend rather than for her mother. As they went on living very different lives—Venetia running Penbedw, Freya roaming the world—their letters were an outlet for confidences, triumphs, irritations, lofty pronouncements, and affectionate exchanges. Freya, the chronic nomad, liked the thought of Venetia's stable life, while Venetia enjoyed the open horizons of Freya's. They encouraged each other to bear their spinsterhood and even to find virtue in it, and often spoke of settling down together when they were old, sharing the pleasures of Wales in the winter and Italy in the summer. "Can there be life everlasting?" Venetia once wrote Freya. "Someday we shall know, but I wish we could know it together."[13]

Little did either imagine that a crisis loomed that would leave the ocean of their friendship as arid as a desert.

. . .

The time Freya spent with the Besses at Le Paradou during July and August of 1935 was a golden interval. Something extraordinary had passed between her and Anton. Whatever "the shattering crisis" had been, it was clear from her happy letters that they had negotiated an understanding. Perhaps she had more of the Mediterranean in her than she realized, or perhaps the exposure to Eastern harems, where sexual references were not only explicit but the dominant topic, had had their cumulative effect. At forty-two Freya, all too conscious of her lack of beauty, longed for sexual fulfillment. Antonin, virile and ruled by the passion for conquest, had assured her that physical unions were "inconsequential," presumably meaning guilt free.[14]

As for Hilda, they would not hurt her. Anton would not be "morally fickle" to his wife, whom he loved first and put first; he was merely giving rein to the animal part of his nature. In his Nietzschean view, the relationship he and Freya shared was a unique bond on a high plane. Together, they had persuaded themselves that it was possible to make of their love "a beautiful, creative and enduring thing for all three," as Freya explained to Venetia a year later.[15] Freya wished to keep Hilda's friendship, recognizing that there would be no hope for a relationship with Antonin if she did not, because he would never leave his wife. These are the reasons it is probable that Freya and Anton became secret lovers that summer at Le Paradou, yet Freya could write sincerely to Venetia: "The more I see of Hilda Besse the more I like her. She is just pure gold all through, and he is a very lucky man."[16]

By August's end war looked likely. Freya feared she would be trapped in France, which might have had its pluses because Anton would be trapped, too, but good sense suggested she get out while she could. By October 1935 she was back in England, enjoying a Welsh autumn with the gentle Venetia, cosseted in Penbedw, free to work on the south Arabia book and think about organizing a return trip to Yemen.

She had also committed to giving a lecture at the Royal Geographical Society about her effort to find Shabwa. In what was revealing itself as a pattern in the face of stress, Freya experienced symptoms of fatigue, weakness, and headaches. At some unconscious level it seems clear that the rest, gentle attentions, and peace Venetia provided at Penbedw recalled to Freya the secure and beautiful time after her accident when her mother had doted uninterruptedly on her injured daughter. Throughout her life illness became a haven and respite from Freya's inward pressures to achieve success. Overall, however, she was happy. She was in love, and loved in return.

Although she thought she dreaded the prospect, the Royal Geographical Society greeted Freya with a huge audience, fairly bursting out of the auditorium. Again, her talk was a triumph, sending her spirits soaring. Sir William Goodenough told her that no woman since Gertrude Bell had been given such a reception. Sir Ronald Storrs declared she was "the most feted person" in London.[17] The Ladies Alpine Club made her its first honorary member. Thrilling as it was, though, she found the effort exhausting, canceled some scheduled broadcasts, and fled back to Penbedw.

An array of creative doctors, whose various diagnoses Freya took with great seriousness, was summoned. She suffered from severe anemia and must take massive doses of iron; a short while later they prescribed adrenaline and salt. She was put on a diet of "six eggs and port" daily and assured that her mysterious maladies were pneumonia, or a "microbe" located in her nasal passages, or a tooth that "woke up masses of poison," or possibly "catarrh in the middle ear."[18] She felt deliciously frail and hovered over. Best of all from her point of view, the doctors were emphatic that any idea of going back to south Arabia by the end of 1936 would have to be postponed.

In the meantime, while the English people mourned the death of King George V and welcomed their dashing new bachelor monarch, Edward VIII, to the throne, Freya toiled away at the new book, to be called *The Southern Gates of Arabia*. She harnessed Anton's help in Aden to have it fact-checked, and he dutifully read it, then gave it over for further scrutiny to his reliable assistant, Mohammed Ali, who had many Hadhrami connections. Both were surprised and distressed that Freya seemed so determined to belittle the achievement of the German photographer Hans Helfritz. As other friends would be in subsequent years, they were taken aback by her competitiveness and considered it petty and unworthy. It was not a pretty sight, this streak of waspishness in Freya's normally beguiling personality—although history is full of tales of intense rivalry between explorers. Anton, admiring her talent enormously, counseled temperance in what was otherwise a marvelous piece of writing.

"I wish I had the time and the peace of mind to review this very fine piece of work. But I must content myself today in criticizing the passages which jar and which, in my opinion, should be modified if not entirely suppressed. The deeds and the misdeeds of Helfritz interest nobody," he wrote. "He is an adventurer whose sole talent resides in the choice of subjects for his camera, as a result of which his photographs are always interesting and often extremely beautiful. From the standpoint of science, literature, the man is a complete nonentity. Why, therefore, pay attention to him? Why even mention him? Even when unflattering, advertisement remains advertisement. You will excuse my impertinence if I tell you that you had better material to hand for your closing chapter." He told her she would be better off showing gratitude to the people who had rescued her. "Freya Stark owes it to her friends, still more to herself, to rise above a disappointment which can be nothing but wounded vanity."[19]

It was good advice delivered with plenty of positive reinforcement, and in part she took it. As a writer and anecdotalist, as well as an artist with a keenly sensitive ego, Freya never willingly refrained from cudgeling characters that she believed deserved disparagement. For her it provided dramatic opportunity—and an armchair way to settle the score. But ultimately she modified her words, and her decision paid off. The shadowy presences of "the German" in *The Southern Gates of Arabia*, like "the Archeologist" who would appear as the antagonist in her next book, added an element of drama and brought a lively note of irascibility to those works—although her counselors were probably right in insisting that she tone it down.

...

In the spring of 1936 Anton's letters were filled with anger at the unfolding jingoism, ethnic hatred, and militarism. He predicted a coming "earthquake." In March, Hitler had reoccupied the Rhineland, violating the Versailles and Locarno treaties. Just weeks later Mussolini occupied Addis Ababa, decisively defeating the Ethiopians while Emperor Haile Selassie ignominiously fled, leaving chaos, massacre, and looting in his wake. In Spain various factions were mobilizing to begin the Spanish Civil War, and by now it was clear to everyone that the League of Nations, which the Americans had refused to join, was finished as a tool for peace and hope. Besse was distressed by this hostile and turbulent international atmosphere, but he also realized opportunity was staring him in the face. While other firms set about reducing their inventories, he recognized that higher prices and increased demand would be war's inevitable harvest. He gave the order to increase purchases of sellable goods. Although his firm was on the Italian blacklist—his large fleet was supplying arms to Abyssinian fighters—and the Italians were placing every conceivable obstacle in his path, he was stimulated by the challenge. Through constant daily crises, such as delivery problems involving Russian sugar or skins for American glove makers, Besse steered his empire from the top floor of his house on Crater Point and made a fortune, extending his new Arabian Airways to Djibouti, Khartoum, and Jiddah.[20]

Yet all the while he corresponded with Freya, worrying about her illnesses, questioning the cures prescribed, advising her on her book, doing one favor after the next. He was giving, he said, "everything that was in me to satisfy you."[21] He said she was a multifaceted star and cautioned her not to let success go to her head. Occasionally he looked for some encouragement in return. "What good, what interest can I bring to a life as full, as delicately crafted, as artistically arranged as that of Freya's? On every level she has today more and better things than I could ever give her—why should I continue to clutter her existence . . . to give her news of a life similar to that of a furrow traced by a decrepit ox?"[22]

More than once Anton must have felt himself skipping to a veritable tattoo of requests. By now Freya expected people to help her—especially if they were rich and powerful and in a position to do so. Once he chided her that he was feeling overlooked amid the scattershot of items she wanted him to take care of. At another point, discussing the difficulties of finding a manager for one of his agencies in West Africa, he momentarily wondered if they should switch places and he get some help from her, then noted wryly: "But you certainly have other preoccupations haven't you? I don't want to be nasty, but often I think that I am for you the bi-monthly French homework; this is the exercise that prevents rust and you have chosen me for this function."

At this point Freya was almost wolfing down the generosity that flowed her way. Anton was not alone in responding to her demands, and he usually did her bidding willingly, apparently content that he would be seeing her soon. "Your manuscript and the proofs are on the little corner table where we read together, your embroidery on a shelf close by the door . . . everywhere Freya, again Freya, always Freya, of whom one speaks a hundred times a day."²³

All the same—Freya could not have helped but take notice—he usually made a point at the end of his letters of invoking his wife's name: "Hilda sends her love" or "Hilda is reading Gertrude Bell and sees you [in it]." Was this a sly tweak?

• • •

At the end of April Anton was on his way to London and would come to Penbedw. Three weeks later, as his ship approached Malta, he wrote, "I will come to Penbedw where, *inshallah,* we shall be alone. This vision of two long days and evenings, in the intelligent silence of this large house which would have so much to say if it could talk, is delicious. Will it come to pass? I do not yet know if I will be alone. I would prefer it but will not put any obstacle in her path if Hilda chooses to come."²⁴

By May *The Southern Gates of Arabia* was ready for publication. During what would be a nervous time for any author, Freya felt fragile enough to check in for a month at a nursing home at 47 Beaumont Street, London, to rest and await the event. The book sold fully half of its first edition; it was recommended by both the Book Guild and Book Society. Jock Murray had decided to raise her royalties and agreed to reprint *Baghdad Sketches*—after Freya told him that another publisher was interested. *The Daily Telegraph* and *Library Supplement* printed rave reviews. *The Times* of London compared her with Jane Austen. The general opinion of the critics was that the book had transcended the travel genre and belonged to literature. Old Sir John Murray, Jock's uncle and head of the firm, congratulated Freya, saying it was a pleasure to publish "a great book." Freya wrote happily to her mother: "I feel rather like a prima donna—so many flowers . . . and the nice little nurses fluttering about as if I were a celebrity!"²⁵ Captain Holt sent two enormous jars of bath salts, while her aging admirer Sir Sydney Cockerell pronounced *The Southern Gates of Arabia* on a par with Charles Doughty. The professionals at the Royal Geographical Society deemed her formidable appendix the most complete summation of material on the ancient southern Arabian incense route to date. Not merely, it was said, was she a gifted writer; she now ranked as a historical geographer. Thrilled, Freya went out to buy a red handbag and two hats "to fit her swollen head."[26]

And then everything fell to pieces.

. . .

On June 11, still in the nursing home on Beaumont, Freya awaited her lover's call. He did not come that evening as she expected. The next morning he arrived, not alone but with his daughter Meryem, deliberately preventing a private conversation. Casually, as if remarking on something as neutral as the weather, he mentioned Venetia, who had just come down to London. He said he had taken her to dinner the night before and to a performance of *Tristan and Isolde*. Freya was stunned. Color drained from her face. How could he have spent an evening with Venetia first? Furious and hurt, she instantly saw conspiracy and rejection: her dearest confidante and her lover, whom *she* had brought together, whom she *depended* on, were seeing each other behind her back. But in Meryem's presence she could say nothing. "Even if I had been able to face it, I could not have put an end to things."[27]

As soon Anton and his daughter left, Freya called the place where Venetia was staying and left a message to meet her at the station, then packed furiously and fled Beaumont Street. Desperate to get out of London, feeling that her world had fallen apart, she called an elderly lady who lived in the Malvern Hills and asked to visit for a few days. At the station Freya waited until the last moment, but Venetia either had not got the message or had decided to ignore it.

As the train rocked on toward Ledbury, Freya scribbled Venetia an urgent note, heavy with reproach: "I hope you will tell me *anything* that happens with him . . . a word from you beforehand would have saved that last humiliation of feeling that things are not being told." She begged Venetia not to let Anton come to Penbedw as they had planned. Instead, she said she would go to Le Paradou and "break it there more gently and so perhaps keep a friendship *though all else must go* (author's italics)."[28]

As it turned out Freya would not go to Le Paradou again for more than a year—and then only to drop in for a casual lunch while traveling in France with friends. Flora, however, went in July. Hilda Besse, ever superb at defraying the fallout from her husband's volatile undertakings, invited her, and, none the wiser, Flora went. The roiled waters closed smoothly over, and not even a close observer would have noticed the outlines of jettisoned friendships rusting beneath the surface.

. . .

Anton understood Freya better than she understood herself, but he did not understand everything about her. He realized that she was exceptionally talented and perhaps realized from the beginning that she had a ruthless streak that ran as deep as the charm so radiantly visible. Tough himself, he must deliberately have chosen to take Venetia to dinner as a way of putting Freya on notice that, yes, he could be used but she did not own him. But if it had been a calculated insult, the strength of her reaction surely surprised him. He could not have guessed at Freya's deep-seated fears that once more she might be rejected by someone she loved and trusted. He could have had no way of knowing how much she dreaded abandonment.

But her pride was hurt as well. "Freya was intensely feminine"—and, as an insightful young friend who knew her later in life observed, "intensely sensual."[29] She was not a woman to be lightly scorned. Her friendship with Anton had been useful, but beyond that he was heroic, charismatic, stimulating—she had been violently attracted. If in fact he had initiated Freya in sexual pleasure, his behavior was all the more wounding. If, however, Freya had spurned his advances and suggested they have a platonic friendship, quite possibly Anton had grown bored with the cost of her demands.

It is interesting that Freya did not hold Venetia as much to account for what happened as she did Antonin. She must have intuited that her silent friend was too timid emotionally to try to lure him away. After her initial blast, she probably recognized that there was little danger of their having become lovers. In fact, she tried to clear the air by writing Venetia several notes in quick succession and was relieved when Venetia wrote back saying to forget about it.

"Yes, my dear, let us forget all about it," Freya responded. "You must not think I minded your *going*; it was *not being told* that I minded, but this is all a fuss and the only abiding sorrow is due to my own mistake. . . . My love to you my dear: do not be angry."[30]

Two weeks later Freya wrote Venetia again, promising this would be the last about the incident:

> I don't want to write any more about A.B. but I do seem to have given and must rectify an unjust impression if I suggested he was ever morally fickle to Hilda. He gives little importance to the physical side of love, and I think he is right so long as the spiritual position is very rigidly kept in order: this he has never failed in

with her, as far as I know, nor ever swerved in his devotion, and this is why they are bound to be happy and, if he had gone on caring for me, he would have been able to tell her as he had promised—or I would. I don't think I have ever caused any woman a moment of real unhappiness. . . .

He was angry now with me for having withdrawn myself, and does not realise that, since he has swerved away from me in spirit, I cannot continue more than a true friendship but no love. The physical is unimportant, I do agree, but only on condition that the spirit is everything and then there can be no compromise: if it is damaged, the whole thing must stop at whatever price of pain, otherwise it becomes mere disorder and licence. I think with you that, if given a chance and a long time, at any rate a very tender friendship may return, but I know I must not compromise now, and if just friendship is not enough for him from me then everything must stop.

She added, full of self-pity: "The only thing I long for now is to get away to the East, far away from everything and everybody."[31]

But Freya did not get much farther than a long visit or two in Devon with her loyal old friends the Wallers at Thornworthy. There was no return to Penbedw, not that year or ever afterward; the friendship was slowly withering. Venetia, stunned by all the emotion, chastely withdrew. In a brief letter to Freya written at the end of June she said: "All of what was good and loving will of course remain of our friendship and if we ever come together again it may help to build a friendship anew."[32]

They continued to correspond intermittently until Freya left for Asolo, followed by a five-month trip to Baghdad, Damascus, and northern Arabia to develop new material for the reissue of *Baghdad Sketches*. Once, during some unseasonably cold weeks in July when Freya was shivering in London, Venetia sent her some warm clothes and Freya wrote back gratefully. There was only one more mention of Antonin Besse. When Freya was still in London, in October 1936, and the Besses were coming and asked to see her, she wrote Venetia that although she was getting well at last, the Besses' arrival made her feel "rather sickish."[33] She did finally see him, but it was a "miserable" encounter, and she didn't intend to see him again.

Antonin, however, was not about to let Freya persist in moral ascendance. A far stronger personality than Venetia, capable of intense emotion not to mention being powerfully positioned to help the Stark women on a number of fronts, he set about to clear the air. A few days after the meeting that Freya described as "miserable" he wrote:

*When the state of your health permits it, and time having done its
work, we will have to clarify a troublesome situation for both of
us. We owe it to ourselves, from the high plane on which we have
voluntarily placed ourselves, an explanation which will leave
nothing in the shade. For me, also for you and for all those that
surround us, it can only be good that our relationship becomes
again* as intimate as it was in the past, at least on the affective and
cerebral planes [author's emphasis]. *You have received from me the
best there is, the most inspiring love and it seems to me that it was
no small thing and should have been sacred to you. This friendship
was tender, noble, based on respect, esteem and admiration, and
should remain as precious as your life itself. Keep me abreast of
your convalescence, of your works, of your movements and tell me
of the fruits that solitude will bring. Very tenderly yours. . . . AB.*[34]

By the end of the year they had resumed a correspondence that would
continue sporadically until the end of Anton's life—and Freya and Hilda
would see each other into the late 1960s. A mocking, ironic note, however,
now crept into his letters—once he said sarcastically that if it hadn't been
for the "cats' scratches and false modesty" in a letter from her, he
wouldn't have known who had sent it, "so charming" was it. But mainly
his communications were warm and full of praise for her accomplishments, and he followed her career with interest. In December he wrote to
congratulate her on receiving the Mungo Park Medal from the Scottish
Royal Geographical Society when she lectured before sixteen hundred
people in Edinburgh. A few years later, complaining to Freya that he was
old and worn out—"white hair, dry and wrinkled skin, ugly enough to
frighten"—he told her: "You are not there yet, and with your nature with
its thousand facets, will never be there. You shall remain . . . until the end:
fearless, indomitable and without mercy, harmoniously conciliating the
inner and outer lives, breaking difficult obstacles in your path."[35]

Antonin had tried to play with Freya, and he had lost, as others would
when they attempted games that tampered with her deepest feelings. He
admired her ruthlessness, as well as her strength and determination. These
were the Nietzschean characteristics they had agreed to admire. He also
recognized a new and more formidable persona emerging, and, having
once called her his queen, he now called her teasingly "Her Most Serene
Highness Freya."[36] But they were never close again. The Besses and Venetia saw more of one another than either did of Freya, although Freya
wrote Venetia from Baghdad in April 1937, almost seven months after
their last correspondence: "Thank you for writing. I have been thinking

often and not with anything but love and just leaving things to time—thinking also what a waste it is to waste the friendship of all these years. So let us leave all the trouble behind us."[37]

And that was that. Gradually the warmth lapsed with distance and Freya's preoccupation with more rewarding involvements. She was incapable of forgetting being wounded by friends—as Bingo Hardie said, "She could turn against people like a lover; she had very passionate feelings about her friends,"[38] and it was simply easier not to see Venetia than to be reminded of something that had been so intensely unpleasant. As Freya had confided to a friend earlier, "When something unpleasant happens, it's better to pretend it didn't."[39] Besides, a war was rushing down on them, and very soon they would all be swept into its vortex.

CHAPTER THIRTEEN

The Archaeologists

Last night I made a list (for myself) of the seven cardinal virtues for a traveller:

1. To admit standards that are not one's own standards and discriminate the values that are not one's own values.

2. To know how to use stupid men and inadequate tools with equanimity.

3. To be able to dissociate oneself from one's bodily sensations.

4. To be able to take rest and nourishment as and when they come.

5. To love not only nature but human nature also.

6. To have an unpreoccupied, observant, and uncensorious mind— in other words, to be unselfish.

7. To be as calmly good-tempered at the end of the day as at the beginning.

I should like to see Gertrude trying to conform to one of them!

—LETTER TO HER MOTHER, JANUARY 12, 1938

ertrude Caton-Thompson, called Caton by her friends, was tall, good-looking, well-dressed, and possessed of considerable hauteur, with a patrician background and income to match. She was an archaeologist and paleohistorian who had trained at University College, London, and in 1921, at the age of thirty-three, announced to her mother that she was off to join the noted archaeologist Flinders Petrie at his dig at Abydos in Upper Egypt. Her mother did not entirely approve of her strong-willed daughter's "working friends," whom Gertrude often invited to lunch at their elegant apartment in Kensington. But if Mrs. Thompson absented herself on those occasions, she was proud of Gertrude's real accomplishments. A sickly child whose beloved older brother had been institutionalized with mental illness, Gertrude grew stronger during a privileged youth attending balls at great houses like Cliveden, Taplow Court, and Bisham Abbey, and riding with the queen's staghounds. Recognizing that their daughter was exceptionally bright, her parents encouraged her academic aspirations. Her focus on Africa came in part from the death of the man she loved, killed by Senussi tribesmen when he was on patrol in Libya.

When she was a fellow at Newnham College, Cambridge, Gertrude was given a grant from the British Association for the Advancement of Science to study stone ruins in British-controlled Zimbabwe. Her conclusions about their origins were as controversial as they were courageous, for she reported back that the Zimbabwe findings indicated the presence of a highly evolved and structured African society, entirely indigenous; they were *not* the product of white Mesopotamian or Greek influence, as prevailing opinion held. This stirred quite a debate in archaeological circles, but Gertrude Caton-Thompson was not the sort to bend when she had arrived at a reasoned view. Such strength of character and firm convictions engendered respect, and by her early forties, when she first met Freya, she was sitting on the governing bodies of Newnham and Bedford Colleges, the Royal Geographical Society, the Royal Anthropological Institute, and the British Association, and was president of the Prehistoric Society.

It was Rhuvon Guest, a linguist and Arabic scholar who had helped Freya with her South Arabian studies, who introduced the two women in 1933. He escorted Freya to a fashionable musical soiree at the house of one of Gertrude's friends. Gertrude, like everyone else, had heard of Freya's travels and prizes, but she admitted in her memoirs, published at the sturdy age of ninety-five, "[I] did not care for what I saw."[1] Precisely what put her off she did not say. But Gertrude was an English snob, more interested in verifiable facts and well-grounded theories than in people— particularly eccentric little women inclined to be coquettish, with odd foreign accents, painted fingernails, and extreme reputations. Besides, given the experience that the two women would shortly share and the abiding dislike they conceived for each other, her memory of this first encounter could easily have been distorted.

Throughout 1936 and 1937 Gertrude and Freya bumped into each other at social events or when mutual friends like Sir Sydney Cockerell brought them together. Whatever her private reservations, Gertrude was interested in the archaeology of Yemen, and Freya clearly was the person to talk to about it. Gertrude had become intrigued with the notion that there might exist a very early link between Rhodesian and Southwest Arabian societies through Red Sea and Indian Ocean traffic, and she wanted to find out if there was any archaeological evidence to prove it.

So far, no properly scientific examination of Hadhramaut archaeology had taken place, although numbers of people, including Freya, had brought back shards indicating a plethora of unexplored ruins. When Freya brought hers to Gertrude for inspection, the archaeologist recognized that some obsidian bits—probably teeth from a saw—were possibly five thousand years old. Both women became excited, and discussions began on mounting an expedition together. Gertrude spoke Arabic poorly and reasoned that Freya's command of the local dialect and familiarity with the region would be of enormous assistance. Freya was impressed by Gertrude's sterling credentials and reputation for professionalism and immediately saw the chance to return to Yemen on an expedition that promised more significant discoveries than anything she had previously undertaken. It should have been a perfect partnership.

At first things went swimmingly. Freya shot off a letter to Harold Ingrams, who had recently been appointed the first British adviser to Mukalla. Could he, she inquired winningly, possibly—lest other archaeologists start "wandering in the Hadhramaut"—reserve any projected dig to her and the remarkably well-qualified Miss Caton-Thompson? "I think we would do you credit and start your administration with the discovery of whatever there may be to discover in the way of archeology."[2] She made clear that the prestigious Royal Geographical Society was willing to back them. Next, through an introduction by the invariably generous Charles Ker, Freya met with Lord Wakefield of Hythe, a millionaire with a record of supporting adventurous projects undertaken by women. She found him small, genial, and white-haired, ready to show her around his office and inspect an array of photographs taken with royal personages and various celebrities whose careers he had helped. She observed that it seemed hardly fair that *he* had to pay the money while *they* had all the fun. Clearly amused, Lord Wakefield offered her a check for fifteen hundred pounds. Later he told Ker that he did it because she didn't look at all like an explorer.

Thanks to Freya's success in gaining Wakefield's backing, plus some money from the RGS combined with four hundred pounds raised by Gertrude, the expedition was able to add a third member. Gertrude wanted to ask an old friend and colleague at Bedford College, Elinor Wight Gardner, with whom she had worked in Egypt and whose style and methods tallied with her own orderly scientific approach. Elinor was currently a lecturer in geology at Bedford College and had recently completed a research fellowship from the British Federation of University Women. Unmarried like the others, she brought a rather easygoing, sweet-tempered nature to the mix, and Freya immediately liked and respected her. Like the others, Elinor had endured the extreme discomforts and hazards of camping in remote areas, shown herself unflappable through floods, cyclones, and other crises of the roughing life, and was not afraid to use a gun.

With things so nicely arranged, Freya—confident that in securing funding she had made her contribution—sailed off to Mesopotamia, leaving the task of assembling the expedition's gear to Gertrude and Elinor—who, after all, were the experts.

. . .

The first bump on what would prove a rocky ride occurred at the very beginning. Gertrude and Elinor arrived in Cairo first in order to purchase a few last necessities. On October 22, 1937, they waited for Freya in a "truly awful hotel" at Port Said, the rendezvous spot for the P. and O. steamer to Aden.[3] Their ship, the SS *Narkunda,* was set to sail at 10:30 the following morning, but there was no sign of Freya. Suddenly, just after dawn, Gertrude heard a loud knocking on her door. A disheveled Freya rushed in, explaining that she had mistakenly gone to Suez and had to race by taxi to Port Said; the taxi had broken down twice, but here she was, and wasn't it all hilarious? Gertrude was not amused.

Nor did Gertrude think it particularly funny when she had to share a sweltering cabin with Elinor on a miserably hot, rough trip down the Red Sea—their portholes were stuck shut—while Freya had somehow managed to get a stateroom to herself. Looking to put things back on a smoother track, Freya suggested they all call themselves by their first names, but it was evident that Miss Caton-Thompson intended to keep their relationship strictly formal. She continued to call Freya "Miss Stark" and clearly expected to be called "Miss Caton-Thompson." Shrugging, Freya turned to more congenial shipboard company. She found a number of people she had met before, including an Iraq Petroleum Company agent escorting two American geologists on an oil survey. She also struck up with two very dignified and turbaned old sheikhs, whom she cajoled into playing deck quoits, watching delightedly as they flapped about in their long gowns.

When their ship anchored in Aden harbor, the residency launch drew up alongside. A handsome young political officer sprang out. Tall and smartly tailored, he introduced himself as Stewart Perowne. He was supposed to be picking up the oil surveyors, he said, but when he learned that Miss Freya Stark, the writer and explorer, was on board, he *had* to meet her: at that very moment he was reading *Baghdad Sketches* and admired it beyond words. Might he have the honor of bringing her and her companions ashore in the residency launch? Showering Freya with a torrent of quotations from Milton and Tennyson, he told the ladies that he was mad for all things archaeological and would love to help them in any way he could. Inviting the old sheikhs to join them and ignoring the oilmen, Perowne handed his passengers into the launch and set out through the crowded harbor.

Suddenly, as Freya watched in paralyzed fascination, a large motorboat bore down on the launch and rammed it broadside, tumbling the ladies into the arms of the horrified sheikhs in a great confusion of knocked off hats and turbans and bodies touching in violation of propriety. It was a comic scene appreciated even by Gertrude and provided an unforgettable beginning for the relationship of Freya and Stewart.

But the hilarity did not last long. Stewart, apologizing profusely, drove the women to their hotel—"a proper Eastern affair, not quite clean," according to Elinor, but worse, it was full. Freya had neglected to reserve rooms. Not until evening could one be found, and the two scientists again had to double up in cramped quarters while Freya went over to stay at the British residency. Gertrude told Elinor that she was getting "a little tired of Freya's unbusinesslike ways." Although Elinor too was annoyed, she was charitable. She wrote to a friend, "Freya does everything by S.A. [seat-of-the-arse] and the feminine touch—which I fear gets her much further than any other method! However, she seems quite a nice person for all that and her red fingernails."[4]

Freya was not free from apprehension herself, confiding to friends that she was feeling "rather peculiar to find myself in a Scientific Expedition," and she wondered "how I shall live up to it."[5]

Stewart Perowne was eager to help—describing the whereabouts of Himyaritic inscriptions that he had discovered in the interior and offering to take all three ladies—but he was most attentive to Freya—to them. Nine years younger than Freya, the son and grandson of bishops of Worcester, Stewart was an erudite and witty Cambridge graduate who had excelled in classical studies. Friends found him extremely entertaining and even a bit flamboyant—he often turned up dressed in jodhpurs, a flowing silk shirt, and Bedouin headdress. Freya was instantly captivated by this dashing chap in uniform but for the time being needed to attend to her role as head of expedition. ("You can't *think* how unsuitable I am for the job," she wrote home all too truthfully.[6])

Unfortunately, Antonin Besse was away in Abyssinia, and it is a good guess that after their recent differences he decided not to instruct his man in charge to extend to Freya the sort of help he had offered previously. The oilmen seemed to have snared the only cook in Aden, so Freya had trouble making arrangements. Finally she managed to unearth a young hillman with long eyelashes named Qasim, who claimed he knew how to make tea, and probably stew, and anyway loved classical Arab poetry. A large portion of their seventy-one boxes, including many personal items and their scientific instruments, had mistakenly been sent on to Singapore. Gertrude called it sheer "imbecility"—and Freya silently thanked her lucky stars that it had not been her fault. What remained had to be sorted and repacked. Worst of all, because it had never occurred to Freya to check on the date, they had arrived at the start of Ramadan, the holy month when the entire Muslim world fasts during the day.* They would not be able to hire workers during Ramadan, so Freya cheerfully counseled her disappointed colleagues to relax and enjoy life in the meantime.

"I find I get through much more with far less exertion than my party," she wrote home. "It is far more useful in this climate to sit quiet and make other people do things. A little chat about their own family affairs does more to get willing and efficient helpers than all the ordering about in the world: I think Elinor Gardner still considers it a waste of time, being used only to Egyptians who can be browbeaten. The Arab has the charming attitude that anything he does is done as a kindness, so it is no good chivvying him about for it. It is a great mistake to look," she reflected, settling down amid the packing cases, "as if you can do everything yourself."[7]

By November 8, 1937, the three were finally on their way to Mukalla, where they were the guests of Doreen and Harold Ingrams. Harold, forty-one and burdened with the responsibilities of his new position, acutely aware of how even the smallest incident could trigger renewed tribal conflict, was not happy that an RGS-backed expedition had arrived in his territory. He was particularly displeased to learn that the women planned to dig in Hureida, a small town in the Wadi 'Amd where some violent clashes had recently been put down by artfully deployed RAF bombs. Ingrams did his best to warn the ladies off, and Elinor wrote home that he wasn't as nice as his wife, was being "obstructive" and trotting out rules about sticking to roads and injunctions about where they could and couldn't go. Gertrude muttered darkly to her companions that they should just "do as

---

* One of the five pillars of Islam, this fast during the ninth month of the lunar year, Ramadan, requires the believer to abstain from eating, drinking, smoking, and having sex during daylight hours. It is an act of discipline for both body and spirit, to help bring communicants closer to God and their fellow communicants.

we like," while Freya, in the middle, tried to placate with smiles, admitting to her mother: "There is no denying we are a nuisance."[8] With temperatures already soaring into the nineties to test them further, the women were unaware that the young Ingrams were privately calling them "the Three Foolish Virgins."[9]

Gertrude and Elinor did relax a bit when Freya took them around the old coastal town and showed them the lovely traditional carved doors with their heavy brass studs and decorative traceries, the dhows silhouetted against the emerald sea, the floppy-lipped camels ringed on the beach, surrounded by women gathering their dung for fuel. While Freya stayed back to take notes and write letters, Gertrude and Elinor ventured out to scout the things that interest scientists, such as erosional levels, microliths, and trihedrals—new terms that excited Freya's curiosity and stimulated her desire to add archaeology to her repertoire of skills.

By November 14 they were on their way into the interior in an ancient truck stuffed with gear and crowded with not just themselves, Qasim the cook, and their driver but very quickly as many hitchhikers as could hang on, including two turbaned sayyids—who after a night on the jol stared fixedly as the ladies struggled to get dressed inside their sleeping bags. Their destination was Tarim, the religious center at the eastern end of the Hadhramaut, which Freya had visited two years earlier. It was a journey of 130 miles, taking two nights and days on a rough, narrow road that snaked around death-defying turns. While the hangers-on pushed, hauled, and coached the truck over ravines and around precipices, Freya noted that their two sayyids "did not trust to predestination" and walked. When Gertrude also declared her intention to walk, Freya could not resist twitting her about her want of courage. Gertrude burned in silent annoyance.

Their supper the first night on the jol was a soup that included Heinz canned beans in which Qasim thought he detected pork. Pork being forbidden and repugnant to Muslims, he refused to eat. Freya, recalling the horrors of the famous Sepoy Rebellion of 1857, when native soldiers in British India's Bengal army mutinied over rumors of pork-greased bullets, suggested this was an ominous beginning. Gertrude imperiously dismissed the possibility. It was Freya's turn to be infuriated.

Years later Doreen Ingrams recalled that Gertrude "couldn't melt." She "always had her nose up in the air" and treated the Bedouin as "coolies" when "in Arabia you would be jolly lucky to be thought their equal—they were not used to taking orders from women." As for Freya: "To do her justice, she would talk to anybody and she had lots of trouble explaining Gertrude's imperious manner to the Hadhramauti."[10] It gave Freya great satisfaction when two little Bedouin boys briefly joined their party and pointed out that Gertrude's hair was badly in need of combing. As for skinny Elinor, they wanted to know, was she a man?

In Tarim the ladies were given a clean, airy bungalow as guests of an Al Kaf merchant prince, and although impatient to get on to their selected dig site at Hureida, they had no choice but to wait out Ramadan, enjoy temperatures cooler than at the coast, swim in the nice pool, and while away the time exploring. Several times on excursions in the surrounding desert, Gertrude had to acknowledge that Freya's silky way of defusing hostile natives could be very useful—if not positively a lifesaver. Although the scientists appreciated the beauty of the religious town nestled against the wadi's grand escarpment and its splendid old houses, they quickly learned to dread the tedious visits to the harems that Freya insisted politeness required. Gertrude was afflicted by sciatica when she had to sit cross-legged on the floor, and she hated having an effusive native hostess spoon-feed her mouthfuls of strange foods while slaves waved overpowering incense under her nose. Elinor strained to understand the local Arabic but had great difficulty with it. She and Gertrude wanted to get on to the task that had brought them. All this dallying was extremely frustrating and, they noted, entirely Freya's fault for not having taken Ramadan into account. But Freya's role for the RGS, to enter native life and describe it ethnographically, was equally difficult to pursue if the scientists insisted on keeping their group apart. So Freya, too, felt frustrated.

By November 21 they were in Seiyun, the largest of the Hadhramauti towns. Again there were housing problems, although Freya finally engineered an invitation to stay at the guesthouse of the powerful local ruler, Sayyid Abu Bekr. But Gertrude was unappeased by the disorganized modus operandi of their expedition head. Unable to forgive Freya for bringing them there during Ramadan, Gertrude was also appalled by Qasim, whom she deemed useless as a servant. Freya was aghast at Gertrude's indifference to the people who were putting themselves out for the women—although what wounded Freya the most was Gertrude's critical attitude toward herself. Elinor quickly became the moderator: "I hope the split won't develop too far—at present they both wail to me and I do what I can to pour oil on the troubled waters!"[11]

Freya reacted to Gertrude's rebuffs by turning on archaeology. "I shall *never* be an archeologist," she sulked to her mother. "I am far too fond of living things and people." As usual she put her own charming gloss on her anger, observing truthfully: "While Gertrude goes wandering with her eyes on the ground for potsherds I am inclined to gossip with all the neighborhood which slowly gathers and drifts along with us offering bits of hopeful rubbish." From Freya's point of view, Gertrude wanted "the Hadhramaut without its inhabitants."[12]

Freya whispered to Elinor that Gertrude was "no traveler" and confided that she did not want her on a trip down the Wadi 'Amd that Freya wished to take at the end of their journey. She wanted to test her theory that a major incense route tributary had once run down to the ancient port of Cana, somewhere west of Bir 'Ali. Having missed discovering Shabwa, Freya saw a second chance for a major find in pinpointing old Cana's precise location.

Then illness struck. Elinor was the first to come down with a sore throat and fever, lying in bed for days in Seiyun while Gertrude and Freya contended over schedules and arrangements, and Freya privately decided that she did not like traveling with women. She was beginning to conclude, she wrote Jock, that she was an "Anti-Feminist."[13]

At last Elinor was strong enough to continue west to Shibam. There the scientists met a measure of squalor for which their previous experience in Africa had left them unprepared. An extremely ancient town, Shibam was crammed on a rock outgrowth less than a mile square. A marvel of tightly packed, multistory, mud-brick houses, this was the place where Freya had been so ill two years before. Gertrude and Elinor were overwhelmed by the flies, the monstrously large mosquitoes, and especially the sewage odors that permeated the labyrinthine alleys. Again it was a struggle to find a relatively decent place to live. Freya implored the help of Anton's agent in Shibam, who finally located a place outside town where dogs barked, roosters crowed, and donkeys brayed through the breathless nights, the air stank foully, and before dawn drummers banged their drums to awaken Ramadan fasters. By day, as crowds of visitors pressed at their door, Gertrude demanded that Freya keep them out. Elinor sank into a relapse.

"I keep the vulgar herd away," wrote Freya sadly. "The results of this attitude were made painfully clear as a peasant woman from next door came up and tried to get in: I shut the door and she went away murmuring that she 'only wanted to see' us and on the way down stole my rings from my bedroom. . . . I am sure if I could have been nice and let her come in for a five-minute chat, she would never have thought of taking anything."[14]

By now the breach between the companions was too wide to bridge. Freya had endured every kind of physical test on her previous journeys and was proud of it. Now she took revenge by expressing her contempt for her companions' weakness in the face of "minor discomforts." She was also concerned that her part of the expedition, to capture a record of domestic Yemeni life, was suffering from the ill will generated by the scientists. Gertrude insisted on boiling their water, which Freya obdurately claimed was "pure" because it came from a well under the cliff. Gertrude countered hotly that it had to be contaminated because everyone bathed and defecated there. Freya had always accepted local customs, even though they were clearly unhealthy, and lived as the natives did, but she now had to defend the fastidious tastes of her companions. In her eyes doing so set up an unacceptable gulf between themselves and the local inhabitants. In fact, their circumstances were wretched. None of them was well—Freya developed dysentery—and it was all they could do to droop through the torrid days.

Gertrude took to bed with a temperature of 102. Sick and angry, Freya did what she always did when she was stressed: retreated to bed as well. Elinor, only slightly recovered herself, was left nursing both. Clearly the unselfish one in the group, Elinor found her patience exhausted. She ached for letters from home and fought back the impulse to flee. In the meantime Freya was railing to Jock Murray about the deteriorated conversation, devoted exclusively to flints and water not boiled long enough. She was also beginning to think she might have just the right idea for her next book: the cleavage between the East and West as seen through the reaction of the scientists to the locals.

On the day of the Id, the riotous feast celebrating the end of Ramadan, Freya staggered out of bed at sunrise with a camera to record the wild ululations, dancing, and shooting. She was gone all day, and Elinor was indignant. Such indifference to one's own welfare was beyond Elinor's comprehension. Then, when Freya returned on the point of collapse and looked to Elinor to nurse her, it was the last straw—especially because Freya was now insisting that she had malaria and had begun dosing herself with quinine even though it made her heart palpitate.

Gertrude and Elinor, convinced that they were all in the throes of sandfly fever, told each other that Freya was possibly a little mad. And to a degree she was. The situation, in which she felt criticized, ignored, and unappreciated, was bringing out all that was most truculent, childish, self-pitying, and neurotic in her character. Elinor would tell Sir Sydney Cockerell later that Freya "had no sense whatsoever as to treatment . . . that she simply fanned through the medical book trying all remedies."[15] Having had one fainting spell a few days before, Freya now gave herself an injection, which brought on severe heart palpitations. Convinced that she was probably dying, she asked to be evacuated to Aden Hospital. Her companions gladly rushed to arrange her evacuation. Elinor accompanied her back to Seiyun, and on December 9 Freya was taken by a Besse plane to Aden.

The Wakefield Expedition to Yemen, 1937–38. Archaeologists Gertrude Caton-Thompson and Elinor Gardner, left, with Freya, as they set off for the Hadhramaut after learning that it was the holy month of Ramadan.

Gertrude Caton-Thompson, archaeologist and fellow of Newnham College, Cambridge. She expected Freya to call her Miss Caton-Thompson, which was not a promising beginning to a long and arduous field trip.

"I hope to goodness the doctor will not let Freya come back if she's not fit," Elinor wrote home wearily. "C.T. is now saying she'll not be left alone with her, which I don't blame her [for]."[16]

. . .

Relieved to be rid of Freya and out of Shibam's pestilence, the scientists reinstalled themselves in Sayyid Abu Bekr's guesthouse in Seiyun, where they slowly recovered and lamented the time lost. The really hot weather would soon be upon them, all work would have to be suspended, and they had nothing to show for the Wakefield Expedition. Finally on December 20, sufficiently recovered but nervous about what new horrors lay ahead, they left for Hureida, ninety-two miles southwest in the Wadi 'Amd. There they were welcomed by the powerful Sayyid Hassan al 'Attas, the local *mansab* or leader. A wealthy religious scholar of considerable regional renown who moved in a cloud of expensive French perfume and conducted himself in "the Arabic equivalent of the Oxford manner,"[17] he was a bit of a dandy, edging his lustrous eyes with black kohl and flashing the magenta lining of his cape. He was solicitous of the exhausted ladies, insisting they lie down on his floor while he doused them with rose water. Then he helped settle them into a reasonably clean house on a steep hillside, well away from sewage drains, from which they could look down on the mud-brick town. Fanatically religious and very poor, the village straddled two regions and had suffered greatly from the ongoing tribal warfare. The scientists noticed that it had no protective walls, only large, white-washed boulders placed at intervals to indicate—they were assured—that murders were not permitted inside the boundaries.

The only other white women the town had ever seen had been Freya, passing through on her previous trip, and Doreen Ingrams. In her charming book *A Time in Arabia,* Mrs. Ingrams recalled that when she arrived after Freya left, the small boys of Hureida peppered her with questions about her belongings and were particularly interested in her shoes. "But rather disappointed, for Freya Stark, one of them told me, had much higher heels." Another boy had added: "In the name of God most high and the religion He glorifies, you couldn't walk in them they were so high."*

The townspeople, astonished that the two scientists had settled among them, optimistically assumed they had come to repair the ruined irrigation

---

* From Doreen Ingrams, *A Time in Arabia* (London: John Murray, 1970), an account of her travels in Yemen's interior. Another anecdote from Mrs. Ingrams's book gives this amusing picture: "I was not left alone as the women were curious to have a look at their guest and both family and friends from neighboring houses soon packed the room. I was writing in my diary at the time and they told me not to stop, for happily Freya Stark had been there since our first visit and had begun a tradition that all foreign women write continuously."

system and watched in perplexity as Gertrude and Elinor, followed by droves of villagers, scouted out where to dig. Little girls, their faces painted in yellow and green, fled screaming from their path. Gertrude simply ignored them. With all the brisk efficiency that Freya professed to despise, she set about the work for which she had come. In no time she had spotted a massive mound of stationary sand and reasoned that something must be hidden beneath. With the help of a huge African slave loaned by the mansab, six tribesmen, and four boys—whom she was prepared to dismiss quickly should they prove "slackers"—she began to excavate. Between the end of December and the first of March, a moon temple dedicated to the pagan god Sin slowly emerged from the sand—the first such discovery to be made in southern Arabia. In and around it Gertrude and Elinor also unearthed some fifty monumental Himyaritic and Sabean inscriptions and extramural shrines, some of which dated to the middle of the fifth century B.C.E.

The archaeologists also excavated some cave tombs, a nasty task that required hours hunched in pitch blackness, inhaling clouds of camel-flavored dust. In the meantime Elinor had begun painstakingly mapping the outlines of a pre-Islamic irrigation system, which indicated that agriculture had once thrived in the valley. Not much pottery was found in the temple, although in the tombs they unearthed glass, tall goblets and curious flanged cups, hundreds of faience and semiprecious stone beads, and Achaemenid seals. A series of skulls found in the tombs later generated considerable interest in paleological circles because of their extreme smallness and feeble muscular development, with a cephalic index of 69.8—lower than any skull series then measured except for areas of the Pacific. Gertrude was later to conclude that this south Arabian civilization was "imitative" and "lacking in original ideas."[18] To this day, not only the significance of their findings but the exceptional care and diligence with which they went about recording them remains an outstanding achievement in the still sparse history of South Arabian archaeology.[19]

. . .

In the meantime Freya, having had a nice rest in Aden, decided to return. She had no intention of being criticized for abandoning her responsibilities as leader of the Wakefield Expedition, so she flew back to the Hadhramaut and was in Hureida by December 27, 1937. In Aden she had entertained many dinner parties with wickedly funny descriptions of her trials with the scientists and was gratified to hear Stewart Perowne laugh uproariously. The disastrous trip would remain their shared joke.

The scientists were not happy to have her back, especially because, less

The Wadi 'Amd, flanked by the high jol, is where the archaeologists made their discoveries, and through which Freya was to travel south by camel on her way to locate the ancient port of Cana on the Indian Ocean coast.

A partial view of the little village of Hureida in the Wadi 'Amd, where Freya and the archaeologists were put up by the mansab, Sayyid Hassan al 'Attas, who also provided them the services of an African slave.

than a week later, Freya was in bed again. Having checked the emotional atmosphere of the house and finding it even chillier toward herself than before, Freya declared that she had "suppressed pneumonia" and packed her bedroom with swarms of tribal visitors, who told her folktales and giggled at her jokes. The scientists grimly went about their work.

Then Gertrude came down with a cold—none of them was ever truly well—and used it as an excuse to remain on the floor above, taking her meals apart. Gertrude's snubbing sparked almost desperate efforts by Freya to win over Elinor. She invented little dramas to capture her attention, unable to see that such ploys were counterproductive. One morning Elinor was awakened by Qasim calling her to come immediately to Freya's room. Freya had fainted three times during the night, she whimpered to Elinor; she couldn't breathe; she had dysentery; she needed a doctor immediately. Resignedly, Elinor sent an urgent message to Harold Ingrams in Mukalla and stayed home from her geological work to care for Freya.

Two days later Ingrams burst into Hureida. He announced that Freya must be sent back immediately to Aden Hospital. He dispatched a runner to get a wireless to the oil surveyors requesting their plane for the rescue. Their pilot was concerned about the risks of landing on a terrain of uneven sand but reluctantly consented and made it in. Then Freya sat up in bed and declared that she would not go with him. There was no way, she insisted airily, that they could get to Aden until after dark. Because it was an open plane, she added, she would only get a worse chill. Everyone was dumbfounded. Gertrude recalled in her memoirs that the pilot declared Freya a "bloody bitch," which, observed Gertrude, "was mild under the circumstances."[20] The episode confirmed all Ingrams's blackest doubts about letting headstrong European women wander in the interior.

A week later Qasim roused Elinor again. Freya was hemorrhaging, but Elinor wrote home that "by now used to her ways I inquired where from before getting too agitated. It turned out that her period had gone wrong, so though a nuisance it was not dangerous and cleared up in less than a day. For the moment there is actually no particular disease she thinks she's got—and really if she has any more I shall go away."[21] Although a person as strongly disinclined to emotionalism as Gertrude and as inflexible in her attitudes could never have tolerated one as needy as Freya, Elinor, in less trying circumstances, might have been more sympathetic. In fact they might have got along very well. But caught in the middle, Elinor took the side of her old friend and colleague, triggering the deep insecurities always lurking at Freya's core. Isolated and ignored, Freya sulked in her bed.

The difficult archaeological work went on. Gertrude was off every morning, toiling in her dusty cave a distant ride by donkey in baking heat.

Elinor spent long hours under the pitiless sun, examining fossilized remains of Paleolithic vegetation in tufa deposits of high ravines that drained into the wadi. At night, listening to explosions as the RAF dropped bombs on a nearby village that was erupting in tribal conflict, she wrote home that she would be grateful when it was all over.

The archaeologists' work was nearly done, and Freya, abandoning hope that she could detach Elinor from her disdainful colleague, resumed talking to both of her plan to go by camel down the Wadi 'Amd. Amazed that she would even bring it up, Elinor snorted privately: "I don't know who she expects to go and pick up the pieces—I shan't!" She added drily: "She is extremely Eastern in her distortion and embroidery of sayings and is always contradicting herself. I would never believe more than a quarter of anything she says."[22]

A few light moments leavened the atmosphere: together the three burned a bit of eighteen-hundred-year-old incense that Gertrude had exhumed; there were visits from the mansab, who invariably turned out beautifully dressed in cashmere shawls and was so holy that his subjects sniffed his hands rather than kissed them. At one point Freya painted his nails with pink polish; at the time he was imposing some stringent measures on his harem, and mischievously she observed that she might be creating a scandal with his wives.

At long last Gertrude decided the dig could be closed. The skulls, inscriptions, flints, pottery, and other findings were carefully packed, and Gertrude paid a formal good-bye call on the mansab, presenting him with eleven Himyaritic inscriptions for his collection. Freya again raised the issue of the Wadi 'Amd. Would they come with her? No, they would not—although Gertrude softened her refusal by noting that since there would not be time enough to do any "serious science," there was really no point. (Later she wrote that she refused to "share an enterprise with someone whose scruples I had learnt to mistrust.")[23] Elinor simply begged off, as she had privately vowed she would. And so the scientists and Freya parted, never to see one another again.

Gertrude and Elinor, eager to get to the coast, went back through the Hadhramaut the way they had come while Freya, mounted on a camel, disappeared to the unexplored regions of the south. At Mukalla the scientists stopped to see Harold and Doreen Ingrams, stunning them with the news that their sickly companion had plunged off into uncharted territory without notifying the resident or getting his permission. Elinor received the distinct impression that if Harold Ingrams had anything to say about it, Freya would not be welcome in the Aden Protectorate again.

. . .

Within two weeks Gertrude and Elinor set sail for Aden, experiencing the usual feelings of gratitude at being served Scotch whiskey in the company of naval officers speaking a cultivated, grammatical English. Bathed, their hair clean, they rejoiced at finding themselves no longer surrounded by small, dusty people plucking at them with hennaed hands. At Aden they gorged themselves on news, including the very bad tidings that Germany had seized Austria.

They called on Antonin Besse, who was exceptionally gracious and helpful, suggesting that they go by the Red Sea to Egypt on one of his ships and stop at the coastal towns of Djibouti and Jiddah on their way. He also invited them for a drive that evening with Hilda, whom they found as likable as her husband. Elinor wrote: "He is a most masterful creature and one can understand how he has climbed from a poor clerk—which is what he was when he first came to Aden—to be the first merchant . . . all over Arabia."[24] He reminded Gertrude of Cecil Rhodes, "compact, purposeful, far-seeing and ambitious for his ideals." Beyond that, she said, "I was struck by his extreme dislike of Freya which, he gave me to understand, was shared by many in Aden." Evidently Anton told Gertrude that "she uses people and returns no gratitude." She added: "I allowed myself to say our relations had been difficult and he replied: 'had I met you I would have taken the liberty of warning you.' "[25] Gertrude, of course, had no way of knowing that painful events had recently occurred between Freya and Antonin, nor that he had been in thrall and then repudiated. Even if he had deliberately provoked her, he would never forgive Freya for turning on him. Yet neither did he wish to break off an association with a writer of such outstanding gifts and prominence.

As Elinor and Gertrude sailed north toward England, each in a spacious cabin of her own with portholes open to the breezes, Elinor mused: "I wonder what is happening to Freya."[26]

. . .

Freya woke up under the shade of a samr tree somewhere deep in the sandy wastes of the Wadi 'Amd to see a Se'ari tribesman sitting beside her, silently observing. And so it was, she reflected. Wherever she went to find solitude on this great, empty earth, from nowhere emerged some form of life, human or otherwise, to share the loneliness.

She lay for a while in the sand, limp from the tension of the past months, the ever-pressing humanity, the constant chatter in Arabic, the struggles with her European companions. She hated having been made to feel incompetent and stupid—and far worse, dreadfully alone. In all the world her darkest fear was being cast as an outsider, yet that was how she had spent the last four ghastly months—an outsider to their exclusive Britishness, their self-satisfied science, flagellated by Gertrude's disapproval and Elinor's irritated compassion. It should not have come as a surprise that Elinor and Gertrude had not accompanied her on this last leg of the journey—yet Freya had let herself believe she could persuade them to come. Their refusal was a final sting. Now privately she vowed that *never* again would she put herself in the position of depending on people who didn't care about her. She would make this a *great* trip. She would *discover* the lost port of Cana—and they would see what they had missed.

With all the zest of which Freya was so capable, and absolutely indifferent to what Harold Ingrams might say when she emerged, she launched off to seek another triumph. Hiring three camels and several Bedouin escorts, and taking Qasim, who was in tears partly from the pain of a suppurating boil under his arm but mostly at having to part from a Hureida girl, they headed south. At best, wending her way by camel through land that even Ingrams had not visited and that remained, to use his term, "unpacified," she hoped she could confirm what historians believed was once the main caravan route to the coast, at whose terminus, Cana, ships had waited to be loaded with frankincense. As far as the eye could see, the horizon was dotted by ominous fortified towers manned by tribal sentries. When they stopped at a settlement, tribal elders converged on Freya for advice. Receiving her as "Beloved of the Government," her interlocutors would disingenuously inquire, for example, how best they should rid themselves of a disliked representative of the local sultan: send a deputation to the British resident, or just murder him quietly?

Halfway through the Wadi 'Amd, at a scattering of mud houses, Freya sickened again. Already debilitated, she was now worn out by the demands of local hospitality, which night after night required that she sit cross-legged on the floor, answer questions of forty men chatting and smoking the hubble-bubble, then visit with the harem to give equal time to the ladies. This time Freya's collapse was not a play for attention. Her guides brought her back the short distance to the slightly larger town of 'Amd, where a runner was dispatched to find Ingrams. One can only guess with what emotions this hard-pressed official heard that Freya was again in need of rescue. In any event, he sent a car bumping down the dry watercourse, only to have another runner meet it halfway to call the rescue off; Freya was feeling well again.

Altering her original plan in order to avoid an area infested by malaria, Freya wended her way for nearly a month—mostly peacefully, although there were some incidents that would have fazed a less courageous traveler—through the network of upland valleys toward the sea. Swaying under a sunshade on her camel, feeling like a passenger "settling into a deck chair" for a sea voyage, she covered well over 120 miles, often riding over nine hours a day through harsh and fantastic country. Descending deep ravines and scrambling over wind-scoured bluffs, she looked for and copied pre-Islamic rock inscriptions, correctly concluding that she was traveling a secondary route and that only at 'Azzan had the main route to Cana begun.

At last reaching 'Azzan, perched between the high jol and the desert, Freya was warned against continuing alone. The territory she needed to cover to reach the sea was very dangerous, and she would only be safe in the company of a caravan that the sultan of 'Azzan was dispatching in the same direction. Protected by twelve soldiers bristling with guns and twenty-seven camels loaded with bales of tobacco, Freya, Qasim, and her camel men crossed the desert to a grim volcanic land, where the camels unloaded at Balhaf. In the meantime the sultan's nephew, who had directed the caravan, had described a place near Bir 'Ali that sounded to Freya like the probable location of ancient Cana. This was Husan al Ghurab, at least six hours farther on. The nephew promised to escort her there. However, the nephew's real agenda was to provoke an attack by the excitable Bir 'Ali tribesmen, archrivals of the 'Azzami, who could be counted on to be much put out by the sight of a female infidel wandering in 'Azzami company through their land. If Freya's arrival sparked trouble, reasoned the cagy 'Azzami—and something unpleasant were to happen—the British might be moved to smash their Bir 'Ali rivals with a few well-placed bombs.

Innocent of these tribal machinations, Freya cheerfully embarked on another camel ride, to discover to her enormous satisfaction more than enough archaeological evidence to prove that this was the site of ancient Cana. Absorbed in copying inscriptions, Freya hardly noticed when two envoys from Bir 'Ali arrived. They would like to come and "shoot," they told her. Tired, thirsty, distracted, and pressed for time, Freya assumed they were talking about giving her a reception of honor. She was very sorry to disappoint them, she said, but would try to accommodate them another day when she had more leisure. When, however, she saw the astonished looks on the envoys' faces and the grin spreading over the face of the sultan's nephew, she realized there must be some misunderstanding. She did not give herself away, and "the envoys departed deeply, if mistakenly, impressed by the equanimity of the female European."[27]

In short order the Bir 'Ali tribesmen returned and this time made it alarmingly clear that Freya and the 'Azzami were to depart immediately. Her request for a boat was menacingly refused, although they gave her party two waterskins for the grueling trip back to Balhaf. By this time it was dusk, and they had to pick their way over black lava in pitch-blackness. Her escorts kept their guns at hand, straining their eyes toward the ridges looming on either side, eerily lit by a dim moon. Finally, at two in the morning, they staggered into Balhaf. It had been an eighteen-hour day—nearly fourteen on camelback. Freya looked at her men's bare feet and saw they were bleeding profusely—but at least no war had been ignited. Ingrams wouldn't be able to hold that against her, she reflected to herself and, ever the star of her own show, drolly noted that the adventure was surely the closest she would come to being Helen of Troy.

By the next morning Freya was on a dhow sailing through the Indian Ocean to Aden, suffering through the aches and chills of dengue fever, a miserable if seldom fatal disease carried by mosquitoes. In her bags she had notes to offer the Royal Geographical Society, including her important discovery of the site of ancient Cana. She also had a valuable Arabic manuscript, several glowing silk gowns, carpets, daggers—and a lizard named Himyar. He was thirteen inches long, with blue gills and a crest like a dragon, and for the time being she kept him in a box. At home she would take him everywhere—causing considerable surprise in restaurants and parks. She fed him nasturtiums and violets, warmed him inside her jacket, and utterly gave him her heart.

· · ·

Naturally, Aden was thrilled to hear the last chapter in the saga of "the Three Foolish Virgins." The dramatis personae—tiny Freya with her reputation for escapades, icily disdainful Gertrude, and bland, plain Elinor—provided plenty of gossip for the small colonial community, fueled as much by Freya's mischievous anecdotes as by anything the two scientists might have said, discretion being more their style. The wags were already having fun with the drama of Miss Stark needing a plane for a second rescue. "Evacuate! Evacuate! A maiden most immaculate!" was the ditty around the dinner party circuit.[28]

Official Aden let Freya's illegal jaunt pass with a scolding. After the incident with the plane, Harold Ingrams had urged the Aden government to recall Freya from the interior, but it was decided that because the expedition was supported by the Royal Geographical Society, there might be resistance to such a measure. Colonel Morice Lake, the shy bachelor officer who had called on Freya during her last hospital stay, was again dispatched to the hospital to deliver a word or two of official displeasure.

Instead the poor man stood before Freya's bed, harumphed a bit, admired Himyar, and told her the government was relieved she was safe. That done, the governor, Sir Bernard Reilly, who quite enjoyed Freya's company, sent word inviting her to stay at the residency after she got out of the hospital.

It would not be an exaggeration to say that Freya got off scot-free in this latest tangle with British officialdom. Her freewheeling methods irked some but amused more. Chiefly it was Harold Ingrams who was annoyed, but the consensus was that he was something of an autocrat in his little fiefdom and would be expected to bridle at Freya's disregard for rules.

Freya couldn't leave Aden without dropping in on Antonin Besse. She found him "rather pathetic, struggling there with all his business and so miserable at the thought of being ill and old—and so incapable of yielding an inch to the exigencies of human existence."[29] She had no intention of forgiving him, so she minimized him—how could she cut him off entirely? Who knew, she might be coming back to Aden yet again.

For now, however, it was time to meet her mother and Jock Murray in Athens. She was eager to introduce them to the scaly little creature she was bringing home. Himyar would be a lot less complicated than others to love.

. . .

Letters and invitations piled up as Freya tottered back to Asolo after her restorative Greek holiday. She looked and acted absolutely flattened, spending as much time in bed as at her desk. In front of her was the awesome responsibility of coordinating her material as head of the Wakefield Expedition for a scholarly report as well as documenting her separate trip to verify the site of ancient Cana. It would be a superb report in the end, the most complete study of the terrain and its people yet produced. She would win the Royal Geographical Society's Founder's Gold Medal for it, but the prospect of putting it all together, as well as preparing a major address for the RGS in London at the end of November, depressed her. She realized it was critical to perform brilliantly, and the prospect was more exhausting than elating, especially because she would have to find a way to deal with Gertrude Caton-Thompson.

While they were in Greece, Freya and Jock agreed that Murray's could get two books out of the journey. One would be a collection of her photographs and the other a Freya Stark travel account. Knowing full well that Gertrude was not alone in having behaved objectionably on the trip, and that Gertrude was well-regarded and had friends in high places, Freya was anxious to put her side forward as quickly and persuasively as possible. She proposed to Jock that the thesis for her travel account should be the arrogance and ignorance with which the British treated peoples of unfamiliar cultures that they, out of ignorance, viewed as "primitive." Gertrude's behavior, she told Jock, would be an excellent vehicle to illustrate her point. Privately he wasn't sure he liked the idea, but it was never easy to countermand Freya, so he decided it was better to wait and see what came out—then deal with it as necessary.

Various magazines also asked for articles. Because Freya needed to defray any ill will from the Ingramses' direction, she set to work on a laudatory piece for *The Times* of London about Harold's efforts to bring peace to the Yemeni tribes. Two years later Harold and Doreen would receive the RGS Founder's Gold Medal thanks in great part to Freya's compliments. As for Sydney Cockerell, who was just as close to Gertrude as he was to her, Freya had written him the moment she was tucked into bed in the Aden Hospital. Things had not gone well, she told her old admirer. Gertrude had "a pedagogic mind not suited to the carelessness of Arabia and wanted to run us on Anglo-Egyptian lines, an effort I was determined to resist: she was very unkind, and I did not wait for seventy times seven before slapping back!"[30] Then she invited him to Asolo to talk about it.

Her old friend seemed sympathetic. Always a bit of a gossip and a dedicated meddler, he was amused by the peccadilloes of his acquaintances, and this dustup among three professional women was not without its diverting aspects. Now seventy-one, retired and with time on his hands, he accepted quickly and went off to stay with Freya and her mother in Italy. The visit was a great success. He laughed at Freya's accounts of her trials with her companions, appreciated the attentions he received from both Freya and her handsome mother, and returned to London ready to take on numbers of small chores, calling himself Freya's "faithful old Secretary" and her "decrepit admirer."[31] A self-professed busybody, Cockerell liked to be in the middle of things; it was never, however, to promote discord but rather out of a sincere desire to assuage it. So he cautioned Freya about the dangers inherent in her suggested approach to the book.

"I think that any venom at all, however little, will do you harm," he wrote when he was back home in Kew. "I know you to be too fastidious an artist to allow your work to be disfigured. . . . If you put [venom] in for your own present satisfaction you will end by taking it all out. It is said that [the American painter John Singer] Sargent had a screen in his studio, behind which he retired at intervals to put out his tongue and clench his fists at his opulent sitters. Having relieved his feelings he returned to his work with a smile. This is how you will behave. Your feelings will have been relieved and neither you nor anyone else will be a penny the worse."[32]

Freya received his comments in silence, wrote back of other things, and continued working on her version of the book. She was prepared to fight back hard. It was as if she fought to keep herself intact, as if making any admissions would challenge the integrity of her very essence. Observant as Freya could be about the behavior of others, she showed herself increasingly willing to ignore unpleasant truths about herself. It was so much nicer just to pretend things were as she wished them to be, and after all, in this lonely world wasn't she her own best advocate and defender?

Cockerell kept Freya in touch with events in London throughout the summer, interspersing his news with accounts of dinners with celebrated friends like George Bernard Shaw, the poet Siegfried Sassoon, the explorer Francis Younghusband, or their mutual friend the archaeologist Leonard Woolley. He praised her for two articles that had recently appeared in *The Times*, noting that the piece on Harold Ingrams had been very timely and well-received. He added that Ingrams had lectured at the RGS and that Gertrude had spoken there as well, "very sincerely and unaffectedly and alluded to no feuds between the turbulent tribes of Thompsoni and Starki. I heard talk all around me of your Times article and several powerful looking women were gazed at intently in the hope that they might prove to be the writer of them! There was also the usual speculation as to your nationality. Your old secretary was mum."[33]

In the meantime Freya doggedly pursued her retributory thesis. At one point feeling a little more optimistic about how her "appalling book" was going, she wrote Jock wickedly: "I must say it is getting to be rather fun—though probably unprintable. I am getting quite fond of my villainess, as one always does. She is a gem."[34]

Her mother and Herbert Young, clearly partisan, had read the draft and found Freya's approach lively and unobjectionable. Several other friends also read the work in progress and approved, relishing the unflattering portrait of the archaeologist. But combined objections beamed to Asolo from Cockerell and Jock Murray in London began to take their toll. From Freya they received querulous letters declaring she had had a headache for fifty days. By the end of July, insisting that she could not continue, that she *must* drop the book entirely for two months, she fled to Partenkirchen for a rest cure.

Nevertheless, she was obliged to struggle on with her foreword to the book of Hadhramaut photographs, to be called *Seen in the Hadhramaut*. Jock wanted it to come out that year and was taking issue with Freya's approach on this piece of writing as well. They were getting nowhere. All the anger Freya felt toward Gertrude had emerged as an angry diatribe against Western gadgets and ideas, which she claimed undermined the ancient character of the Yemeni people. They would be "Woolworthed" into uniformity, she raved in the latest draft she sent Jock. The West came into a country, was her argument, unaware of the harm it was doing, not to *give* but to take away, making the inhabitants dissatisfied with what they were but not taking the trouble to guide them "through the labyrinth of what they would become." It was like a man, she said, leaving a bottle of prussic acid around "promiscuously among the ignorant."[35] It was as if she alone were ready to understand and appreciate the value of these old societies.

By now in desperation Jock was relying on Cockerell to negotiate the wild shoals of Freya's indignation, and the two were regularly lunching to discuss how far they should let her go. Again Cockerell came to the rescue, calming her with reason. "I am not sure that we can legitimately withhold modern inventions and amenities from backward communities unless we are so much in earnest as to be prepared to go without them ourselves," he wrote.[36] He also warned her against upsetting the Ingramses with too severe an indictment of their modernizing efforts in the Hadhramaut. Eventually, grudgingly, Freya made the emendations. Before the year 1938 was over *Seen in the Hadhramaut* appeared, dedicated to Viscount Wakefield of Hythe, to a general round of applause for being the first such pictorial portrayal of this remote area.

But the struggle over *A Winter in Arabia* would continue for nearly two more years, as Europe staggered from one blow to the next. Hitler's armies crashed into Czechoslovakia, and Mussolini seized Albania. When at the end of July 1939, just weeks before the start of the Second World War, Cockerell received yet another draft and saw that Freya had not modified her description of Gertrude, he did not pull his punches:

> Your references to her are undignified, ill-natured, and in questionable taste—quite unworthy of anyone so perfect in most respects as yourself, and calculated therefore to tarnish your reputation.
>
> It might easily have been foreseen, and it was foreseen by me, that two admirable women so differently constructed as GCT and yourself would be oil and water in cramped and uncomfortable quarters under the strain of heat, glare, dirt, smells, noise, illness and mosquitoes. I am told that Arctic explorers similarly get on each others' nerves.
>
> [Gertrude] has never breathed to me a syllable against you, knowing you to be my friend. But I can well imagine that if she

were writing a book, and chose to bring you into it, she could find
some traits and peculiarities to dwell upon that irritated and even
exasperated her. Such little things suffice. Does not Dickens
remark somewhere that the Romans must have annoyed other
people very much with their noses?

There now, that is how I feel about it and how a great many
other people are bound to feel. I expect you will condemn me in
your mind (if not on paper) as an obstinate and fussy old prig,
quite unsuitable for secretarial duties. But then you knew quite
well the sort of thing I should say, so why send me the stuff and
ask my opinion if you don't want to listen? I give you permission
when you write a chapter on secretaries to introduce all the venom
you please! Yours affectionately, SC.[37]

Freya destroyed the letter—it is not among her effects although it was
her habit to keep everything that Cockerell wrote. But at least she
responded: "You are a dear friend. I don't think you are judging from a
quite abstract viewpoint, but it [is] impossible to do so and no one really
can judge of the thing who knows the people."[38]

Clearly relieved but still pursuing his theme, Cockerell wrote back:

I honestly believe that what I wrote to you on 30 July was dic-
tated mainly by a jealous regard for your reputation. It seems to
me that in this matter your usually exquisite perceptions have got
out of focus, so that you cannot see that the GCT motif is as inju-
rious to your book as a maggot in a ripe pear. Tolstoy said to me:
"If you want to influence others, do it by your personal example."
Your personal example in Arabia has been like Doughty's. You
have won the confidence and affection of those you travelled with
and dwelt amongst. This is manifest to the reader—and is the best
possible lesson—you need no foil to drive it home. Think how
hateful it would be if Doughty had been accompanied by some
intolerant Englishman. Had this actually been the case he would
have kept it out of his narrative. He was too great an artist to
allow such a thing to come between his readers and his main
theme—which was, like yours, Arabia and its inhabitants.[39]

Advice administered with so many graceful spoonfuls of sugar was not
difficult to take. More than two years after Freya had written her first
draft, after a new global conflict had begun and she was back in Aden for
a third time working for the British Ministry of Information, she finally

capitulated to the demands of Cockerell and Jock—to whom she had once raged: "Not God Almighty could I let loose with scissors in my book!"[40] Worn out by the protracted dispute as well as happily distracted and deeply involved in war work, Freya let Jock pull the barbs from Gertrude's lacerated character and publish an acceptable—to his lights—book. She wrote him: "I feel so unhappy about my book and rather wish it were suppressed: so many things and proportions have altered. Anyway, I am glad, I *may* tell you, that you are pruning away all the unkind pieces, for I feel now that you and Sydney were quite right [about] the Archeologist. . . . I should not like really to be unkind to her when either of us *might* be blown up at any time!"[41]

And so the painful saga ended. *A Winter in Arabia* was finally published in 1940, with a preface by no less a figure than Sir Kinahan Cornwallis, soon to be sent as ambassador to Iraq, where he would see Baghdad through the difficult days of an Arab revolt against British authority. He enthusiastically endorsed both the author and her thesis: "The average Englishman is not blessed," Sir Kinahan opined, "with an exaggerated sense of imagination in his dealings with other races, but it is to be hoped that all who read Miss Stark's pages will learn the difference between the right way and the wrong, and profit thereby." As for the Ingramses, they had the gratification of seeing the book dedicated to them.

. . .

There is a postscript to this story.

Little did Freya know that the wily old scholar, ever meticulous, with literary history always in mind, had preserved drafts of his letters. It was almost as if he anticipated that after his death someone would write about the feud, and he wanted his role in it clearly recorded. Nor could Freya suspect that he would show the letters to Gertrude, who was deeply offended when *A Winter in Arabia* came out, even with its emendations. Presumably Cockerell hastened to Gertrude not just to ensure that he stayed on good terms with both women but also in an effort to heal the breach. He wanted to show her evidence that Freya actually felt contrite.

After Cockerell showed Gertrude these drafts, she wrote back that she had heard that "F.S. was maliciously reading choice bits from her m.s. about me to her friends . . . about the cheapest form of amusement I had ever heard of, and the nastiest. But now, from what you say in your last letter, I think perhaps she did not really stoop as low as that. And I will make amends by not any longer believing she did."[42]

Gertrude went on to cap a distinguished career by election to the British Academy. In 1953 she received the Royal Asiatic Society's Burton

Medal for "eminent services in Oriental exploration and research," which did much, she told friends, to compensate for the miseries of the Hadhramaut. Elinor Gardner became a fellow of Lady Margaret Hall, Oxford, and, while she did not write a book, a collection of her letters relating to this trip were placed in the archives of the Royal Geographical Society. The women assiduously avoided bumping into one another, though Cockerell remained on the best of terms with both Freya and Gertrude.

Chapter Fourteen

London Prepares
for War

> *There are few sorrows through which a new dress or hat will not send a little gleam of hope, however fugitive.*
>
> —Beyond Euphrates

*I*n the fall of 1938 Freya was back in Asolo after her rest cure in Austria, uneasy over so many signs pointing to war. The German Reich had annexed the country in March and now focused its voracious appetite for lebensraum on the Czechoslovak Republic, the one remaining democratic outpost in Central Europe. Surrounded on three sides by the militarist new Germany, with the leaders of France and Britain pressing them for concessions to avoid war, the Czechs called up four hundred thousand men to protect their borders. Other countries were also mobilizing. The French had summoned their reservists, putting a total of a million men in arms, while Mussolini was making alliances with a corrupt Yugoslav government. Seemingly Great Britain alone refused to face the dreadful reality of imminent war and was doing virtually nothing to prepare itself. Instead, in mid-September Prime Minister Neville Chamberlain flew to Germany to confer with the German chancellor at his hideaway at Berchtesgaden on what could be done to avoid a second bloody conflict in barely a generation.

In Asolo, her introduction to the picture book finished but still wrestling with the travel book, Freya joined Flora and Herbert Young in gloomily following developments. It seemed impossible that Europe could avoid war, but if it came Freya wanted to go immediately to England to volunteer her services. Flora and Herbert, now seventy-seven and eighty-seven respectively, feeling themselves too old to face the upheaval if they didn't absolutely have to, decided to see what happened before abandoning their beloved home. English and American friends had been slipping away all summer as Mussolini staged military pageants to get the Italians in the proper frame of mind. Because Asolo was so small and Fascists were everywhere, Freya, Flora, and Herbert feared their mail was being read, and they arranged for Lady Gwendolen Iveagh to send them a coded signal when she reached England and had a chance to consult with her brother-in-law Lord Halifax. Olga was the code word they decided would signify "peace."

In the last week of September, Chamberlain returned from a second futile meeting with Hitler, at Godesberg. In his briefcase were still more of the dictator's ultimatums, but to these he felt he could not submit despite his wish to do almost anything to avoid war. The despairing Czechs ordered full mobilization, and the world was certain the awful moment was at hand. From England came Lady Iveagh's telegram: "Olga dying." Those in Asolo's foreign community who had not already done so left immediately. Freya hastily gathered her belongings and with her little lizard boarded the train for England, joining the streams of panicked travelers rushing home—or into exile.

She stopped in Paris and found it strangely empty. Now that she had some cash, war or no war, Freya was determined to get a little something from the couture houses. On September 29, while she was ordering a spectacular hat of ostrich feathers that was sure to put, she thought dreamily, "a cold glitter" in the eyes of other women,[1] Chamberlain was in Munich, caving in to a smirking Führer in the gravely mistaken view that he was securing "peace in our time." The abandoned Czechs, soon to be annihilated as a free nation, wept at their fate.

For a brief and foolish moment many in England allowed themselves to believe that the crisis had safely passed, that the policy of appeasement had succeeded. When the British prime minister returned to London, crowds surrounded 10 Downing Street and sang "For He's a Jolly Good Fellow." But Freya was sure that Chamberlain had committed a disastrous and dishonorable blunder, that appeasement would never stop Hitler, and that the wider outbreak of hostilities was only a question of time. Yet the celebratory atmosphere in London that winter seemed also unreal. In six months the world would be at war, but for now the city scintillated with all the dazzle of a grand ball.

Initially Freya settled into 7 Airlie Gardens in Kensington as a guest of Margaret Olivier. The combined tension of getting her Royal Geographical Society lecture prepared and dealing with "the appalling book" took its customary toll. She suffered a bout of extremely low blood pressure, an old affliction, while Mrs. Olivier, "an angel of goodness," nursed her, alternately letting her rest, entertaining her friends, and never, never mentioning Viva Jeyes's diamonds.[2] Instead, now that Viva was gone, Margaret slipped gently into the role of looking after Freya when she came to England, and Freya would regard the Oliviers as a second family. Margaret's daughter and her granddaughter, inheriting the lovely house in turn, continued the hospitable tradition to the end of Freya's long life.

The winter of 1938 was a glorious season of friends outdoing themselves to entertain the celebrated traveler. Freya was feted, discussed, and raved about. Newspapers, radio broadcasters, and even brand-new television wanted a piece of her time and paid her for it—she always gave good value. To one dinner after the next she floated off swathed in "yards and yards of tulle,"[3] in a cloud of expensive perfume, with one of Viva Jeyes's diamond pins sparkling in her hair. It only added to her flamboyant reputation that Himyar often came with her. She draped the lizard around her neck or kept him warm under her jacket and bought violets for him at a shilling a day. She had fashioned a tiny harness for him to wear, and weekend hostesses rushed to see that he got hot-water bottles and heating lamps. Their households would be thrown into confusion when he escaped, only to have him turn up in unexpected places like the kitchen flue.

Freya fretted about Himyar; she often returned home to find him nearly strangled in his harness and felt guilty at having left him. She confided to friends that it was remarkable that a creature so small and ugly could deal so gallantly with such a strange and unfriendly world. No one, thought Freya to herself, could understand better than she.

As the wounds from the Caton-Thompson episode healed, she breathed a sigh of relief that apparently no negative fallout was going to make life unpleasant. She could preen in her applause, even though the struggle with the book and the pressure of her impending lecture kept her popping in and out of bed. Nothing detained her, however, from maintaining a busy schedule of seeing new friends like Vita Sackville-West and her husband, the diplomat Harold Nicolson, who agreed with Freya that Chamberlain's appeasement policy was a terrible mistake. Many people she met at this time became lifetime friends, like the travelers Ella Maillart and Peter Fleming; his brother Ian, who created the James Bond novels; Fitzroy Maclean, the writer; Elizabeth Monroe, the Middle East specialist; Sir Charles Bell, who traveled among the Tibetans; the superintellectual Huxley clan; and Thomas Boase, the Oxford art historian. She saw Stewart Perowne, brought to London by the Colonial Office to learn radio broadcasting in the event of war; the two shared any number of friends.

There were lunches, teas, and dinners with the authors Rose Macaulay ("so bitter"), Virginia Woolf ("a beautiful, ascetic, dreamy face"), and Max Beerbohm ("just like his books, the most charming adjectives popping out of his mouth").[4] People could entice guests to dinner by promising that Freya Stark would be there. Aristocrats invited her to their stately houses. She stayed with Sir Henry and Lady Angela Hoare of Stourhead and the David Cecils of Hatfield House, where Henry VIII's young daughter Elizabeth had survived her dangerous youth to become Britain's greatest queen.

Freya and the Arabist and former political officer Frank Balfour hit it off immediately. He was the nephew of Lord Balfour, whose famous 1917 declaration promising British support for a Jewish National Homeland was now causing such difficulties for the British in Palestine. Frank Balfour, like Freya, was very pro-Arab and confided to her that his uncle "must have been dotty" to have endorsed the policy he did.[5]

Anxious to make her own views known, Freya supported a Palestine refugee aid organization and sprang at any chance to advise the government. Lord Halifax, now foreign secretary, having been helpful to her more than once and respecting her abilities, called her to his office to talk about Yemen, and she warned him of the strong Italian presence there. With Sir Sydney Cockerell she also called on Lord Stanley Baldwin, the former prime minister. Much as Baldwin impressed her, he also amazed her. The statesman seemed taken aback when Freya remarked that Italy was preparing for war. "War? War with whom? Nobody wants war," drawled the man who could easily have been the country's next leader. Freya concluded that while Baldwin might have integrity he lacked "knowledge about the outer world . . . younger men is what we need."[6]

An increasingly self-confident Freya, flirtatious, feminine, and fashionably turned out, threw herself into muscular arguments with establishment policy makers. Their company, it was now clear to her, was far preferable to that of their wives. Her experience with Gertrude and Elinor had confirmed that men were much nicer and far less critical, and Freya thirsted for their attention. Indeed, though she tried to appear modest and unassuming, more than ever she strove to use her formidable intelligence to keep at the front of the pack. Her genuine passion for the beautiful and expensive clothes she now ordered from Paris reflected in part her wish to make a dramatic entrance. If she couldn't be beautiful, at least she could be the most fascinating woman in the room. Her earlier insecurities and shyness were being fast buried under a solid sense of her own importance—an exhilarating feeling that even she recognized might be a little dangerous.

Freya was startled but not completely displeased at one dinner party when the aging authoress Elinor Glyn fixed her with a piercing stare and declared that inside her diminutive self there lurked "a man, a young man pure and enthusiastic . . . caged in a woman's body."[7] Evidently the actress had glimpsed the masculine element in Freya's nature, the tough, competitive drive that could be ruthless. To most, however, she was thoroughly female, a spellbinder as skilled as any professional actress. As for Freya, she sensed herself ready to perform on an ever more challenging stage.

. . .

On the evening of November 28, 1938, the Royal Geographical Society was packed with a glittering array of lords and ladies, scholars, and men of great reputation, in all some eight hundred, including the dean of Westminster Abbey; Mrs. Neville Chamberlain; Lord and Lady Iveagh and her sister Lady Halifax; Lord Allenby's widow (Field Marshal Lord Allenby having died in May 1936); various Huxleys, Nicolsons, and Balfours; and finally of course both Jock Murray and Sir Sydney Cockerell. Neither Gertrude nor Elinor was there. The RGS chairman, Admiral Goodenough, by now Freya's ardent admirer, opened the meeting with lavish praise for the famous explorer, who sat serenely in an elegant Paris gown, waiting to be introduced.

For more than an hour, Freya recounted the challenges and accomplishments of the Wakefield Expedition, which she, no archaeologist herself, she noted modestly, had enjoyed the great privilege of leading through the heat and rigors of Yemen. Their successes belonged to the tireless labors of her colleagues, but she had been most fortunate, and would have to admit rather proud, to find at the end of their journey the lost port of Cana. When she finished the audience expelled a long communal sigh, followed by thunderous applause. Lord Wakefield rose to intone: "I do not know that I have listened to a lecture that has gripped my heart and imagination more than that to which we have listened tonight." Her work—which, he did not have to add, had been possible thanks to his support—had rendered "a great service to the cause of Civilization." Stewart Perowne was next: "I have seen Miss Stark on the job, and I have heard what those among whom she and I lived thought of her. I assure you that it halved the burden of one's task to be able to say, when criticized as a minion of the British Government: 'But there *is* Miss Stark.' "[8]

For Freya perhaps the greatest compliment was from Lady Violet Leconfield, the tall, handsome, and powerful mistress of Petworth, one of Britain's greatest houses, where Freya had recently enjoyed her first encounter with the exalted habits of the very privileged. Lady Leconfield had been a fellow of the RGS for years, and it was thrilling to have this awesome dowager tell her assembled social set that Freya was clearly one of "the greatest of living travelers."[9] Freya felt clasped to the bosom of the aristocracy.

The newspapers wrote it up. Everyone marveled that so slight a creature could have braved so much—apparently with "all the ease" of "a saunter over Dartmoor."[10] Sir Leonard and Lady Woolley gave her the use of their house and staff at 12 Royal Avenue, in Chelsea, while they went to India for the winter, so Freya decided to do a bit of entertaining of her own. With the pressure of the lecture off and a spate of articles out of the way, all her usual symptoms of illness vanished, and she plunged into the business of entertainment with gusto. Only once did she remember to have dinner with Venetia. It was "all right," she wrote her mother afterward, "but no particular pleasure. She has had Anton Besse to stay this year and she always goes to Jock for news of me: I cannot feel real friendship again. But it is as well to patch it up with a decent outwardness."[11]

. . .

Nobody was more excited by Freya's laurels than her mother. Now that her daughter was certifiably successful—if not in the way that Flora had originally hoped—she could view Freya's triumphs as an extension of herself. The weight of power at last was shifting in Freya's favor as Flora did her best to serve. "My little girlie," she wrote happily, sending along a muff, "*all* through your own efforts—and that is a consolation to me, who have done *nothing*." She told Freya of the complimentary letters she received from friends: "It is so nice to feel that these nice people really love you." In an anxious postscript, however, she cautioned her triumphant child to avoid the dangers of "wit with a bite." People too clever are admired, she said, but "they can also be feared and finally avoided."[12]

But Freya seemed in no danger of being avoided. The earl of Iveagh and his generous wife, Gwendolen, continued to be good to her, entertaining her at Kenwood, their glorious eighteenth-century Robert Adam mansion on Hampstead Heath. They even introduced her to a member of the Royal Family, Princess Alice, Countess of Athlone, the granddaughter

Freya always regretted that she had not been born a beauty, but she was endowed with enormous charm, courage, and energy; she was a fascinator who knew how to cast a spell over any room. This photograph was taken in 1940, when Freya was forty-seven.

of Queen Victoria and cousin of George VI. Her Royal Highness had recently crossed Saudi Arabia, the first such visit by European royalty, and been enormously impressed by Ibn Saud, the tall, handsome warrior-king. Freya was even more impressed by Princess Alice. In all her life Freya would never cease to be awed by the pageantry associated with monarchy. As one embarrassed godson reported years later, in a royal presence Freya "went to her knees."[13]

The Iveaghs also included her in all the festivities surrounding the marriage of their twenty-year-old daughter, Lady Patricia Guinness, to Alan Lennox-Boyd, an extremely promising young man, a friend of Winston Churchill and a future cabinet minister. Because Lord Iveagh was the enormously wealthy chairman of Arthur Guinness & Co., the wedding, held at the Iveaghs' country estate in Suffolk, was a major social event. Freya enjoyed every minute—not least because her new admirer Stewart Perowne, thirty-seven, and the bridegroom's attractive, unmarried brother, Donald Lennox-Boyd, thirty-two, swept her into their orbit of attractive officers. Somehow it did not seem to matter that Freya was about to turn forty-six. In London they became a merry threesome. If her companions were a touch arch, a mite epicene, she resolutely did not notice. Badinage was their style, and Freya excelled at giving as good as she got. As far as she knew, Donald was an officer in the Scots Greys. She was not aware that he was actually an intelligence officer. He and Stewart told her that if war came she should sign up for work with the Ministry of Information—but in the meantime they gaily discussed plans for a reverse trip together north to south along the incense route. It all seemed wonderfully fun—and when Freya departed at the end of February, Donald was calling her his "Valentine."[14] After a last lecture before the Royal Central Asia Society, where Harry St. John Philby asked her tough but not unfriendly questions, she boarded the Simplon Express for Italy and home.

. . .

To her credit, Freya had not been as confident in London's sophisticated society as she had tried to seem. As she wrote Cockerell, she felt a bit like Cinderella, for whom "the clock has struck twelve." She reflected that "for the first time in my life I have had a swim in the Social World, and begun to find my feet among its reefs and pleasant places, and found that it is a good world too if one can bear in mind to live there *sans peur et sans reproche*—fear of other people or reproach from oneself."[15] It had frightened her a little with its overwhelming glamour, and she was wise enough to suspect it.

Harsh reality greeted her return. Italy was well along in its preparations for war. Flora was away in America with the Beaches, who had sent her the fare for a visit, so to Freya fell the sad task of hiding silver and asking friends to keep household valuables in case they were forced to evacuate. Suddenly her spirits took a free fall. Nothing had really changed: she was still unwedded, alone, with little money—and she would probably be forced into exile. The manuscript of the book that she now always referred to as "appalling," that she had fled from the previous summer and neglected during the frenzied London winter, *had* to be finished, somehow. She was still being prodded by Jock and Sydney Cockerell. Above all else, to make life seem insupportably dreary, little Himyar had died in the freezing north some weeks before. She had written her mother at the time: "I can't think or speak of him without crying. It is absurd for so tiny a creature—but I think he and I were alike in lots of ways, both rather small and lonely in our hearts. It may be ridiculous to care so much, but after all there is less difference between us and a lizard than between us and God and we expect *Him* to feel an interest."[16]

But who was there to *really* take an interest in Freya?

Seeking movement as an antidote for depression, in the middle of March she departed for Syria with a copy of William of Tyre* in her pocket to see what could be made of a tour of Crusader castles. T. E. Lawrence and Gertrude Bell had both written about these fortresses. In fact Lawrence's survey, done for his Oxford bachelor of arts thesis, is still regarded as one of the most authoritative investigations ever undertaken. It was a worthy subject for anyone who considered herself a historiographer and expert on Arabs—and Freya tried to approach the undertaking with enthusiasm, despite her malaise.

When she reached Hama she suffered a shock that further depressed her: A telegram was waiting from Jock announcing that he was engaged. Freya not only had never met his intended, but had not even heard Jock mention Diana, even though Freya and Jock had spent her last weekend in London together. She felt angry and betrayed. The fact that the world was facing almost certain war and young people seemed to be throwing themselves into marriage made her feel old and neglected. She could barely rally herself to send the happy couple a return telegram of congratulations and suggested in following letters that Jock must be too busy with his bride to give *her* book the attention it required.[17] Jock, understanding the source of her jealousy, tried to placate her with a long philosophical letter.

---

* Archbishop William of Tyre (circa 1130–1185) wrote a famous chronicle, *The History of Deeds Done Beyond the Sea,* a detailed account of the Crusades and Latin Kingdom of Jerusalem, 1095–1184. He also wrote a history of Mohammed's successors, unfortunately now lost.

*Stewart Perowne, British colonial officer in Baghdad
and Yemen, often wore Arab headdress. The son and
grandson of bishops, Perowne captured Freya's interest
from the moment they first met in Aden in 1935.*

Not long afterward, in mid-April, a worse blow came. Having scrambled through rocky fastnesses above the green Orontes Valley searching for Assassins' castles, Freya arrived in Aleppo to give herself a bit of luxury at the Baron Hotel, one of the very few in Syria that offered European plumbing.* There she found a letter from Stewart Perowne containing the awful news that Donald Lennox-Boyd had been murdered in Berlin in mysterious circumstances. Only the week before, Donald had written an affectionate letter addressing Freya as "My dear Valentine."[18] Alone in her hotel, she grieved and brooded, and gave in to dangerous fantasy: Hadn't Donald been in love with her? Hadn't she just lost the love of her life? Miserably she wrote Sydney Cockerell to find out what he could about the murder.

Over time Freya would convince herself that Donald and she had been lovers and that they'd intended to marry. She not only asserted this fantasy to friends as if it were fact but published it in her memoirs after the war. Donald's nephew, Simon Lennox-Boyd, said it was a preposterous claim, and he had been amazed when Freya declared it to him years later, her eyes misting with tears. "It was well-established that my uncle was homosexual," he stated firmly in an interview in 1990. He added: "His remains were brought home from Germany by my mother, his ashes in a jar. The family never knew exactly how he died, whether he was shot or poisoned, but they learned that he had been in intelligence work." Adding that the family also learned that Donald had been arrested by the Nazis in a gay bar, Lord Boyd pointed out that Freya never showed anyone in the family the letter supposedly containing Donald's marriage proposal, nor does this letter exist in the Austin archives. Instead, the sad truth is that Donald Lennox-Boyd was an outstandingly attractive, wealthy, and socially connected officer on whom Freya focused her need to think of herself as loved and courted—to be *married*. Just as Elinor Gardner had perceived, Freya was increasingly unable to disentangle what was real from what she desired to be real. For Freya fantasy was like a nomad's tent, offering shelter from hostile elements over which she had no control when clouds from a hurtful world obscured her Pleiadic beacon.

By now the list of damaged relationships in Freya's life had grown long. She had lost Guido; dropped Viva Jeyes; lost Vyvyan Holt, Venetia, and Anton; and her two archaeologist friends were now enemies. Was she unable to sustain an intimate bond? Was the fault hers, or theirs? Did

* The Baron Hotel still exists, although it is no longer luxurious and its plumbing is no longer modern, as the author discovered when staying there on a visit in 1998. Even so, it is marvelously atmospheric, and its guestbook is a wonder of names, including Freya Stark, T. E. Lawrence (who left without paying his bill), Lord Allenby, King Faisal, Harry St. John Philby—to name just a few.

she, at some level, wish to avoid getting too close to anyone, conducting relationships by correspondence? Is that why she so loved to travel— because it was easier to manage a relationship when there was distance in between? Contemplating this trail of broken friendships must have frightened her profoundly, increasing the loneliness that dogged Freya despite her efforts to accept separations with equanimity, as merely "a reluctance to depart from familiar things."[19] Her genius was her rich imagination, and as Antonin Besse had seen, obstacles in her path were brushed aside and any truth unacceptable to her powerful will was suppressed, altered, or otherwise shaped into more bearable contours. Freya's need for unqualified admiration was becoming insatiable.

Lonely and forlorn, Freya continued her search of ruins along the Orontes for another week, until she decided, in what had become a characteristic reaction to difficulty, that she should return to Aleppo and check into the hospital there run by French nuns. They gave her tisanes, poultices, and sympathy for just under ten shillings a day while she wrote desolate and self-pitying letters to her mother, Herbert Young, and Sydney Cockerell, and cheered herself with the cockeyed notion of bringing back to Asolo a young Nosairi guide who was exceptionally good-looking and had proved adept at washing her underthings, bringing her tea in the morning, and making her feel that he would throw himself on a scimitar for her if necessary.*

Isa, "Jesus" in Arabic, seemed to think the idea of a career change as appealing as Freya, who was soon back in Asolo cajoling the highest authorities in London to help get him a work permit. It seemed unlikely that an Arab servant would be suited to life in a tiny north Italian town, but then neither had a lizard from Yemen been a usual choice as a pet.

In July, Freya was back at the Villa Freia in a glum state of mind. Even the prospect of her trip with Stewart Perowne down the incense route seemed insufficiently consoling. Better was the beginning of a lifelong friendship with Bernard Berenson, the celebrated art connoisseur, who lived just outside Florence in a lovely villa, I Tatti. Freya received the first of many letters from him on August 20, 1939: "I am eager," wrote the delicate old aesthete, "to see more of you, a great deal more, to explore the

---

* Nosairis, known today as Alawites, or Alawis, because they believe that Mohammed's son-in-law Ali was an emanation of Allah, belong to an obscure and very secret sect that, like the Druze, was an offshoot of Shi'ism. Orthodox Sunnis do not even consider them Muslim; they were generally among the poorest groups in Syria and are chiefly to be found in the Latakia area. Their doctrine is thought to combine Babylonian star worship with elements from Isma'il-ism and Christian Gnosticism. The Alawites have, however, acquired considerable respectability and a new measure of prosperity since Hafiz al-Assad, an Alawite, became Syria's strongman.

Pacific of your heart."[20] These were the sorts of sentiments that Freya preferred to hear.

By the end of August she had arrived in London to find that Stewart had already been summoned to Aden, while Vyvyan Holt and other friends in the military waited for their postings. The giddy metropolis of the previous winter was tense, full of sandbags, khaki uniforms, and people carrying gas masks, while trenches were being dug in London's beautiful parks. Hospitals readied for the casualties expected from Hitler's first air raids.

Then, on September 1 banner headlines blazed on every newsstand. Germany had attacked Poland, leaving Britain and France no option: two days later they declared war. The long months of uncertainty were over. Abruptly the mood and tempo of the city changed completely and Freya's with it. There was a summons from the Colonial Office asking her to join the new Ministry of Information being organized under the direction of Professor L. F. Rushbrook Williams. Freya found herself a "South Arab" expert at a salary of six hundred pounds and—she noted with satisfaction—the only woman in the group. In a matter of days she was sharing a table with Sir Kinahan Cornwallis, the lanky, husky-voiced, blue-eyed veteran of Arab affairs and (some said) lover of Gertrude Bell who had escorted Emir Faisal to Iraq to take his throne in 1921 and stayed on as adviser until 1935.*

Attracted to Cornwallis, Freya settled down to make herself useful, and they quickly became friends. It occurred to her that it might be ever so nice if Sir Kinahan wrote a foreword to her book, completely finished at last and accepted by Jock, and it was not long before he consented to do so.

The government recognized that Freya had plenty of skills; not only was she intimately acquainted with many areas of the Middle East and spoke a number of Arabic dialects but she was also fluent in Italian, German, and French, understood Persian, and even had a smattering of Greek. The Home Office was concerned with how the Arabs would react in the coming conflict. There was no guarantee that the Middle East would stay neutral; Germany and Italy were already hard at work, with their agents fanning out through Turkey and Iraq, as well as west through Egypt into the Maghreb. Freya had warned Lord Halifax that there was a large Italian presence in Yemen. Now she found herself being invited by Malcolm MacDonald, the colonial secretary, to come for a chat.

It was a fine exchange. In perfect harmony the traveler and the cabinet

---

* There was a considerable difference in age between Sir Kinahan and Gertrude Bell. Even so, according to the recent biography of Bell by Janet Wallach, Bell fell in love with him, but her passion remained unrequited, a probable contributing element to the depression that led to her suicide.

minister discussed the need for building a good postwar foundation for a democratic Arab world that would, of course, be happily disposed to British commercial interests. Freya even suggested that the British develop an Arabian school after the war in the spirit of the American missionaries whose splendid American University in Beirut was everyone's model. They agreed that there could be no hope of enlisting Arab sympathy if strong steps were not taken to curb Jewish emigration into Palestine, as MacDonald, its chief author, urged in the recently issued white paper, a stunning reversal of previous British policy. The government, MacDonald assured Freya, intended to stand firm against any more "Zionist nonsense."[21]

This "Zionist nonsense" was none other than the age-old drive of Jews to return to Eretz Israel, the land of their Old Testament forefathers. The previous decade had seen ever-increasing clashes between the arriving Jews and the Arabs who had called Palestine home for the past two thousand years. Even before the Balfour Declaration endorsing a Jewish National Home was issued in 1917, British policy had supported the Zionist drive. As Arab opposition grew more intense, the British administrators had put it down violently, cooperating with the Haganah or Jewish defense force, which they allowed to arm itself, unlike the Palestinians, for whom bearing arms was illegal. Between 1937 and 1939 many Arabs were hanged, were killed by British troops in acts of unofficial retribution, or saw their houses dynamited if they were suspected of harboring guerrillas. But now, anxious to cultivate Arab sympathy, the British declared their intention to cap Jewish immigration at half a million and guarantee achievement of an Arab Palestine in ten years.

When Freya left the secretary's office, she was optimistic. She had a role to play in a just war defending the country with which she passionately identified. Stewart Perowne had asked for her assistance in Aden, where he was also working for the Ministry of Information, and she had accepted the reassignment with pleasure and anticipation. At her request the ministry gave her three films on English life to take in her suitcase. On October 8, her heart filled with emotion as she bade good-bye to friends and the anxious city she might not see again, Freya began a journey across nine frontiers to take her stand for democracy in southern Arabia.

PART FOUR

THE *Warrior* NOMAD

*I wanted space, distance, history and danger,
and I was interested in the living world.*

—THE COAST OF INCENSE

CHAPTER FIFTEEN

A Recruit in Yemen

> *The art of smuggling should not be despised. It is less expensive than war and . . . has a spice of danger of its own.*
>
> —TRAVELLER'S PRELUDE

The British had a big job before them—and propaganda was key. From Palestine to Iraq, from Aden across the Red Sea to British Somaliland and up through the Sudan to Egypt, the British Empire was uneasily poised to go to war on soil that belonged to predominantly Muslim peoples, alight with their hot passion for self-rule. They were thoroughly cynical about the machinations of all European powers and had been exploited long enough to become masters at the game of treaties, allegiances, and intrigue. It was the job of the Ministry of Information, together with a number of other quickly constituted intelligence services, to persuade the Arabs to actively support the Allied side—or at least to keep them neutral. At the same time they tried to assess the strengths and intentions of the enemy forces.

To complicate matters Italy had not yet declared itself. For desperate months the Home Office's position was to avoid any measures in the Middle East and Africa that might provoke Mussolini, although to many observers this was a fool's dream because Italy's aggressive intentions were obvious. In the precious interlude before Italy chose sides, England faced the task of gearing up its armies and armaments, which had languished under Chamberlain's appeasement policies. The breadth of the challenge was becoming stunningly apparent: it would fall chiefly to British leadership to coordinate in the Middle East and elsewhere one of the most far-reaching and complex military operations ever conceived, involving armies from different nations—Canada, South Africa, Australia, New Zealand, India, Indochina, and eventually the Free French—speaking different languages and holding to different religious beliefs and cultural values. In the Middle East a highly sophisticated intelligence-gathering apparatus was essential.

In Cairo it was getting started. From various parts of the British Empire came men who knew how to listen and how to whisper. One obviously needed undertaking was to remove the nearly one thousand Germans, many of them Nazis, who lived in Egypt. Fortunately Ali Maher, the Egyptian prime minister, seemed willing to cooperate, so this was done with dispatch, and the lot were quickly incarcerated in two well-guarded schools. For the time being that left large numbers of Italian nationals—businessmen, diplomats, officers, and spies—free to create trouble in the streets of Cairo and Alexandria, but there was nothing to be done about them until Italy threw off its cloak of neutrality.

General Archibald Wavell, the British Middle East commander in chief, believed deeply in clandestine operations. Various units were hastily set up both to counter Fascist influences and to gather intelligence. Directly under Wavell's command were Colonel Walter Cawthorn, a young Australian officer who would head the Middle East Intelligence Center, and an old friend of Wavell, Colonel C. M. Thornhill, a member of the highly secret Special Operations Executive, or SOE. Among the men looking for ingenious ideas were Colonel Iltyd Clayton of Military Intelligence and Reginald Davies, former area representative for the Alexandria Municipality and now the local bureau head for the Ministry of Information. In due course there would be many more agencies engaged in propaganda of one form or another—counterespionage, sabotage, and the like—and they often stumbled over one another. Freya would meet all of these men and work for some directly. She was never affected by their bureaucratic tangles, for as was often said during the war, she should not be interfered with, having friends "in the highest places."

. . .

Freya was tired when she arrived for a brief stopover in Cairo. But as she made her way in a horse-drawn calèche through the racket and bustle of the crowded city, she felt renewed. No sooner had she passed through the bougainvillea and rustling palms around the Metropolitan Hotel and settled herself in her room than bellboys clamored at her door with messages.

There was a pile of party invitations from old Middle East hands—for Cairo's gaiety during the war was to become legendary. She also learned she was being sought by several of the start-up agencies.

All these men were familiar with the influence that Gertrude Bell had had on Middle East policy and were eager to enlist the talent of another female pundit. Before she continued on her way to Aden, Freya had talked with not only Cawthorn (and met his wife, Mary) but Colonel Clayton, Davies, and possibly Thornhill as well. In any case it was agreed that since she felt she should proceed to Aden as planned—and as she had promised Stewart Perowne she would—they could use her for a special mission into the medieval capital of Sana'a in the high Yemen. She would report back to Cawthorn's Middle East Intelligence Center. With the approval of the Ministry of Information, the plan was designed, funding was obtained, and Freya sailed down the Red Sea to Aden.

As the hot winds of Arabia swept over the ship's prow, she mused on the strange and wonderful turns suddenly bringing together all the interests that had fired her imagination as a young woman and were now giving her a chance to serve her country in its moment of peril.

. . .

By the middle of November 1939, Freya was writing happily to Flora and Herbert from Aden: "Stewart tells me that the daily bulletin has a bite in it since I came."[1] Settled into two fusty rented rooms furnished with massive Victorian furniture and photographs of royalty, Freya looked out from her balcony at Aden harbor crowded with British warships. Immediately below was the office that Stewart had set up with an English secretary, various Parsi assistants, and a twenty-three-year-old Arab translator who stayed unruffled and natty in a white suit and silk cravat no matter how frantic the activity Freya and Stewart generated.

Freya was much amused at having the "son of a bishop" as her boss and with admiring eyes watched as he "swooped in and out, long-necked and bald-headed like a young vulture . . . sipping honey even from Government telegrams, embellishing them with Scriptural quotations."[2] Her job was to write pamphlets, occasionally censor incoming films, and turn Reuters newspeak into prose for the radio broadcasts Stewart had trained for the previous winter in London. They both agreed, given the Arabs' love of poetry, that a way to encourage pro-British bravado in noble hearts was to scatter verses from Wordsworth translated into Arabic through their copy—what could be more stirring? These were then beamed across the Red Sea, as well as nearer to home in Aden's central square, near a huge statue of Queen Victoria in

The Imam Yahya's summer palace, an impregnable fortress perched on a massive rock in the Wadi Dhahr outside Sana'a.

In Sana'a, Freya was guided every evening through silent, narrow streets on her way to show her propaganda films to members of the court or privileged others. This recent photograph shows a mansion typically whitewashed with gypsum in the old walled city that the imam's guards locked up every night.

billowing bronze petticoats, where crowds poured from the mosque after evening prayers.

In no time Freya and her boss had settled into a cozy intimacy leavened with much teasing on her part and bossing on his. She relished the settled, almost married feeling of Stewart coming to her balcony every evening for a glass of vermouth and quiet talk before they went out to one of the interminable parties that were an important part of life in this remote outpost. She was growing quite "dependent," she wrote home, and Stewart quite "possessive . . . he *hates* it if I go to a party by myself."[3] Many mornings they met before dawn to ride on the beach under the stars. None of this was lost on Aden's tight little colony, and there was considerable talk about just what sort of relationship Freya and Stewart had.

Antonin Besse, whom Freya had resumed seeing twice a week or so, scrambling in the hills as they had in the past, or riding with Hilda, did not like Stewart, which Freya professed not to understand, although it secretly pleased her. Behind his back she and Stewart called him Sidonia, after a character in *Tancred,* a novel about the Crusades by Queen Victoria's clever prime minister Benjamin Disraeli. Antonin was getting "crochety" but amused Freya when he railed that he couldn't seem to stop making money on the war.

To cap her happiness she had sent for Isa, the handsome Syrian Nosairi servant, who she was confident would wash her unmentionables and keep everything properly pressed. And without telling anyone except those who had to know, she organized the trip to north Yemen she had concocted in Cairo.

· · ·

To venture into the imam's territory was a courageous undertaking. At no point did Freya act without the help and support of Stewart, in whom she confided all but the request of the Cairo agents that she return to Egypt afterward. Ever feminine in her approach, she offered to send her reports through Stewart, giving him carte blanche to rewrite them if he wished or even send them in under his signature—as if everything she did was by his order. Freya was happy to promote Stewart's success. The Aden governor, Sir Bernard Reilly, and Colonel Morice Lake, the two bachelor officials who had served in Aden since before the First World War and had been good to her on her previous trips, were fully informed, as was the much-tried but much-appeased Harold Ingrams, still resident at Mukalla. Since they were officially tied by the Home Office's policy of no provocations to Italy, Freya's trip had to be the friendly visit of the traveler, although in fact her mission was to assess the strength of the Italian influence, discover what if any military help Italy was giving the imam, learn where the imam's personal loyalties lay, and do what she could to counteract the force of Axis propaganda. As she reported to Malcolm MacDonald in London, the trick was to get into the harems "in a quiet way and give a straightening twist to the news."[4]

That Freya gained entrance to northern Yemen was a triumph in itself, because visitors were firmly discouraged and journalists completely unacceptable in a country where the seventy-six-year-old imam was absolute ruler. This fierce tyrant was quite capable of putting anyone who displeased him into his dungeon; he had kept two of his own sons there despite the pleading of their mother, his favorite wife. He was aware, and so were the British, that the Italians would have liked to use his kingdom as a base for air strikes. British and French Somalilands were less than an hour's flight across the Red Sea, while the Anglo-Egyptian Sudan could be made vulnerable a few hours farther on, and then there was Cairo itself. The imam knew the strategic importance of his domain, but because he lacked antiaircraft equipment, there was much to be said for neutrality. The sympathies of his court, however, tended to lie with the Italians, who had long been a presence in Sana'a, whereas the British in the south were regarded with suspicion. If the Italians joined Germany in war, there would be a lot of pressure on the imam to throw North Yemen's lot in with the Axis. Playing for time, he decided to admit the English sightseer.

In February 1940, accompanied by Isa—who was revealing an unexpected grudging side to his character, including *not* liking to wash Freya's unmentionables—as well as a Somali driver, his two helpers, and a Yemeni cook, Freya departed by ship with a movie projector and three films hidden beneath the clothes in her suitcase. Disembarking at Hodeida, on the Red Sea coast, she bantered her way through Yemeni customs, where she assured the guards that what she had was a portable commode. Then her party began the long, lurching climb over sand dunes, torrent beds, and boulders, initially circling south before ascending more than eight thousand feet into the mountains to reach Taiz, the imam's southern capital. The fortress gate was opened by a manacled prisoner, and Freya was greeted by the local governor in an enormous white turban. He told her that his wives were away but she should stay in his empty harem. In the middle of the night she was awakened by the tinkling of a music box being played close to her ear. The governor, it seemed, was sitting by her side in pitch-blackness. Would she like another blanket? he whispered. Trying to breathe calmly, she thanked him but said she just wanted to sleep. For the rest of the night she could not be sure if he was still in the room.

After reaching the ancient walled city of Sana'a at last, Freya stayed two months in the imam's religious fastness, wandering through narrow, unpaved streets, marveling at the vertiginous stone buildings, some more than ten stories high, whose windows and doors were outlined in sparkling white gypsum. Slim, dark-eyed men wearing long white *thobes* and curved daggers swaggered between goats and chickens as female figures floated silently by in black, occasionally revealing a dainty hennaed hand or foot. No music or radios were allowed in the public squares; only those few enjoying royal favor were granted the privilege of a radio to listen to the news from Rome and Berlin. But the imam had long accepted medical missions from both the Italians and the English. The Italians used their hospital as a cover for bringing in technicians with submilitary equipment, and they used their medical staff to infiltrate the court. The English had only two overworked doctors—one of whom was a pacifist—and a tender young internist, whom Freya found "much at sea" in political waters.

In due course the new arrival was invited to tea by the foreign minister's wife, who greeted her swathed from head to toe in veils. Freya lost no time casually mentioning that she had a movie projector, adding demurely that *of course* she would never do *anything* to offend the imam, but perhaps some of the lady's friends would enjoy watching a film or two? As she had hoped, the lady exclaimed that they "*must* see it!" One night Freya was alerted that the entire royal harem was on its way to view her films. Because her male helper was not allowed in the presence of ladies, she had to struggle alone with her ignorance of all things mechanical to set up the projector as wives, daughters, female servants, and princes of the blood surged about her in the darkness. To her vast relief, images finally appeared on the screen. She felt, she later said, like "an amateur at a seance" who tries to summon the Devil and "the Devil appears."[5] Her audience loved the films, gasping at the sight of British warships, booming artillery, and fighter planes roaring from airfields. From then on, night after night, Freya slipped through Sana'a's narrow streets following a veiled guide to another multistoried house protected by a thick, nail-studded door. Strangely enough, the favorite film of most audiences turned out to be one showing grazing sheep and rose-covered English cottages.

Excluded because of her sex from the imam's *majlis,* or weekly reception, Freya sent her cook to listen and report. At every possible opportunity she promoted the British view with members of the court who asked to see her. A prince or sheikh would toss his cloak at one of his wives "as if she were a hatrack"[6] and invite Freya to settle down and give her thoughts. She was a competitive and tireless infighter, loving the thrust and parry of besting the Italians in the sequestered harems, where the game was mostly played, never overlooking a chance to belittle the claims of the other side. Several irate members of the Italian community stopped speaking to her. The question of Palestine, she quickly discovered, was dominant. "Anything to do with it touches them profoundly," she reported back by messenger. "The whole of Yemen is built on religion: the cry of Islam is very strong: and it is a fact that every Yemeni I have spoken to has put Palestine in front even of the question of his own borderland! I have everywhere repeated Mr. MacDonald's assurance that H.M.G. means to stick to the White Paper, and this has had a good effect: but I believe that every effort should be made to circulate anything favorable in the Palestine situation."[7]

It was hard work, and there were moments when she drooped in discouragement. Once an old sayyid spat at her in the street, probably more out of religious impulse than political scruple, but it was unnerving. She wrote: "You can't think how tiring it is to come and push oneself into a strange place where one isn't particularly wanted; to be a sort of monster and have to wear down everybody's prejudice by the mere delicacy of behavior."[8]

But by keeping a keen ear open and asking the right questions at the right moments, Freya was able to send back to Aden details on the whereabouts of arsenals and garrisons, the amount of coffee going to Italy as payment for armaments, and an estimation that between regular and reserve there were about thirty thousand troops in the Yemeni army. The condition of the troops, she reported, was poor because the national habit of chewing *qhat,* a narcotic leaf that reduces appetite and drive, had weakened many men. She also noted that the officer corps was mostly made up of tottering old Turkish officers left over from Ottoman days.

Before Freya left she achieved what she had most hoped for. One evening as she was showing her films, she felt a stirring that convinced her the imam himself had slipped into the room. Feigning innocence and dying to meet the old man, she maneuvered through the dark toward the mysterious figure. Suddenly she was surrounded by a solid wall of retainers, preventing her from getting close to the sacred presence. Even so, when she heard the gasps of amazement over the British military displays, she was confident that she had made her point.

At the end of March it was a relief to leave a place that, for all its exoticism and beauty, she found grim, fanatical, and backward, with "a feeling of secret horror and intrigue."[9] Although the heat in Aden would be unbearable, Freya was eager to be heading back—all the more so when a telegram arrived from Stewart saying that he was down with a fever in the hospital and urging her to return to him. She responded eagerly.

The Foreign Office wired that they were deeply appreciative of Miss

Stark's efforts. When Yemen stayed neutral during the war, Freya's courageous penetration of north Yemen's curtained imamate was given the
credit. Henceforth throughout the war the British government adopted
a policy of sending propaganda films along with any traveling British
official.[10]

. . .

"Stewart treats me as if I were his wife—and he always expects me to be
there, but never tells me the probable programme beforehand," Freya confided in a letter to Sydney Cockerell, who had recently sent her a copy of
his just-published book, *Friends of a Lifetime*. "I keep him in a state of
mild but continuous exasperation: do you think that is a sign of love or
hate? It seems quite pleasant anyway."[11]

Stewart, who had quickly recovered from his illness, was now meeting
Freya nearly every morning to ride or swim or sail. As Aden sweltered and
people struggled to stay awake in the lethargy of the monsoon season,
they worried together about the state of the world or laughed over Isa's
latest outrage, for the once so promising servant had turned out to be a
drunken liability, given to launching into violent tirades about religious
issues and thumping antagonists over the head. Grinning, Stewart said he
was delighted that Freya would have to sack Isa and forfeit the considerable sum she had paid to bring him from Syria.

In pleasant propinquity the two discussed the proprieties of male-
female relations. A current now seemed to thrill through their conversations. Freya coquettishly reminded Stewart of the night in Taiz when she
was alone and the governor crept into her room. As before, she went to
considerable pains to give him the credit for her ideas. She gently prodded
him into promoting the idea of a Volunteer Aden Arab Police Force. "If
we can rouse the feeling of service, we can count on loyalty in difficult
times," she argued.[12] She also urged that the new force include women
wardens because in an attack men would not be allowed into the harems.
London adopted the plan, and news of its inception was broadcast widely.
Stewart, credited with sponsorship, was clapped on the back while Freya
looked on with shining eyes.

Freya could not help having the almost certain conviction that Stewart
was about to propose. He was not like Vyvyan Holt—or Antonin Besse—
whose strength and authority had awed her. Yet as the two of them
hunched over the radio listening to the news that Germany had invaded
Denmark and Norway, or over dinner and a glass of wine, she found herself touched and anxious about him and knew he depended on her. She
caught him looking at her and had an excited sense that he was holding

something back. But days passed and he said nothing. Then the BBC reported the evacuation of Dunkirk. The Besses were in a plane crash that left Antonin encased in a body cast; he never fully recovered from this accident. Freya urged her mother and Herbert Young to leave Italy but sensed they were not getting her letters. Grimly, she decided to draw up her will. "There is only one thing to hold on to really," she wrote Jock. "We shall hold on or *die*. In my heart I have already said goodbye to all things: even to Asolo, though a dull pain comes when I think of my old people in the garden there. I wish they had got away."[13]

Finally, on June 10, 1940, Italy declared war on Great Britain and France. The bombing of Aden began immediately. It had been hard for Freya to endure the slighting remarks of the British about the lack of bravery and capacity of the Italian people, whom she loved and understood, but she never doubted that Mussolini would bring them into war. Stewart, who had not believed Italy would declare, suddenly became irritable and anxious, losing weight and barking at Freya when she went out riding in the middle of an air raid. Unlike Stewart, she found the exploding bombs and thundering guns exhilarating. She was more fascinated than fearful when their office shook to its foundations and wished she were back as a nurse in the field. Impatient to be directly involved, Freya jumped at the chance to work as an interpreter for some recently captured Italian seamen.

The hero of the hour was the captain of the British *Moonstone,* a little trawler with only a gun or two that miraculously shot out the conning tower of an emerging submarine, killing all the officers but one, whom Freya was asked to interrogate in Italian. She suggested she stroll with the young officer along the beach, where they could see British ships that had been hit the night before in a raid and were still smoldering. Probing deftly, she asked enough of the right questions—she who shunned all things mechanical—until she discovered a missing navigational detail that she reported. As a result two enemy submarines were sunk. It was Freya's second major coup—and again a telegram full of praise for Miss Stark arrived from the Foreign Office.

Then Freya was asked to go up to Cairo for a Ministry of Information conference. Neither Stewart nor Harold Ingrams saw any objection, so Freya was soon in a Red Sea convoy. No sooner did she scent the cool air of the Mediterranean and survey the sparkling Gulf of Suez than she was seized with a passionate longing to share the enormous excitement that there must be in Cairo. "I hope in my heart of hearts that there may be no conveyance back to Aden for a month," she admitted to Cockerell in a letter.[14] There were so many friends she wanted to see, so many suggestions to make that she was positive could be useful. In Cairo, the command center of Britain's defense, she reasoned she could contribute so much more than in Aden.

Sure enough, the men from the Ministry of Information urged Freya to stay on; both Reginald Davies and Colonel Thornhill asked her ideas on propaganda offensives. In particular, Colonel Clayton of Military Intelligence had the idea of a "whispering campaign" in Iraq, where Nazi agents were suspected of fomenting an uprising against the government.[15] Field Marshal Wavell invited her to lunch, as did the British ambassador, Sir Miles Lampson. Freya again embraced opportunity.

• • •

It was dreadful with Stewart. They had a fearsome row over it. When he learned that Freya had been asked to work in Cairo at double the salary, he tried to prevent the transfer, telegraphing his superiors that she could not be spared and insisting that the request was completely out of order. Harold Ingrams, now serving as acting governor to the Aden Protectorate, was also annoyed because his office had initiated a regional propaganda broadcast and the loss to the program of someone as able as Freya would make difficulties. Freya felt guilty and torn, but she also believed that if she could float an idea she had for a propaganda program, Stewart could be brought up to work with her. He could even run it, because a man would ultimately be needed to head anything serious. Somewhat stunned at the fierce opposition from Aden, and dreading the thought that Stewart might never forgive her, she wrote a long explanation for her decision to Ingrams, rather emotionally declaring that she was feeling "like dust and ashes."[16] She managed to get a ride on a Blenheim bomber back to Aden and spent a stormy week listening to her colleagues vent their resentment. Freya became hurt and angry too; one friend remembered seeing a scrawled note on one of the documents in the office: "If Stewart is going to be so rude about me, he'll have to marry me."[17] Eventually outvoted by their superiors, Stewart and Ingrams had no choice but to let her go.

Stewart accompanied Freya to the ship, saw to it that her bags and her large hatbox were safely stowed, and bade her good-bye. On the way up the Red Sea, the convoy was bombed and strafed. Defying the captain's orders, Freya stood on the deck watching plumes of water shoot up around her and the guns of the accompanying destroyers flash "like sparkling gold."[18] In the majestic turbulence she thought she saw the glory of a helmeted Athena emerge from the clouds, sword in hand, prepared to smite the enemy.[19]

CHAPTER SIXTEEN

Glittering Cairo

> *The want of a regular education*
> *never caused me any regret,*
> *but the absence of beauty has*
> *always been disappointing.*
>
> —TRAVELLER'S PRELUDE

*S*urely there will never again be anything quite like Cairo during the Second World War. In an atmosphere as heady as the perfume of jasmine climbing the walls of young King Farouk's palace, England's best and brightest converged to wage the battle for Western civilization. Pashas and nabobs, diplomats and prime ministers, merchants, military brass, and even at one point two kings in exile conducted business, and everywhere, from the wide terrace of Shepheard's Hotel to the Kit Kat Club, Madame Badia's, and the Muhammed Ali Club, spies listened and reported. Refugees from Eastern Europe tumbled out of ships into Cairo's streets. People quickly learned to tell the wide-brimmed hats of the Australians, the diamond-shaped *czapkas* of the Poles, Free French berets, conical crowns from New Zealand, Indian puggarees, and in due course the cockaded olive green caps of the routed Greek army.[1]

Most military and diplomatic wives and their babies were evacuated in 1940, after General Wavell made his first lunge at the Italian army in the Western Desert, but the privileged and clever managed to stay by their officer-husbands, performing nursing and clerical duties. The richest set themselves up in handsome villas and competed fiercely to give spectacular parties, attended by other sleek women in diamonds and their superbly tailored escorts. There seemed to be a fete every night at which young officers danced into the wee hours, then rose at dawn to join those less well-connected in snub-nosed tanks grinding through a moonscape on their way to battle. There in the desert they fought the enemy through sandstorms and explosions. A single canteen of water and a cigarette was luxury. The ones who survived were changed forever, but they didn't talk about it. Instead, they returned to Cairo to dance again.

Presiding over the diplomatic and political sides of all this was Sir Miles Lampson, the British ambassador—the *only* ambassador in Egypt. The British had not relinquished their hold on a country so vital to their empire, although the Anglo-Egyptian Treaty of 1936 gave an extremely restive Egypt some gains in independence. All other countries were represented by mere consulates or legations. No man was more powerful than the six-foot-six giant who contemptuously referred to King Farouk as "the Boy" and was heartily loathed by the ambitious young monarch, who returned the favor by calling Lampson "the Buffalo." Lampson's elegant gray frock coats and polka-dotted bow ties did not entirely soften his "considerable personality—strong, unscrupulous and entertaining," according to Harold Macmillan.[2] Lampson and his much younger Italian bride, Jacqueline, called Jacqui, lived in the sprawling colonial villa that was the British embassy. From its columned veranda a view of lawns and gardens spilled to the Nile—and anyone who was anyone came to inhale Britannic imperial power.

Lampson had reigned over the Veiled Protectorate since 1933, when he arrived as high commissioner, and he acutely understood the attraction Berlin and Rome held for various Egyptian parties, especially King Farouk, who encouraged Italian advisers at his court, where intrigue teemed in every palace corridor. It amused the Egyptians that Sir Miles's wife was the daughter of a well-known Italian physician who once practiced on Harley Street, London, but was now the Italian Army's surgeon general. One famous story described how Lampson warned the king that he must get rid of his Italians, and Farouk retorted that he would when Lampson got rid of *his*. The loyalty of Mrs. Lampson was never in question, however, and she continued through the war as the highly visible first hostess of Cairo.

Politics was not a sphere that belonged to Sir Miles alone, although he would have preferred that it did. It was the job of General Sir Archibald Wavell to run the war, and wars are weighty with political considerations.

A muscular, bullnecked professional soldier with an ear for poetry and an eye blinded in World War I, Wavell was respected and trusted by his troops for his commitment to good supply lines and sound equipment as well as for his personal bravery. He made a point of visiting the soldiers at the front lines and thought nothing of flying long distances in a small, unescorted plane. Several times he crashed yet invariably emerged unscathed from the wreckage.

Wavell was a curiously gentle man, a general who disliked killing yet had been a tough military administrator in Palestine a few years previously, dealing harshly with Arab ambushes, snipings, and holdups. Wavell not only caught and executed two Arab sheikhs who were insurrection leaders but also hunted down the infamous grand mufti, religious head of the Palestinians, whose inflammatory oratory and constant plotting were the scourge of Jews and British alike. The mufti, however, disguised in women's clothing, escaped and surfaced again and again, to make trouble throughout World War II. Finally, it had been Wavell's idea to create the half-British and half-Jewish special "night squads" employing tracking dogs, which the Arabs came to dread.

Now in Cairo as commander in chief, Middle East, Wavell faced an awesome challenge. He was responsible for the land forces defending three million square miles, including the Suez Canal, the Strait of Hormuz, and the Dardanelles, as well as the critical oil pipeline that ran from Mosul west to Haifa. His troops were outnumbered five to one by the Italians when the war started, and before long he would face General Erwin Rommel, the greatest of German commanders. The further responsibility of this man, whose taciturnity Prime Minister Churchill found irritating in the extreme, was to retain the goodwill of Moslems throughout Turkey, Syria, Palestine, Transjordan, Iraq, Iran, Saudi Arabia, the Aden Protectorate, Yemen, Egypt, and the Sudan. Never in the history of warfare had one commander had to deal with so many countries, political crosscurrents, cultural differences, or troops from different nations.

Fortunately, he had learned from a good teacher. Wavell had fought under Field Marshal Lord Allenby in the First World War and had an opportunity to study him closely when he wrote Allenby's biography.[3] Allenby had creatively employed various tricks to make the army's task easier, so Wavell learned the value of clandestine operations and was quick to seize on unorthodox methods and unusual people. Just as Allenby had placed stuffed horses in Palestinian orange groves to fool the Turks in 1918, Wavell used dummy tanks to deceive the Italians in the Libyan wastelands in 1940 and soon afterward engineered false dust trails that successfully threw German aerial scouts off the track.

Some of his choices of personnel and operations put him at logger-heads with Lampson, whose embassy was running its own intelligence units—creating a byzantine and competitive atmosphere—but Wavell defended his agents against the protests of the Foreign Office. With his alert ear for talent, it was no surprise that news of Miss Freya Stark's arrival would interest him.

They had met briefly in 1939 in Ankara, when Wavell was there to talk with the Turks and Freya was on her way to Aden. She had been impressed with his air of "friendly granite," and there are those who believe that Wavell was drawn to Freya for her fantastic hats. (His subordinates laughed about Wavell's doodles of ladies' headgear—his aide-de-camp kept a file of some of the most outrageous ones, created during tedious briefings.) Freya and Wavell hit it off and began a friendship that lasted to the end of his life. Most women dreaded sitting next to the silent and preoccupied general at dinner, but not Freya. She and the general shared a love of poetry, and Freya, who was fairly confident of her reservoir of remembered poems, had to admit that the general outclassed her. She was wise enough not to make him talk about the war but got him to quote long passages from Oscar Wilde instead. She found the general more comfortable than the arrogant ambassador and gray-haired, plump Lady Wavell less intimidating than the stunning Jacqui Lampson.

Very soon after her arrival in Cairo, Freya visited General Headquarters, the sprawling warren of offices near the embassy dubbed Grey Pillars. She wanted to propose an idea conceived in Aden when she had interviewed a number of Italian sailors. Rather overwhelmed at finding herself alone with the commander in chief in his map room, she haltingly unfurled a scheme to "reeducate" Italian prisoners who were disillusioned with Fascism and send them behind enemy lines, where they could raise and supply partisan bands. Wavell listened in silence. Freya waited nervously, wondering whether she had overreached. Finally Wavell said quietly: "I have no men to spare."[4]

It was true. He was already fighting on three fronts, and soon it would be five. The general continued, however, to ponder the usefulness of Freya's plan and later asked Peter Fleming, who was sent to Egypt to give crash courses in assassination and explosives and to recruit and train Italian agents, to look into it. Although Fleming opted to concentrate on sabotage in northern Greece, a plan similar to Freya's succeeded when the Americans used both Mafia connections and partisan support to prepare for their landings in Sicily in 1943.

Clearly Freya could be a valuable asset. Wavell's old friend Colonel Thornhill at the Special Operations Executive was collaborating with her on "A Memorandum on Anti-Italian Propaganda in the Middle East," which was soon circulating in intelligence circles. Colonel Walter Cawthorn, the head of the Middle East Intelligence Center, who had sent Freya on her mission to the imam's court, now talked to Wavell about sending her to Baghdad. In the end, however, Rushbrook Williams's Ministry of Information kept her in their Publicity Section, and she was directed to report to the Ministry of Information's man in Cairo, Reginald Davies. The decision demonstrated Lampson's strength in interdepartmental struggles. The strong-willed ambassador considered the need for a propaganda offensive in Egypt by far the most pressing priority—and he got his way. Their resulting plan was Freya's idea, a scheme to create a secret society like those that had so fascinated her when she first came to the East. It would be called the Ikwan al-Hurriyah, or Brotherhood of Freedom.

· · ·

Initially, Sir Miles thought Freya should hold a salon where important Egyptians could be entertained. Freya knew better; they needed to reach the ordinary people, the junior bureaucrats, camel drivers, policemen, small shopkeepers in the souk, country families, those whose loyalty would eventually hold the country—or not. She also knocked down the notion that the society's members be paid by the embassy. If this enterprise were not voluntary and attended out of genuine interest, she argued, it would have no chance of success. Bribing people to adjust their beliefs was both cynical and repugnant.

Freya drew parallels with other secret societies, where men had gone underground to achieve their goals. She cited especially the Muslim Brotherhood or Ikwan al-Muslimin, which British intelligence knew had been attracting young Arab military officers since the 1920s and secretly training them in weapons practice, which the British authorities had banned. A pan-Arab organization, its members swore absolute fealty to Islam with a gun and a Koran in a darkened room. Dedicated to eradicating corruption and foreign domination, the members of the Muslim Brotherhood organized themselves into small cells that welcomed membership of the fellaheen, or peasants. (Two young members during the war were Lieutenants Gamal Nasser and Anwar Sadat, but neither Freya nor anyone else could suspect the future roles they would play.) Freya's idea was to create an equally compelling model and cadre of idealists. She envisioned an infinitely expanding network, an Arab brotherhood nursed by benevolent British administrators that embraced all religious groups and promoted hope for a postwar system along secular democratic lines.

Ambassador Miles Lampson and Lady Lampson, his beautiful young Italian wife, in 1940. They led the social whirl that continued on in Cairo despite the fighting nearby in the Western Desert.

General Archibald Wavell, a tough soldier who disliked killing and loved poetry, met with General Charles de Gaulle, leader of the Free French forces, in Cairo in 1941.

. . .

To begin, Freya was put in touch with officials and British civilians who had Egyptian friends. These first members were to reach out to more acquaintances and form new "cells." As the project got under way Freya assured her superiors that if all went well and she were given sufficient support, the "Brotherhood" could swell to twenty thousand members within a year.

It was hard work to start from nothing, but throwing her heart and soul into the project with an almost messianic zeal, Freya soon was supervising discussion groups all over the city as new members joined. Inviting people to her apartment for nonalcoholic teas, she mixed English and Egyptians, and dusted the occasions with glamour by including beautiful women and an occasional visiting VIP. She called on friends to volunteer time or at the very least attend a party or two. Often there would be a speaker to discuss topics that might relate to the war's progress or nationalist hopes for the future. Although at first the Egyptians who attended came from the professional classes, eventually the working poor in the cities and fellaheen in small villages attended. As in the Muslim Brotherhood, whose genius had also been to include the fellaheen, these neglected Egyptians saw in these gatherings a rare opportunity to air their concerns and anxieties about everything from National Socialism or British postwar intentions to their intense desire for land reform. Freya trained her staff to respond with simple, heartening, and clear answers—and if the staff were uncertain about what British policy was, they cleared their answers with the Foreign Office. But it was Freya's gift for communicating, her warmth and sparkle, and the interest she took in individual problems that really greased the wheels.

. . .

"Oh Stewart," Freya wrote in September 1940, "it is rather nice to have dinner with no one drunk about, and to sit at a table with embroidered linens and lovely fruit piled in bowls of amber glass. I have just bought peach-colored towels for my bathroom and a bath mat to match as well as bath salts. There is a lovely spare room, canary-colored furniture with a terrace on the river and the barges and their big sails just below. . . . I have asked Mrs. Cawthorn if it would be proper for you to come and stay: *almost* anything is proper in war time one gathers."[5]

Freya missed Stewart. She was having a splendid time and working furiously, but it would be better if he were there too. She knew he was still angry because he couldn't resist asking in his letters how her "conscience" was. She had settled into an attractive apartment on the island of Zamelek, near the fashionable Gezira Sporting Club, where polo and tennis were played by the chic, wealthy, or well-connected—even Wavell himself, preoccupied as he was, often took an early-morning ride or hit a golf ball before returning to Grey Pillars to run the war. The strangest thing about Cairo at this tense time was the contrast between the city's gala atmosphere and the carnage of a desert war being fought almost within earshot. It moved Freya, and many others during these wrenching years, to see white egrets feeding peacefully by houseboats along the Nile and to know so much dying was scarcely a bird's flight to the west.

By now Freya had two assistants. The first, Pamela Hore-Ruthven, was a stunning young blonde related by marriage to Ambassador Lampson. Pam's husband, the Honorable Patrick Hore-Ruthven, whose father was governor-general of Australia, was an officer in the Royal Fusiliers and a gifted amateur poet. Pat would be away for weeks at a time as a commando in the Western Desert and then would return to play polo at the Gezira Club, dine on houseboats on the Nile, or go duck shooting with Sir Miles. This outstandingly attractive couple, known as Pat and Pam, were driven to parties by a chauffeur wearing a fez. Lunching one day at the embassy soon after her arrival, Freya was introduced. Conceivably Freya sensed a serious—or at least adventurous—side to Pam, or maybe it was simply that she knew Pam's good looks and connections would be useful. In any event Freya took the young woman aback by suggesting she come up to her room and help her pack for a weekend. Pam soon found herself both packing for her new acquaintance and accepting an invitation to become Miss Stark's assistant in the new propaganda effort.

In her memoirs, written in her eighties, Pam recalled her first impression of Freya as "a very round small person with a pair of the sharpest, most knowing little brown eyes beneath a fantastic hat."[6] The two women were a study in contrast: Pam, tall, young, and impressionable; Freya, short, experienced, and iron-willed. In no time Freya had engineered Pam's release from "re-writing dreary situation reports" at GHQ. This Irish Anglican clergyman's daughter, whose life had been relatively sheltered despite a fair amount of travel, was launched on an adventure she would never forget. Hours previously devoted to "a wild and careless life" were now passed under Freya's tutelage, listening to the hopes and dreams of young Egyptians or riding into villages to talk to tribal elders as children clamored at their horses' heels. Sometimes they would go to an experimental farm and be told that the war effort was driving up prices and people could barely afford to eat. Pam heard Egyptians' anger toward and sense of betrayal by British rule, and learned for the first time how much they identified with the struggles of the Palestinian people to hold their homeland.

Freya's other assistant was Lulie Abu'l Huda, a vivacious, dark-eyed daughter of a former prime minister of Transjordan. Lulie spoke Arabic and came with some rather formidable qualifications. Not only was she a princess of the old Ottoman aristocracy but when Lulie decided to go to Oxford her mother packed up her palace in central Cairo and, veiled in black, accompanied her daughter so that she might get a proper education. Related to many influential people in the Arab world, Lulie needed no training in the problems confronting the ikwan and possessed her own hot passion about the justice of British policy in Palestine.

With Freya as their leader and the clerical help of a Coptic secretary, the women built their network. Together they churned out a weekly bulletin, ran discussion groups, attended teas, and enthusiastically promoted an optimistic conviction that Britain would win the war. "Persuasion" and goodwill, Freya told them, "not Propaganda," were what they were about—the very words Mrs. Humphry Ward had spoken in London so many years earlier to the antisuffragettes. All three worked to the point of exhaustion, but Freya especially was bent on making a success of her idea.

Only one dark thought clouded the pleasures of her present life: concern for her mother and Herbert Young in enemy Italy. She had begged them to get to Switzerland or the United States while there was time. Her last telegram had been urgent. But no letters from Asolo arrived. And then at last word came that the Fascists had found a means to revenge Freya's successful mission to Sana'a.

· · ·

At two o'clock on the afternoon of June 24, 1940, fourteen days after Italy declared war, two well-dressed men and a carabiniere brigadier knocked on the door of Casa Freia in Asolo. They had come, they explained, to take Signora Stark and Signore Young for questioning in Treviso.[7]

Flora, by then seventy-nine, and Herbert, a frail eighty-nine, had seen things go from bad to worse. Coal was running out, the *municipio* had requisitioned all the brass and copper pots, and there was almost no meat in the market. Through the cold winter Herbert sat for days running his fingers desultorily over his Pianola and bursting into rages against the Fascists while Flora tried to keep them self-sufficient by raising potatoes and even sheep. She had done her best to get them out of Italy, but Switzerland was refusing any more visas and money cabled to them by friends in the United States was confiscated. Finally they had no choice but to wait out the war, even though their house, one of the most spacious in Asolo, had been requisitioned by the Fascist administration and they were banished to two small rooms on the top floor.

When word came from the highest level of Mussolini's government that Flora's daughter was a spy, the old couple were immediately detained as possible collaborators. They were sent to the Treviso prison, one of the worst in Italy, where their passports, rings, pens, and Herbert's tie and suspenders were confiscated, and the efforts of friends to intervene were unavailing. Even Mario, now a Fascist official, protested this treatment of his children's grandmother. John and Lucy Beach, who had closed their house and returned to still-neutral America, were helpless at such a distance, as was Lady Iveagh, hunkered in London under a rain of German bombs.

As weeks went by and the old couple languished, it fell to the daughter of one of Italy's most powerful men to plead their case. Contessa Marina Luling-Volpe, whose father was Mussolini's finance minister and owned Villa Barbaro, the famous Palladian villa at nearby Maser, had been impressed by Flora's efforts to help poor girls at Mrs. Beach's tessoria. Horrified to learn from her father that the Fascists intended to send Flora and Herbert to a concentration camp, Maria demanded he obtain their release.

Eventually, on July 15, their jailers unlocked their cells. But Herbert and Flora were not set free. Instead they were sent to a small hill village, where they were kept under surveillance for three more months. This experience of prolonged stress broke Herbert's health. He died of cancer barely three weeks after returning to Asolo. Flora lived another year and a half, brought to California by the Beaches. At first she appeared to have regained her robust former self, reconnecting at last with Freya by letter and even writing a short piece about her imprisonment, later published by John Murray as *An Italian Diary*. She herself did not live to see its publication because the Foreign Office felt such a memoir should be suppressed until the end of the war.[8]

On October 27, 1942, Freya heard from Lucy Beach: "A doctor has thoroughly examined her and thinks there is a growth and she can't possibly recover. He has ordered a narcotic to be given at night or when she needs it. . . . It has been a bitter thing to accept. I longed so to keep her for you Freya, but if it's God's will we must accept. I will try to make her last days as happy and comfortable as possible. . . . I asked her if she wanted you to come and she said by no means. Your country needs you. She said 'Bless her, bless her, bless her.' "[9]

On November 12 came the last cable: "Mother went peacefully and without pain. Love Lucy Beach."[10]

· · ·

Freya wrote Sydney Cockerell. Flora "was not so much a mother," she said, "as a very vivid, entrancing presence. . . . I feel as if no one in all the world belongs to me and it is rather like being in a room far too big for one."[11]

Without the parent whom as a child she had loved almost too much, from whom she had painfully striven to separate herself, Freya could begin to bury her anger and resentment against the person whose over-whelming presence had oppressed her youth. She blamed Flora for many things: the uncertainty of her childhood, the estrangement from her father and loss of their easy Devon life, the disaster of Vera's marriage, and, per-haps most of all, a betrayal of Freya herself. At some deep level she never felt that Flora had loved her as much as she needed to be loved. Probably this was the reason for Freya's later passionate attachments to friends whose devotion to her was unqualified, who made her feel absolutely pri-mary. Although in later years her mother had focused on her daughter and her successes the greatest part of her formidable energies and talents, an emptiness in Freya remained unfilled. She never entirely shook off her early sense that she was only one of many in her mother's affections. Now it was too late to gain that special place.

When the news of her mother's illness came, Freya was deeply involved in writing the first volume of her memoirs, encouraged by Cockerell. After Flora's death she used the writing to understand their complicated rela-tionship and came to a forgiveness and reconciliation she could not have achieved had Flora been alive. But even though the portrait that emerges gives full credit to Flora's beauty and drive, she remains elusive, as if her daughter's feelings toward her were simply too powerful and complex to share—even, perhaps, to comprehend.

· · ·

It was not easy to convince the Egyptians attending the ikwan meetings to throw their lot in with the British, who were being pummeled by nightly air raids in the Battle of Britain. One after another the European allies had collapsed before the enemy, leaving Britain to carry on alone. But to con-sulters of tea leaves, it seemed the Nazis and their Fascist allies were sure to triumph. In the boulder-strewn expanse of Egypt's Western Desert, above the impassable salt pans of the Qattara Depression, General Wavell continued his bloody skirmishes with Marshal Rodolfo Graziani's Italian army, but he was making no headway. Despite being badgered constantly by Churchill to mount a major assault, the cautious general was reluctant to risk his men until he felt his underequipped army was ready. Finally, on December 8, 1940, Wavell launched a surprise attack at Mersa Matruh, continued a drive through Egypt, seized Sidi Barrani by December 12, and crossed into Libya before Christmas.

The effect was galvanizing. Everywhere people took heart in what, at last, was a major British victory. Churchill, who had constantly deviled Wavell for not being sufficiently aggressive, was so carried away when he heard that the Australian Light Horse Regiment, a mechanized unit, had won the day at Sidi Barrani that he astonished Parliament with a thundering speech about a cavalry charge.[12] In Luxor, Freya and Pamela Hore-Ruthven joined the Lampsons' splendid Christmas party by Karnak's great temple, where champagne flowed and the ambassador and his wife led dancing into the night. By day, with two air marshals in tow, Freya and Pam galloped into the Valley of the Kings to lie in the sun and raise their glasses. With renewed zeal they added sixty new members from Luxor to the ikwan.

As all eyes focused on Wavell's three fronts—his armies were fighting in East Africa and the Sudan as well as Italian Cyrenaica—the delirious news came back from the desert of thirty-eight thousand prisoners taken, plus valuable supplies of guns, gasoline, and armored cars. Long columns of defeated troops were marched back into Egypt, prodded by a handful of British soldiers. Surrendering Italians even begged war correspondents to accept their arms. Bardia was taken in early January 1941, and Wavell sent Lieutenant General Richard O'Connor, later captured by Rommel, on to Tobruk, where the Italian resistance collapsed in hours, opening a vital port to British supply ships. Another twenty-five thousand Italian troops and fifty tanks were captured at the cost of fewer than six hundred casualties.

London was intoxicated by Wavell's victories. Churchill, usually annoyed by Wavell's laconic style, now cabled in grateful brevity: "St. Matthew, Chapter VII, Verse 7" ("Ask, and it shall be given you; seek, and ye shall find; knock, and it shall be opened unto you"). Wavell, desperate for more aircraft and learning that a delivery was finally on its way, responded: "St. James, Chapter I, first part of Verse 17" ("Every good gift and every perfect gift is from above").[13] Much of the Italian Army was now in disorderly retreat westward toward Benghazi.

Mussolini fired Marshal Graziani, and Freya invited the Wavells to dinner. "We had a quiet domestic evening, only six, and talked about anything but the war, and General Wavell sat twinkling with his one eye and quoting poems about Samarkand and talked about the Caucasus. He is just the most modest man in this world and no one would think he had just brought off one of the biggest victories of the war," Freya wrote to Lucy Beach.[14]

By the beginning of February 1941, Benghazi fell, putting all Italian Cyrenaica in British hands. Wavell had eliminated the remainder of the Italian Tenth Army with a bold and unorthodox maneuver. Instead of going by the coast road, he sent his commanders over an uncharted route through the desert, risking unknown conditions and uncertain water sources with so little food and supplies that the strategy could well have spelled disaster. Instead the Italians, who far outnumbered the British, had been caught by surprise. The Italian commander handed his revolver to a British subaltern of the Rifle Brigade whose only remaining antitank gun had wiped out three of the last five Italian tanks. As for the British, of 350 tanks only 10 were still operable. The First Desert Campaign was over. Wavell had fought the first war ever conducted with modern equipment in desert conditions. It was an overwhelming victory by an army desperately short of guns, tanks, trucks, ammunition, and especially gas, fought against extremes of cold, dust, sandstorms, and mirages. With his armies advancing into both East Africa and the Sudan, Wavell should have been allowed to rest and reconnoiter. But that did not reckon on Greece.

The small Greek Army enjoyed several victories that winter. Woefully underequipped and suffering terrible privations in the snowy Pindus Mountains, the Greeks had nevertheless beaten the Italians back to Albania. The Italians simply ran, leaving their guns and heavy equipment behind—the sight of an unarmed Greek, it was said, was enough to send whole battalions into flight. For a time it looked as if the war would be won and there would be peace by spring. But in Berlin, Hitler had been watching Wavell's victories and the bravery of the Greeks with growing frustration. He and Mussolini met at the Brenner Pass to discuss the failure of the Italian Army, and not long afterward the Luftwaffe appeared over the Mediterranean in increasing numbers. Hundreds of German aircraft attacked Malta and the British air bases in Sicily. More menacing still, General Rommel had arrived in Tripoli on February 12. He ordered the bombing of Benghazi to begin at once. At the same time Churchill came to a decision that would alter the course of the war and Wavell's career.

One day Pamela Hore-Ruthven was summoned on rather short notice to dinner with the Lampsons at the embassy. She found herself and Jacqui the only two women in the company of the ambassador, General Wavell, the chief admiral, and the chief air marshal. Foreign Minister Anthony Eden and General Sir John Dill, chief of the Imperial General Staff, who had just flown in together from London, were also there. The young woman noticed something "sad and worried" in General Dill's manner.[15]

Earlier Churchill and the Home Office had prodded Wavell to intervene on behalf of the hard-pressed Greeks, presumably to show the United States that they were prepared to aid even the smallest in the stand against tyranny. At the time the Greek dictator Metaxas had turned down British help so as not to provoke a German invasion. Wavell, his troops and supplies exhausted, had been relieved. As he had told Freya earlier, he had "no men to spare." But then Metaxas died, killed by overwork and a heart attack—although some say poisoned—and his successor reopened the question of British relief. Churchill, forever interfering with his generals, decided that Wavell must send troops and equipment to Greece whether or not he felt he had the resources. Eden and Dill had come to Cairo to deliver the message.

It was a deeply disturbing day for Wavell. Pamela Hore-Ruthven pointed out in her book that,

> with only 500 miles to go, the Eighth Army was already half-way to Tripoli. . . . With Tripoli gained by the British, the Axis would have retained no foothold in Africa. I suspect that Dill's air of sadness arose from the fact that he disagreed with his orders, as any good soldier must, seeing he was being asked to withdraw a victorious army to untenable positions, while his seasoned troops were replaced with inexperienced recruits. Rommel himself later confirmed that "no resistance worthy of the name" could have been mounted by the Axis if the momentum of the advance had continued.
>
> There was much bitterness in the desert army as to why so decisive a series of victories was never followed through. It seemed to us that all the advantages we had gained, at the cost of many courageous friends and comrades, were being heedlessly thrown away.[16]

Freya was one of many who never forgave Churchill. Ever afterward she would say to friends: "Churchill was a big man, but Wavell was a *great* man."[17] All her yearning for heroism found a focus in the beleaguered general, whose photograph would be foremost among her pictures, transferred from mantelpiece to mantelpiece wherever she lived.

Now Wavell had a fourth front. Uncomplaining, he halted his advance, pruned away what weary troops he could from the various campaigns, and found enough transport ships still afloat to send to Greece sixty thousand men. He was dangerously overextended. Incredibly, Churchill had

Flora Stark in Pasadena, California, after she escaped to America from Fascist Italy, where she had been imprisoned. She stayed with Lucy and John Beach, who cared for her during her final illness.

Pamela Hore-Ruthven, Freya's lovely blond assistant in the Ikwan al-Hurriyah, whose husband died of wounds in the Western Desert. She remained a close friend to Freya all her life, naming her godmother to her first child and frequently visiting Asolo.

also offered help to Turkey, but Turkey elected to remain neutral. Together with his air and naval commanders, Wavell flew to Athens to discuss plans for an intervention that was against all military reason. The story went around that on his way back to Cairo he had been spotted reading *Alice's Adventures in Wonderland.*

On April 3 Rommel's Afrika Corps launched a surprise attack on the British outposts in Libya, and ten days later his Panzer divisions had reoccupied Sollum and Bardia; Tobruk would be encircled less than a week after. Then, early in the morning on April 6, German troops that had been massing on the Balkan borders poured into Yugoslavia and Greece. A new, terrible phase of the war began.

. . .

Freya, Pamela, and Lulie had been indefatigable in their efforts to make a success of the brotherhood. Starting out with 12 members, the ikwan had grown to 524 registered members by the end of February, and while the Foreign Office was smiling on their work and funding additions to the staff, they desperately needed more help. Freya wrote Stewart, as always begging him to come up, pointing out that it was time a man took over: "You know how little ice our sex cuts in the oriental mind. I think if we want really to make a big thing of it, a more impressive standard bearer is required."[18] But Aden was getting ready to receive a huge influx of Italian women and children from Abyssinia, across the Horn of Africa. As a humanitarian gesture, the British had decided to accept the refugees fleeing the vicious tribal warfare that erupted as British troops approached the Abyssinian capital, Addis Ababa. Stewart wrote back, why didn't Freya come help him in Aden? Autumn, autumn, she promised; things would surely be easier by then. Then lovingly: "Golden words are said about you: I give a little extra gilding when the opportunity occurs. I don't want to compare you to a lily exactly. . . . The Italians are not expected to last many more months and we have an unpleasantly German summer before us. I wish so much you would come here to take over."[19]

. . .

It had always been assumed that Freya would take the ikwan idea to Iraq, where anti-British feeling was even stronger than in Egypt. Now, with Germany turning south and probably next to the east, it was feared that a drive into Iraq and Persia should be expected. She planned to leave in a fortnight. Pam and Lulie knew the ropes, so Freya could safely put her burgeoning committees in their care.

She and Pam had recently enjoyed the most marvelous of triumphs: entrance to Al-Azhar, the oldest university in the world, founded by the Fatimids in 972, where a student spent at least thirteen years in religious studies before graduation. At any international academic procession, a representative from Al-Azhar was always given precedence in the line, and neither the government of Egypt nor any leader in the Arab world could hope to be taken seriously without acceptance by its venerable scholars. It was a citadel of extraordinary influence, and a great deal of Nazi and Fascist effort had been directed toward winning over Al-Azhar. To her mother Pamela wrote: "We were told it would be impossible to get in there. Freya can accomplish anything and it is fascinating to see her sitting among them all in her quaint clothes, they in their delicious robes listening and melting and smiling."[20] Freya, too, felt it capped her efforts. It was almost unprecedented for a woman—and a Christian and foreigner at that—to have been given such a hearing.

In *The Arab Island,* the book she wrote in 1945 to state the Arab position to an American audience in the midst of a passionate domestic debate about whether to recognize Israel as a state, Freya recalled these extraordinary exchanges—and expressed gladness that she had devoted time to studying the Koran: "It was here that I came to realize, from the theologians of the Azhar, on what democratic foundations the theory of Islam is built. Text after text they would quote, from Quran, or tradition, or history of the first caliphs, the Guided Ones; and this appeal, of the original democracy of Islam, would time and again brush away all the arguments of our enemies, which at that season were being poured like a deluge over the Arab world. I believe, indeed, that it was this fundamental tradition, so opposed to despotic doctrines, that chiefly kept the Arabs on our side."[21]

· · ·

Freya had been giving herself day and night to her work. She had suffered with flu several times, her usually low blood pressure was very low, and she said she was beginning to feel like "a sheep dog, yapping here, running there, trying to keep the flock together."[22] Now she was expected in Baghdad, and she looked forward to the change. She was also assailed by an urge to write again. Confidentially she wrote to Stewart: "How I begin to hate democracy but don't, don't say this abroad. I don't really, but I feel the Committee is just too much with us. I long for a camel or even a donkey. There is a lovely feeling of spring about, all the fields full of young flax or corn or beans or flowers—a war or an office seems monstrous."[23]

By the end of March she was on her way east. Ringing in her ears were the words of Prime Minister Churchill himself, whom she had met when he came to Cairo for conferences. When they were introduced, Freya wrote Stewart, he told her that he had heard so many things about her. "When I replied I hoped they were good, he remarked that it is much more interesting not to inspire only praise . . . so I think the worst."[24]

CHAPTER SEVENTEEN

The Baghdad Siege

> *Such delicate goods as justice, love and honour, courtesy, and
> indeed all the things we care for, are valid everywhere; but they
> are variously moulded and often differently handled, and
> sometimes nearly unrecognizable if you meet them in a foreign
> land; and the art of learning fundamental common values is
> perhaps the greatest gain of travel to those who wish to
> live at ease among their fellows.*
>
> —PERSEUS IN THE WIND

*F*reya's spirits soared on her release from the
"pharaonic microbes" and exhaustion of Egypt. She very much
wanted to visit Teheran again, if she could fit in a little trip to Persia
between responsibilities in Iraq, so she wrote her old friend Gerald
de Gaury, one of the attractive intelligence officers from Baghdad
days who was posted there. Meanwhile, she arrived in Baghdad to
find the city in the midst of a coup d'état.

The British were well aware of Baghdad's strategic importance to
Hitler. By occupying Iraq he would gain control of the Persian Gulf
as well as the critical pipeline from the Abadan oil fields in Iran.
What neither the British nor anyone else knew was that Hitler was
secretly preparing to invade Russia, with whom he had recently
signed a nonaggression pact. Preoccupied with conquering the
Balkans and Greece, he was not in a good position to move into the
Middle East until that region was put in order with the Nazis' spe-

cial brand of savagery. But Hitler did not suspect the degree of impatience felt by a small clique of violently anti-British Iraqi generals popularly called the Golden Square, whom the Führer had been cultivating. For a long time they had plotted to seize power and had communicated this to Berlin. Berlin had urged delay. But their hot-headed leader, Rashid Ali al-Gaylani, was determined to make his move.

On the day Freya took a room in the Tigris Palace Hotel, a seedy place with appalling plumbing but one of the best available, her old friend from the Ministry of Information Sir Kinahan Cornwallis arrived to present his credentials as the new British ambassador. At the same moment Rashid Ali's troops surrounded the palace, made prisoners of the six-year-old king and his mother, and searched every room for her brother, the regent, Abd ul-Illah. Four doctors stood by with a certificate attesting to his death from a massive heart attack. But the fortunate regent was safely curled under a rug at the feet of the American ambassador, being driven past Iraqi guards to the British air base at Habbaniyah, fifty-five miles west. Sir Kinahan could find no one to whom to present his credentials.

For the moment the city remained calm, alert, awaiting events. Rashid Ali proclaimed a new government with himself as the head, and Freya wandered out to admire Baghdad's two recently completed bridges, a splendid new gateway of Assyrian monoliths, and the trees that had been planted along the boulevard. In a rather bemused mood she pondered the changes that had taken place in her own life and in the world since she had settled into her smelly quarters thirteen years ago wondering if the mummy of a long-dead Assyrian was rotting below. She was no longer bewildered and poor, she was a respected colleague of many of the most significant decision makers of the war. Strolling into the souk, she was happy to hear herself addressed as "my sister" even while the shopkeepers were tearing down all the British war posters from their windows.

Captain Vyvyan Holt, still Oriental secretary, looking distracted, came around to pick her up for a ride as in the old days. Freya's one-sided love for him had long been a thing of the past. They talked about the situation and its probable outcome. In the meantime the phone lines to the palace had been cut, the little king's British nurse was tasting all his food as a precaution, and trucks full of Iraqi soldiers were pouring into the city. Like Sir Kinahan, Freya was appalled that the British position had deteriorated so badly, although Holt's intelligence team had done its best to keep the Foreign Office informed on the Golden Square's plot. Later it would be revealed that Britain had penetrated the Iraqi code but, unwilling to give away such an important advantage, allowed the coup to proceed. For the moment, however, Freya knew only that her job was to counter anti-British sentiment.

She set immediately to work to create a pro-British ikwan in the city, dashing off a note to Rushbrook Williams in London about her plans. They must start by getting several dozens of the "most suitable" British to round up all their Iraqi friends so that by autumn, she optimistically speculated, they would have "a fairly large area of prepared or friendly soil." But she admitted it would not be easy with "most of the voices of the country in enemy hands."[1] Both the chief newspapers, the *Bilad* and the *Istiqlal*, as well as the broadcasting station kept up a steady stream of anti-British propaganda. With most Iraqis looking to Germany as their savior from British domination, Freya reflected that people were feeling "Better the Devil they didn't know to the Devil they did." One of the most outrageous rumors floating about was that the British had caused the death of the queen's husband, King Ghazi, three years earlier.*

The British did have their supporters—some of the rich, some of the powerful tribal sheikhs, and some patrician families who had thrown their lot in early with the British. These elite classes were reluctant to share power with the struggling middle classes and especially the poor, among whom nationalist stirrings were strong, heightened by the war. If Iraq were to have a European mentor, even many of the rich, however, preferred that it be Germany. The Iraqis had little understanding of National Socialism or the German attitude toward people they considered "inferior." Instead, it was whispered in the marketplace that Hitler was a secret convert to Islam.

Furthermore, everyone loves a winner, and at this point Germany showed every sign of coming out ahead. In North Africa, General Rommel had reclaimed Benghazi from Wavell in a bloody battle, and the Germans were pulverizing the Greek and British troops. In addition, the former mufti of Jerusalem, Haj Muhammad Amin-al-Husseini, whom Wavell had chased from Palestine several years earlier, was back in Baghdad. His incendiary oratory was rousing the populace to new heights of anti-British fervor.

---

* The truth was less flattering to the image of the young monarch, the son of the first Hashemite king, Faisal, although the British *had* been worried that he lacked his father's steady hand. Ghazi, spoiled and intemperate, died in an accident of his own making. He had been listening to his favorite radio program when the sound went out. Furious, he leapt into his sports car and rushed out to his summer palace on the Ramadi Road, thinking he could catch the rest of the broadcast there. Crossing the railroad track, his car flew out of control and hit a telegraph pole, which fell on the car, killing him instantly. At the time the event inflamed the people's worst suspicions, and they rioted around the British consulate. When the consul appeared on the steps to reason with them, they bludgeoned him to death.

The circumstances of Ghazi's death remain an important issue in Iraq, where some are trying to revisit the question to fuel anti-Western sentiment.

One day Freya met him at the house of her friend the Christian Arab writer George Antonius, whose monumental *The Arab Awakening* remains a seminal work in the Pan Arab nationalist movement. Naively, Antonius believed that Rashid Ali's new government promised hope for Arab independence, and, as a Palestinian, Antonius was attracted to both the mufti's gospel of freedom from the colonial yoke and his unyielding opposition to Zionism.

Surprised and intrigued to find herself in the company of a man who was regarded as the chief thorn in Britain's side, Freya observed the mufti closely. "I . . . was impressed but not won by his very vivid personality," she wrote. "He seemed to radiate a feeling of friendly danger. He had a gloomy sayyid beside him whose looks were just hatred personified but the Mufti himself seems to take his enmities in the detached and good-humoured Arab way. I must say I should rather like to get to know him better if it could be done."[2] This was not to happen. The handsome, blue-eyed, youthful-looking cleric, descended from one of the most illustrious Palestinian families, was deeply embroiled in fomenting as much trouble as he could in Baghdad and elsewhere.

When his intrigues in Iraq were successfully put down, the mufti fled to Berlin with Rashid Ali. Throughout the war he engaged in every possible scheme to sabotage an Allied victory, outliving Hitler and continuing his passionate mission to save his land from the Zionists. Al-Husseini was without scruple, a man who rejoiced in every murder or misfortune he could conceive of or share in for every Jew anywhere—not merely in Palestine. At this time neither Freya nor especially Antonius—who insisted to her that the mufti and Rashid Ali were merely patriots and not puppets of the Reich—had any idea that British intelligence had broken the Italian radio code and could overhear the plotters' communications with Berlin.

The War Office realized they could not ask Wavell for any troops for Baghdad, so they turned to the government of India. Luckily, the Tenth Indian Division was concentrating at Bombay for shipment to Burma to strengthen the British position against the Japanese. As the Indian troops landed at Basra, there were demonstrations in the streets. Driving back to her hotel, Freya's taxi was surrounded by mobs of students with banners screaming slogans. They engulfed the car, kicking it and spitting. While her driver muttered, "Dogs, sons of dogs," Freya fixed her face in an interested smile and called out to the spitters through the window, "*Ya meskin. Ya meskin* (Poor things. Poor things)," as they banged on the car.[3] She refused to let herself be frightened and forced herself to be sympathetic. Nonetheless, when she got back to the hotel she sent Jock Murray a list of her scattered possessions—just in case.[4]

After a few more days the city seemed to have settled down; there was hope that the crisis could be resolved by diplomatic means. Rashid Ali, aware the Germans were too busy with Greece to help, had opted to play for time. Freya, eager to join Gerald de Gaury in Iran, decided it was safe to take a short leave and headed off. She spent several mornings being painted by de Gaury, who was not only a good amateur painter but in later life the author of many entertaining books on the East. He was also spectacularly good-looking and always perfectly turned out in uniform. From the time they met in 1929 in Baghdad, he had been a frequent visitor both to Asolo and to La Mortola. Oddly, Freya never seems to have been drawn to him as a lover, although he was evidently not homosexual.

In Persia, Freya found an old world trying to stumble into the new, a sight that she increasingly viewed with regret. In obedience to Reza Shah's directives to Westernize—the soldier shah was known to take his riding crop to anyone in traditional dress—women were no longer sweeping about in long black chadors but had adopted drab scarves. They looked ashamed, she noted sadly, to appear so naked in public. With equal reluctance men had been forced to put aside the handsome, wide-skirted *sardari,* or frock coat, and elegant fez. Instead, the shah commanded men to adopt a European fedora—whose brim the pious regarded as an obstruction to prayer.

Freya also found Teheran overflowing with Axis "technical advisers," most of them under twenty-five, just the right age to serve as soldiers. But after a week a premonition that action would commence any minute brought her racing back to Baghdad by train from Kermanshah. At the Iraqi border, guards put her in police custody in the railroad rest house, and, fearing they would try to prevent her from going on, Freya commenced a tremendous fuss about requiring a lady's maid. The guards, unprepared for such a strenuous prisoner, let her go. Early in the morning of May 2, she arrived at the British embassy in a horse-drawn carriage under a parasol. She was the last person admitted as the embassy gates were locked by Rashid Ali's soldiers and the Siege of Baghdad began.

. . .

It was precipitated by a second wave of Indian troops landing at Basra. The Iraqis protested, asking for help from Germany and Italy, then marched on the British-built Habbaniyah airport and surrounded it. At two in the morning all British subjects in Iraq were requested to gather at prearranged places. One hundred and thirty-two women and ninety-nine children were sent on RAF buses to Habbaniyah with the Golden Square's permission. They were evacuated to India, leaving behind their husbands,

Haj Muhammad Amin-al-Husseini, the blue-eyed grand mufti of Jerusalem, an implacable foe of Zionism whose plots against Jews and the British created trouble throughout the Middle East during the war.

Captain Gerald de Gaury, one of the British officers in Baghdad to whose circle Freya was eager to belong. Reputed to be the illegitimate son of Lord Kitchener, de Gaury hosted Freya in Teheran before she headed back to Baghdad and became a captive in the Baghdad Siege.

Ambassador Kinahan Cornwallis in the garden of the besieged British embassy during the uprising of the Golden Square, 1941. This photograph was taken by Freya.

who were herded into the embassy. At five a scattering of British planes roaring out of Habbaniyah attacked the Iraqis.

In the embassy, 366 men and a handful of women, whose lack of British papers disqualified them for evacuation, gathered in a house with toilet facilities for 10. Men started work immediately digging latrines and wastewater sumps in the garden.[5] When Freya arrived she found an enormous bonfire being fed by the contents of office files. A big V of white sheets was spread out on the lawn to indicate their existence to RAF reconnaissance planes. Although all radios had been requisitioned by their Iraqi jailers, they had managed to hide a few. After the gates were barred, the compound was ringed with Iraqi guards while Iraqi police boats patrolled the side that faced the Tigris. Ambassador Cornwallis, "a rugged, tall old bit of weather-beaten rock,"[6] opened the grand piano in the salon, revealing a store of Lee-Enfield rifles, which were distributed. Sandbags were arranged against the walls and barbed wire strung about the garden. One man noticed a friend dropping little parcels down a disused well in the courtyard. His friend was the British officer who had been advising the Iraqi Air Force, and the packages were vital parts of the only serviceable Iraqi planes.[7]

It was quite a Lucknow atmosphere, Freya thought, not for the first time remembering the terrible nineteenth-century Indian Mutiny. She was issued a blanket and pillow and went upstairs to find a balcony on which to settle, marveling at the cooing of doves inside and crackling of rifle fire outside. Nineteen other women—Armenians, Jews, Yugoslavs—put their bedding on the roof. Day after day, as the temperature soared to 114 degrees, the men stripped to their shorts and the women did what they could to stay cool. One man recalled in his memoirs that he had teased Freya by saying he now knew what it meant to be "stark naked" and noted that she was not amused. But he also credited her: "With her fluent local Arabic and her aplomb and bonhomie, she became our most useful contact at our gates with the Iraqi police posted here, and helped us to buy fresh meat and vegetables to leaven our Spartan fare."[8]

With a mixture of baksheesh and badinage, Freya befriended the guards. One friend recalled her chatting through the railings of the main gate when a British plane flew over and the guard began firing with his rifle. Freya pointed out that the plane was beyond range, and the man said, "You know best, Madam," and put down his rifle.[9] She joshed with the police whose boats were tied to the river entrance, asking about their catches of fish. Once, when the mufti had preached a particularly incendiary sermon in town calling for holy war, a guard urged: "Become a Muslima and I will keep you myself."

In the meantime Wavell was confronting the dreaded fifth front. With armies fighting in Eritrea and Abyssinia, holding back Rommel's thrust into Egypt, hounded from Greece, and in retreat to Crete, he now had to focus on Iraq. He had heard the news of the coup on his birthday and was reported to have remarked, as usual, "I see." With superhuman calm he set about organizing what troops he could, a ramshackle column of infantry supported by a few armored vehicles gathered from throughout Palestine. This ragtag lot he dubbed Habforce and sent out on a practically waterless route stretching some five hundred miles over the desert to Iraq. Along the way they were joined by the Arab Legion, the pigtailed Bedouin fighters organized by the celebrated desert leader Lieutenant General Sir John Glubb, affectionately known by his men as Glubb Pasha.

Although Berlin responded by sending Messerschmitts to the Iraqis, they could spare only a few; too many German aircraft had been destroyed in the assaults on Greece and Crete. Berlin also sent an air commander to take charge, but typical of Rashid Ali's undisciplined troops, as his plane circled the city Iraqi soldiers commenced to fire randomly at it. When the German aircraft landed no commander emerged. They had put a bullet through the throat of their adviser.

The siege lasted a month. Outside the compound fires burned, bombs thudded nearby, and the sky flamed red as oil tanks exploded. Occasionally an RAF plane dipped encouragingly above the compound, scattering leaflets and even mail. On their radios the embassy's occupants heard the peculiar news that Hitler's assistant Rudolf Hess, apparently even crazier than the Führer, had landed in Scotland. In the awful heat most men slept in the garden, but officials had rooms in the mansion and Freya was often invited to dine with Ambassador Cornwallis and Vyvyan Holt. One evening she managed to sweep in dressed in an evening gown. Another time, when the heat overwhelmed her and she felt unwell, Holt let her rest in his office, but she steadily encroached until he complained rather churlishly that it was beginning to look like "a boudoir."[10]

Holt, whose close friend was the Iraqi foreign minister, also negotiated for supplies—which variously included tins of brilliantine, Kotex, medicines, even at one point mothballs. Looking at the list over his shoulder, Freya commented that this last item was surely "the suggestion of a pessimist."[11] A policeman, bringing in a heavy load of cosmetics and feminine requirements, said he couldn't understand how "a harem about to be murdered could still be thinking of face powder." But Freya retorted that she, for one, intended to die "with her face in proper order."[12]

So the days passed, livened by explosions that shook the windowpanes and a mob outside shouting slogans. Although bullets from a sniper's rifle ricocheted off her balcony columns as she brushed her hair, Freya continued her walks in the embassy's garden. The aim of the Iraqi gunners, she felt, left a great deal of room for improvement. With Cornwallis she discussed the possibilities of escape, and they agreed it would be difficult. On May 19 the water was cut off. "Very inconvenient," noted Freya, observing the garden bushes covered with drying underclothes from laundry the day before. When lectures and entertainments were organized, Freya decided she "would not submit to any education while here. . . . I sat through half a lecture on Iceland about which I have not the faintest curiosity and then strolled in the hot and restless wind to see the river still flowing swiftly."[13]

Both attracted and repelled by the constant intimacy, fearing the siege would be protracted but not really in doubt over their ultimate rescue, Freya observed the community's behavior and approved of her countrymen's resolute efficiency yet was touched by the differences between East and West. By day the Europeans organized, held lectures, and got their laundry done. At night, however, they would sleep apart from one another. The Easterners, whether Parsi or Sunni, Shi'a or Hindu, gathered around their kitchen fires in tight fellowship. Only a Christian's polluting hand dipped rashly into a believer's dish could provoke an outcry. It had always fascinated her too that Eastern men showed open affection—holding hands, kissing one another, draping an arm over another's shoulder. The Westerner, especially the British male, allowed himself no such outlet.

Early in the morning she watched the sun rise over the Tigris River beneath her and found it very beautiful:

> So much *water*; it looks like a solid thing, some great dragon
> hurtling to the sea and the ripples are the swing of its muscles as it
> moves. Its light has a million little breaks where every ripple
> pushes up a tiny crest, so that it is a multitudinous light, holding
> shadows in its heart like happiness, or grass in sunshine. And the
> houses on the other side have fascinating detail: dark mouths of
> steep streets that go down: a pointed *bellam* moored here or there
> below the walls: small patches of garden, a trellis of vine or orange
> where some rich Jewish merchant now lives in fear. The jade green
> bridges upstream and down, whose curves make the only hills we
> have for miles and the finger-minarets and domes, make the view
> more like a book than real life. One can't think of this as real life
> after all.[14]

Instead, she thought of Venice and its broad lagoon. With all the punitive and threatening talk she heard around her, Freya wondered what would be done to punish the Iraqis when the embassy compound was freed. As she had mused in a note to Sydney Cockerell at the beginning of the coup d'état, she hoped that the British would respect Iraq's hopes: "I think that to push back a government onto a people who are not ready to lift one finger for it themselves is a *bad* cause."[15] She was persuaded that British policy in Iraq had congealed in support of an ossified and repressive leadership that had dangerously ignored the voices of younger, reform-minded elements—and this must be changed if the Arabs were to stay neutral.

On May 24 their radios broadcast the news that Wavell's rescue force was twenty miles away, with Glubb Pasha's Bedouins riding in the lead. At Basra the Indian Army was preparing to fight its way north up the Tigris. But if encouraged by those developments, the besieged turned despondent to hear the fate of Crete—the losses had been terrible and the Germans were murdering civilians with a cool brutality that made Iraqi excesses seem mild.

At 6:00 P.M. on May 30 the noise of gunfire and explosions dramatically escalated. A servant was seen hurrying out to unlock a small door within the gates. Suddenly a grim procession of Iraqis entered the compound. They had come, they announced, to discuss an armistice with Sir Kinahan Cornwallis. Someone was sent to arouse the ambassador from a siesta, and the delegation waited as he put on a shirt and trousers. When he appeared an Iraqi colonel greeted him with a truculent harangue about "the legitimate aspirations of the Iraqi people." Sir Kinahan yawned, rose to his full six feet, five inches, and declared in his perfect Arabic that he had had "the honor of accompanying King Faisal I to Baghdad and assisting him with *making* the first Constitution for the State of Iraq."[16] Having established that he knew as much or more of Iraqi history as the delegation, Sir Kinahan sat down to work out practical arrangements.

By this time the advancing force had crossed the Euphrates and was approaching Baghdad. As RAF bombers continued razing the western Iraqi defenses, an agreement was concluded for a meeting between British officials, representatives of the regent, and Iraqi rebels, to take place at a canal on the outskirts of the city. To Freya's delight, His Majesty's spokesman turned out to be none other than Gerald de Gaury, who had made a spectacular dash from Teheran to an Iranian port. He had hailed a passing battleship by frantically waving his gold-crested attaché case and got a ride in a British plane from Basra to Palestine, where as adviser to the regent he joined the forces marching to Baghdad.[17]

Now de Gaury's and the regent's representatives stood on the marshy bank of the canal in the predawn gloom waiting for the Iraqi team. As minutes passed and no one from the Golden Square appeared, the regent's representatives, afraid they were targeted for assassination, jumped into de Gaury's car and drove off. British troops forced them back, and they returned just as the rebel team approached across the canal. One participant recalled hearing de Gaury and another tall figure hailing each other cheerfully across the water: "Hello, Gerald!" "Hello, Ghazi!" Ghazi, one of the Golden Square rebels, had been at Sandhurst with de Gaury.[18]

And so ended the Iraqi coup d'état of 1941. Rashid Ali escaped to Berlin, but others of the Golden Square, including Ghazi, were put in prison and the regent and his ministers were reinstalled. The city streets, however, boiled with hatred. At least one British observer noted that the regent's prime minister, the forceful, pro-British Nuri Pasha, made a point of sitting himself in corners, away from windows, and keeping his back toward the wall.* Those who had been locked in the British compound were now released to find their houses looted, vandalized, and even in some cases defiled with excrement during a terrible day of rioting that erupted throughout the city.

The Iraqi police stood back and even abetted the looters. Snipers aimed at any Western face, and for days it was safer to stay at the embassy than move about in town. Most tragic was the fate of the great Baghdad Jewish community, the oldest (twenty-five hundred years) and most prosperous in the world. Before British troops could restore order, Ghazi Street ran with blood. Jewish men, women, and children were massacred. Christians and other minorities were attacked and killed as well in a spasm of bloodletting that extended to Mosul, Kadhimain, and other cities. But by far the greatest number of victims were Jews. The survivors of this community, which had brought so much to the quality of life and richness of the country, which had lived in peace under the benign tolerance of the Ottoman Turks, now packed to leave, taking their fortunes and varied abilities with them.

Freya, like all the other witnesses, was horrified and saddened at such vicious behavior from the people she admired. It was as if all the civilizing centuries had done nothing to cure a barbaric sickness lurking in their hearts; as if, like their ancient Assyrian ancestors, they would lay waste

---

* Nuri Pasha would not survive the later coup in 1958, when the little king and the regent were assassinated by the military, paving the way for the appearance of Iraq's present dictator, Saddam Hussein. Nuri's mutilated body was then dragged through the streets. Freya would dedicate *Dust in the Lion's Paw,* her account of the war, to him and other Iraqi friends who died in the coup, as did hope for a democratic, pro-West Iraqi nation.

innocent and enemy alike. No person with any decency could say the slaughtered Jews were anything but innocent, yet Freya and her colleagues saw the Arabs' anger as frustration with British support for Zionist ambitions and felt they needed to drastically alter their policy—and quickly. The Soviets, who would be engaged in their own fight for survival within weeks, were not yet offering themselves as patron and alternative to the Arabs—but if something were not done, some, like Freya, foresaw that this was an increasingly real possibility.

. . .

The ceremony that restored the little king and his government took place on the first of June with the sound of a band playing to a crowd of grim faces. Freya was the only woman in attendance. Later people would talk as if she had been the sole woman held in the embassy compound—and so her legend grew. It was true that she had played a significant part in shoring up morale and keeping communication open with the Iraqi guards. Her good humor with their jailers had contributed significantly to an optimistic atmosphere—people remembered this and were grateful. During the tense weeks of captivity, her compassion and insights on the issues that angered the Iraqi people about British policy had a lasting impact on many who heard her.

Two days after the restoration ceremony, Freya was collected by her friend Colonel Cawthorn and flown back to Jerusalem with a group of officers. There would be much to do now. She was eager to influence a situation whose outcome could have profound and long-reaching implications for the future of Western relations with the Arab world. "Britain has come to be associated with what is rigid, self-interested, and superannuated," she warned in one of a series of articles for *The Times* of London.[19] But for the moment she saw no alternative to British authority in Iraq and could not help but be carried away by the display of British might that had brought about her rescue. Landing in Jerusalem that night, she and her companions celebrated with champagne.

Now, with everyone else, Freya turned to watch Wavell's commanders and de Gaulle's Free French march together to defeat the Vichy government in Syria, lest Hitler entertain any more thoughts about German hegemony in the Middle East. On June 21 Damascus fell. On July 10, Beirut. On Bastille Day, appropriately, an armistice was signed making de Gaulle and his Free French the new masters of the Arabs in Syria.[20] By then Hitler's armies had stormed deep into Russia, determined to succeed where Napoleon had failed.

The Brotherhood

*Perseverance is often praised, but it is not so often realized that
another quality must accompany it to make it of any value—and
that is elasticity; perseverance in only one direction very often
fails: but if one is ready to take whatever road is offered, and to
change the chosen way, if circumstances change, and yet to keep
the end in view—then success is infinitely more probable.*

—BEYOND EUPHRATES

n June 1941 suspicion and fear riddled Cairo.
Evelyn Waugh was part of an elite commando group that had just
arrived. Going to confession one Sunday, he realized that behind the
grille the priest was asking more than personal questions and he had
the cleric arrested as a spy.[1] It was a clear sign of the poisonous feelings seething in the hectic city.

Suddenly from Churchill came the abrupt command that Wavell,
whose abilities the prime minister had never regarded highly, should
switch positions with the commander in chief of India, Field Marshal Sir Claude Auchinleck. Churchill even denied the exhausted
leader the two-week leave he had requested. It was a shocking
moment for everyone in Cairo, where Wavell was widely admired,
and it contributed to growing fear as Rommel's Panzer divisions
surged into Egypt. Only the crucial port of Tobruk was holding fast.

On June 10 Miles Lampson recorded in his diary: "Freya Stark looked in in the morning, just back from Bagdad. She said they had a most exciting time during the month they were shut up there. They were kept under strict guard and the garden controlled by machine guns on the surrounding roof tops. On the whole she looks extremely well and seems to have enjoyed herself quite a lot. She's a great girl."[2]

To no small degree the knowledge of Freya's "machine of public opinion" made the British in Cairo feel more secure. Knowing that thousands of neutral people could be enlisted voluntarily in support of their cause gave considerable psychological solace at an alarming time. When Cornwallis requested her transfer to Iraq, Lampson was unwilling to let her go. "Miss Stark's organization in Egypt," he telegrammed the Foreign Office on July 7, 1941, "cannot be left without guidance. . . . Miss Stark may spend some time in Baghdad but I cannot relinquish Miss Stark for permanent attachment to your staff."[3]

Freya was aware of the competing claims on her, and she basked in the attention while working herself to the point of exhaustion. By the end of 1941 there would be 144 committees and several thousand men and women established in cells from Upper Egypt to the delta. It was a shot in the arm for Freya when Major Ralph Bagnold, the strange little man who had created the famous Long Range Desert Group nicknamed the Desert Raiders, whose surprise attacks became myth in the Desert War, told her that her ikwan was considered a success in the highest circles. He said that in the beginning nobody in intelligence had believed that she could really carry off her networking idea—but it was now conceded that she had.

As word of her work grew, so did Freya's stature. And just as her talent had admitted her to London's intellectual and social circles, she now blazed in the society of wartime Egypt. Miss Stark had become one of the experts whose knowledge was invaluable. If the old dream still held, surely she was in a position to become a true Tharaya, one "who illuminates the world." She must have marveled at how her early interest in the secret Druze and the Assassins had led her to a role at this extraordinary moment of history. Yet now she was intrigued by a different kind of closed community.

Freya had been wise enough in London to view with a degree of skepticism the rich and privileged world that had rushed her. Now that the same snobbish and class-conscious society that had dominated English life at home had transferred itself intact to Cairo, she seemed less able to resist the notion that she had a right to be—that she *belonged*—with these titled, pedigreed, and carelessly elegant people. She wrote, "One feels no one can be much better than the best of our aristocracy; so conscientious, so anxious to play their part rightly, so self-reliant, so careless of all voices except that of their own conscience—and so refreshingly direct. I am surprised that I seem to fit so easily into a world with which after all I have so little to do—but I suppose we do share the same values, interested in outside things and not so much in oneself, and that is perhaps fundamentally aristocratic."[4]

Freya was now in grave danger of being seduced by the dazzle of this set, and increasingly it showed in her behavior. She had not lost her sympathy for the simple people of the world, or what Kipling had called "the common touch," which was in part the secret of her success in building the ikwan with such optimistic energy and warmth.[5] But the romance of the elite excited her, and in their midst she fell victim to an impulse to imitate their ways and behave rather high-handedly to those who were not in a position to object. It was a division in her personality that she never resolved: attraction to the glamour and society of the privileged coupled with the need to be refreshed by simple folk in remote places. Her fears of being consigned to outsiderhood had never been entirely conquered, and adulation stimulated her desire to punish those who were not her eager partisans.

As a result several assistants were sent packing while others were mindful not to incur her displeasure. Gerald de Gaury told her people were saying that if Freya disliked you, you were "sent away." An observant young woman who met her in Cairo in November 1941 and later boarded at her house in Baghdad, Hermione Ranfurly, wrote in her diary: "Woe betide those who stand in her way—they will be defeated with a dexterity and force which will surprise the most stubborn opponent. I like her very much."[6]

Welcomed to the inner circles both of the Foreign Office and Grey Pillars, Freya now was regarded as one of the most respected experts on the Arab world. Yet a scholarly reputation could not supply her deepest needs. She still yearned for affection and, still fearing she was not pretty enough, looked for signs that she was loved. As she wrote Cockerell in 1941, "I should so hate to be neglected."[7]

In the meantime it was awfully nice to have the government pay for her socializing. Freya was enjoying a salary and living expenses beyond anything she had known. Her flat was spacious and charming, and she filled it with desirable people. She was a hostess on the level—almost—of Lady Jacqui Lampson or Momo Marriot, daughter of the American financier Otto Kahn and wife of Brigadier John Marriot, who was directing the Sudan campaign. She was part of an elite coterie regularly dining with VIPs like Charles de Gaulle ("a Rodin sculpture . . . roughly cut and very sad"), the journalist Eve Curie ("an interesting fiery creature with . . .

The old Ottoman house overlooking the Tigris where Adrian Bishop entertained the best and the brightest of British officers serving in Baghdad—and Freya.

Freya, always passionate about clothes, enjoyed wearing romantic costumes. Here she poses with Peggy Drower, Stefana Drower's daughter and the last of her assistants in the Ikwan, in the garden of Freya's bungalow at number 14 Alwiyah, Baghdad, 1943.

rather repellent French hardness"), the English socialite Lady Diana Duff Cooper ("Her eyes are like the blue sky . . . quite literally dazzling"), or her husband, the politician Duff Cooper, Churchill's good friend, whom she had met in Cairo and with whom she had begun a lifelong friendship.[8] She also came to know the lovely Joan Ali Khan, who had scandalously left her husband, Loel Guinness, to marry the handsome playboy Ali Khan, son of the Ismai'li billionaire who had been so helpful to Freya on her first trip to Aden. Before long Freya had both Joan and Ali working for her, using Ali's influence with the Persians to set up cells in the Shi'a communities of Cairo and later in the Shi'a holy cities of Iraq. When the prince and princess of Greece came to Cairo, Freya gave a dinner for them at her flat.

Not everyone fussed over her. When she was introduced to the prime minister's magnetic son Randolph Churchill, he turned his back on her in midsentence. Freya was incensed, telling friends that he was "a quite unsufferable young man with appalling manners," and took pleasure when others remarked that this egotistical, overweight, and alcoholic ne'er-do-well was doing the Allied cause more harm than the Germans "simply by being himself."[9] It must have hurt a lot, however, to know his reputation for preferring only beautiful women.

But such nonadmirers were few or were very quiet about it. Most responded like Lord Sherfield, one of Harold Macmillan's civilian advisers to the Allied Army and later British ambassador to the United States: "She wasn't beautiful. She had a little bird-like face. But she had a luminous personality." He remembered Freya arriving in the middle of a dinner party in Tunisia in 1943, when the Americans had landed in North Africa: "This tiny person in a turban wore amazing clothes, sort of draped all around as if she had dressed herself in curtains. Within a half hour, everybody was eating out of her hand. She absolutely captivated the group."[10]

At the same time she impressed them, Freya made people laugh: with a whispered joke to the ambassador ("What did the brassiere tell the top hat? You go ahead and I'll give these two a lift")[11] or by a disarming eccentricity like the moment caught by Hermione Ranfurly at a picnic: "Freya Stark, dressed in a hideous sporting jacket, spun on her own mills in Italy, and snake gaiters topped by a large double-brimmed felt hat, was a sight for the gods, and her running commentary to her donkey made Sir Walter Monckton laugh so much he nearly fell off his mount."[12]

When the photographer of the fashionable, Cecil Beaton, arrived as an official war photographer, he asked to be introduced to Freya so he could take her picture. Gerald de Gaury wrote her that "he is coming your way. He asked what you were like and has the impression that you are a formidable dowager. My impression of his impression is that you are a cross between Agatha Christie and Mrs. Asquith."[13]

. . .

Freya was loath to leave Cairo to begin anew with the ikwan in Baghdad, but duty and Ambassador Cornwallis prevailed. After months of bouncing between the cities as the two ambassadors haggled over who should have her and Rushbrook Williams in London reminded them that she was "anyway on loan from Aden," in February 1942 she was finally assigned to the Baghdad embassy as second secretary. Her new status, she told friends delightedly, gave her the right to send her letters by diplomatic pouch. Privately she believed she had stepped on the all-important first rung toward an eventual career in the Foreign Service.

In Baghdad anti-British sentiment remained strong. The trials of Rashid Ali's followers were agitating the city, already tense at the prospect of a planned British invasion of Iraq's Shi'a neighbor, Iran. As the German Army piled up victories a few hundred miles to the north, rumors abounded. The headmistress of the best girls' school was said to have asked for exams to be advanced by two months so they might be finished before the Germans arrived. It was not going to be easy to launch the ikwan in such an atmosphere. But Freya got to work, gathering groups in a congenial spirit, probing their concerns, and spreading her particular brand of warmth, faith, and conviction that any reasonable person would surely prefer the democratic way.

If Baghdad wasn't Cairo, it was filled with good friends. General Wavell stopped by on his way to India, telling the embassy staff that he had come to see Freya because he had heard that she bought seven new hats. Freya, who had long used her closeness to Cornwallis and Lampson to urge that Stewart be transferred from Aden to head the ikwan, now had the satisfaction of seeing it happen. He was appointed director of publicity. If he had feared finding himself under Freya's authority, he could be relieved that she was his assistant instead, responsible for public relations, and she was even happier about such a position because she had always believed women were more effective when they took second place to men. That is, unless they dared to pay her less.

Briefly there was a flap over her salary. Freya met the usual formula of lower compensation to female government employees with unequivocal threats to resign, so it was settled that she be paid as much as her boss. Otherwise, she preferred not having to be responsible. She had no need to exert power by being boss herself; she was quite at ease with the considerable power she possessed. She hated processing papers and had, she declared, "an allergy" to numbers. Stewart, who knew the government's insatiable appetite for tidy accounts, wrestled continually with Freya's cheerful disregard for them. The less contrite she was, the more indignant he became, but it was hopeless. "I feel that the items are like very shy wild animals," she declared, "which I have to trace in and out of their elusive columns."[14] The new head of the ikwan in Cairo, Christopher Scaife, met her midyear in Jerusalem to review the Cairo records and suffered the same frustrations Stewart had. Freya, quite enjoying Scaife's predicament, wrote, "He was awfully pedantic and couldn't see why I had classified a typewriter (bought) under the heading 'telephones': they all seem to me the same sort of mechanical idea, and telephones were the only heading that had any money left."[15]

Vyvyan Holt, still advising Cornwallis, was also in Baghdad, so Freya was surrounded by men she enjoyed, and they accepted her as one of their own. Among them was Adrian Bishop, a brilliant adviser from intelligence, with whom Freya had spent many stimulating hours during the siege and, like all the rest, admired extravagantly for his wit and genius. Bishop often hosted the group in his old Turkish mansion on the Tigris and, unlike the others, got away with patronizing Freya a bit. When she talked rather more at dinner than Bishop deemed acceptable, he said: "Now little Freya, if you keep silent for some minutes, there will be a prize for you."[16]

Seton Lloyd, already making his reputation as a distinguished archaeologist, was a lodger in the house and in his memoirs remembered a time marked with stimulating conversation and considerable hilarity—conducted in the uniquely understated British way. At one dinner, which coincided with the spring flooding of the Tigris, water began gurgling through the floorboards. Bishop paused midsentence to indicate the noises should be ignored. "Half an hour later," Lloyd remembered, "we were sitting with our trousers pulled up to our knees and no further comment had yet been made; but, after a pause in the conversation, he observed—'I think, gentlemen, that we might now transfer ourselves to more comfortable seats for our brandy.' "[17]

Although the government had paid for Freya's transfer and helped her furnish her house in Baghdad, it was not enough to pay for a cook named Jasim, two houseboys, a gardener, and a weekly seamstress. Freya might have had an allergy to government accounts, but she was vigilant when the money was her own and showed great ingenuity in stretching it. With every intention of entertaining with flair, she decided to take in paying lodgers, although, to her pique, when Cairo HQ heard about it, they reduced her living allowance.

Freya had no idea that her brashness was being quietly marked by some who considered her too outrageous. She even suggested to the ambassador's wife that she lend her two servants from the embassy. Lady Cornwallis was appalled. If some, like Hermione Ranfurly, were amused at Freya's resourcefulness and ability to maximize every opportunity, others were less so as whole embassies and untold numbers of pilots at one time or another found themselves involved in ferrying Freya's souk purchases throughout the Middle East. Lesser mortals had no more chance of withstanding Freya's combination of charm and nerve than of resisting a tornado, but unfortunately for Freya neither did they forget. She was evidently unable to see the danger in allowing herself to believe she could get away with anything. In the long run, however, this blindness would hurt her career and keep her from fulfilling the enormous promise so many saw in her.

In the meantime she was indulged. Elizabeth Monroe, a Middle East authority and one of Freya's Foreign Office liaisons, said that if Freya ordered too many napkins one had to be careful or one would find oneself buying a dozen back from her. "It is easy to become cross with Freya," Mrs. Monroe said, "but difficult to remain so. She is such good value! Her intelligence is her greatest gift and asset, perhaps the explanation of her power to infuriate, and still to melt. It is her actual presence that produces the melting effect, all the men adore her."[18]

One young man, Nigel Clive, just graduated from Oxford and assigned to political intelligence, became one of Freya's paying guests—at Stewart's suggestion. Nigel was from a good family, and Freya, interested in such people, liked him immensely. Later, dissatisfied with the too-easy life in Baghdad, Nigel volunteered to serve behind the lines in Greece during the 1946–1949 civil war, but he helped with the ikwan long enough to become a lifelong friend. Nigel was one of the many young men who petted Freya, escorted her to parties, told her she was adorable, and wrote her extravagant letters about how she was "the thief of Baghdad," stealing their hearts. Throughout the war and long afterward, Nigel added his notes and cards to all the others from young men describing their postings so miserably far from "Freya-dom." When Nigel swore that he was in love with her, she seemed to take him at his word. According to Nigel, it never occurred to her that men *weren't* in love with her and poised to do her favors.[19]

But there was something amiss. Not Nigel, not Seton Lloyd, but many of these young men were homosexual. Adrian Bishop was. It was not discussed aloud, but Bishop, who resembled Oscar Wilde, had been involved in a sexual scandal that only his brilliance and the wartime emergency caused the Foreign Office to overlook. Later he was killed in a fall off a balcony in Teheran under rather peculiar circumstances. Pat Domvile, the officer who had dropped the Iraqi plane parts down the well during the siege and was a relative of Stewart Perowne, was gay—as was Christopher Scaife.

Although Freya seemed both unaware of and uninterested in homosexuality in general and in her circle in particular, she did once ask Nigel about Stewart. Why, she wanted to know, was he not married?

"You *are* absurd! Everyone knows," Nigel remembered saying, taken aback that Freya apparently was unaware that Stewart was gay.

"Come on, Nigel. What don't I know?" Freya persisted.

"That Stewart is *queer*."

Freya looked thoughtful. "I don't think for a minute there's anything peculiar about Stewart Perowne," she finally answered.

"I'm using 'queer' in the technical sense," said Nigel.

"What does *that* mean?"

" 'Queer' in the technical sense means 'homosexual.' "

"Oh. Like the ancient Greeks!"[20]

And that was that. Freya declined to explore the subject further. She clearly found the company of homosexual men safe. With them she could flirt yet be relieved of having to deal with authentic sexual tension. She needed to be a queen, and they gratified her desire without making more troubling demands. Always in love with being in love, and from every testimony a sensuous, very physical woman, Freya nevertheless was getting through a war that was producing romantic liaisons at every turn without connecting to an appropriate lover of her own. Could this have been by unconscious intention?

Clearly there were many ingredients in Freya's contradictory makeup: an uncertain, lonely, and traumatized childhood; the bullying unofficial stepfather, Mario; her parents distant and her father weak, her mother having refused to let her establish herself as an individual. All these elements simmered, chaotic and unresolved, as Freya bargained for love and reassurance—so long as she did not have to risk her most tender, deepest, private self. Her naïveté, her eagerness to be loved, her readiness to play their games, apparently brought out a protective impulse in the men around her. They laughed together about her flirtations, which were sometimes comically inappropriate, but to her face they were kind and competed for her company; it was all just part of her eccentricity, as harmless and innocent as her famous blue hat with the clock hands that pointed to the hours of assignation: five to seven o'clock.

With women, however, it was different. Stories merged into Freya's legend of the way she treated young female assistants, especially the pretty ones who were, "like slaves," made to do personal errands, even sometimes to press her dresses—not altogether unlike, one supposes, the duties her mother had once exacted of Freya. Peggy Drower, daughter of Freya's old Baghdad friend Lady Drower, followed Pam Hore-Ruthven as her assistant and spent two years trying to get repaid for the cost, not to mention the enormous effort, of packing up Freya's belongings and sending them to Asolo after the war. As her reward Freya urgently requested her to leave her teaching position at London University and move her husband and herself to Asolo to run the tessoria.[21] Any woman too young or tender to stand up to Freya was used mercilessly—those who dared resist soon found themselves elsewhere. Even if the girls were daughters of friends—and they often were—they were mobilized with evenhanded efficaciousness.

A more appreciative victim was the same Hermione Ranfurly who had observed Freya so keenly in Cairo. Now in Baghdad as personal secretary to General Maitland Wilson, in charge of the Persia-Iraq command in 1942, Hermione was dark-haired, vivacious, and a countess to boot. She had successfully outmaneuvered the entire military when they tried to evacuate her in 1941 along with other wives. She jumped ship in South Africa, escaped back to Cairo, and waited in hiding until her excellent secretarial skills were recognized and put to use. A strong-minded young woman whose husband had been captured by Rommel, the countess made up her own mind about people and was not easily pushed around. Arriving in Baghdad, she was delighted to be a boarder at Freya's pretty bungalow. In her diary, published in her eightieth year, Lady Ranfurly noted: "She is priceless; when I asked her what I should pay for board and lodging she just said, 'Whatever you earn I'd like three quarters of it.' It was said so charmingly I agreed and now I'm rather short."[22]

Hermione and Nigel Clive would explode with laughter behind their landlady's back at the appallingly bad meals served at Freya's table, often consisting of boiled cat or wild dog. Sometimes, on good days, they got camel. Yet as Hermione said, "Freya has a magic all of her own: she gets on well with high and low—old and young—and with all nationalities."[23]

Pamela Hore-Ruthven was a young woman whose good looks Freya seemed willing to forgive, especially since she was cooperative and had excellent connections. "I was very biddable," said Pam, who openly admired the remarkable Arabist who had so expanded her intellectual vistas.[24] Very quickly after Pam started work with the ikwan in Cairo, Freya began depending on her so much that she and her husband laughed secretly together over how possessive Freya had become. Although it was clear that Freya liked Pam's husband, it was equally obvious that she was jealous of the young couple's relationship. When Freya went to Baghdad in 1941, she flooded Pam with insistent letters until she agreed to come to Iraq and be her assistant. Freya didn't know it, but Pam was pregnant and Pat didn't want her to go. In the event, Freya won the struggle—for a time.

Pam landed in Baghdad in the fall of 1941, two years before Hermione, and Freya put her to work furnishing her spacious bungalow, sending her off to the souk to buy mattress-ticking curtains, bedspreads, and kilims. Pam enjoyed her tasks, the company of the intelligent men in Freya's circle, and the special warmth with which Freya always treated her. Freya, for her part, sighed to her mother about the impact Pam was making. "She is a great asset: I think it shows that I am really nice to have anyone about who eclipses one so utterly."[25] But to Cockerell she admitted that having beautiful Pam about stoked her fears of "getting so elderly and never beautiful." Freya said that it made her "wistful."[26]

But "wistful" was hardly the emotion Freya felt when Pam received too much attention. One evening at a dinner party Pam, because she was married, was seated in the place of honor at her host's right hand. Freya, her amour propre profoundly injured, froze the party with arctic indignation. For the first time Pam realized how much Freya resented being a spinster.

Not long afterward Freya and Pam went on ikwan business to the holy cities of An Najaf and Karbala, accompanied by a police escort. Although Pam was quite aware of the proprieties and had brought with her appropriately modest clothes, Freya insisted that she don a voluminous shirt and long skirt from her own suitcase that were not only hideous but hot. Pam, pregnant and unwell, was not happy.

Still, such discomforts seemed trivial compared with the spectacle of the holy cities that Freya opened up. Shown to the "stranger's quarters" of a mosque, Pam was deeply impressed to be a witness to an all-night discussion with the mullahs. She never forgot the sight of Freya settling in to what became a marathon political round with white-robed and turbaned mullahs who avoided looking at the ladies directly. Through the night, installed cross-legged on a gorgeous Oriental carpet, Freya was the personification of British imperial dignity, raising her right hand as she reverently uttered the word *democratia,* and letting it fall expressively when she intoned the dread names of the Axis dictators.[27]

When Pat got leave Pam wanted to return to Cairo and for the first time found herself engaged in a war of wills with Freya. Unwilling to let her go, Freya argued that women who could *ought* to be doing war work. Pam shot off hotly that it was soldiers who won wars and a woman's job was to love them and be there for them when they weren't fighting. It was not a battle that Freya was going to win. Pam left for Cairo, and it was the last time she would see her husband; he was killed fighting in the Western Desert. When Pam headed sadly back to Ireland to have their baby, she asked Freya to be the godmother. It didn't matter to Pam that Freya could occasionally "be difficult." She understood perfectly that Freya's lapses merely revealed the exceedingly needy and wounded spirit lurking behind all that talent and drive.

· · ·

The British of the older generation are apt to ask one another what "sort of a war" they had. "I had a great war," someone will say, while the other will admit to having had "a boring war." Freya had a ripping good war by any measure. Short of having been a general or an ambassador or even the prime minister himself, it is hard to imagine how she could have traveled as much as she did, impressed so many significant players, or had such a splendid time. When her friend Ambassador Cornwallis suggested she take her golden tongue to America to explain the British position on Palestine, Freya was completing two busy, productive, and fulfilling years in Iraq.

She worked, she said, "inhumanly hard." Day after day, through heat and dust, she met in large and small rooms all over the country with Iraqis asking difficult questions, pumping out her enthusiasm and faith in a democratic future, taking pride in bringing together Bedouin sheikhs and engineers or lawyers or carpenters and peasants, soothing ruffled feelings between one tribe and another, urging cooperation between Iraqi officials, and cheering on her staff. She even did her best to get committees started in the army, a delicate bit of maneuvering, for a law prevented political activity in the Iraqi military. She attended ceremonies at the Iraqi court, and her advice and insights were constantly sought by both British officialdom and highly placed Iraqi ministers, including her friend Nuri Pasha, the prime minister. Yet she almost never failed to find time to get her weekly facial or have her nails manicured or clatter off in high heels to dinners at the palace or British Club wearing some extravagant new evening costume.

Stewart, she knew, was often more than a little envious of her success. Cornwallis knew it, too, and told her so: "Stewart is as jealous as the devil," he said in 1942, when Stewart was giving Freya a hard time over her budget.[28] They wrangled like children when he insisted that he would make no more disbursements unless Freya detailed every item. Freya had managed several times to get leave for rest that the other hardworking assistants could not, and it rankled Stewart. He felt more than a little green over reports that the besieged soldiers of Tobruk were reading Freya's books, or that General Smuts of South Africa had told Miles Lampson that he had committed many of Freya's pithy observations to heart. At one point Harold Nicolson stood up in the House of Commons to publicly praise the work Freya had done with the ikwan. But it was impossible not to acknowledge that she worked harder than anybody, and Stewart inevitably came around to apologize—even when he learned that she had gone over his head and got Cornwallis's approval of her budget.

A nineteen-year-old university student, Nizar Jawdat, whose father would serve four times as prime minister of Iraq, was dragooned into the ikwan office on Rashid Street for several months of work. Fifty years later he remembered Freya's "phenomenal intensity and attention." Jawdat, later driven out of Iraq by the same coup that felled Nuri Pasha and now a Washington, D.C., art dealer, said: "She was far more focused than Perowne, who was all over the place. She would ask all sorts of questions and suddenly you realized that she was on to something and she'd go after it." Perowne, according to Jawdat, although "charming, suave, and good-looking," had a "mean edge" and enjoyed "sticking the knife in."[29] Nor did Perowne listen as carefully as Freya did to Jawdat's ideas and suggestions.

The truth was, Stewart was far more interested in the goings-on at court than in the struggles of nation building. What really captured his enthusiasm as public relations officer was getting a properly royal atmosphere established for this newly created Hashemite kingdom and its young king, only two generations away from life in a Bedouin tent. Stewart loved being an impresario of royal pageants, going so far as to obtain a disused royal carriage from the Buckingham Palace mews. He even designed the uniforms for a royal bodyguard. For a "Royal Hadiitha Hunt" he collected a pack of hounds to chase jackals—there being no foxes—and had bowler hats mailed by diplomatic pouch for the bemused Arabs to wear as they clinked their British stirrup cups. The old hands called his addiction to traditional British protocol, ribbons, and decorations Perownia and exchanged meaningful looks behind his back.[30] Although he was courtly and generous to his friends, and impressive on archaeological and historical subjects, Stewart evidently did not demonstrate to his superiors the seriousness deemed essential in dealing with the great events unfolding in the Middle East.[31]

• • •

Between late May and early June 1942, Rommel's battering ram finally crashed through Tobruk's defense, and twenty-eight thousand British defenders were captured, profoundly disheartening the hard-pressed British Army. At that very moment Churchill was in Washington, D.C., and the decision was made to send the first American-built Sherman tanks to aid the British Eighth Army, which was now backed up to El Alamein, only sixty miles from Alexandria. The German sword was pointing directly at the heart of Cairo, and the canal itself was in deadly peril. Despite the entrance of the Americans into the war, it was a dire moment. Malta had taken relentless pounding, while German U-boats sank Allied ships in catastrophic numbers. In Russia, German troops were pouring over the North Caucasus plains; Sevastopol had been taken, and in late summer the Germans advanced on Stalingrad. By September Russian soldiers were grappling hand to hand in the streets with German troops.

With typical British resilience, most people tried to be upbeat, and none more so than Freya. Still, like all the others crowded around their radios, Freya could not help wondering if Britain would be defeated. Reassuring herself that America's intervention would turn things around, she found herself hoping once more that her job as second secretary would translate into postwar diplomatic work. Things could work out for her just as they had for Gertrude Bell—her "Siamese twin," as she ruefully put it[32]—since the comparisons never ceased to irk her.

Eager to keep her options open, she periodically reported to her superiors that she hoped His Majesty's Government would be wise enough to continue a purely cultural and nonpolitical presence in Iraq after the occupying armies and political officers withdrew and hinted broadly that she could see a role for herself in such a plan. She said, and she strongly believed, that Britain would be wise to send high-caliber teachers and organizers on goodwill events through the British Councils to stoke the stuttering flame of pro-British sentiment. Astutely, she urged that the council personnel keep as clear as possible from current official Iraqi circles, something that most traditional Foreign Office people were reluctant to do. Imperial instincts die slowly, and it was hard for those long used to conducting the affairs of colonial people to face the hard fact that Britain would have to modify its part in a postwar Middle East—or not play at all.

The old guard, committed to maintaining its power bases, would fight democratization while Freya supported the yearnings of the effendis, the newly educated class of bourgeois who wanted reform. "One can have very little sympathy with the pashas of Egypt who keep their villagers on two and a half piastres a day, or the profiteers of Iraq whose cellars are stuffed with corn while the people go short of bread."[33] Freya saw clearly that hope for stability in the area meant resistance to reactionary elements, and she hoped that her ikwan could play a nonviolent, modernizing role.

Along with her friend Nuri Pasha and others, she anticipated the formation of an Arab federation after the war. But whether it would be Nuri's hope for a unified Syria, Lebanon, Palestine, and Transjordan with semiautonomy for the Jews in Palestine, or a pan-Arab league led by Egypt, no one could guess precisely. Freya and the other Arabists knew that cooperation between the Arabs—especially between the two sworn enemies Hashemites and Saudis—would not come easily. And there could never be stability if the fate of the Jews and their passionate insistence on a state of their own were not confronted imaginatively.

• • •

In August of 1942, when Freya was on a rest leave on Cyprus, a telegram arrived from Wavell:

> MISS FREYA STARK WOULD BE USEFUL IN INDIA IN CONNECTION WITH PROPAGANDA ITALIAN P. OF W. [PRISONERS OF WAR] PROVIDED SHE CAN BE SPARED AND WILLING TO STAY FOR 3 MONTHS INDIA. FAIRLY STRENUOUS WORK AND CONSIDERABLE TRAVELING. IF WILLING CAN YOU ARRANGE MILITARY PASSAGE BY BOAC TO GWALIOR.[34]

Never mind that she was exhausted. For a trip to India to stay with her commander in chief in viceregal splendor, Freya could find the energy and leave the ikwan—even though she knew its rapid expansion was putting pressure on the harried staff. Despite the injured looks from her colleagues, she submitted her request for permission to go.

The flat answer came back from Cairo HQ: "Request denied." Determined, she tried again, pleading that she would spend just a fortnight and pay her own way. One can only imagine the pleasure her bureaucratic critics took in denying Freya this special opportunity. For a long time she heard nothing. "Cairo is . . . like the whirlpool of Niagara, things go round and round slowly but never get out," she wrote Jock Murray in frustration at the end of January.[35] When she heard that Christopher Scaife in Cairo was telling people that her request was nothing but "flightiness," she began moping about her work, eventually coming down with gastric flu and malaria, and looked so pitiful that her colleagues became alarmed and begged her to take the leave. Finally Cairo consented: she could go, but for a fortnight only.

By February 1943 an ecstatic Freya, still suffering from intestinal difficulties, was settled with the Wavells in Delhi, noting that the ever-present cows in the crowded streets "had the air of petted beauties who have lost their figures"[36] and that on a ride with the c in c she had been catapulted over the head of her horse and as a result was having great difficulty curtsying. The days flew by.

Because the scheme to interview prisoners of war had been laid aside, Freya came up with a new idea, one that incidentally provided an opportunity to see parts of Persia she had not previously visited while collecting information from consulates about local opinion. Wavell was all for her reporting anything she might hear about Russian political activities along Persia's sensitive borders, especially at Meshed, where Russian agents were known to be active, so her proposed expedition had his blessing. It would be a glorious excuse to see the Himalayas and have a splendid new adventure without having to make a single pitch for democracy. So Freya bought a car for a thousand pounds, candidly admitting to a number of friends that she anticipated selling it for a huge profit in Baghdad. An RAF air commander, John Hawtrey, one of the young men who had competed to be her dancing partner in Baghdad and called her "adorable," now sprang to accompany her, declaring it would give him a chance to inspect air supply stations if he got leave from the air marshal in Delhi—which he did.

It was not easy to find spare cars or extra tires or gasoline, but with Wavell's intervention Freya soon had a dove gray Plymouth loaded with gas cans and was scattering people and animals from the road on her way to meet Hawtrey in Quetta, a hard drive north through Afghanistan and the Bolan Pass, the ancient so-called route of the conquerors. When they rendezvoused in Quetta she was glad to discover that Hawtrey was carrying a revolver. They both knew that plenty of bandits along the way would be exceedingly interested in such a rarity as their little gray car.

In high spirits the two started out on a four-thousand-mile journey the first part of which took them south of the stream-threaded Chagai Hills of Baluchistan, then north the length of Iran to Meshed, Persia's holiest city. The burial place of Imam Reza, the Eighth Rightly Guided One, Meshed had been torn by rioting as recently as 1935, when the inhabitants tried to resist the sacrilege of the shah's new clothing regulations, taking refuge in their mosques, from which they were forced out at machine gunpoint. Freya learned from the British consul that an ikwan network would be useful there but would have to be delicately handled because of the Russian influence seeping over the border through Turkmenistan.

When they discovered that the road to Teheran west along the Elburz foothills had been washed away by spring floods, Freya and Hawtrey backtracked six hundred miles south on a roundabout route that took them along the edge of the pitiless Dasht-e-lut, or Lot's Desert, and through the famous caravan cities of Kerman, Yazd, and Isfahan. Along the way they stayed at British consulates or army posts while Freya probed for information on local political sentiment, learning that anti-British feeling was running high everywhere in the country. Where there were RAF landing fields, Hawtrey inspected their conditions.

The trip was a tremendous lark, and Freya and Hawtrey were easy companions for nearly three weeks. "Johnnie's opinion of my driving," she wrote, "is terribly unflattering—but no quarrels, which shows how unlike he was to Gertrude (miaow) and it really was most restful: every sort of desert and never a bit of propaganda."[37] They bumped the final miles into Teheran nearly a week after they had been expected. Neither dared dally any longer, especially Hawtrey, whose leave had been up for a week. Anxious to catch whatever lift he could get to Delhi, he was poised to jump on anything going to Baghdad. Freya, having no desire to tackle the dangerous route west around the Zagros Mountains to Iraq alone, decided to sell the car in Teheran.

According to Betty Holman, whose husband, Adrian Holman, was the Teheran consul, Freya, their guest, asked if she could use the help of their Armenian chauffeur in something having to do with her car. Her husband, fond of Freya after having lived through the Baghdad siege with her, gladly assented. The next thing Freya's hostess knew, the Holmans' chauffeur, quivering with excitement, dashed into the canteen where she worked waving five hundred pounds and asked her to put the money in the safe for him. It seemed that the chauffeur had gone that morning with Freya for a business discussion over glasses of tea with two Persians. When the Persians departed the car vanished with them—and Freya remained, holding five thousand pounds. She turned to the chauffeur and thanked him for his trouble with this staggering tip.

That evening, in response to the Holmans' stunned inquiries, Freya merely smiled and changed the subject. Her hosts, however, were embarrassed. They felt compromised and worried that they might be associated with the sale of what appeared to be semiofficial property in wartime without proper permits.[38] Ambassador Sir Reader Bullard, who had entertained Freya on a previous visit, was furious, immediately severing any further connection with her. There are no more letters from this distinguished diplomat in Freya's vast file.

Doubtless the official who issued her a purchasing permit in Delhi expected her to deliver the vehicle to the government car pool in Baghdad, where she would be reimbursed. But to anyone later bold enough to ask, Freya seemed imperturbably confident that she had acted sensibly and in self-protection. Had her car, privately purchased, been stolen—as it well could have been if she had tried to drive alone the rest of the way to Bagh-dad—the government would not have compensated her for the loss because the car was not in fact government property, only government-sanctioned.[39] At the time it had seemed out of the question to wait around in Teheran for the proper documents to be processed. So—rationalized the woman raised in Italy, where a little extralegal dealing to get around central authority was part of the culture—the solution was to dispose of it immediately on the black market. And that's what she did.

Freya and Johnnie Hawtrey just managed to squeeze themselves into a brigadier's car for a grueling race through the night to Baghdad. Perhaps out of contrition Freya spent the next several months visiting widely scattered committees in Iraq on a schedule so punishing that both her assistants and the embassy staff became concerned for her health.

Repercussions from the car sale lasted the rest of Freya's life. People never ceased to spin versions of how Miss Stark had purloined a government car and sold it for an outrageous profit. Depending on the teller's bias, the much-embellished tale was recounted with indignation or high humor. Freya was never officially reprimanded—or if she was she never let on. Nor did Lord Wavell mention the incident, continuing to correspond affectionately about her hats or poetry or some example of bravado that reminded him of her. Freya, seemingly unfazed by all the fuss, referred to it only passingly in her autobiography: "The history of my car caused some scandal, for I sold it for a splendid profit as soon as I got to Teheran, having omitted (by ignorance and not intention) to get the diplomatic permit to which I was entitled."[40]

The legend continued to grow that Freya Stark could get away with things because important people liked her and protected her. Nobody else, it was whispered resentfully, could engineer such a holiday when others were killing themselves at work or literally being killed in the field. As detractors fumed Freya's fans grew more vociferous in applauding her resourcefulness. Yet the incident hurt her. The official world, which Freya had so hoped would award her a diplomatic job, now began to share evaluations on the colorful Miss Stark. She was an extraordinary creature—talented, unusually courageous, and delightful company, it was agreed—but she did not appear to be the sort of team player that the Foreign Office embraced in its fold. In the world of diplomacy it was important to play by the rules. Wavell, Cornwallis, Lampson, and countless others would remain her friends, but from the brotherhood Freya most admired and to which she most desired to belong, the British Foreign Service, she never received a serious postwar overture.

Nevertheless, Freya's wartime contribution was authentic and measur-

able. The Ikwan al-Hurriyah would later be considered one of many foot-
notes to the mighty effort assembled by Western democracies to blunt
Nazi and Fascist ambitions in the East.[41] And it did enjoy an epilogue. In
July 1943 Cornwallis and the Ministry of Information decided that Freya
should embark on a lecture tour in the United States on the Palestine issue.
She consented to go, turning over her budget and reports to her successors, Christopher Scaife and Ronald Fay in Cairo. The enemy was in
retreat by now, and the previously uncommitted were rushing to the
ikwan in droves. There were thirty-four thousand members in May; by the
end of the year over forty thousand had joined from hundreds of towns
and villages throughout Egypt, Iraq, and Palestine. Only in Palestine,
where Lulie Abu'l Huda struggled to enlist the wives, sisters, and mothers
of men already engaged in a life-and-death struggle with Jewish militants
over who owned the land, was it difficult to recruit Arab members.

There was good reason for Ambassador Lampson in Cairo and Rushbrook Williams in London to be concerned about the size and strength of
Freya's "lusty child." Both during and after the war there were fears in
the Foreign Office that in the wrong hands the network could become a
double-edged sword. Debate went on over what should be done about it
after hostilities ceased. In Iraq the issue was made moot when the postwar
government simply abolished the ikwan as British troops and advisers left
the country, while in Palestine it quickly fell victim to the clash between
Jewish settlers and Arab landholders. But Egypt was different. The British
were not ready to relinquish either their bases or their control of the Suez
Canal, and maintaining a pro-British vehicle to influence opinion seemed
good policy. By 1947, when Miles Lampson retired, the embassy was paying the costs of supporting an ikwan with seventy-eight thousand members belonging to forty-eight hundred committees, although its purpose
was defined as nonpolitical and entirely educational.

But these were the troubled years that preceded the military coup by
the Egyptian Free Officers. In the autumn of 1951 the Wafd party repudiated the Anglo-Egyptian treaty, and the British were forced to introduce
stronger and stronger countermeasures against pronationalist guerrilla
activity. A virulent newspaper campaign had begun against the ikwan,
which by then had become deeply suspect. There were bomb threats in
Cairo against ikwan offices, and a bomb actually exploded outside the
office in Alexandria. By 1952 it was clear the British position in Egypt was
untenable. The ikwan's membership files were ransacked, and Ronald Fay,
who had stayed on as director, was quietly told by the embassy to leave the
country. Only days later, just before a frenzied mob burned the center of
Cairo, the Ikwan al-Hurriyah was officially banned. On the night of July

22–23, Egyptian army units, many of whom were members of the secret Muslim Brotherhood, seized the capital's key locations, and the Egyptian Revolution triumphed, led by thirty-four-year-old Colonel Gamal Abdul Nasser. Ironically, a year later, following an assassination attempt on Nasser's life, the Muslim Brotherhood was suppressed.

As for Freya, in August 1943 she was ready to be briefed for her American tour. Leaving Baghdad with Stewart Perowne, in *his* car, she conferred with Syrian politicians in Damascus, talked with the Zionists in Palestine, the emir of Transjordan, the politicians of Egypt, the military officials who had led the triumphant sweep into Tunisia; she even had a fleeting morning exchange with General Dwight D. Eisenhower, who had landed in Algeria. At last, feeling exuberant and well-versed on regional opinion and politics, she headed to London to confer with the experts at the Ministry of Information. From there Freya would cross the Atlantic Ocean to talk the perplexing Americans into good sense about Palestine.

CHAPTER NINETEEN

An American Tour

> *Life is real; life is earnest.*
> *How I wish it weren't.*
>
> —ON A TROOPSHIP,
> MID-ATLANTIC, 1943

*F*reya lay in a hospital in Halifax, Nova Scotia. At the end of October 1943, two-thirds of the way across the Atlantic on a troopship, she had begun to suffer acute abdominal pain. Fortunately, the ship docked just in time for her to be rushed into surgery before her appendix burst. Even so, a life-threatening and painful peritonitis had set in, and it took nearly a month to recover. Now, with pink returning faintly to her cheeks, Freya gazed out her window, ruminating on the full schedule that awaited her in New York, Washington, D.C., and Chicago. She dreaded the prospect of pitting her tired wits against America's prevailing pro-Zionist and anti-British sentiment. "Even a Zionist can't give one appendicitis without some supernatural assistance," she wrote peevishly to Stewart.[1]

As she fretted, her mind drifted to the question of her future. What would happen to her when the war was over? How would she fit into the new postwar order? It would be a different place, that was clear, where America, not Britain, would lead. She would be happy if, when things settled down, she were awarded "a little Vice Consulate by some quiet shore,"[2] as she confided to Stewart, imagining days in some well-appointed official residence composing reasoned essays and entertaining evening guests.

Utterly blind to the possibility that her formidable energy, and what she would surely have called occasional testing of tedious regulations, might have left enemies in her wake, Freya indulged in a bit of self-pity. She had served her country unstintingly and would give her best again for Britain in America. Even so, it would be hard when the war was over, knowing that she was alone, without her mother or Herbert to care what became of her.

For now, however, she had a job to do. She recognized that Britain's great empire would go, but she hoped her country would not abdicate entirely its chance for moral leadership. She wanted Britain to fulfill its promises to the colonial peoples she had learned to respect. "I have been thinking with more and more certitude on the wrongness of all our ways on becoming utilitarian at the expense of human relationships . . . the human relationship is what counts: and now that I have had time to think it all over, this has come to me so clearly that I feel I can lay hold on it as a definite philosophy and guide," she wrote Stewart.[3] Nations, at bottom, were just like people; both needed friends. Britain's former colonies would soon be independent. Already policy makers were talking about the inevitable competition over their resources and allegiance. Britain would be wise, she felt, to keep relations warm with the peoples of the East—or it would be left far behind the United States and the Soviet Union.

As for the goals of the Zionists, Freya, like her Arabist colleagues, was certain that they were incompatible with any reasonable vision of a harmonious Middle East, but the Americans were in an election year, and both Republicans and Democrats were endorsing a Jewish Commonwealth in Palestine in their platforms. Good fencer though she knew she was, as Freya rested in the enforced quiet of Halifax, she braced for an unpleasant reception.

Since late 1942 the world had grown aware of Hitler's deliberate policy of exterminating "inferior" people: the retarded, insane, homosexuals, gypsies, resisters, intellectuals, but especially and particularly European Jews. The extent of German savagery, however—the fact that two-thirds of all the Jews in Europe were being systematically gassed in specially constructed crematoria—still was not fully grasped by the general public. The Zionists, though, understood all too well and were fueled by their anguish. They were determined to save the Jews who survived, get them to Palestine, cooperate with the British militarily but do whatever they could to undermine the white paper, and, above all, establish beyond challenge a Jewish nation.

Freya knew the British were caught in a seemingly impossible bind. If they continued to allow the Jews to flood into Palestine, the resident Arabs would be overwhelmed by refugees far better organized, funded, and equipped to struggle over possession of the land. The effort to keep the Arabs neutral in the war might be lost, and Arab antagonism would bode ill for future British negotiations over oil. For Arab or Jew, British policy appeared to be both intolerable and inhumane: whichever way the British turned they committed an injustice against someone. But until the war ended and the Palestine Mandate question could be taken up by the United Nations, what option did they have but to continue their present policy of interning or removing the arriving refugees to Mauritius?

In 1940 the British had intercepted two ships on their way to Palestine and removed 1,700 refugees to the SS *Patria* for transfer to Mauritius. The Haganah, the Jewish Defense Force, attempted to disable the ship by planting a bomb on its hull. When the bomb misfired and blew up the ship, 200 people drowned.[4] In 1942 the British colonial secretary, Lord Moyne, denied entry to Palestine to 769 Romanian Jews escaping from a Black Sea port on an unseaworthy cattle boat, the *Struma*. The Turks blocked the vessel's passage; it foundered and sank, with only 2 survivors.[5] Worldwide Jewry protested furiously, while to the Americans Britain's actions seemed almost as barbarous as Hitler's. Such incidents gave ammunition to the Zionists' lobbying efforts in the U.S. Congress.

To Freya, and to her Arabist colleagues close to the drama in Palestine, the actions of the Jewish terrorist groups were appalling. In Baghdad at the time of the *Struma* incident, she quickly learned that in Jerusalem, in revenge, Zionist extremists had murdered the deputy police inspector and rigged bombs to the house of her friend the high commissioner Harold MacMichael. At the inspector's funeral, mines were then discovered hidden along his funeral route. Freya was all too aware that she could have been in the mourning party. Therefore, when she arrived in New York she had a very different perspective from that of the Americans she had come to influence.

· · ·

In New York, Freya was luxuriating as the guest of Mrs. Otto Kahn in her mansion at 1 East Ninety-first Street. Mrs. Kahn and her two daughters, whom Freya had met in Cairo, like a number of wealthy American Jews, were deeply ambivalent about the Zionist goal of turning Palestine into a Jewish state and were horrified by the methods of secret groups like the Irgun and Stern Gang, who engaged in extortion and arms stealing as well as acts of terrorism against innocent civilians. The Kahns wanted nothing to do with men like Menachem Begin and Yitzhak Shamir, who organized violent plots aimed at British officials. Eager to demonstrate their distance from the Zionist cause, they entertained Freya for nearly a month, introducing her to prominent opinion makers from the worlds of theater, publishing, business, and finance.

With everyone, Freya found herself arguing—intelligently, pleasantly, but constantly. From New York she went to Washington, D.C., where she met with government officials, members of Congress, cabinet members, and the owner of *The Washington Post,* Eugene Meyer, and argued some more. Because most of these Americans seemed not to have heard of the second clause of the Balfour Declaration, she recited it, trying not to seem preachy. Over and over she assured her listeners that the British had fulfilled the *first* part of the declaration—facilitating a National Home in Palestine for the Jews—and now had an obligation to fulfill the *second:* "Nothing shall be done," she repeatedly quoted, "which may prejudice the civil and religious rights of existing non-Jewish communities in Palestine."

In her most polite English manner, she suggested that it would be fair to everyone if people would only agree that nothing should be done without the Arabs' consent. "We musn't *impose* solutions," she ceaselessly explained. She predicted that an Arab federation would be created after the war that would surely make room for a Jewish community. After all, in traditional Islam there had never been racial prejudice against Jews; that was a Christian habit. And it hardly made sense, she insisted, to make the Palestinians pay with their homes and lands for injuries done to Jews by European Christians.

Wined and dined, presented before women's groups and newspaper editors, Freya was stung by the criticism hurled at her. Not only harangued about Palestine, she was faulted by opponents of Britain's colonial policies. In the privacy of her room in the evenings, she would fume that the Americans had apparently forgotten that Britain had stood *alone* as the bulwark against Hitler for *years* before the United States bothered to help. And England was *still* fighting. Sometimes her irritation surfaced and she would bark, "There is a *war* on. When it is over, *then* we can address these problems."[6] In the meantime she had to endure with as much grace as possible those who repeatedly pointed out that Britain would be taking second place after the war.

When she was introduced to Clare Boothe Luce, the wife of Henry Luce, founder and editor of the influential *Time* magazine, Freya reported to London that Mrs. Luce looked at her "as an enemy on sight, with lovely eyes firmly fixed on the middle distance." A playwright, polemicist, and later ambassador to Italy, Mrs. Luce announced flatly that the British had no right to be in India and should remove themselves immediately.

Freya responded that Britain needed time to avoid a massacre between Muslims and Hindus. Mrs. Luce retorted: "Let there be massacres. Why should the white races have a monopoly on murder?" Freya, barely restraining herself, suggested that Mrs. Luce might like to adopt a "Freedom for Fratricide" slogan. Mrs. Luce stared coldly back as Freya offered her most dazzling smile.[7]

Freya was amazed by American women. She could not decide whether they were insufferably efficient, their blue hair and set faces "stonily out for culture," or whether she approved of them because they didn't seem "to mind being middle-aged."[8] She thought the numbers of women who turned out for "issues" lunches like those given by the Foreign Policy Association a remarkable phenomenon. "The hand that rocks the cradle seems to go on rocking indefinitely in all sorts of unexpected places," she reflected.[9]

Alice Roosevelt Longworth, daughter of Theodore Roosevelt and the acid-tongued queen of Washington society, was one woman Freya found refreshingly different, "full of gaiety and malice."[10] By now convinced that most Americans were marginally uncivilized, Freya enjoyed talking to someone interested in Greek civilization in Bactria and so committed to daily exercise that, by way of demonstration in the middle of lunch, Mrs. Longworth picked up her foot and used both hands to wrap it over her shoulder. Freya found this delightfully eccentric and felt more at home.

Everything Freya heard or said was dutifully reported to her "other end" in London, Elizabeth Monroe, the Foreign Office Middle East specialist responsible for handling her tour. They were amusing letters, livened with remarks on how bad the hats and how good the shopping but mostly descriptive of policy discussions and the people she met. Occasionally some of the self-pity Freya felt seeped into her reports, as when she complained the tour was like being "an unarmed Christian in the arena with no particular method for dealing with the lions."[11]

To add to her difficulties, it was whispered that a secret British cabinet committee was revising Palestine policy and might come around to recommending partition. If true, this was alarming news. If the Palestine issue were to be settled and the 1939 white paper policy that she had been dispatched to America to defend officially disavowed, Freya would be left hanging by her government, a fool in the eyes of all who had heard her. Although she peppered Mrs. Monroe with inquiries and asked for reassurance that Britain intended to stick by the white paper, no satisfactory response came from London.

As it happened there was a young scholar in the British Foreign Office in Washington responsible for keeping Whitehall up-to-date on weekly political developments in America. Posing as a journalist, Isaiah Berlin was actually an intelligence officer with a secret channel into the heart of the British government, and he had learned that there *had* been a change of view about Palestine within the prime minister's committee. When Freya looked him up in Washington, however, he concealed this information. "So we chatted," recalled the man who was later considered one of this century's great intellects. "We got on extremely well. Our views could not have been more different. She wanted the Zionist movement suppressed; I wanted it to succeed. I said nothing. It was not my business." He confined himself to reminding her that many of the politicians, like Churchill and Duff Cooper, were Christian Zionists. Freya responded that politicians come and go but the Civil Service stays, and the old hands in both the U.S. State Department and the British Foreign Office were on her side. Their view, she insisted, would eventually prevail. Looking back, Sir Isaiah said Freya's tour had been doomed from the start: in both London and Washington the momentum generated by the pro-Zionist forces had become irresistible.[12]

Churchill never announced his cabinet's change of policy, because the following year Lord Moyne, who had been a target of Zionist resentment ever since his involvment in the *Struma* affair, was murdered by the Stern Gang. The assassination of his close friend temporarily cooled Churchill's ardor for Zionism, and in November 1944 he told the House of Commons: "If our dreams for Zionism are to end in the smoke of assassins' pistols, and our labors for its future to produce only a new set of gangsters worthy of Nazi Germany, many like myself will have to reconsider the position we have maintained so consistently in the past."[13]

The debate over Palestine was destined to continue until 1945, when the war ended, Churchill was defeated in the succeeding election, and Franklin Roosevelt died. It would fall to a new generation, led by Clement Attlee and Harry Truman, to see the Zionist dream come true.

. . .

As Freya continued west on her American tour, reporters had a field day writing up "the female Lawrence of Arabia." *The New York Times*, *Newsweek*, *Time*, *Collier's*, *Vogue*, *The Christian Science Monitor*, the *Chicago Daily News*, the *San Francisco Chronicle*, and many others all published articles. "If a small, sloe-eyed, soft-spoken Englishwoman now visiting in Chicago hadn't learned Arabic during a three-year invalidism in Devonshire," began a typically exaggerated story in the *Chicago Times*, "Rommel's army might have reached Cairo."[14]

Freya simply twinkled beneath her hat brim and patted the hand of

When Lord Balfour issued his famous declaration announcing official British support for a Jewish national homeland, Palestine erupted in the greatest violence yet seen. Here, a Jewish home in Hebron has been ransacked by Arab rioters.

Violence was not confined to the Arab side alone. Here, the home of a well-to-do Muslim family near the Jewish quarter in Jerusalem has been looted by Jewish rioters.

whichever reporter happened to be standing by. She only denied she had ever been or was now "an agent," although this was how she was frequently described.[15]

Not surprisingly, with the November election looming, politicians seized on all the publicity. On March 29, 1944, Representative Emanuel Celler, a Brooklyn Democrat with a heavily Jewish constituency, rose in the U.S. House of Representatives and loosed a broadside: "Mr. Speaker, it is tragic indeed, to have Britain seal the doors of Palestine against Jewish immigration. . . . But the British Ministry of Information adds insult to that injury by importing into this country one Miss Freya Stark. She is a paid 'agent provocateur' . . . spreading lies concerning the Palestine Jews in her efforts to justify the infamous MacDonald White Paper which bars Jewish immigration into Palestine.

"She is a decided mischief maker," the congressman fulminated, "a sort of modern Molly McGuire trouble breeder. She bears watching. She is a Judeaphobe and an Arabophile. She is the usual stooge of power politics. We want none of her kind in this country. It is amazing that the British Ministry of Information, a creature of the British Government, allows this woman to make these outrageous statements to the American public."[16]

The British embassy in Washington rushed into high gear to counter the charges. Miss Stark was a "world-famous authority," read the hurriedly written statement to the press. She had been "granted leave by the Ministry of Information to deliver lectures in Chicago," and the ministry was merely "defraying her traveling expenses as an officer." That she should have been given the opportunity to speak to "other educational parties" while in America was purely incidental.[17] In fact, of course, Freya was being paid to do exactly the job she was doing. But the embassy saw fit to disclaim any official government sponsorship of her mission.

Freya accepted the rationale behind the embassy's stated position, but she was indignant at—and a little frightened by—the congressman's venom. Quickly, she penned her own comment to *The New York Times*: "I wish to put on record that I am in no sense anti-Semitic, that indeed I am not anti-Zionist except insofar as I feel that their establishment in Palestine can only rightly be made by agreement with the inhabitants of the country and not by force."[18]

Then she wrote Sydney Cockerell: What on earth did it *mean* to be a "Molly McGuire"?[19]

· · ·

It was not long before the tempest had boiled across the Atlantic, and London was asking for an accounting of Miss Stark's activities. Geoffrey

Mander, a member of the House of Commons, requested that the minister of information, Brendan Bracken, a close friend of Churchill, be summoned before the House to explain the matter. Exactly what was Freya up to in America? On April 27, 1944, *The Times* of London reported the following exchange:

> MR. MANDER: Can the Right Honorable Gentleman give an assurance that there is no foundation for the statement that Miss Stark has gone out to spread pro-Arab propaganda?
>
> MR. BRACKEN: Miss Stark is a distinguished scholar who has been followed through the United States by a number of persons anxious to traduce her, and I wish to put it on record that she has nothing to do with propaganda for Arabs or anyone else.

At this point, a third member of Parliament chimed in:

> MR. KEELING: Would not the Right Honorable Gentlemen agree that she is one of the greatest authorities on the Middle East and is a most admirable person to represent British culture in America?[20]

This ringing endorsement in Britain's highest body did much to consolidate Freya's position—not to mention buoy her spirits. The papers quickly rounded up statements from old friends like Sir Ronald Storrs, who tut-tutted in the *Evening Standard:* "I have known Miss Stark for years and the idea that she is grinding axes for anybody seems to me not only baseless but ridiculous."[21]

And Sir Sydney Cockerell, never willingly absent from a good brouhaha, weighed in simultaneously: "Miss Stark knows the Arab world as very few have ever known it. She speaks about it not as a propagandist but as the leading authority."[22] He then skipped over to Parliament to deliver into the Right Honorable Geoffrey Mander's hands a copy of the little diary Freya had kept of her first visit to the East. Cockerell had edited it over the last year, added a glowing introduction, and given it to Jock Murray, who had just published it as *Letters from Syria* to the usual praise. The timing of the book and the publicity Freya was receiving made a very happy confluence of events.

. . .

By the beginning of April 1944, Freya was more than ready to come home. She had done what she had been asked to do, but she had experienced a great weariness with her thankless job. The position she had defended was right, she believed deeply, but in the end she felt defeated and hopeless. There was nothing more she could do or say, so why try? At least she had visited Lucy and John Beach in California and sorted through her mother's papers. She had even got to Canada to do the same with her father's affairs. When she left the Beaches, Lucy wrote an old friend from Asolo, Lady Anne Lawrence: "You know I've not seen Freya for six years and I find that she has grown very much. She has great poise and authority. Her lines are clear and firm. Flora would be very proud of her. But she is the same dear person, quite unspoiled, and it has been a joy and a comfort to have her here. We hated to have her go."[23]

Heading home to England, where the Allied invasion wings were "trembling and unfolding," Freya concluded that she hadn't much liked America despite finding certain individual Americans appealing. The trip, she felt, had been "like going to the dentist: so much of one's substance gone, only to get hurt."[24] Besides, wasn't there something wrong with a country that treated its black people the way the Americans did? She had seen the shabby ghetto called Harlem in New York and the notices in buses in Washington requiring "Colored" to sit in the rear. "It is rather the same sort of idea which sees no harm in filling Palestine regardless of its feelings, and much nearer the Nazis than people like to say."[25] After all, she had seen how rich and vast America was, with room enough for all sorts of people. It was a bitter thing, she concluded, that with their space and land and opportunity, the Americans were so grudging about accepting Jewish refugees.

She had felt little rapport with a nation that seemed so materialist: raw, loud, standardized, energetic without profundity, "a moneyed wilderness." Oddly enough, the Americans she had most enjoyed, whom she had consistently found the most "sympatique," were Jews. Not the ones who had heckled her at lectures or written vitriolic letters but the thoughtful ones who had been, in her view, far and away the most interesting and cultivated of the people she had met: American Jews, she decided, were the ones "most out for ideas."[26]

On D day, June 5–6, 1944, the Allies landed at Normandy. The massive reconquest of Europe began. In London a few weeks later, Freya watched doodlebugs, the dreaded German V-1 rockets, buzz murderously over the city. "How good to be back in dear old London," she scribbled to a friend, "so shabby and knocked about and wearing her rags so toughly."[27]

. . .

It would be a long time before Freya recovered from her American visit—arguably, she never did. Failure, criticism, and most of all rejection had always been frightening to her, and America had rejected views she held at her very core. In later years friends like Pamela Hore-Ruthven remarked that after America, Freya avoided getting into controversies over Palestine. After the war she wrote no more books about Arab lands—which were rapidly metamorphosing into military dictatorships while a state called Israel, even before it was recognized by the United Nations in 1948, clearly existed. She regretted this extraordinary triumph for some because of the cruel harvest it would leave for others, but there was nothing she could do about it.

Although detractors periodically surfaced to accuse Freya of anti-Semitism, she was both comfortable with and accepting of the great varieties of people who always made travel a fascination for her. She believed, she said, in "pluralist societies," and she disliked any form of "religious extremism." Her objections to Zionism were philosophical and political, not racist, and she pointed out that it was unfair to equate her anti-Zionist position with anti-Semitism. She was sympathetic to the Zionist dream of a homeland for Jews, safe from a world that repulsed, isolated, and ultimately murdered them, so long as, she would point out, it were not exclusionary. She foresaw that the creation of a Jewish homeland that displaced Arabs to fulfill the dream would spawn a legacy of violence lasting for years to come.

PART FIVE

THE *N*OMAD QUEEN

*There ought to be more time—or at least
some arrangement by which those of us who
want more get it and those who have too
much of it could get rid of it.*

—REMARK TO A FRIEND, 1934

CHAPTER TWENTY

Mrs. Stark

> *People who have gone through sorrow are more sympathetic*
> *than others, not so much because of what they know about*
> *sorrow, but because they know more about happiness. They*
> *appreciate its value and its fragility, and welcome it wherever it*
> *may be. The Puritan attitude which grudges happiness belongs*
> *only to those who have never entered very deeply into life.*
>
> —BEYOND EUPHRATES

On May 8, 1945, the war in Europe was over, but Freya was not able to witness the rapturous celebrations in London and Paris. She was in India, tearing up and down the subcontinent for Lady Wavell, who had asked her to come back and set up another prodemocracy network. This time the target was Indian ladies, whom Freya would presumably inspire to discuss the future of India in kaffeeklatsches and teas, although it was more than a little questionable whether rajas' wives were the best conduit for conveying democratic ideals.

It didn't take long for Freya to see she wasn't getting far. The women weren't much interested, nor for that matter was Lady Wavell. It was hard for anybody to work up enthusiasm for yet another British-sponsored effort when the days of the British in India were clearly numbered. But having spent two draining months the previous summer at Thornworthy, Devon, finishing *The Arab Island*, her book on the Arabs for the American publisher Knopf,

Freya had leapt at the Wavells' invitation to come to India the previous November. It had solved the problem of what to do next and had given her a paid opportunity to witness the twilight of the British Raj.

Thanks to Lord Wavell, she had even managed to be in Simla during the great conference on India's future attended by Gandhi, Jinnah, and other nationalist leaders. Unfortunately, she developed blood poisoning through an insignificant wound and became quite sick. But Lord Wavell came to her room, sat on her bed, and described the history-making events unfolding next door. He hoped, he told her, the British would be able to withdraw in stages and prevent the awful massacres that he correctly anticipated would occur between Muslims and Hindus if independence were not carefully orchestrated.

The gravity of future issues notwithstanding, Freya, like everyone else, was profoundly war weary. All she really wanted was to get to Italy and see her beloved Asolo. After all these years the yearning was overwhelming. In April 1945 Freya heard that Verona, so close to Asolo, had been liberated. To Pam Hore-Ruthven she wrote: "I feel as if there were an earthquake inside me."[1]

At last released by Lord Wavell, Freya traveled to Venice with fresh lemons, olive oil, sugar, and flour stuffed in her baggage. True to form, she was the first civilian to get past the restrictions of the military authorities. Others less well-connected would not get permits to return to Italy for months. On July 25, 1945, Freya was on her way to Asolo. As she drove past exploded tanks and crossed temporary bridges, she was heartened by glimpses of peasants on their way to church dressed in their Sunday best. There was poignancy, she mused, in the sight of people trying to maintain a normal life in the midst of terrible loss and dislocation. At last she found herself passing beneath Asolo's old Roman arch, by the sixteenth-century fountain, and finally, incredibly, walking through the gate of her house. Her heart beat wildly, her eyes were luminous with unshed tears. After nearly seven years Emma, the maid, opened the front door as if nothing had changed.

It was a glad reunion, although the ghosts of the old people haunted every room. The servants, Emma and the gardener Checchi, were relieved to have Freya back, and she was grateful to find Casa Freia intact if down-at-the-heel after serving as the regional Fascist headquarters. Flora's lace curtains had been savaged to adorn a Fascist baby's cradle, the insides of Herbert's prized books had been ripped out to light fires, and the laurel bushes had been butchered to discourage snipers. But there were cheering moments as villagers arrived bearing the household possessions she had hidden what seemed like a lifetime ago.

The silk factory, she was thrilled to discover, was still limping along; Flora had willed it to her secretary, Caroli Piaser, and Freya now asked to buy it back.[2] Caroli, a quiet, unruffled woman, glad to have the well-connected English lady returned to town and grateful for a job as her secretary, agreed, quickly making herself helpful in countless ways. The whole town was reduced to "neolithic foraging,"[3] as Freya wrote friends, and Caroli showed herself adept at this, as well as at maintaining the house, supervising the tessoria, and keeping up with Freya's increasingly voluminous correspondence—roles for which she would be amply rewarded when Freya died.

As Freya sought to rebuild her life, the town did the same. The war had left bitter divisions between those who had been Fascists and those who had been partisans; the Communist Party was growing in influence, and beneath the rubble a new level of bribery and administrative corruption had set in. Freya found herself acting as an "unofficial liaison" officer.[4] People came to her door night and day to air their problems and recount hair-raising stories of Nazi cruelties. From Dronero the sad news came that her two nephews were dead. Paolo had been captured by the Russians and died in a prison camp,* and Roberto, who had joined the partisans, had been shot by the Germans. Her niece, Costanza, called Ceci, was the only one of Vera's children to survive the war.

When Ceci came down for a visit, Freya was overjoyed to see her pretty niece, hear her "laugh like springtime," and meet her husband, Franco Boido, a boy from Dronero whom Ceci had married the previous year.[5] Franco had been captured by the Germans the day after their wedding and severely beaten. But Ceci, Freya noted approvingly, revealed the family's resourcefulness when she got him released with a judiciously placed bribe and a gold bracelet.

Finally, but unenthusiastically, Freya saw Mario. "What I feel about my brother-in-law is unprintable," she wrote Jock Murray. She was shocked by his haggard appearance; she told Jock that all Mario's vices were now in his face, "so that one does get punished in this world after all."[6] When Mario refused to give Ceci jewelry that had belonged to Vera, Freya decided she would give her niece the house at La Mortola. The house needed much repair after all the shelling the coast had endured, and it seemed a satisfying irony that it should be done with di Roascio money. Freya looked forward to a long and happy relationship with this precious remaining family member.

---

* Although Freya tried hard over a period of years to learn Paolo's fate through various Russian contacts, neither she nor anyone else received specific news of his death. She concluded that he did not survive a Russian prison camp. He was never heard from again.

. . .

As Europe rebuilt, Freya settled down in Asolo. *The Arab Island,* her sensitive and engaging account of the important transitions taking place in Arab lands, had been enthusiastically received in America, and she hoped it would help the Americans understand a region she felt they knew alarmingly little about. Jock Murray prepared to bring out a British edition. By default it seemed, Freya found herself once more looking to pen and ink to define who she was and how best to continue making her mark. She had been a participant in the greatest conflict the world had ever seen and been deeply moved by the heroism she had witnessed. But had all the sacrifice achieved a just world? She sensed that as people struggled to recover from the legacy of destruction, the issues might not be so clear-cut. Would there ever again be heroes on the scale of those like Wavell and the others she had known? Increasingly Freya found herself drawn to the history of antiquity and began rereading the classics, fascinated in particular with the greatest general of them all, Alexander the Great. In the meantime she felt an enormous sorrow for her impoverished country and, ever the patriot, wanted to continue serving England—if there were only a way.

A small hope was still alight for that "little Vice Consulate by some quiet shore," so when the Allied Military Government offered her a job doing more public relations work, Freya leapt at the chance. This time she was to create "reading centers" the length of Italy, providing newspapers and periodicals to a citizenry readjusting to freedom. In the coming national election the defeated Italians would decide whether to keep the Savoy monarchy or establish an Italian republic. The British occupying forces reasoned that reading centers would reintroduce the Italians to the Free World and reestablish good terms between the two countries. Freya needed the income and was thrilled to learn the government would put a car at her disposal. The young Ministry of Information officer in Rome who would be her boss, Michael Stewart, was somewhat taken aback when Freya, who could never resist maximizing an opportunity, asked if he would mind calling her salary an "allowance" so she could avoid both English and Italian taxes. It was hard to object to someone as charming and famous as Freya, so he smiled and agreed. Yet he noted, as others had, that it was not the way people in official capacities were expected to behave.[7]

. . .

No sooner was Freya in possession of a large government car than she invited friends from rainy London to share the Italian sunshine. In no time she was racing about the countryside with the cartoonist Osbert Lancaster and Lulie Abu'l Huda, her former assistant in Cairo, as they tore into cathedrals and added their lunches to the government tab—cramming in reading centers between sightseeing stops. New friends like the journalist Alan Moorehead and his wife, Lucy, arrived, also the writer Patrick Leigh Fermor. Pam Hore-Ruthven came with her two young sons; Freya's Baghdad friends Nigel Clive and Gerald de Gaury visited, too, and even Christopher Scaife, with whom she was back on good terms. They chatted in the garden against a racket of workmen installing spectacular new marble bathrooms, shell-shaped sinks and tubs festooned with canopies. "I have decided never to save any money *ever*," Freya drawled languidly over the uproar, "and to collect things that are beautiful . . . as a protest against this dreary evenness."[8] She also decided that it was time she wore mink. Friends regaled one another with stories of how poor Jock Murray was besieged with demands that he send four thousand English pounds in return for Freya's copyrights so that she could buy herself a fur coat. Declaring such a deal imprudent, Jock stood fast. "Absolutely not," he shot back in a telegram.[9]

When her chauffeur sideswiped a man who later died, and then an American deserter stole the car, the government terminated Freya's position. Officialdom had lost patience with Miss Stark's famous prodigalities and ingenuous machinations at government expense. As always when there was nothing she could do to change things, Freya accepted her disappointment cheerfully and bought a secondhand Vespa, which she drove erratically, arriving windswept at parties in satin and diamonds, and as often as not crashing into a wall to make the thing stop. Friends shuddered as they passed her roaring over twisting roads on her way to Florence to see Bernard Berenson at I Tatti or Marina Volpe at her glorious Palladian villa at Maser.

If anything, there were even more invitations from London than before the war, as well as requests for articles. It was so chaotic to have Freya visit, what with the "continual bells and tells," as one friend put it,[10] and varieties of little services required that Jock Murray usually ended up as host, letting Freya run his wife ragged with her hairdresser, theater, luncheon, and dinner appointments while Freya concentrated on filling in what she announced were gaps in the education of the younger Murrays, several of whom were her godchildren. She bought them a pair of gerbils so they could "learn about sex," but the gerbil mother attacked her husband and ate her babies, so the lesson was not a success.[11]

At Windsor Castle Freya visited Pam Hore-Ruthven, now a viscountess and extra woman of the bedchamber to the queen. Freya chided her for

In October 1947, Jock Murray hosted a splendid reception for Freya and Stewart Perowne at the publisher's Regency mansion at number 40 Albermarle Street, off Piccadilly. Freya was fifty-four, and Stewart forty-six, when they married.

becoming a snob but fluttered excitedly, Pam noticed, in the presence of Their Royal Majesties. Pam, who was far from snobbish, only smiled as Freya then sailed off for yet another grand country weekend with her growing set of fancy friends, Lady Nancy Astor of Cliveden, Lady Sybil Cholmondeley of Houghton Hall, Lord David Cecil of Hatfield House, the Nicolsons at Sissinghurst, the earl of Amherst or the earl of Grafton. In turn, she invited them all to visit her at Asolo. But there was one person whom Freya especially wanted to come.

. . .

Stewart Perowne had spent visits of nearly a month in Asolo. Freya was a little puzzled that he slept so much—staying in bed until noon, then returning to his room after lunch for a nap that lasted until teatime. She had recently embarked on a new book, which would come out in 1948, *Perseus in the Wind,* a little peroration on personal values that both Jock and Sydney Cockerell considered an extremely dubious undertaking. They had strongly advised her to stick to travel writing and resist this disturbing inclination to philosophize. But since the war Freya had taken to the role of pundit like a fish to water; her deft aphorisms were frequently quoted. Her friends no longer heard her mention anything about government service. She had stubbornly proceeded with the book despite what Sydney and Jock thought. Now she was grateful for Stewart's odd rest habits and the quiet they afforded. Little did she realize how much the visits meant to him.

In Baghdad he had been dealt a crippling blow. His superiors at the Colonial Office had told him that, now the war had ended, there was no prospect of further work for him in Iraq. He was dumbfounded. Except for Aden the entire span of his foreign service had been spent in Baghdad. He knew the Iraqi community, the court, the tribes. Now they were telling him that not only would he not be needed where he was most expert but there was a good chance the Colonial Office would not offer him employment anywhere else either.

The news was a defeat of his own hopes and the expectations he knew his father entertained for him. At Haileybury, the school founded by the East India Company whose distinguished alumni included Lord Allenby and Clement Attlee, Stewart had graduated second in his class and a superb athlete. One friend who later became the vicar of St. Paul's Knightsbridge remembered: "I rather hero-worshiped him—he was so refreshing as a boy. He had a way of standing aside and being amused by life."[12]

From Haileybury, Stewart went on to Cambridge. But the joy the young scholar found in his immersion in classical archaeology and architecture was extinguished when he learned that his mother, to whom he had been exceptionally close, was dying of cancer. Now his brothers, who from childhood had called him "the ginger cat" because he kept his own counsel, found it harder than ever to know what he was thinking.[13] Although his father hoped his talented son would make a career in the church, Stewart obtained a graduate degree in classics from Harvard University and returned to Britain to join the Colonial Service.

Freya, long titillated by the fact that Stewart was "the son and grandson of bishops of Worcester," settled into her chair at the dinner table, encouraging Stewart to describe the formidable Perowne family. His paternal grandfather had been the bishop of Worcester and an authority on the Psalms through his dazzling command of Hebrew, Aramaic, and Arabic. Stewart's father, Arthur W. T. Perowne, was first the bishop of Bradford, then succeeded his father as the 107th bishop of Worcester. Hard as the young Stewart tried, it was difficult not to feel eclipsed by Dr. Perowne's long shadow; perhaps that contributed to his decision to choose a different path.

During the restful weeks Freya provided in Asolo after the war, Stewart told her later, he privately confronted an emotional crisis: "I was desperate," he said. "I saw no future, no light."[14] His apathy and exhaustion were evidence of depression, but it was neither his style nor his upbringing to confess the depth of his discouragement to his hostess. He confided enough so she could encourage him, then set himself to be an entertaining guest. He talked about attending the celebrations in Damascus for Syrian independence from France, ending their mandate. Bevies of young Syrian beauties, he told her, followed the speeches by opening the bosoms of their gowns and letting fly pigeons—the "soul of free Syria." But the befuddled birds fluttered aimlessly, and at least one settled on the helmet of a soldier. Freya laughed and laughed.

After this visit Stewart returned to Iraq to wrap up his duties and ten months later went to England for a discouraging round of talks with foreign and Colonial Office officials. Then he came back to Asolo for another heartening visit with Freya. She was sympathetic about his career problems, telling him that as far as she was concerned he should have expected "a real welcome . . . after all your years of such successful work. I am sure they want you very soon and then will be all smiles and favours." She suggested that his troubles could be the result of the envy of others and the closeness he had enjoyed with the Iraqi court. If that was true, she told him kindly, "it gives a chill to the spirit and takes all the *joie de vivre* out of one's work."[15]

Two months later Stewart wrote that he had finally received an appointment. On August 22, 1947, he announced: "I'm going to Antigua (which rhymes with 'intriguer'), shall I send you some rum and slaves?" Although he considered it "banishment" and "ironically humiliating" and having nothing to do with what he was expert in, he was relieved to have this Caribbean posting, where he would be colonial secretary, a rank just below ambassador. He urged her to come for a visit.[16]

Two weeks later he followed with an electrifying letter:

> *My dearest Freya. Will you marry me? I really can't think of any*
> *good reason why you should—or I would have asked you before.*
> *But you do know me with all my imperfections. You know how*
> *inadequate and selfish I am. You also know how quite happy*
> *and how much more aware, and generally useful to society I am*
> *when I am with you. I feel that without you, the future is drab*
> *(not that I ought to try to appeal to you that way) but with you*
> *I think it might be the kind of adventure at which you are so*
> *outstanding an artist.*

He suggested that she telegraph her response so that he could tell people "the good news," then he would go on to the Caribbean, and she would follow as soon as her book and bathrooms were completed. He would allow her, he said, to revisit Italy in the spring "like Persephone," but "only for a bit!" and added: "I'm not as attractive as Pluto, but still, I hope you may find it possible to take me on, for worse, if not for better! Because I have come definitely to the conclusion that it may well be a very good thing for us both." Signing himself "your loving Stewart," he added that he feared his letter sounded "impertinent," but he was leaving it just as it was.[17]

It was everything, everything, Freya had ever wanted. Marriage at last! Of course she loved him. Hadn't she worked to help his career for years? Stewart's proposal had been a long time in coming—and she was as flabbergasted as she was deliriously happy. Also, deep down, she could not help being more than a little anxious—but she couldn't think about that now. She sent a telegram back: "Yes, of course—darling."[18]

Their friends were stunned. Many were alarmed. Few doubted that Stewart was homosexual, and those who knew Freya best worried that her persistent innocence on the subject meant trouble. Beyond that, there was the difference in age. Stewart was forty-six, Freya, fifty-four. Nevertheless, there were those who claimed the liaison made sense for them both, assuming that two such well-known Arabists would have much in common, even if their relationship did not include sex. Despite Freya's flirtatious ways, many friends wondered if she might not be sexually neuter, so surely little harm could come from a friendly professional partnership. They assumed it would be in the nature of a "grand literary alliance." Little did anyone suspect the powerful hope, the buoyant expectations, that now surged in Freya's breast.

. . .

She sat down to scribble notes, announcing to friends that "the most peculiar thing has happened."[19] First to hear was Nigel Clive, now in British intelligence in Athens as the Greeks fought the Communist partisans in a civil war. The closest of the devoted young male admirers Freya had gathered during the war, Nigel found her letter discomfiting. Still in his twenties, he never considered that their little flirtation was anything more than lighthearted banter. Her letter, however, revealed that Freya had entertained what struck Nigel as some sort of absurd fantasy about what might have been between them: "If you had been old, or I young, we might have lived our lives together: or perhaps we might not have cared for each other or not realized it. As it is, we hold hands across a river of time. Nigel, darling, please remain my dearest of friends."[20]

Touched and amused that she viewed their friendship so romantically, Nigel wrote back assuring Freya that they would be friends forever, but he did not remind her of their conversation six years ago in Baghdad, when she had asked why Stewart was not married. Relieved by this evidence that her support network was still solidly intact, Freya went on to inform Pam. "I expect you were as surprised as I still am, and I hope not quite as alarmed," she wrote on September 22.[21] On the same day to her friend Bernard Berenson she wrote: "I can't help thinking I shall make a very unsatisfactory wife, but one never knows."[22]

A number of her closest friends felt that they had an obligation to tell Freya outright that she could be heading into a disaster. Probably Sydney Cockerell, who prided himself on his truth telling, cautioned her on what she should expect. At any rate there is a curious hiatus in their steady correspondence during these weeks. The next letter from her "old secretary" was very short, expressing a resigned wish for her happiness and regretting that, at eighty, he was too feeble to attend the ceremony. When Freya arrived in London, her suitcases bursting with gossamer pink nightclothes for her trousseau, Diana Murray told Jock that she refused to attend such "a grotesque event," but Jock gamely arranged to give a party for Freya.[23]

On October 7, barely five weeks after his proposal, Stewart and Freya took their vows before the altar of the venerable and socially favored St. Margaret's Church, Westminster. Leslie Perowne, Stewart's younger brother, was best man, and Jock gave Freya away. "The worst thing I ever did," he said later.[24] The wedding was followed by a large reception at nearby St. Ermine's Hotel. Wilfred Thesiger, well-known for his travels among the Bedouin of Iraq and Arabia, remembered that only the tall green feather of Freya's hat could be seen floating "like a periscope" above the sea of guests.[25] Stewart's brother vividly recalled silently shaking his head as Freya signed the church register with a flourish, giving her age as a full five years less than it was.[26] Pam Hore-Ruthven helped Freya pack, and she too was distressed to see the abundant supply of peekaboo underwear Freya was taking along. Friends waited nervously for the honeymooning couple to return.

. . .

Testimony about the honeymoon differs, but it became another source of riotous speculation by Freya's friends and acquaintances for years afterward. The Countess Anna Maria Cigona, Marina Volpe's sister, resented the attention Freya always received but remembered hearing Caroli Piaser say that on the morning after they arrived she knocked on their bedroom door to bring their mail and discovered Stewart alone in bed clasping an armload of roses. She also said that Freya was furious at Stewart for losing his luggage to a thieving baggage handler; when the couple stepped off the vaporetto in Venice, the fellow vanished with the bags down a dark alley.

However, Freya said to Pam that the days had flown by and that while Stewart had been naive about handing his handsome bags to just anybody, their loss was merely the wages of sin from traveling with such smart luggage. Nothing of grave importance had been lost, only forty-nine little rosebushes that they had brought from an English nursery to plant in Asolo—and would Pam please come visit very soon and bring forty-nine little replacements?

As for Stewart, his subsequent letters to Freya glowed with love. On October 26 he left for Venice to go to London and thence to the Caribbean. "Darling . . . it has been the most wonderful fortnight—so short—none ever shorter in time, so long and deep in love. Il piccolino agrees!"[27] What this actually meant one can only speculate, but it certainly suggests something intimate and sexual between them; later, in the nearly daily stream of caressing letters from Barbados, Stewart referred to their sleeping together: "How I wish I were back in our charming bed rolling to the middle, with Maria bringing in the breakfast and you putting it into my lazy mouth (you can't do it here—it would be regarded as 'foreign' and 'immoral')."[28]

It would not be surprising if Stewart and Freya had made love on their honeymoon. As a man of his time, and especially as a bishop's son, Stewart wanted to be straight, wanted to please his urgent partner, whom he genuinely loved and very much admired. He yearned for the legitimacy and blessing of marriage as eagerly as Freya ever could have. He wrote from London that he felt sorry for his unmarried friends, although he continued to be amazed "that you should have paid me the compliment, done me the unique honour, conferred on me the sole privilege of being your husband."[29] He called her his "darling wife" and himself her "adoring husband." Over and over he wrote that he missed her terribly: "I do miss you so much, and am so delighted that our fortnight of reality can so obliterate years of unreality," signing: "Dearest love for always . . . *Eternamente*—what a pretty word!"[30]

After bidding good-bye to friends at Cambridge, Stewart spoke happily of the scholarly atmosphere and sense of tradition at his alma mater: "I wish you were here to see things for me. You always make me feel like a blind man relying on a guide, you see so much."[31] When he suffered an attack of rheumatism, he said it was so hard "without you to be cherished by day and night—an aspirin is really no substitute for a wife."[32]

. . .

By the time Stewart was established in Barbados, in the rather grim, small house the government had allotted them, his eagerness for Freya's arrival was spilling from every letter: "I love you more and more and can bear you not being here less and less."[33] He worried that she would be disappointed by their circumstances and tried to do what he could to make the house attractive before she came, although he told her that all the real decisions he intended to leave to her. In the meantime, he said, he was inviting no one over; everyone would just have to await his *wife's* arrival.

Freya had obviously sent some anxious inquiries about money, how they should share costs, and what arrangements ought to be made for her travel. Stewart attempted to allay her concerns. "Our first aim must be to get Asolo solvent, I agree," he wrote her. "But as we shall not be living there for some time, we must also think of Barbados, which is to be our *home*. I can provide all the basic requirements. But a bit extra will ease the shocks of life for you. If therefore you can make the 'hairpin money' correspond to what you would spend, whether you were in London or Italy (roughly), excluding capital charges, just . . . support of Freya, then I think we can get along." He told her also that he had changed his will, leaving her all his books, goods, clothes, and money—which would amount to "only about 2 quid," he added apologetically, but he wanted her to have it for her lifetime—then what was left could go to his brother Leslie and a niece.[34]

That in their absence from each other they were having fantasies of marital intimacy is clear by a response to an inquiry from Freya: should she bring nightgowns? "Yes," Stewart responded, "nightgowns are necessary. Not so much on account of [the ambassador's wife] as the servants. Here, one usually sleeps with no more than a sheet on one, and it would not do if Myra [the servant] came in and found you completely Rokeby. She'd tell a shocking tale and I should have to resign. So bring plenty of nightgowns."[35] He told her they had twin beds side by side.

As for Freya, whether it was, as she claimed, the strain of the book on which she was furiously laboring to finish or anxiety about the realities she might face when she joined Stewart, she now decided to defer her departure for a month. Her decision provoked more amused gossip among their friends. Lady Wavell's comment, "Freya Stark is interrupting her honeymoon to write a book on Love," enjoyed wide circulation.[36]

There is more than a little poignancy in knowing, however, that Freya was working at this time on the essay in *Perseus* devoted to sorrow. It would have been more accurately entitled "Rejection," for Freya was revisiting the bitter episode in her young womanhood when her sexual passion for her fiancé had been spurned. Without precisely identifying it as the time she went with Viva Jeyes to confront Guido in a hotel in Bologna, she vaguely alludes to waiting by a window looking into a brothel and watching prostitutes parading naked in their room.

Would she again be denied what every other being on earth seemed free to enjoy? Would she again discover that even prostitutes were better off than she? Could her husband reject her as Guido had when she was an innocent and desirous twenty-six-year-old if she rejoined him? And could she ever trust another man enough to consign herself and her freedom into his care? As Freya composed this chapter, the memory vividly awakened, a forgotten ache stirred; with it came an old fear: she must never be rejected again.

• • •

Freya knew she was taking a big step. Writing Stewart that the work on the house was finished, she admitted that "I am feeling so unflatteringly sad at leaving. I wish you were *here*."[37]

Stewart, however, was suffering no such reservations. He was impatient to have her with him and eagerly wrote that he had ordered her a pearl necklace for her birthday. Again and again he talked of how proud he was of her ability and reputation and warned her that she would be treated as a "Famous Person."[38] She should prepare some remarks for the press, he cautioned. With her arrival in Barbados imminent, Stewart anticipated the changes their new life together would bring: "I wondered, as I walked naked about the house, whether I can still be so free and easy when you are here, and just how much of the cupboard, dressing table and mirror space I shall have to give up, and how many clothes I shall have to put in a dressing room, and which it will be and how much dressing I shall have to do in it."[39] But it seemed a delicious anticipation.

At last, in the middle of February, Freya and Stewart were reunited. Almost immediately she was unhappy. The island was pretty and green, with neat fields of sugarcane and old parish churches, and they could ride in the morning, but Freya hated the official duties that Stewart assumed she would undertake. She wrote Pam two weeks after her arrival, "I am just bored to death with being an official wife, but you needn't say so to anyone around." The house, although small, had been arranged very nicely by Stewart, brightened by rugs and accessories he brought from the Middle East, and she had the help of an elderly cook and two black menservants. "I think them nice people with such gentle voices, and no hurry or longing for more work than necessary; as they immediately realized that I sympathized with this attitude to work, we got on very pleasantly."[40] However, the colonial community was suffocatingly provincial, self-important, and small-minded, and Freya found the racial divisions that permeated the island extremely distasteful.

But the real issue, from Freya's point of view, was Stewart. To both Jock and Pam she claimed that he was bustling about as "the Perfect Civil Servant and Priestly Son," and it was obvious she felt neglected. He was acting, she confided to Pam—asking her to hide her letter—like "a middle-aged married man far too busy to dally with [his] wife or anyone else: how much preferable to have a Blonde somewhere on tap and make it up to me in the intervals! I was awfully unhappy but am getting a bit tough now and there is perhaps a hope that his views on the Good Life may change. Oh Pam!" she wailed, prepared to indict the entire male sex, "what idiots they are!"[41]

Jock also knew things were going badly when Freya wrote that she felt "caged. . . . Don't repeat this Jock, but I did look down into an abyss and am still very wobbly."[42]

Freya's plan and Stewart's expectation had been that she would stay until October. By April, however, she was writing friends that she felt "imprisoned in a dewdrop"[43] and was returning to Italy in June. More explicitly to Jock she wrote: "This marriage business is not going at all nicely. I had a miserable time, and now the decision is made and I feel better, like after an operation. Perhaps a summer away may do good. I don't want to quarrel and I won't, but I will just go. And this would be such a dear little island with anyone who was a little bit in love with me."[44]

· · ·

It was all so understandable. Both spouses had duped themselves about what lay in store. The reality of Freya, with her corsets and stubby figure and yearning for passion, must have presented an arduous challenge to Stewart's nature—for all the romantic fantasies induced by their mutually deluding correspondence. Freya had left her glorious new bathrooms to come to an intellectually constricted community and life with a poorly paid medium-rank civil servant who was unable to sleep with her. No matter what the gossips might have said, those who knew Freya best spoke of her extreme femininity, her flirtatiousness—as one godson stated, she exuded "a very powerful physical presence; she was distinctly not neuter."[45] In this moment of truth, the tension must have been fierce. Both were profoundly disappointed and depressed.

Stewart must have been not only taken aback that Freya had no interest in the role of official wife but also concerned about the repercussions her flight might have on his career—about which he remained very insecure. There was no question that such a distinguished consort was a great asset, and Freya was perfectly aware that in this respect she had the upper hand. Further, she had no intention, ever again, of languishing in an unhappy situation. Ever since she had gained freedom by going east, Freya had recognized the importance of effective action. But could she acknowledge at all that she had brought this pass upon herself?

So Freya returned to Asolo. Her affectionate correspondence with Stewart resumed, but deep problems had surfaced. At this point neither had any intention of calling off the marriage; they both liked their new status and assumed things could work out. Freya set about using her considerable influence in diplomatic and Arabist circles to get Stewart out of Barbados and into a posting that they both would like better. He felt that he had let her down, but for the time being there was nothing he could do but stick to his job—and he missed her. "Freya! The house is like a grave!" he mourned a day or so after her departure. "So empty and silent—though fortunately not so empty as it was before you came. Your presence is about, in the most smiling and beneficent ways. But it will be hard to put up with echoes and shadows only."[46]

It was hard to suppress the hurt he felt: "At least you will allow that you're happier without *me,* than without anyone else! *Love, love,* nothing but *love.*"[47]

Freya sent him a silk suit from the tessoria and told him not to worry about pensions or a foreign service career but concentrate on making a good literary life together in some congenial place. Still, Stewart was understandably nervous about his future. "I admit that Barbados is boring (the most boring place I ever was in, and the most alien to me) but I *do* have to work here. You know that I'd rather be with you in Asolo all the time, but that can't be. So I rather selfishly assumed that during the six months of the year you contracted to marry me for, you'd identify yourself with *my* goings-on, Plutonic, admittedly, and then return to be Proserpine for the other six. But clearly, I had not got the rule of Plutonic Affection right!!"[48]

Stewart could not bring himself to use the term *platonic*, but clearly he was saying theirs had to be a platonic relationship. Freya, however, wanted to know more. Visiting Berenson at I Tatti, she evidently confessed to the old scholar that they were having difficulties. Apparently Freya told Berenson that she wanted things clarified; she wanted to know exactly what it meant when Stewart didn't sleep with her. Could he change?

"I have been thinking over all this year, full of strangeness, and find rather to my surprise that I do not really love you less! How astonishing!" she wrote on their wedding anniversary. But she added, "I think you have left something lying between us, untold. Whatever it was, it will not make me think less of you or care less for you."[49]

The time had come for candor. Stewart felt compelled to tackle the delicate issue. And so began an agonizing correspondence. He introduced the subject lightly, describing a pleasant dinner with friends: "Everyone [was] I think, 'queer,' which is the argot for homosexuality, and so much more euphonious. And yet their talk was alive, full of ideas and content," he went on, hoping to explain the pleasure he took in their artistic company.[50]

Freya was dissatisfied with vague allusions, and more probing letters from Asolo arrived in Barbados. One night, as if he had drunk too much wine to make the task easier, Stewart took the bull by the horns in rapid, barely punctuated sentences:

> It is difficult to say what "normal" is—my friend a counselor of St. George's Hospital always refuses to use the word and in both men and women, you have a wide and graded range from ultra-male to ultra-female with naturally mostly people in the middle ranges . . .
>
> Now for myself, I put myself in the middle group. I have ordinary male abilities. I like male sports some of them, and I love the company of women. In fact, I find it hard to exist without it. At the same time, I am occasionally physically attracted by members of my own sex—generally. For some even pleasurable reason—by wearers of uniform.

Why, you say, did I not tell you? It was not deceit dearest—
what you said . . . about my being honest means anguish and so
deeply. It was just shame, and a feeling that as the leaning was so
detested (by me) it would be kept down and that union with you
would cause it to disappear, as the sun puts out the candle.

What actually happened was that a neurosis started I was so
anxious to be "normal" that I fretted and fretted until the frustra-
tion set in!

I see now how wrong I was not to trust you. You realize that
this horror has been with me even since adolescence, and that it is
a terror, and a humiliation. At one time I spent much time and
money on a psychiatrist. But it was no good. So I say "it might
have been a club foot or a harelip."

That is the story. Since you on your side say that all that mat-
ters is love, (as if you hadn't always said it and shown it) you
make it so easy for me to tell you. . . .

Perhaps I should admit that since we've been married I have
averted my eyes from even the most handsome uniforms and that
you need have no fears that I shall ogle the Horse Fleet.

Well, that's a burden lifted, and, I hope dissipated. And now its
off, the old guilt complex feels much better. A long kiss darling. S.[51]

. . .

Stewart had made a clean breast of his dark secret to his wife. This was a
time when a homosexual orientation was officially unacceptable in the
service that had become his career. It took courage to tell Freya, and he
assumed and hoped that she would respect him. For the time being she
did. She was touched by his honesty and evident remorse when he confessed to her: "It makes you feel a liar and a confidence trickster that you
have obtained love under false pretenses."[52]

When he begged her to come out for Christmas, she agreed, and both
thought it would be a good idea to avoid Barbados and take a holiday in
Mexico and British Honduras (now Belize). When he declared: "Homosexuality is *hell* . . . your loving sinner, S," Freya believed that she could
save him.[53] With that, in a mood of tempered optimism, she crossed "the
weary ocean" in November and stayed with her husband through
March.[54]

Sadly, however, the issue between them could not be so easily laid to
rest. In April, once more alone, feeling "empty and rather dazed," Stewart
went to his doctor. He was told that while he suffered from low blood
pressure, otherwise he was physically fit, just run down and needing rest.

"I think it is largely mental, and that for two reasons, or from two sources. First you," he wrote miserably. "The realization that I am not a good husband is very upsetting—a continual worry. It is bound to be so: maybe it is much better to be a worried bad husband than a complacent one. I'm much better than I was, so far as realization goes. Only that *does* mean a strain—a wrench from the crooked to the straight, all the harder at my set age. I'm in between at the present juncture, I hope. So let us trust the swing will continue. Only when spirit and flesh are at odds, there is bound to be an inward fatigue."[55] Second, he went on to say that it was hard to be working in a setting so uncongenial—indeed the whole world was seeming dark to Stewart. With the threat of global atomic war, the murder of Count Bernadotte in Palestine, and the ominous glare of Communism's "red lanterns" shining over Eastern Europe, he felt more and more, he sighed, like St. Jerome at work in his cave while Civilization was dissolving around him.[56]

His letters no longer vibrated with the energetic descriptions of life among the sugar planters or thoughtful commentary on art and music and politics that had once enlivened them. At one point Stewart said pitifully that he missed the Arabs, who always "tell one how beloved one is. . . . I miss so much being told I'm loved. I hope that is not very childish . . . but even if it is, it is true."[57] It was Freya's love he really sought, of course, although he claimed it was that of the people he was working with in Barbados. His father's recent death was another blow. As he grieved Stewart confided to Freya that members of his family seldom talked openly to one another, and although he loved them very much and respected them, he had never felt it possible to take them into his confidence about personal problems. Now any possibility of understanding and forgiveness had been buried with his father.

. . .

In the meantime, Freya was tripping back and forth to London on a gay social round. She was also deeply absorbed in writing the first volume of her autobiography, which would ultimately emerge as a masterpiece of the genre. Some months earlier *Perseus in the Wind,* the collection of twenty meditations on "eternal verities," had come out to excellent reviews, including what was positively a eulogy from Harold Nicolson in *The Times.* Pleased, Freya sent it off to important friends, including the dowager Queen Mary, whose flattering response was duly filed in Freya's growing archive of letters from the royal, rich, and famous.

Best of all, Freya had the satisfaction of hearing both Cockerell and Jock Murray apologize for their "bad advice" against the project. She had made her essays a weave of personal recollections and observations on literature and history that showed off her breadth of learning in elegant commentaries on subjects such as love and sorrow, tolerance, happiness, and travel. Perhaps she had Stewart in mind when she reflected on the importance of words:

> *We seem to have forgotten the dignity of the only instruments, among all our inventions, that can carry and make articulate the thoughts, the soul of man. Even when used without so high an intention, words may yet be innocent and make a pleasant noise in the world, like brooks on moss or stones, or the wind in trees. But their misuse perverts the divine. And we have now come to a pass where truthlessness is tolerated, and even expected in politics, diplomacy, advertisement, the education of children and the privacy of marriage. The depth of our degradation of words may be measured by the surprise any newspaper editor would feel if his news were criticized merely for being untrue.*[58]

Many thought it her most brilliant work, and friends like Edwina Mountbatten, Sybil Cholmondeley, and Nancy Astor told Freya they kept it on their bedside tables. Stewart wrote from Bridgetown that he had overheard someone saying, "This book could not possibly have been written by a woman." He had proudly responded: "In fact, *Mrs* Perowne wrote it."[59]

Despite the book's success, Cockerell hoped Freya would not give in to a tendency toward embroidered prose and sententious opinions. She was now sending him drafts of her autobiography, and he believed it was far superior to the meditations of *Perseus,* which skated perilously close to smug—although her prose was too delightful, her insights too keen, and her ability to distill the essence of an idea too original not to win his admiration. Like her vivid letters, he considered the autobiography fresh yet wise, altogether a pleasure to read. Her letters, he would write her four years later when he was confined to his bed at Kew, "were pure enchantment. . . . I do not see how they could be bettered by the greatest letter writers of all times."[60] He was adept at flattery, but he was also truthful, and because he was a collector and anthologizer of letters himself, his was high praise that would be echoed by many others when her collected letters were eventually published.

While Freya composed for Stewart—and myriad others of her grateful correspondents—the effortless descriptions of people and places, thumbnail sketches that captured the atmosphere of visits to Hatfield House,

Sissinghurst, Cliveden, Ditchley Park; talks given on the BBC; Laurence Olivier acting; an archaeological evening with Sir Leonard Woolley— Stewart languished in Bridgetown, absorbed in repentant and anxious thoughts. He desperately wanted their marriage to work and wondered if it could. Unable now to see Barbados except through Freya's negative lenses, Stewart found his once bright days had turned to leaden duty. He simply endured and pined to share the fun that his talented wife was describing.

"It is never dull to hear of your doings," he wrote, "particularly when they are mixed up with our friends. We have too many I agree. Why can't we send them to Christie's, like other treasures? To be sold at auction, on Thursday next, a friendship in perfect condition, twenty years old, with one of the choicest characters of this or any age. What business we would attract."[61]

Despite all the apparent fun, however, Freya continued to be obsessed with what Stewart was up to. She persisted in probing the wound. How did he spend his days—and evenings—she wanted to know. "I'm always in bed by ten," he assured her, "generally soon after nine; yet I wake at two or three, oppressed with *sin*. Sin is most tiresome," observed the bishop's son, "because if you don't think about it, you fall into it, like a ditch, and if you do it is very upsetting. It is a phase, part of the 'unwinding process,'" he finished bleakly. "It will pass and meanwhile it is very unpleasant. But then, reformation always is."[62]

The "ginger cat" was trying hard to talk of personal things, engaged in an agonizing war against his own nature. Coming as he did from High Anglicanism, he saw his homosexuality as a sin against God rather than as, for example, an inherited genetic condition. For the sake of their marriage and his immortal soul, he continued to struggle. The American journalist Stewart Alsop had recently been in Barbados, and his comment to friends that Perowne was "coldly intellectual" revealed the degree of depression suffered by this normally courtly and gregarious man.

In the meantime Gerald de Gaury had visited Asolo again, and Freya did not keep from Stewart some unflattering comments made by their dashing friend. What exactly de Gaury said is not clear, but he was known to be mischievous and obviously had referred to Stewart's days in Baghdad's homosexual circle. "Yes, always tell me," Stewart responded. "I was so foolish, last year, not to tell you. Not only foolish, but wicked. Because now that I have told you, instead of accusing me of false pretenses, as you might, you have shown me and *given* me, the way of return. I'd almost written 'escape' but it is not that. It is the *way back*."[63]

Freya could not disguise her curiosity. She wanted to know *exactly* what had gone on; had there been a scandal? Determined to be truthful, Stewart braved up to this too:

> *You say "You must have got yourself into a mess and have suffered from it." Well, as I have told you, it wasn't much of a mess—just the perpetual fear of being in one—but it is true that I wasn't brave enough to tell you what it was! Now that, through no bravery of my own, I have told you, I feel all right.*
>
> *But I might have got into a mess, I will tell you when we talk it all out, of so many who did—men you and I knew and loved— some we still do. . . . When I left Baghdad in 1946 I was desperate—I saw no future, no light. But the moment I reached Asolo, all was well. I wrote to [a friend] and told him what a wonderful peace you gave me. But then I went back and into the depths again. Again, in 1947, you hauled me to the heights, and, like a drowning man who has reached the land he had always meant to reach, I felt that I could not leave it. . . . You are the only woman whose future I really felt I would wish, however humbly, to share.*[64]

There was nothing more that Stewart could offer Freya. He was willing to tell her everything, and she was ravenous to know it all. She was tireless in her quest, forcing him to confess, to repent, and to reform. Before this Freya had never been truly dangerous. At worst she had been guilty of using someone willing to be used—but she always gave much in return. Before Stewart she had never invested deeply in another human being, or asked for his soul—now the question was, would she cast the treasure away?

There is little doubt that he did his best to sleep with her, though it must have been a Herculean task, and he probably succeeded. One's heart goes out to a man willing to reject his own nature to satisfy a woman he loved and admired extravagantly but who, in her late fifties, half bald, thickset, and thick-ankled, had lost whatever allure she might have had. Nobody ever said Freya was pretty, although Archibald Roosevelt, grandson of Theodore Roosevelt, agreed with others that she was "far from being as homely as pictured" and that in fact he had been surprised on finally meeting her to discover how attractive she was: "You would never have guessed from her photographs," he added.[65] But if Freya had been Aphrodite herself, Stewart's task would still have been impossible.

· · ·

Stewart and Freya's marriage got one last shot. As with everything else, Freya had tirelessly sought a better position for her husband. She had boldly informed one high-ranking official that the Colonial Office was in danger of being responsible for a divorce. As usually happened with something Freya wanted badly, she got her way, and Stewart was offered the job of adviser to the Ministry of the Interior, Cyrenaica. It meant that he would be working for the Foreign Office rather than the Colonial Office, which they both considered an improvement in rank and, presumably, career security. Even better, this put them back with the Arabs on the blue Mediterranean in North Africa.

Cyrenaica was the eastern part of Libya, the fourth largest country in Africa, where much of the Desert War, including the Battle of Tobruk, had been fought. It appealed to them both because of its rich history of Phoenician trade, Punic Wars, and plethora of Greek and Roman ruins. Libya had been occupied by the Vandals, the Byzantines, the Fatimids, the Normans, and ultimately the Ottoman Turks—"a sort of palimpsest of histories," as Freya put it.[66] Beyond the delightful prospect of archaeological jaunts, Libya excited the couple because it was on the cusp of postwar change. An Italian colony since 1911, the country was now jointly occupied by the British and French and temporarily divided into three provinces—Cyrenaica and Tripolitania, administered by the British, and the Fezzan, governed by the French. In 1949 the United Nations had called for Libyan independence by the beginning of 1952. They both agreed that Stewart could find a real role to play there, especially because they were already acquainted with Sayyid Idris, the leader of the Senussi, a Sufi religious order that had carried on a long resistance to Italian colonial rule, who was now expected to become King Idris in a federated monarchy.

· · ·

They started out with hope. Christmas had been spent quietly at Asolo, where Stewart read the galleys of *Traveller's Prelude,* Freya's brilliant account of her early years, dedicated to Sir Sydney Cockerell, who had urged her to write it. She had written Stewart before he arrived that she was feeling a bit like Anne of Cleves waiting for Henry VIII: "Oh, dearest, do you think we *can* make a success of it after all?"[67] And he, quoting the poet James Elroy Flecker, had affirmed, "We *can* take the Golden Road to Samarkand!"[68]

The azure Italian sky was cloudless the morning he arrived, and Freya hoped this was a good omen. Her financial position was looking up with an increase in royalties from her publisher. With vintage dexterity she had also outmaneuvered the Bank of Italy, which tried to claim her English dividends. Having had a wearing autumn filled with book deadlines and visitors, she was now determined to keep their schedule as free as possible. The holidays passed quietly; after Christmas they embarked on a romp through Tuscany to Rome on the Vespa. Snow and hail fell over the Italian hills, and friends reported: "Freya is killing Stewart."

And then, by March 1950, they were in Benghazi, the capital of Cyrenaica. They were assigned to a dreary little semidetached house, so they found a nicer place outside the town with a walled garden, and soon Freya was coping with all the problems of moving in. She waited impatiently for their furniture to arrive and dashed off to enjoy the countryside, keeping an eye out for land mines buried in the most innocent places. She turned a squadron of Arab workmen loose on the house, and because their beds had not yet come, borrowed several operating tables from the local hospital, which, she said to friends, "skated about" on the floor during the night.[69]

At first her letters to Cockerell, Berenson, and her scores of other friends were filled with delight in the beauty and history of the place. But by April it was evident that things were going badly again. "It is a frustrating feeling not to be able to get to one's proper work," she wrote peevishly to Jock of interruptions and delays and constant racket in the house. "I had an idea that my proper work was to love and be loved, but it isn't: it is just to write books, so what is the good of not doing so?"[70]

Lavender Goddard-Wilson, the young wife of the British resident's secretary, meeting Freya at this time, confirmed that Benghazi was every bit as provincial as Barbados had been. The community was composed mostly of Sudan service staffers, who were not very sophisticated and who hardly knew what to make of Freya. Mrs. Goddard-Wilson, however, found the famous Traveler fascinating and felt sorry that such an interesting person had to put up with the small British community's "suburban mentality." Freya, she said, did not make much effort "to muck in" with them, although she did reach out to the local people. Instead, she spent most of her time writing. Like Pam Hore-Ruthven, Mrs. Goddard-Wilson felt privileged to accompany Freya on visits to Libyan ladies' harems, where she was impressed by Freya's skill and diplomacy: "We would sit on magenta and puce sofas arranged along the walls. Freya taught me how to deal with Eastern silence. In the West we are apt to regard silence as catastrophic, but in the East it is admired. Freya would waft a conversational sally into the room and wait. Then from across the room, a lady would respond. It was very dignified and I learned a lot. She was a brilliant listener with extraordinary eyes that never seemed to miss anything. She would listen for a while and then out would come some surprising and trenchant remark. I learned a new way of thinking about the world from watching her."

By contrast, Mrs. Goddard-Wilson thought Stewart "a rather Regency character" in the sense of being mannered and somewhat distant. And in her view he couldn't resist delivering arch opinions that did not endear him to his superiors. Current national issues never interested him as much as the ancient world, and he liked nothing more than to declaim on Hadrian's character or the ramifications of European princely houses. "He had a dilettante's mind. But Freya knew more," said Mrs. Goddard-Wilson.[71]

Unfortunately for Stewart, Libya was swarming with British diplomatic personnel involved one way or another in the transition to federation. Although he tried conscientiously to perform his duties, hurrying between the department heads and the office of the British residency, he soon felt underused and too frequently countermanded. He shared his frustrations with Freya, but, emphatic and certain herself, she simply could not understand those who were not and became less and less inclined to sympathize with someone who in her view lacked authority and strength. She had helped him all she could, but no amount of knowing the right people was going to transform Stewart into a take-charge administrator. She could not do his job for him or give him the self-confidence he lacked. They were utterly different, and, as Stewart later told Pam, he always felt "that little hand at my elbow, urging me on."[72] Although Freya never mentioned the model of the successful homosexual-lesbian marriage of Harold Nicolson and Vita Sackville-West, it is likely she had heard the gossip about their union and understood exactly what it meant, despite her insistent naïveté. But whereas Harold was forceful and successful and Vita not only respected but needed him, Stewart was weak, and weakness was the one thing Freya could not abide.

· · ·

It was a tragic situation, really, for them both. As Mrs. Goddard-Wilson said years later, "All Freya wanted was to be cherished, and Stewart couldn't." Instead he depended on her, which was what she didn't want. He could be intimate through correspondence but not when they were together. By August 1950 Freya was in flight again. "I came away sadly yesterday—sad, sad reasons," she wrote Stewart from Cairo.[73] She stayed away until late fall. It was now just a question of time. Renewed uneasiness about his job exacerbated their problems. Stewart heard that the Foreign Office did not intend to renew his contract after Libyan federation. Nor did the Senussi officials seem eager to employ him. Although he did his best to get "assurances," he received none from any quarter, despite various friends trying to advise and help.

After Christmas, when Freya rejoined him, the picture was no brighter, and in March she again retreated to Asolo: "Things are so sad and superficial between us," she wrote, "that I have long been feeling that they cannot go on as they were. . . . I don't know whose the fault, anyway it doesn't matter. . . . Half a dozen people around us tell me their hearts more intimately than you do. Better just to come and go as friends and that I will always be. There is nothing but true affection in my heart."[74]

Either Stewart did not attempt to respond or the letter is missing. But what could he say, other than what he had already nakedly admitted? "Everything you say is better than what I do," he would write, abject in her absence: "I feel as if I were running on batteries and not on the Dynamo."[75] He was affectionate, admiring, but he could not give more than he had given, especially when she was under the same roof, yearning for more. Instead, he sought her advice about his job.

For the preceding three years she had lobbied again and again for him and consistently offered sound counsel on policy as well as stratagems for winning. He should give people, she said, "a feeling of safety, by being always ready to advise and never grasping the credit, so they will come to rely on you without a feeling of danger to themselves or their vanity." But he was never as well-organized as she nor as astute in maneuvering the shoals of office politics. He was easily distracted by other things, invariably finding archaeological ruins more congenial. "I feel that you have been sometimes injudicious," she wrote, "in not putting first things first (I may be quite wrong); one must delegate work, but only when one is sure that it will be carried on. In fact, one is never free of the responsibility until the job is finished. You must make people realize that you do mind, deeply, if the little country is a success or no."[76]

The trouble was that Stewart was not interested in the complex internal tensions of a federating Libya, although her encouragement, he told her, gave him hope and he would try harder: "We are too good to waste— or at least you are," he added humbly.[77]

But Freya was hardly in danger of being wasted. She was receiving enormous attention for *Traveller's Prelude,* a triumph when it came out in October 1950. Vita Sackville-West raved about it in *The Spectator,* saying that she could not review it, she was too abashed, and could only write an open letter to Freya declaring: "Your book and your life are both too rich and too thick for me: they shame me into a realization that my own life has been poor and thin compared to yours. I am the sparrow watching your eagle; the mouse lying between the paws of your lion."[78] The praise was unqualified from every quarter. Miss Stark was "a great writer and this is a great book," stated *The Observer,* marveling at her "exquisite balance of humour and wisdom, the book's 'strange excellence.' "[79] "She has had the strength to turn everything she has experienced . . . into nourishments for her brain and heart," extolled the Sunday *Times.*[80] The author's ability to paint landscapes vividly in words or to capture a character's vital essence was repeatedly remarked on, as well as the emotional impact the account of such a striving, optimistic life had on its reviewers.

Freya was now declared to have produced a fine body of work. She had proved herself a brilliant stylist, deep thinker, and affecting writer—all above and beyond being an authoritative and entertaining commentator on travel through the Arab world. Glasgow University informed her that she would be honored with a doctor of law degree ("Did you ever hear anything more exhilarating? So many laws I have broken!"),[81] and the Royal Central Asia Society announced that she would receive their Percy Sykes Medal.

The ceremony in London fell on Stewart's birthday, and he wrote despondently from Benghazi that all *he* had ever done "was amass a wonderful collection of friends—and that's a sort of exploitation really."[82] Life at the moment seemed unrelievedly bleak and lonely, although recently he had decided that he too should write and had embarked on what he called a "fizzy" novel, envisioning it as a gossip fest playing with their diplomatic circle. When he showed it to Jock Murray, who admitted it had problems, again Freya tried to buoy him up with good advice: "You thought of getting by with much less hard work than necessary. The lighter the work, the more polish it requires, like the shine on shoes. . . . [Jock] is very cautious, so I think it is not at all a discouraging verdict, though evidently, like most authors, you must sweat over it a bit. That is the real hardness of writing, the *hatred* one feels for one's work before the end."[83] To cheer him she suggested that the porch she wanted to add to Asolo should have their initials etched into it.

Then came the final blow. Stewart received a letter from the Foreign Office announcing the termination of his employment. He was not even to be given a pension, just a cash settlement. Freya argued for him when she was in London, but by now she was deeply discouraged and suggested that he might be happier doing something different. How about getting a degree in archaeology? In the Cyrenaica desert he had discovered the ancient Greek city of Aziris, the first European settlement in Africa, mentioned by Herodotus and Ptolemy, high on a jol overlooking the sea. He could publish something about it, as he had in Aden when he found inscriptions and sculpture at two fifth-century sites. Archaeology might beckon as a prospect, but at the moment at least it was not a job.

There was nothing for it but to pack up and join Freya in Italy, where she was working on the next volume of her autobiography, *The Coast of Incense,* which she intended to, and did in fact, dedicate to Stewart. Friends, including Lady Edwina and Lord Louis Mountbatten, the last viceroy in India, had put in good words for him, so for three months, from November 1951 to the end of January 1952, he was given the job of liaison for the Arabs to the United Nations in Paris. Freya joined him at an inexpensive little hotel, where, she wrote to a friend, "I have the spare bed as if I were one of Stewart's suitcases." The government was paying him almost nothing, so they had to eat at bistros "like impoverished students."[84] Stewart disappeared all day at the Palais de Chaillot, where, Freya wrote Berenson, "speeches go on as continuous as Tibetan prayer wheels and with the same sort of hopes attached."[85] Because her husband's role was minor, Freya could attend only a few of the glamorous gatherings. So she confined herself to taking black-veiled Iraqi or Syrian wives to the couture houses and enrolled to take drawing lessons at an atelier where her parents had studied sixty years before.

Altogether she and Stewart had a barren sojourn, seeing each other very little and communicating even less. Britain's diminished stature was discouraging too. "The Middle East is a headache and we shall be very lucky if we weather it with any credit at all," Freya wrote a friend. "I should have liked to see us out of Egypt five years ago: now it is difficult to do so, and no thanks if we do. The whole of Asia is shutting down again, gradually, like an oyster. I do hope Asia Minor will keep open."[86]

Freya had had enough. When she left Paris, she left Stewart. She talked to a lawyer to arrange their separation. She wanted to be emphatic about it: they would agree to inform friends "discreetly"; Stewart would be welcome from time to time to Asolo; they would return to their independent lives. Above all, Freya would be known "for business and social purposes as 'Mrs. Freya Stark.' "[87] At least she had captured the title she and her mother had always wanted her to have. From now on Freya was a married lady—albeit one with the maiden name that she had worked so hard to make known.

Freya went off by herself into the Apennines, walking for several weeks along deserted trails, legs aching, stopping with peasants and eating dinner in their kitchens by the fire. The mountains were still snow-covered; she got a cold but kept going, lonely and self-pitying, until her fatigue lessened and the early spring sun revitalized her spirits. Gradually she began to feel "convalescent, a nice lizard-like feeling on any warm stone."[88] But in those weeks she prepared a new face for the world. Privately she believed that life with Stewart brought too many burdens with too few rewards. She was hurt and disappointed, emotions that now turned into bitter anger. She would "pull out the eye that offends."[89] She was not about to drown with Stewart. But with all her exhilarating strength and ferocious capacity for self-justification, Freya would have to persuade herself as well as others that their breakup was entirely Stewart's fault. He did not love her; she could not live "falsely"; love was "a sacrament"; and it was "impious" to live a charade. Although most of her friends accepted her rationalizations and were relieved to think such an ill-starred adventure had finally sputtered to a close, there were a few who realized just how deeply Stewart had been hurt.

He was also angry. He had opened his soul to her. No one, except perhaps his long-dead mother, had ever seen him so naked. He had plumbed the depths in their correspondence, he had abased himself. In October, before the United Nations conference, at her urging he had again gone to consult a doctor on his sexual problems and reported back what the doctor had advised: "I don't do any good by worrying about being homosexual, that I didn't ask to be, and that I can't alter it. And guilt over being so, and having attractions to other men, is out of place and wasting. He said naturally both of us, having been free and independent for so long, have to yield and give. That is something you *can* learn, and I said we are learning it."[90]

But Freya was long past adapting to anyone. Either *he* would adapt or it would be no good. On March 26 he wrote her a long letter. "I'm by no means unaffectionate by nature," he defended himself.

> But I can't stand the feeling that all the time I'm expected to be what I'm not, and doing what I can't do. No one can; nor can anyone live in a continual state of tension. It is very strange that having written so lucidly about your mother you should not see how much you resemble her! It is unconscious I know; but such is your instinct of always having your own way, *that even when we are walking arm in arm, you pull like a spirited horse all the time, when you ought to be allowing me to guide you for a change.* Of course that is magnificent when it's applied, as you have so notably applied it, to individual achievement. Where would you have got without it? But it does not *adorn* a wife. It isn't endearing. And without endearment, passion or principle or anything

else, has no little hooks to catch hold by. . . . I hope you'll think it over very carefully—and think not talk. If you discuss me with other people, you naturally only do so with people who are going to agree with you, or else they wouldn't talk at all, which is bad of you. I've never discussed you with anyone, except Sheridan [Russell], at your particular request. . . . It isn't other people's business.[91]*

Stewart remained true to his word. Only to Pam Hore-Ruthven did he mention "the little hand always pushing at my elbow." But Pam was on his side. She felt that Freya had used Stewart, even though Pam loved Freya and they remained close. His brother Leslie remembered Stewart's lips tightening when Freya's name was mentioned, but he did not remember his brother ever breathing a word of criticism against his wife—and Stewart gallantly let Freya remain his wife in name. In 1952 he went to work for the Anglican bishop of Jerusalem, designing and setting up refugee camps on the West Bank. And he began to write, as he had longed to do. Very soon there was a stream of books: on the early Christians, the Jews, Classical Greece and Rome—some eighteen in all. A few were very good, especially his biography of Hadrian, and some were not so good, at least from the point of view of scholars who took issue with his idiosyncratic views on the demise of the Roman Empire. But they were fun and easy to read, and those looking for a taste of the past enjoyed having Emperor Vespasian described as resembling President Dwight D. Eisenhower, or Hadrian likened to Prince Philip.

Stewart and Freya avoided each other, writing occasional, carefully cordial letters and asking a friend who had lately seen one or the other—in a careless tone—to report. Stewart kept up with a wide and often distinguished circle of friends. He began to relax, not trying any longer to hide his sexual preferences. John Julius Norwich remembered being somewhat taken aback on a visit to Malta, a favorite vacation place since Stewart's posting there in the thirties, when Stewart asked the name of "that spicy young" naval officer who had brought them ashore.[92] Others remarked that there was usually a coterie of admiring young men surrounding him when he lunched at the Traveller's, his London club. As he allowed himself more freedom, Stewart gave rein to his creative side, entertaining his

---

* Sheridan Russell's friendship with Freya went back to before 1928. He eventually married Michael Stewart's sister, having given up his career as a pianist. He became a social worker and was always poor; Freya was good to him, inviting him and later his wife for holidays in Asolo. He was a strong Freya loyalist, and she asked him to talk with Stewart about his sexual problems.

friends in a less guarded way than in the past, sending them into transports of hilarity as he sang arias from *Madama Butterfly*. Stewart lived into his eighties, writing, traveling a bit, regarded affectionately by a host of friends, and he never spoke to anyone about his marriage.

It was not just to Freya that Stewart behaved in an exemplary way. He showed himself decent and honorable to many, and his friends considered him truly kind. In sum, Freya had missed a chance to work out a life with someone with whom she shared a great many things, a man, one suspects, who would have been good to her in her old age. Stewart died at the age of eighty-seven in 1989. His funeral was held at St. Paul's, Knightsbridge, presided over by the Anglican bishop of Gibraltar. Like many of Stewart's obituarists, the bishop could not resist quoting from a published letter by the eminently quotable Freya: "Long necked and bald-headed like a young vulture," she had written from Yemen to her mother long ago, "he hovered with out-spread wings at the central desk, pounced on the strange language of Whitehall, disembowelled the files with an epigram at incredible speed, and was out again, followed by the adoring gaze of Ali the office boy, who would always contrive to stand, covered in purple ink, a pace or two behind him."[93]

She had caught the man's essence with her swift, unfailing pen. But the man himself she let go.

CHAPTER TWENTY-ONE

The Endless Horizon

> *If we are strong, and have faith in life*
> *and its richness of surprises, and hold the*
> *rudder steadily in our hands, I am sure*
> *we will sail into quiet and pleasant*
> *waters for our old age.*
>
> —LETTER TO A FRIEND, JULY 1934

*F*or Freya that first summer of 1952 was dreadful. She had so loved the idea of being married, yet now worse than ever loneliness yawned before her. She brooded, but she was constitutionally unable to admit fault. Instead she tried to line her friends up on her side—just as Stewart had asked her not to do. "Did you know Stewart was a pederast?" she would inquire and then weep softly or propose an arduous walk in the mountains.

All that summer she was in a ferocious mood, and Caroli, her secretary, or Emma, the cook, often felt the lash of her tongue. When an invitation came from a rather effeminate and rowdy group of artists renting next door, Freya tartly refused. "This place is full of pansies and lesbians," she wrote Jock crossly—although shortly afterward, so amused by the efforts of one of them to meet her, she invited him over and watched him comport himself "like a Plymouth Brother."[1]

Freya was also feeling disenchanted with her niece, Ceci. At first thrilled to be reunited with her sister's pretty daughter, eager to take her on educational trips and open windows on rich intellectual vistas, Freya was hurt when her niece seemed to prefer "to play with her ski instructors" and resisted being lectured on the verities.[2] Ceci would argue, seem ungrateful—and then by way of apology admit that Freya's brilliance made her feel "inferior," a confession so alien to her aunt's exuberant and determined nature that she heard it with impatience and incredulity rather than sympathy. Freya would stay long weeks of the summer at L'Arma, but she was too overbearing a guest, and Ceci resented playing host to Freya's court. Gradually Freya ceased coming. In 1979 Ceci suffered a massive stroke, and she died in 1981. She left a son, Paolo, Freya's last blood relative, but the estrangements between his mother and great-aunt had taken their toll, and Freya's relationship with Paolo gradually withered.

The redoubtable machinery that whirred indefatigably once again geared up to absorb her disappointment, dispose of cast-off expectations, repair itself, and prepare for new challenges. As always, "something interesting" was not long in coming: Lord Balfour's nephew David Balfour invited Freya to join his yacht, the *Elfin*, for a sail along Turkey's Lycian shore. Organizing herself for a three-month tour, she planned first to sail with the Balfours, then move on to Ankara for several weeks as a guest of her Baghdad friend Seton Lloyd, now director of the British Institute of Archeology. From there she would seek simple lodgings in the countryside and in Istanbul be put up at the British embassy because Freya was now invited everywhere, and if she wasn't she'd write a bewitching note inquiring, might she possibly visit a few days?

Travel had long been Freya's palliative, and once again it served her well. Turkey promised just the fresh challenge she craved, and she immediately started to study the language and refresh herself on the major Greek and Roman authors as a new ambition stirred. Why not "illuminate" both herself and the world on the fascinating subject of this country? With eleven books on the Arabs now behind her, she had no desire for the moment to say anything more about them other than the occasional public comment. She had done enough of that in America, only to be bruised. Besides, she was thoroughly discouraged by the hash the Arabs were making of things. Egypt had seen years of violence against the British establishment, and King Farouk had been deposed by a military coup that brought in the flaming nationalist hero Colonel Nasser. In Iran, Mohammed Mosaddiq had abruptly nationalized the oil industry, to which Britain responded by organizing an oil boycott. Syria was in ferment; there was agitation in Tunisia and Algeria; the old Imam Yahya had been assassinated in North Yemen, and it looked like neither his successor nor the British in Aden could hang on much longer.*

But Turkey was another matter. A country at that time on good terms with its more regimented Arab neighbors yet also a friend to Europe, Anatolia had always been the gateway between East and West. Here Freya could train her formidable powers on the mighty events that had shaped Western civilization. It was a subject that had drawn her for a long time, and Turkey, with its rugged mountain chains, ravishing coastline, and sweeping plains, was barely noticed by tourists. Freya could travel around fairly freely and observe the glorious stage on which Agamemnon besieged Troy, Alexander routed Darius, Cleopatra seduced Antony, and golden Byzantium fell to Mehmet, the Ottoman conqueror—the very stuff that stirred Freya's soul.

In no time she was cruising in Turkey's crystal blue waters, causing a sensation by diving in for a swim where a shark had just been sighted and cajoling her host to bring his boat dangerously close to coastal shallows because she had spotted a ruin on a bluff that they simply *must* see. Balfour complied, utterly smitten, with a prayer for his boat. When she disembarked to continue alone over Turkey in a taxi, he urged her to return for a second season.

It took all Freya's resources to recover from the disaster of her marriage and to face the loneliness of these first travels by herself after the war. She would seek "the realms of gold," she said.[3] Restless movement was still the best balm when life threatened to overwhelm her. For a decade she threw herself into Turkey and its history—these are "our own *origins!*" she would exclaim. Passionately, she sought to recapture the rapture of her first journeys twenty-five years earlier. With Herodotus as her guide, her head covered by one of the ruffled bonnets she had taken to wearing and her eyes occasionally brimming—tears of joy, she insisted—she clambered over Hellenic ruins, often astonishing her driver by declaiming verses from Thucydides as she teetered precariously on a fallen column. The classical world had been harsh and insecure—as well as filled with grandeur. Why wasn't this a place for her to feel at home?

She found the Turkish people a refreshing change from the Arabs. They might not say such original things or be so inquisitive, she thought, but it was a lot easier at the end of an exhausting day to be served dinner peacefully by a silent Turkish wife so she could read without the whole family

---

* In fact, Yahya's son Ahmad resisted the forces of revolution until his death in 1962, when the Yemen Arab Republic was founded. The British pulled out in 1967, and the protectorate became the People's Democratic Republic of Yemen.

clamoring to visit at all hours of the night. As for Turkish men, they were *extremely* virile. "It's almost frightening to feel so unsafe, even at my age!"[4] she trilled to Jock, who was glad to see a return of her old high spirits.

Through the fifties Freya labored over a series of travel books that no English-speaking tourist visiting postwar Turkey failed to carry along. More than any author Freya opened up Anatolia, and the country soon swarmed with tourists. Every summer and fall she climbed in the Taurus Mountains, visited friends on the Hellenic coast, crossed the great Anatolian plateau to Lake Van in the east, or swam in a hat and large woolen bathing suit in the Black Sea. She went to Elazig and Erzurum, where the Tigris and Euphrates Rivers originate, wandered along the Maeander River, checked out Crusaders' castles, and surveyed the great battlefields of the past. Rather like the fourteenth-century Italian poet Petrarch, who declared he wished he had been born in an earlier age, Freya had accepted that she was happier in antiquity.*

"Alas, I see nothing but squalor ahead," she lamented of the general state of the Cold War world. In 1956, when she visited Lawrence Durrell on Cyprus, Greek Cypriots set off a bomb in his garage. That same year she was appalled by the aggressive actions taken by the British, French, and Israelis against Egypt after Nasser nationalized the Suez Canal. Even more, in 1958 she was grief-struck to hear—she was in Trebizond at the time—that the young Iraqi king and her friend Nuri Pasha, the prime minister, had been murdered in a military coup. She dedicated the final volume of her autobiography, *Dust in the Lion's Paw,* to the slain Iraqis.

Through her late sixties Freya continued to take tough trips alone by foot, or mule, or taxi. They were coin for her writing, and she did need money. Although Freya was loath to admit anything so crass— she always stated that she traveled purely for pleasure—the truth was the books were an important source of income. The first of her Turkish travelogues, *Ionia: A Quest,* in 1954, was followed by *The Lycian Shore* in 1956, both companionable ruminations on the virtues of past and present. Her ambitious third in 1958 was *Alexander's Path,* in which Freya duplicated the brilliant young Macedonian's marches from Phrygia to Pamphylia and re-created the strategies of the Greeks against the Persians. *Riding to Tigris* appeared in 1959, written after a journey through Kurdish Anatolia during which she was often feverish

---

* "I devoted myself, though not exclusively, to the study of ancient times, since I always dislike our own period; so that, if it hadn't been for the love of those dear to me, I should have preferred being born in any other age, forgetting this one; and I always tried to transport myself mentally to other times." From Petrarch's *Letters to Posterity.*

and once caught herself wondering what every traveler eventually must ask: "What *am* I doing here?"

Eventually she admitted in a letter to Victor Cunard, the journalist: "I don't believe I can go on doing these escapades for very many more years. There is a very wearing span between the day's delights and the awful depression of the nights when all the troubles of the flesh come upon one: food, insects, washing so difficult, and amiability to too many strangers at once in a foreign tongue."[5]

Her public remained faithful, and all four Turkish books did well in both England and America. U.S. Supreme Court Justice William O. Douglas called them "a collector's item,"[6] and Freya's literary friends applauded them in reviews and rightly pronounced them classics because they illuminated not only Turkey but what was universally true in human behavior. Even so, they represented a change from Freya's earlier spontaneous descriptions of Arab societies. She was now solely interested in using her journeys to elucidate history and her philosophy of life. Autodidact that she was, she thrived on learning, and romantic that she was, she was happiest invoking the triumphs of the ancients and pondering the relevance of the past. Some found her writing more erudite than they liked despite the lovely language, exquisite insights, and grandeur of landscapes deftly "painted with words."[7] Although Freya would always enjoy a devoted following, she was too intellectual to appeal to a truly mass audience.

Jock knew this. Proud of publishing her, loving her despite the advantage she continued to take of his time and office, he worried about Freya. He knew that money was constantly a problem, and now she insisted she wanted to do a book on the Romans in Turkey, which he was sure would have no commercial interest. Of course Freya didn't listen. She was convinced she could make a great contribution to scholarship by "debunking" the notion that the Romans had brought prosperity to the East, arguing instead that Rome's eastern policy had been a disaster, weakening the empire by pushing too far from the center until the Romans confronted the Persians, a far more powerful and dangerous enemy. All this drained the imperial treasury and ultimately spelled Rome's ruin. Excited by her thesis, declaring the "beastly Romans" to have been "brutal Fascists,"[8] Freya pored over their "blood-stained annals"[9] and took six years to do the book, finishing in 1966, when she was seventy-three.

When Jock turned out to have been right, Freya shrugged. The 479-page book was politely received but did not do well. "One no longer speaks a familiar language when one talks of the Classical world" was all she said.[10] Nevertheless, Arnold Toynbee and Harold Nicolson declared it an impressive undertaking, agreeing it was intelligent, formidably re-

The triumphant nomad, wearing one of the dresses she had made from exotic fabrics obtained during her travels—Asolo, 1960.

Freya at eighty-six.

Freya with Her Majesty, the Queen Mother.

searched, and well-written. Her friends were suitably impressed, although privately most thought it heavy going. Her faithful readers vainly sought through the endless footnoted pages some resemblance to the charming descriptions of people and places they had once counted on. Much more to their liking was the delightful anthology of Freya's previous writings, *The Journey's Echo*, that Jock and she had put together three years earlier. If Freya was crushed, she did not complain—nor did she tackle anything like it again. She had proved to herself she could do it, and that was all that mattered.

By now Freya was facing old age—yet still she traveled, enduring discomfort for the reward of beauty and revelation before some remote panorama. Often she criticized the encroachments of ugly modern "improvements" on lovely old habitats, but preservation was a cause, and Freya had long since decided she would leave causes to others. Just as she could never have survived as a diplomat or a foreign service officer, the ambition she had reluctantly abandoned at the end of the war, Freya did not tolerate tedious chores or impingements on her time other than those of her own creation. Her inquisitive, restless spirit required freedom of movement. Probably she would never have been happy in a traditional marriage, as Minnie Granville's husband had noted so long ago when he said if she had a husband she would be "clipped and spoiled." She was incapable of acknowledging this about herself, yet at some level she must have realized that her unfettered life allowed her to do what she wanted.

Since she had freed herself from her mother long ago, Freya had followed her own genius. She had imagined herself the star in many roles over the years—explorer in Persia and Luristan, Mata Hari at the imam's court, English plenipotentiary during the war, and humble pilgrim wandering through Turkey's ancient ruins. She amused friends by saying that she wished she'd been a clothes designer or a land surveyor and that her greatest disappointment was not having been born a great beauty. But in truth Freya had seized her life and made it a richer adventure than any of those who pitied her in her youth could ever have conceived.

. . .

When Freya was still in her late sixties, she announced, "The young must be illuminated," and embarked on a series of trips with her numerous godchildren who were of an age to see the world.[11] Much like her old mentor Professor Ker, Freya had always liked having children around, "as long as you don't step on them," as she said when their parents started bringing them to Asolo as babies.[12] Later, as university students, they came on their own, gathering around her in the garden to argue over philosophy and

politics, attending Freya on the Arabs or the Greeks while she drew them
out about their romances and hopes.

Accompanied by an alternating cast of godchildren, with one hauling
her false-bottomed suitcase lest some morsel of antiquity be denied her by
customs and another in charge of her "monstrously heavy Remington
typewriter,"[13] Freya variously guided them to the Greek island of Skyros
to mourn at Rupert Brooke's grave, dragooned archaeologists to walk
them over the Acropolis, roused them in the middle of the night to see
dawn break over Troy, and ministered to their hangovers in the morning
by insisting they eat a coddled egg and fish. One night in an obscure Turkish village where Freya had installed them in a rather surprised headman's
house, a baby girl was born; she was promptly named Freya Stark.

The godchildren admired Freya's ability to sleep anywhere, on any surface, as well as the ingenious organization of her camping gear. The boys
chuckled over her innocence, and the girls fumed that she favored the
boys—which she did. More than one girl brought along by a godson was
stunned by Freya's imperious treatment, as if girls were fit only to wash
the camp dishes while Freya discoursed on Rome with the boys. But they
all remembered being excited and challenged, and all marveled at Freya's
energy and eagerness to push on long after they themselves were exhausted. When she was seventy-two, two godsons accompanied her on
a trip through the Taurus Mountains in an arctic windstorm that blew so
hard they had to hang on to her ankles lest she blow off her mule—yet
under her hat brim her eyes glittered with pleasure. Both boys studied Arabic and the Middle East as a result of her influence.[14]

. . .

On returning to Asolo, Freya kept the house in an uproar of distinguished
guests, whom she fed so indifferently that returning friends brought their
own wine and cheese. No one was allowed to interrupt Freya's mornings,
which were devoted to writing and keeping up with her enormous correspondence. After lunch there were siestas and often a long climb in the
hills, followed by superb conversation at dinner.

As old friends died Freya mourned "an emptying room."[15] Lord
Wavell, Antonin Besse, and Duff Cooper were gone. Sir Sydney Cockerell
was bedridden and stone-deaf, although letters continued to arrive from
Kew in an ever more microscopic hand. By the late sixties, however, Cockerell too had died, followed by Sir Leonard Woolley, Sir Kinahan Cornwallis, Lord Halifax, and many old friends from the Baghdad days.
Bernard Berenson, whom Freya had watched sink deep into age "wrapped
in red velvet with a red velvet cap like some very old Doge by Tin-

toretto,"[16] was perhaps missed the most. The venerable aesthete had dedicated his last book to Freya, and she returned the favor by dedicating *Alexander's Path* to him. She had loved their comfortable discussions, observing him rather like an admiring daughter who wants to learn how a parent confronts death. They had talked a lot about the hereafter, but Freya never committed herself to a specific faith. As she had said before, she preferred to "wait at the gate."

Freya's appetite for luxury remained as powerful as in the days when she had commandeered government vehicles to ferry her acquisitions. She went first class if one of her rich friends paid for it—but her own money went to purchase beautiful things, paintings and books, and her house glowed with tessoria silks and fine antiques. When she was seventy she took some friends to look for property not far from Asolo at Montoria. It was raining. The view, she breathed, was nothing less than "a Giorgione landscape."[17] She bought two hills and embarked on a building spree, a *folie de grandeur* that soon had friends and accountants scrambling for ways to save her from bankruptcy. Not to be dissuaded from building an enormous house, Freya envisioned a retreat for brilliant *dilettanti*—delight takers—rather like those assembled by Lord Burlington or the members of Queen Cornaro's dazzling court—and begged friends to join her "sleeping among the nightingales."[18] Unfortunately, her enterprise turned out to be more like the Moloch of the old Dronero factory, inhaling all her money as friends ducked her entreaties to buy a floor, rent a floor, wouldn't they like to move in permanently?

While the conversation around Freya's pool and in the spectacular garden she created "was heady stuff,"[19] friends were wise enough to avoid full-time commitment. "You'd think my property was medicine, it is so hard to make any want it," she complained.[20] Her "sordid" struggle to keep the mansion solvent went on for ten years, until finally, to everyone's relief, she sold it, took an apartment in Asolo, then hopped on a train for Switzerland with her underclothes bulging with banknotes she had hidden to escape the border guards. In Geneva she negotiated a 15 percent life annuity that turned out to be so disastrous for the bank it annually dispatched a representative to Asolo to verify the incredible fact that the old lady was still alive.

Ever traveling, crisscrossing Europe, going up to Castle Mey to stay with the Queen Mother in Caithness, Scotland, revisiting Yemen and other haunts, Freya even returned to the United States as the guest of an American couple who had bought a Palladian villa near Asolo and were enchanted by their neighbor who seemed to know everybody and to have been everywhere.[21] Once or twice Freya made a bad choice in a traveling companion and, concluding midtrip that he was either ignorant or uncouth or, as in one case, daring to write a rival account—declared him "a tourist, not a traveler" and treated him dreadfully.[22] Several such victims returned home lacerated and brimming with outraged anecdotes, which only stoked the fires of Freya's legend.

In the last decades of Freya's very long life, she traveled extensively through the Far East, Persia, Central Asia, India, and North Africa, and at eighty wrote up her excursion into a nearly inaccessible area of Afghanistan in an amusing account entitled *The Minaret of Djam*. A Swiss woman so liked the book, in which Freya expressed a desire to own a camper, that she wrote offering to buy her one. Thus arrived in Asolo the Dormobile, which, with Freya at the wheel, was dangerously "inclined to wander" through fences and into cow-filled meadows.[23] Freya was obliged to agree, and her license was finally permanently revoked in her eighty-fifth year. "I shall never master the automobile," she declared and contented herself with horseback riding instead.[24]

. . .

At age eighty-two Freya was knighted, making her a dame officially as well as in fact. That same year she decided her letters should be published. *All* her letters, she said, as Jock's eyes grew large—everything she had written since Flora had saved the first scrap in 1914, everything that she could ask back from friends who, it turned out, had generally saved them. So began a stupendous exercise in retrieval. Jock refused to be pushed into another hopelessly uncommercial project, so Freya sold the Jacopo Bassano, the Edward Lears, the Prendergast watercolors, her Yemeni silver jewelry, and published them herself in eight handsome volumes.[25] She pressed Lucy Moorehead, whose husband, Alan, had been paralyzed by a stroke in 1967, to edit them. Heroically, Lucy agreed. When Lucy was killed in a car accident in 1979, Freya turned to Lucy's daughter, the journalist Caroline Moorehead, who finished the job. It took ten years, and, perhaps more than anything Freya ever did, this panoramic collection of sparkling sketches and memorable observations covering more than three-quarters of a century of life richly experienced stands as her epitaph. Her project "was not vanity," she insisted, "just a human story stamping itself on paper . . . a personal mirror reflect[ing] a period of interest never to be surpassed in our world."[26] Freya was ninety-two when the last volume appeared, and when Caroline Moorehead published a condensation of them in 1988, the writer Jan Morris wrote in her review, "I do not wish to gush . . . but Dame Freya really is wonderful."[27]

When Freya was eighty-seven, her old friend Veronica Bamfield visited

Asolo and found her jumping down the stairs, three at a time. "I've been strictly, strictly forbidden," she whispered, holding a finger to her lips, "but it *is* such fun!" Lord Iveagh's family had turned their beautiful villa into what quickly became an alluring destination for Veneto visitors, the Hotel Cipriani. A little worried that Freya might not be eating well, they arranged for her to dine there daily. For years afterward guests in the dining room would inquire of the manager, who *was* that diminutive old lady in the spectacular hat? If he were shown sufficient appreciation, the manager usually escorted a guest to Freya's table, where he (or she) would be treated to bouquets of aphorisms and drolleries to amuse the folks back home.

Up to London, off to Greece, Freya continued to travel until she was ninety, periodically interviewed by newspaper reporters or television teams, who always found her good copy. In 1977, when she was eighty-four, the BBC filmed her making delphic pronouncements on a leaking raft in the Euphrates as it slowly sank. At eighty-eight she was filmed riding a mule into the Himalayas via Langtang to the Tibetan border. It worried the TV crew that by evening she was so stiff she had to be lifted off and carried to her tent.[28] Freya confided to friends she had hoped to die there in the lofty mountains. Sadly, however, her stout heart kept beating as her beautiful mind began to falter. "A thing with a long name has been getting into my neck," she told her neighbor, meaning arteriosclerosis.[29] Generous friends kept a vigilant eye on her shrinking portfolio and made sure she had nurses to look after her. On her ninety-first birthday the town of Asolo held a splendid fete to celebrate, and the Queen Mother dispatched the Royal Household Cavalry to perform elaborate drills. Freya sparkled and laughed on the podium, but it was evident that she no longer fully understood what was going on.

Not long before, she had said to a friend: "Waiting for death, my dear, is very much like being in an old-fashioned steam train, setting out on a journey. You let down the window by a leather strap, and your friends are on the platform waving goodbye. And then the blasted train doesn't move."[30]

But Freya and her friends had made their adieus, and it was now just a question of time. Freya's striving spirit had long since wrenched the most from life. Beginning with little, she had made much, and for years had been able to enjoy the satisfaction of seeing her books regarded as classics and her adventures included among the annals of famous British women of courage. Willful, determined, charismatic, and exploitive, she was a resilient and optimistic artist who had stood against the ignorance that she knew existed equally in East and West. Her writing documented nearly a century of extraordinary change in the Islamic world, and while she had not been able to affect British policy in a direct way, she had kept the flag aloft for decency, civility, and compassionate understanding. Above all, her serene conviction that the study of history—all history, from ancient Mesopotamia to modern times—not only afforded the greatest pleasure but was civilization's best defense had been a message widely heard.

Her appreciative public had long forgotten to call her "intrepid." They now said how "wise" Dame Freya was, how "durable" in both her person and her work. It was true that she never deviated in her personal search for those underlying truths that anchor all people, nor, like a true Tharaya, did she ever flag in her effort "to illuminate the world." Therefore, on May 9, 1993, as spring flowers perfumed the Venetian foothills and Freya breathed her last, she could depart in peace to join the realms of gold.

Surely one of the most electrifying experiences to befall a biographer is to learn a major new fact about his or her subject after the intense study has concluded, the book wrapped in its shiny new dustcover, and, at last, deposited on bookstore shelves.

This happened to me. A few months after *Passionate Nomad* was published, I was put in contact with a remarkable family of women, the descendants of Elizabeth Cady Stanton, the famous American feminist. It seemed they possessed some family papers that connected them to Freya. At first the family was a bit hesitant to share something that had been kept secret through several generations. But true to the sturdy values of their celebrated ancestress, they resolved to come forward in the interest of historical truth. In due course, therefore, I was sent two documents, and this is what I discovered:

Freya Stark was illegitimate. Robert Stark, the beloved, even mythologized parent who had migrated to Canada, was not her biological father.

At first I was astonished. But the more I thought about it, the more certain I was that the emotional events recounted in the two documents had truly occurred. Suddenly things hidden and unexplained made sense. It was a tale that not only confirmed important aspects of Freya's character, but also clarified a crucial piece of her past, quite possibly known by her at some point in her life and carefully concealed thereafter.

The two documents were written by Elizabeth Cady Stanton's granddaughter, Nora Stanton Blatch DeForest Barney (1882–1971) when she was in her seventies. One was an unpublished version of a memoir for the benefit of Mrs. Barney's children describing her youth and including a train of events that led to the birth of Freya Stark. The other was a six-page longhand letter to Freya, presumably composed in Cuba while Mrs. Barney was traveling there in 1952. It states that Mrs. Barney had just finished reading Freya's autobiography, *Traveller's Prelude,* published in 1950, and, realizing that Freya believed she had been born prematurely, in Paris, felt an obligation to give her the true story. Although the memoir gives a fuller version of Freya's birth, from a biographer's point of view the letter was by far the most provocative, addressed as it was directly to

Freya. Why was there no evidence of this letter or any other correspondence from Mrs. Barney or her mother in Austin, at the Humanities Research Center where all Freya's other correspondence reposes if, as Mrs. Barney notes, their families were both interrelated and close friends? Had Mrs. Barney ever actually sent a copy of it—or did she shrink at the last minute from a deed that could hurt too much? According to her family, it was Mrs. Barney's habit to draft a letter in longhand, have it typed by her secretary and then mailed. If a copy of this was in fact sent, what was Freya's reaction? With gentleness and sympathy Nora Barney had undertaken to spell out the facts as she knew them, beginning her letter with: "So now, dear Freya, if you don't want to know, just throw this into the wastepaper basket."

The following is the story, drawn from both accounts, of how, as a child of nine, Nora Barney traveled with her mother, Harriot Stanton Blatch, along with Flora Stark and two companions, on a very special and critically eventful adventure to Italy.

During the 1880's Freya Stark's mother, Flora, had become a close friend of the daughter of Elizabeth Cady Stanton, Harriot Stanton Blatch, who had married an Englishman, William Henry Blatch of Basingstoke. The friendship is not really surprising as Flora was not only a second cousin of Harriot's husband and a first cousin to her own husband, Robert, but she and Robert were also in-laws, as William Henry Blatch's sister Kitty had married Robert's brother, William Playters Stark. The two brides, one from Italy and one from America, apparently shared a certain disdain for the provincialism of Basingstoke where the Blatches lived and Torquay and Chagford where the Starks lived. They were only a few years apart in age, Harriot being five years older, and held similar views on a number of liberal topics. Harriot cared passionately about economic injustice to the poor. Flora, although an artist first and foremost, was equally interested in helping the underprivileged, especially women. In her memoir, Harriot's daughter Nora remembers them in their bloomers, bicycling through the countryside and likely discussing how to improve the world.

In the late fall of 1891, the two decided to travel to sunny Italy. Mr. Blatch was left to tend the brewery that was his family's business, and it is unknown where Robert Stark was. Instead of their husbands, the women departed in the company of a third friend, a Miss Atkins*, and a young man who was an admirer of Flora's and who had spent the previous

*This friend is referred to as Miss Anderson in the memoir, and Miss Atkins or Atkinson in the letter.

month biking and frolicking with the two ladies in Basingstoke. His name was Obediah Dyer, and he is described in the narrative as a well-to-do young man from a prominent family in New Orleans. The adults left by train, nine-year-old Nora and her nanny, Elizabeth, traveled by sea, and they all joined up in Sorrento at the Cocumella Hotel. While little Nora worried about Italian smells and the locals' distressing habit of beating their donkeys, Mr. Dyer seemed "completely swept off his feet by Flora. I do not wonder," writes Nora in her memoir. "I adored her. She was very tall with the most beautiful carriage and walk I have ever seen to this day—not beautiful but statuesque."

A few weeks later, a trip by boat to Capri was planned, but as Harriot Blatch was pregnant and did not trust "the perils of the sea," roughened at that time of year by winter winds, she sent Nora and the nanny, Elizabeth, along, accompanied by Flora and Mr. Dyer. They visited the Blue Grotto, and then Nora and her nanny returned—but not with Flora and Obediah. "Elizabeth sputtered about it all the way back on the boat, but of course I didn't see why," Nora notes in her memoir. They were greeted, she says, by "rather blank looks" from the ladies who had stayed behind. When Flora and Obediah eventually rejoined them, there were more trips, one to Vesuvius and another to Pompeii. Then after several more weeks, Flora abruptly departed for England. The female friend was surprised, Nora's memoir recalls, "but mother didn't seem surprised at all. With the attraction gone, Mr. Dyer also left and then in May, mother, Elizabeth, Miss [Atkins] and I sailed back to London and Basingstoke."

One is left to infer that Flora realized she was pregnant and hurried back to her husband's embrace. In any event, about a month later, when Harriot gave birth to a sister for Nora, Flora and Obediah were back at the Blatches' for another prolonged visit. Young Nora, who had been packed off to a boarding school she despised fled back to Basingstoke, only to find Flora looking "very big indeed" and Mr. Dyer, attentive as ever, settled in a nearby hotel.

Here begins the crux of Nora's story as recounted in her memoir. "I was so glad to get back . . . I didn't care where I slept, and there was always Elizabeth. She and Father welcomed me home whether truant or not. Elizabeth kept mumbling and grumbling about Flora. I knew nothing of the facts of life except that kittens were inside cats and babies were inside mothers. One day a very important doctor arrived from London—a distant cousin, Dr. Coupland, and the next day, in November, Flora had a little girl in the room where Helen and I had been born. Elizabeth mumbled 'Premature! Ridiculous! Nail-perfect, nine months to the day . . .' the significance of which I did not understand until years later."

After attending Flora, the doctor departed immediately for London, directing Nora's father to register the birth. "After he left, Mother and Flora set upon Father and told him he just couldn't, and shouldn't register it. Father kept protesting, but he finally gave in—as was usually the case.

"All this time Mr. Dyer was hovering around, and now his attendance was constant," continues Nora's narrative, describing how she and various cousins teased him. "He was really, as I look back on it all, a very charming, generous, conscientious young man, small with flashing brown eyes." She decided she admired him enormously when one day she and her cousins tipped him out of a swing and catapulted him into a bush. The youngsters fled, hid, and eventually, emerging for tea, saw him limping, but silent about the mishap. "He knew our gratitude was unbounded and through the years to come I never forgot it." In the meantime he hung over Flora and the baby, Nora recalled, and never left her side.

"Then one day I heard mother say a very strange thing to him: 'It is unseemly that you stay longer.' What, Nora describes herself wondering, did "unseemly" mean? She begged her mother to let Mr. Dyer stay on, but Harriot only replied that Nora was "too young to understand." Shortly after, Mr. Dyer left.

Apparently very soon after this, Robert Stark himself arrived to greet his "premature" first child. Nora remembered overhearing her mother reporting "in glee" to Flora: "He accepted it!" while, she said, the nanny "scowled but held her tongue."

Through this whole episode, Nora's father never commented. "Father," said Nora, "never opened his mouth on the subject. No doubt the non-registration was a very painful thought." Robert Stark collected his wife, his baby daughter and, according to Nora, together they departed for the Continent. The drama was over. The Blatch household "sank back into the old routine." The month of the birth had been November, 1892—not Freya's stated birthday of January 31, 1893.

Later, Harriot Blatch relocated to America to assume the role her mother had designated for her, carrying the torch for women's suffrage. Yet, Nora remembers, the incident continued to trouble Harriot, and she felt remorseful at having sent Obediah away.

One has to wonder how it could have been that two women, presumably steeped in emancipated thinking, could have opted for preserving a conventional and obviously unhappy marriage when a love match was possible. That women learn to think for themselves was one of Harriot's first principles, as it had been for her famous mother. Divorce was certainly not unheard of, and Robert and Flora had lived miserably together for fifteen years. Obediah Dyer, as Nora wrote in her letter to Freya, "was deeply in love and desperately wanted your mother to divorce Robert . . . and marry—but for some reason your mother would not." It seems baffling that Flora threw away a chance for happiness at last, especially as she left Robert in the end and consigned herself and her children to a life of poverty.

As for Obediah Dyer, Nora tells Freya in the letter that "when I saw you in 1929 for the first time since you were a baby I was struck by the likeness." She adds that her mother, Harriot, always wondered if Freya's sister, Vera, was not also Obediah's child, "but she knew little of what went on after your mother left." Presumably, therefore, the Blatch family and the Starks did not see each other often, if at all, after Flora left Devon to live in Italy.

The Blatches got a second chance to play an important role in the Stark women's lives when Obediah Dyer died. For years he had been sending gifts to both Nora and to Freya via Basingstoke—dolls and other presents suitable to children of the age Nora had been when he last saw her, but no longer appropriate for growing young women. Apparently concerned not to do anything that would connect him directly to Freya, Obediah evidently asked Harriot to help him deliver an anonymous bequest to Freya of 2,000 English pounds. In her revelatory letter to Freya, Nora asks: "Didn't it strike you as strange that suddenly out of a blue sky came $20,000?" This is presumably what Nora's family thought the gift was worth in dollars.

In conclusion, Nora tells Freya, "Well, that is all in the past. Your mother, my mother, Elizabeth, Father, the doctor, all are dead and I am 70. So you are just as much as I am one-half American. Believe me, I write all this because I thought you might want to know. Mr. Dyer's life was one more turned upside down by your mother."

Having unburdened herself of the secret that had burned so long, Nora ends her letter in an effort to find meaning and possibly a way to soften the blow she was inflicting: "Just what the beginnings are seems to make very little difference nowadays. In fact, more is expected of those born out of wedlock because statistics show that given half a chance that is where genius is born. After reading the Freya Stark story which will go down as history, I am wondering how many other men and women of genius really had fathers they never knew. With all good wishes, your cousin, Nora Stanton Barney."

Could it be that Freya never knew? It seems there was a real effort to keep the secret. Even so, servants talk. Basingstoke was a small town and the Blatches stood out. The Blatch and Stark cousins evidently remained close and even Flora and Freya returned episodically to England for visits and might have encountered the Blatches. In the light of these disclosures, it is understandable that Flora and Robert's brother Playters disliked each other. He probably knew his sister-in-law had betrayed his brother. If Robert also knew the truth and felt humiliated it makes sense that he cut loose from his beloved Devon and escaped to a new life in Canada. There is no evidence, however, that he was not fond of the little girl who was supposed to be his even if he was not the one who gave Freya the critical gift of money that enabled her finally to embark on her life of travel. Probably, however, he did help her buy the house in La Mortola.

Freya was an exceptionally bright and sensitive child who might well have correctly interpreted hints that all was not right with her origins. But, as her intimates acknowledged, she managed to erect a wall about herself and they respected her strong need for privacy on personal matters. By the time Nora Barney's letter arrived—if it did—Freya would have been sixty and at the height of her glory. She could hardly have welcomed Nora's news. There is abundant evidence that Freya wove fantasies to shape truths more to her liking—and certainly the Paris story of her birth was the more agreeable tale. As for the two bachelors who went through the snowy streets of Paris to buy a layette, that could fit. It was probably nearly December when Flora and Robert got to Paris and Herbert Young and Herbert Olivier might easily have gone out to find clothes for the "premature" baby.

Nora was right to say Freya was a genius. With little formal education, through neglect, poverty, and loneliness, she had triumphed. She had suffered a brutal injury in early adolescence, that tender period when a young person first gains a sense of attractiveness and desirability—and was left disfigured and uncertain. Those scars healed, at least on the outside. Inside, one has to assume, there was a permanent wound, an unspoken vulnerability. Her relationships suffered because of it. If she knew, or even if she just sensed that she was born out of wedlock, this blow to her self-esteem would have been another goad to accomplishment. It would have been imperative for Freya to validate herself—to prove her legitimacy in the eyes of the world, to demonstrate that, yes, she was Dame Freya Stark, traveler without peer.

. . .

A final word of gratitude is due the person who put me in touch with Elizabeth Cady Stanton's family, Professor Ellen DuBois of the University of California, Los Angeles. It was from Professor DuBois that I finally realized the golden potential of the Internet when she posted a notice to me on Amazon.com, suggesting we get in touch. I did, eagerly, and it turned out that Professor DuBois had written an excellent history, *Harriot Stanton Blatch and the Winning of Woman Suffrage,* published by Yale University Press in 1997. She had also edited a version of Nora's memoir for *The History Workshop Journal* in 1987 with permission from the family. However, with admirable delicacy she confined mention of the incident that concerns us here to a footnote. Professor DuBois told me that she buried the information because she did not know if Freya Stark had any living relatives. Immersed as I was with my own book and Middle Eastern history, I do not believe I would ever in my wildest imaginings have looked to the heroines of the American suffrage movement for information on Freya Stark. So I can only conclude that the world is small and the Internet is serendipitous.

Jane Fletcher Geniesse
January 2001

Books by Freya Stark

The Valleys of the Assassins. London: John Murray, 1934.

The Southern Gates of Arabia. London: John Murray, 1936.

Baghdad Sketches. London: John Murray, 1937.

Seen in the Hadhramaut. London: John Murray, 1938.

A Winter in Arabia. London: John Murray, 1940.

Letters from Syria. London: John Murray, 1942.

East Is West. London: John Murray, 1945.

Perseus in the Wind. London: John Murray, 1948; reprint, London: Century, 1984.

Traveller's Prelude (vol. 1 of autobiography, 1893–1928). London: John Murray, 1950.

Beyond Euphrates (vol. 2 of autobiography, 1928–1933). London: John Murray, 1951.

The Coast of Incense (vol. 3 of autobiography, 1933–1939). London: John Murray, 1953.

Ionia: A Quest. London: John Murray, 1954.

The Lycian Shore. London: John Murray, 1956.

Alexander's Path. London: John Murray, 1958.

Riding to the Tigris. London: John Murray, 1959.

Dust in the Lion's Paw (vol. 4 of autobiography, 1939–1946). London: John Murray, 1961.

The Journey's Echo. London: John Murray, 1963.

Rome on the Euphrates. London: John Murray, 1966.

The Zodiac Arch. London: John Murray, 1968.

The Minaret of Djam. London: John Murray, 1970.

A Peak in Darien. London: John Murray, 1976.

Rivers of Time (a photographic collection with Alexander Maitland). Edinburgh: William Blackwood, 1982.

PRIVATELY PRINTED

Freya Stark Letters, vol. 1 (1914–1930), ed. Lucy Moorehead. Compton Chamberlayne, Salisbury, Wiltshire: Compton Russell, 1974.

Freya Stark Letters, vol. 2 (1930–1935), ed. Lucy Moorehead. Tisbury, Wiltshire: Compton Russell, 1975.

Freya Stark Letters, vol. 3 (1935–1939), ed. Lucy Moorehead. Tisbury, Wiltshire: Compton Russell, 1976.

Freya Stark Letters, vol. 4 (1940–1943), ed. Lucy Moorehead. Wilton, Salisbury, Wiltshire: Michael Russell, 1977.

Freya Stark Letters, vol. 5 (1943–1946), ed. Lucy Moorehead. Wilton, Salisbury, Wiltshire: Michael Russell, 1978.

Freya Stark Letters, vol. 6 (1947–1952), ed. Lucy Moorehead. Wilton, Salisbury, Wiltshire: Michael Russell, 1981.

Freya Stark Letters, vol. 7 (1952–1959), ed. Caroline Moorehead. Wilton, Salisbury, Wiltshire: Michael Russell, 1982.

Freya Stark Letters, vol. 8 (1960–1980), ed. Caroline Moorehead. Wilton, Salisbury, Wiltshire: Michael Russell, 1982.

Over the Rim of the World: Selected Letters, ed. Caroline Moorehead. Wilton, Salisbury, Wiltshire: Michael Russell, 1988.

Bibliography

LETTERS (PUBLISHED AND UNPUBLISHED)
Freya Stark papers at Humanities Research Center, Austin, Texas
Royal Geographical Society: Elinor Gardner letters
Private: Freya Stark correspondence with Pamela Hore-Ruthven Cooper
Private: Freya Stark correspondence with Peggy Drower Hackforth-Jones
Private: Sydney Cockerell papers, including letters from Sydney Cockerell, Minnie Granville, Lady Anne Lawrence, Lady Gwendolen Iveagh, Sir Denison Ross, Lucy Beach
Private: John Beach letters, including letters from Lucy Beach, Lady Gwendolen Iveagh, Freya Stark, Flora Stark

FILMS AND BROADCAST TAPES
Bowen, Sarah. BBC program
Luke, Colin. *A Desert Voyage,* BBC London, 1977
Norwich, John Julius. BBC program

REFERENCE
Encyclopedia of Islam, ed. by Houtsma, Wensinck, Gibb, Heffening, and Levi-Provencal, vol. 4, S–Z. Leyden: E. J. Brill; London: Luzac & Co., 1934.
The Meaning of the Glorious Koran. Text and explanatory translation by Marmaduke Pickthall. Karachi: Taj Co.
Atlas of the Islamic World Since 1500. Francis Robinson. New York: Facts on File, 1982.
Atlas of the Arab World: Geopolitics and Society. Rafic Boustani and Philippe Fargues. New York: Facts on File, 1991.
Cultural Atlas of Mesopotamia and the Ancient Near East. Michael Roaf. New York: Facts on File, 1990.

GENERAL
Ascherson, Neal. *Black Sea.* New York: Hill and Wang, 1995.
Bell, Gertrude. *The Desert and the Sown.* 1905; reprint, London: Virgo, 1985.
Betts, Robert Brenton. *The Druze.* New Haven: Yale University Press, 1988.
Birkett, Dea. *Spinsters Abroad.* Oxford: Basil Blackwell, 1989.
Blunt, Lady Anne. *A Pilgrimage to Nejd.* 1881, John Murray; reprint, London: Century Publishing, 1985.
Blunt, Wilfrid. *Cockerell.* New York: Alfred A. Knopf, 1964.
Bury, G. Wyman. *The Land of Uz.* London: Macmillan, 1911.
Caton-Thompson, Gertrude. *Mixed Memoirs.* Gateshead, Tyne & Ware: Paradigm Press, 1983.
Clarke, M. *Stories from the Arabian Nights.* New York: American Book Co., 1897.

Clive, Nigel. *A Greek Experience: 1943–1948.* The Chantry, Wilton, Salisbury, Wiltshire: Michael Russell, 1985.

Cockerell, Sydney Carlyle. *Friends of a Lifetime,* ed. Viola Meynell. London: Jonathan Cape, 1940.

Cockerell, Sydney Carlyle. *Such Good Friends.* London: Rupert Hart-Davis, 1956.

Collins, R. J. *Lord Wavell 1883–1941: A Military Biography.* London: Hodder & Stoughton, 1947.

Cooper, Artemis. *Cairo in the War: 1939–1945.* London: Hamish Hamilton, 1989.

Cooper, Pamela. *A Cloud of Forgetting.* London: Quartet Books, 1993.

Daftary, Farhad. *The Ismailis: Their History and Doctrines.* Cambridge: Cambridge University Press, 1990.

de Gaury, Gerald. *Traces of Travel.* London: Quartet Books, 1983.

Doe, D. Brian. *Southern Arabia.* New York: McGraw-Hill, 1971.

Doughty, Charles M. *Passages from Arabia Deserta,* ed. Edward Garnett. Middlesex: Penguin, 1931.

Fagan, Brian M. *Return to Babylon: Travelers, Archeologists and Monuments in Mesopotamia.* Boston: Little, Brown, 1979.

Footman, David. *Antonin Besse of Aden.* Basingstoke, Hampshire: Macmillan Press in association with St. Antony's, Oxford, 1986.

Fromkin, David. *A Peace to End All Peace: Creating the Modern Middle East 1914–1922.* New York: Henry Holt, 1989.

Grafftey-Smith, Laurence. *Bright Levant.* London: John Murray, 1970.

Guthrie, Grace Dodge. *Legacy to Lebanon.* Richmond, Va.: Grace Dodge Guthrie, 1984.

Helfritz, Hans. *The Yemen.* Trans. M. Heron. London: George Allen & Unwin Ltd., 1956.

Hitti, Philip K. *Capital Cities of Arab Islam.* Minneapolis: University of Minnesota Press, 1973.

Hitti, Philip K. *The Near East in History.* Princeton: Van Nostrand, 1961.

Hopwood, Derek, ed. *Tales of Empire: The British in the Middle East.* London: I. B. Tauris & Co., 1989.

Hore-Ruthven, Patrick. *Joy of Youth: Letters of Patrick Hore-Ruthven,* ed. Ethel Anderson. London: Peter Davies, 1950.

Hourani, Albert. *A History of the Arab Peoples.* Cambridge, Mass.: Belknap Press of Harvard University Press, 1991.

Ingrams, Doreen. *A Time in Arabia.* London: John Murray, 1970.

Ingrams, Harold. *Arabia and the Isles.* London: John Murray, 1942.

Izzard, Molly. *Freya Stark: A Biography.* London: Hodder & Stoughton, 1993.

Kahn, Margaret. *Children of the Jinn: In Search of the Kurds and the Country.* New York: Seaview Books, 1980.

Kaplan, Robert D. *The Arabists.* New York: Free Press, a division of Macmillan, 1993.

La Valle, Francesco. *Freya Stark in Asolo,* trans. Graziano Guadagnini. Magnifica Communita Pedemontana dal Piave al Brenta-Asolo, 1984.

Lampson, Miles. *The Killearn Diaries 1934–1946.* London: Sidgwich & Jackson, 1972.

Larsson, Theo. *Seven Passports for Palestine: Sixty Years in the Levant.* Longfield, Sutton, Pulborough: Longfield Publishing, 1995.

Lewis, Bernard. *The Assassins.* London: Weidenfeld and Nicolson, 1967.

Lloyd, Seton. *Ancient Turkey: A Traveller's History of Anatolia.* Berkeley: University of California Press, 1989.

Lloyd, Seton. *The Interval: A Life in Near Eastern Archaeology.* Osney Mead, Oxford: Alden Press, 1986.

Longrigg, Stephen. *Iraq, 1900–1950.* London: Oxford University Press, 1953.

Louis, William Roger. *The British Empire in the Middle East: 1945–1951.* Oxford: Clarendon Press, Oxford University Press, 1984.

Mackey, Sandra. *Passion and Politics: The Turbulent World of the Arabs.* New York: Dutton, 1992.

Mackey, Sandra. *The Iranians: Persia, Islam and the Soul of a Nation.* New York: Dutton, 1996.

Macmillan, Harold. *War Diaries.* London: Macmillan, 1984.

Maitland, Alexander. *A Tower in a Wall: Conversations with Dame Freya Stark.* Edinburgh: William Blackwood & Sons, 1982.

Mansfield, Peter. *A History of the Middle East.* London: Penguin Books, 1991.

Mansfield, Peter. *The Arabs.* London: Allen Lane, 1976; New York: Viking Penguin, 1990.

Marco Polo. *The Travels of Marco Polo,* trans. Ronald Latham. London: Penguin, 1958; New York: Viking Penguin, 1986.

Marechaux, Pascal. *Arabia Felix: Images of Yemen and Its People.* London: Thames & Hudson, 1980.

Marr, Phebe. *The Modern History of Iraq.* New York: Westview Press, 1985.

Mernissi, Fatima. *The Forgotten Queens of Islam,* trans. Mary Jo Lakeland. London: Polity Press, Blackwell, 1993.

Middleton, Dorothy. *Victorian Lady Travellers.* London: Routledge and Kegan Paul, 1965.

Monroe, Elizabeth. *Britain's Moment in the Middle East, 1914–1956.* London: Chatto & Windus, 1963.

Monroe, Elizabeth. *Philby of Arabia.* London: Faber & Faber, 1973.

Mottahedeh, Roy. *The Mantle of the Prophet: Religion and Politics in Iran.* New York: Pantheon, 1985.

Nicolson, Harold George. *Diaries and Letters: 1930–1964.* London: Collins, 1971.

O'Brien, Conor Cruise. *The Siege.* New York: Simon & Schuster, 1986.

Perrin, Noel. *A Reader's Delight.* Dartmouth: University Press of New England for Dartmouth College, 1988.

Philby, Harry St. John. *Sheba's Daughters.* London: Methuen, 1939.

Philby, Harry St. John. *The Empty Quarter.* London: Century Hutchinson, 1986.

Phillips, Wendell. *Qataban and Sheba.* New York: Harcourt Brace, 1955.

Raban, Jonathan. *For Love and Money: A Writing Life.* New York: Harper & Row, 1987.

Ranfurly, Hermione. *To War with Whitaker: The Wartime Diaries of the Countess of Ranfurly, 1939–1945.* London: Mandarin, 1995.

Rodinson, Maxime. *The Arabs,* trans. Arthur Goldhammer. Chicago: University of Chicago Press, 1979.

Roloff, Beny. *The Thrones of Earth and Heaven* (photographs by B. Roloff and texts by Freya Stark, Jean Cocteau, Bernard Berenson, Rose Macaulay, Stephen Spender). London: Thames & Hudson, 1958.

Roosevelt, Archie. *For Lust of Knowing: Memoirs of an Intelligence Officer.* Boston: Little, Brown, 1988.

Roshwald, Aviel. *Estranged Bedfellows: Britain and France in the Middle East During the Second World War.* Oxford: Oxford University Press, 1990.

Runciman, Steven. *A History of the Crusades, vols. 1–3.* Cambridge: Cambridge University Press, 1951.

Russell, Mary. *The Blessings of a Good Thick Skirt: Women Travellers and Their World.* London: Collins, 1988.

Ruthven, Malise. *Traveller Through Time: A Photographic Journey with Freya Stark.* New York: Viking Penguin, 1986.

Savory, R. M. *Introduction to Islamic Civilization.* Cambridge: Cambridge University Press, 1976.

Searight, Sarah. *The British in the Middle East.* London: East-West Publications, 1979.

Simmons, James C. *Passionate Pilgrims.* New York: William Morrow, 1987.

Smith, Charles D. *Palestine and the Arab-Israeli Conflict.* New York: St. Martin's Press, 1992.

Stark, Flora. *An Italian Diary.* London: John Murray, 1945.

Storrs, Ronald. *Orientations.* London: Ivor Nicholson & Watson, 1937.

Tabachnick, Stephen E., and Christopher Matheson. *Images of Lawrence.* London: Jonathan Cape, 1988.

Thesiger, Wilfrid. *The Life of My Choice.* Glasgow: William Collins, 1987.

Tidrick, Kathryn. *Heart-Beguiling Araby: The English Romance with Arabia.* London: I. B. Tauris & Co., 1989.

Trench, Richard. *Arabian Travelers.* London: Macmillan, 1986.

Von Hammer-Purgstall, Joseph. *The History of the Assassins,* trans. Oswald Charles Wood. London, 1835; New York: Burt Franklin, 1968.

Wallach, Janet. *Desert Queen: The Extraordinary Life of Gertrude Bell.* New York: Nan A. Talese, 1996.

Waugh, Evelyn. *When the Going Was Good.* Boston: Little, Brown, 1934.

Wavell, Archibald. *Allenby: A Study in Greatness.* London: G. G. Harrap & Co., 1940.

Wheeler, Mortimer. *Splendours of the East.* London: Weidenfeld and Nicolson, 1965.

Wilson, Jeremy. *Lawrence of Arabia.* London: William Heinemann, 1989.

Notes

PROLOGUE

1. Quoted by Maria Aitken, in an article about Freya Stark (hereafter FS) in *Sunday Telegraph,* January 31, 1993.
2. Vita Sackville-West, *Spectator,* November 24, 1950.
3. FS, *Beyond Euphrates* (London: John Murray, 1951), p. 4.

1. THE BEGINNING

1. FS to Flora Stark, January 21, 1928, in FS, *Letters from Syria* (London: John Murray, 1942), p. 46.
2. FS to Venetia Buddicom, November 23, 1927, in ibid., p. 3.
3. FS to Robert Stark, November 24, 1927, ibid., p. 4.
4. FS to Robert Stark, May 30, 1923, in *Freya Stark Letters,* vol. 1, ed. Lucy Moorehead (Compton Chamberlayne, Salisbury, Wiltshire: Compton Russell, 1974), p. 71.
5. Interview with Noelle Kelly, 1989. Lady Kelly described a dinner party she gave when the author Fitzroy Maclean asked what had attracted Freya to the East and her answer was "Clearly, it was oil."
6. FS, *Traveller's Prelude* (London: John Murray, 1950), p. 324.
7. FS to Mrs. Aidan Thompson, December 27, 1927, in FS, *Letters from Syria,* p. 31.
8. FS to Viva Jeyes, December 22, 1927, in ibid., p. 26.
9. FS to Lady Waller, February 12, 1928, in FS, *Letters from Syria,* pp. 65–66.
10. FS to Mrs. Herbert Olivier, January 14, 1928, in ibid., pp. 40–41.
11. FS to Flora Stark, February 2, 1928, in ibid., pp. 74, 76.

2. A NOMADIC YOUTH

1. FS, *Traveller's Prelude* (London: John Murray, 1950), p. 6.
2. Ibid., p. 34.
3. Ibid., p. 26.
4. Interview with Barclay Sanders (Mrs. Theo) Larsson, 1989.
5. FS, *Traveller's Prelude,* p. 44.
6. Freya always gave this as her birth date. However, at least one friend, Evelyn Lambert, remembers noticing an earlier date on her passport, and the date on the tomb of Freya's sister, Vera Stark di Roascio, is 1893. It seems that Freya was actually a year older—possibly even more—than she let on, making her at least 101 when she died.
7. Barclay Sanders Larsson, the granddaughter of Herbert Olivier, often heard this story repeated by her grandparents and parents as she was growing up. Interviews, 1989, 1990, 1993.

8. FS, *Perseus in the Wind* (London: John Murray, 1948; reprint, London: Century, 1984), p. 45.

9. Ibid., p. 48.

10. FS, *Traveller's Prelude,* pp. 37, 38.

11. Ibid., p. 38.

12. Ibid.

13. Robert Stark to FS, February 16, 1931, in the archive at the Harry Ransom Humanities Research Center, University of Texas, Austin (hereafter HRC).

14. FS, *Traveller's Prelude,* p. 62.

15. Ibid., p. 46.

16. Ibid., p. 49.

17. Ibid., p. 62.

18. FS to Stewart Perowne, August 8, 1948, in *Freya Stark Letters,* vol. 6, ed. Lucy Moorehead (Wilton, Salisbury, Wiltshire: Michael Russell, 1981), p. 66. The delightfully antiquated term *louche,* according to *The New York Times*'s language guru William Safire, "originally French for 'cross-eyed,' is rooted in the Latin *luscus,* 'blind in one eye.' In English, early in the nineteenth century, *louche,* pronounced 'loosh,' came to mean 'oblique, not straightforward,' and in a shameful linguistic abuse of a physical disability, has since pejorated to 'disreputable, indecent.' "

19. FS, *Traveller's Prelude,* p. 73.

20. From Lucy Beach's letters to her mother, shown to the author by her son John Beach in Bedford, New York, 1994. Flora Stark became the manager of Mrs. Beach's tessoria.

21. Flora wrote an account of her Dronero experience that is in the HRC.

22. FS, *Traveller's Prelude,* p. 73.

23. Quoted from Flora Stark's typewritten account of her years in Dronero, in the HRC.

24. FS, *Traveller's Prelude,* p. 88.

25. Ibid., p. 228.

26. FS, *The Zodiac Arch* (London: John Murray, 1968), p. 45.

27. FS, *Traveller's Prelude,* p. 85.

3 · A LONG SIEGE

1. FS to Flora Stark, February 1, 1914, HRC.

2. Interview with Sheridan Russell, 1990.

3. Vera Stark to FS, December 19, 1912, HRC.

4. FS, *Traveller's Prelude* (London: John Murray, 1950), p. 134.

5. Ibid., p. 86.

6. Ibid., pp. 128–129.

7. Ibid., p. 147.

8. Ibid., p. 151.

9. Ibid., p. 160.

10. Ibid.

11. Flora Stark to FS, September 1, 1916, HRC.

12. FS to Flora Stark, August 25, 1916, HRC.

13. FS to Flora Stark, August 9, 1916, HRC. Edited version included in *Freya Stark Letters,* vol. 1, ed. Lucy Moorehead (Compton Chamberlayne, Salisbury, Wiltshire: Compton Russell, 1974), p. 2.

14. FS to Flora Stark, September 6, 1916, HRC.

15. Ibid.
16. FS to Flora Stark, October 13, 1916, in *Freya Stark Letters,* vol. 1, p. 10.
17. Flora Stark to FS, October 1, 1916, HRC.
18. Flora Stark to FS, November n.d., 1916, HRC.
19. FS to Flora Stark, December n.d., 1916, HRC.
20. FS, *Perseus in the Wind* (London: John Murray, 1948, reprint, London: Century, 1984), p. 123.
21. Ernest Hemingway wrote about the retreat in *A Farewell to Arms* (1929).
22. Margaret Jourdain to FS, December 22, 1916, HRC. Miss Jourdain was a supporter of young writers and an expert on early English furniture at the Victoria and Albert Museum; she lived with Ivy Compton-Burnett, the writer, and was probably her lover.
23. Freya included an edited version of her war diary in *Traveller's Prelude.* Quotation on p. 205.
24. Ibid., p. 142.
25. FS to W. P. Ker, February 18, 1921, in ibid., p. 260.
26. FS to Robert Stark, July 12, 1921, in *Freya Stark Letters,* vol. 1, p. 56.
27. FS, *Traveller's Prelude,* p. 323.
28. Details here are from a letter from Olivia Barker, wife of Oxford professor Ernest Barker, to FS, written on October 23, 1950, HRC, making a number of small corrections and emendations to *Traveller's Prelude,* which Mrs. Barker had just read and found "enthralling." Mrs. Barker has one of W. P. Ker's goddaughters with him on the mountain when he died.
29. FS, *Traveller's Prelude,* p. 308.
30. Ibid., p. 249.
31. FS to Robert Stark, May 22, 1922, in *Freya Stark Letters,* vol. 1, p. 61.
32. FS, *Traveller's Prelude,* p. 313.
33. Ibid., p. 325.
34. Ibid.

4 · THE MYSTERIOUS DRUZE

1. FS to Flora Stark, March 11, 1928, in FS, *Letters from Syria* (London: John Murray, 1942), p. 85.
2. FS to Flora Stark, March 15, 1928, in ibid., p. 88.
3. Ibid., p. 89.
4. FS to Venetia Buddicom, March 16, 1928, in *Freya Stark Letters,* vol. 1, ed. Lucy Moorehead (Compton Chamberlayne, Salisbury, Wiltshire: Compton Russell, 1974), p. 154.
5. FS to Flora Stark, April 1, 1928, in *Letters from Syria,* p. 100.
6. The visitor to Damascus or Hama today can see the two handsome palaces in those towns built by a member of this illustrious clan, Assad Pasha el-Azm, an Ottoman governor during the eighteenth century who by winning the trust of the Syrian people after years of good stewardship incurred the suspicion of the sultan, who therefore had him strangled.
7. James C. Simmons, *Passionate Pilgrims* (New York: William Morrow, 1987), ch. 6.
8. FS to Penelope Ker, April 4, 1928, in *Letters from Syria,* p. 109.
9. FS to Mrs. Aidan Thompson, January 26, 1928, in ibid., p. 50.
10. FS, *Beyond Euphrates* (London: John Murray, 1951), p. 9.
11. Molly Izzard, author of *Freya Stark: A Biography* (London: Hodder & Stoughton, 1993), was fortunate to interview Francis Edmunds before he died.

12. FS to Venetia Buddicom, May 5, 1928, in *Letters from Syria,* p. 94.

13. FS, *Letters from Syria,* p. 138.

14. Robert Brenton Betts, *The Druze* (New Haven: Yale University Press, 1988), p. 11.

15. FS to Flora Stark, May 11, 1928, in *Letters from Syria,* p. 148.

16. The following exchange with the French officers was documented by Freya in her article "France in the Jebel Druse," *Cornhill Magazine,* November 1928.

17. FS to Flora Stark, May 5, 1928, in *Letters from Syria,* p. 149.

18. Ibid., p. 150.

19. FS, "France in the Jebel Druse," p. 547.

20. FS to Flora Stark, May 14, 1928, in *Letters from Syria,* p. 161.

21. FS, "France in the Jebel Druse," p. 547.

22. FS to Flora Stark, May 14, 1928, in *Letters from Syria,* p. 164.

23. FS, "France in the Jebel Druse," p. 547.

24. Ibid.

25. Ibid.

26. FS to Flora Stark, May 15, 1928, in *Letters from Syria,* p. 169.

27. The author heard this view expressed by several sources, including Nizar Jawdat and the wife of a Kurdish chieftain's son who had provided hospitality to Freya and been insufficiently thanked.

28. FS, *Letters from Syria,* p. 189; Freya was quoting Francis Edmunds's letter to Venetia Buddicom.

29. Simmons, *Passionate Pilgrims,* p. 59.

30. Gertrude Bell, *The Desert and the Sown* (London: William Heinemann, 1907; reprint, London: Virago, 1985).

31. FS to Venetia Buddicom, June 28, 1936, in *Freya Stark Letters,* vol. 1, pp. 37–38. Also mentioned by Malise Ruthven in "Making History," *London Review of Books,* June 19, 1986. I am grateful to Mr. Ruthven for his excellent comparison of these two remarkable women.

32. FS to Herbert Young, January 6, 1929, in *Freya Stark Letters,* vol. 1, p. 187.

33. FS to Sydney Cockerell, May 21, 1943, in *Freya Stark Letters,* vol. 4, ed. Lucy Moorehead (Wilton, Salisbury, Wiltshire: Michael Russell, 1977), p. 289.

34. FS to Flora Stark, May 25, 1928, in ibid., p. 172.

35. FS, *Beyond Euphrates,* p. 42.

36. Ibid., p. 7.

37. FS, "France in the Jebel Druse," p. 548.

38. FS to Robert Stark, July 2, 1928, in *Freya Stark Letters,* vol. 1, p. 174.

39. *The Encyclopedia of Islam,* ed. Houtsma, A. J. Wensinck, H.A.R. Gibb, Heffening, and E. Lévi-Provençal (London: Luzac, 1934), p. 740.

5. AH, BAGHDAD

1. Leonard Huxley was the father of Aldous, Julian, and Andrew, a trio of famous Huxley writers and scientists.

2. Herbert Young to FS, February 15, 1926, HRC; also published in FS, *Traveller's Prelude* (London: John Murray, 1950).

3. FS to Robert Stark, July 29, 1928, in *Freya Stark Letters,* vol. 1, ed. Lucy Moorehead (Compton Chamberlayne, Salisbury, Wiltshire: Compton Russell, 1974), p. 175.

4. FS to Flora Stark, September 19, 1928, in ibid., p. 177.

5. FS to Flora Stark, February 3, 1929, in ibid., p. 188.

6. FS to Robert Stark, April 7, 1929, in ibid., pp. 190–192.
7. FS to Robert Stark, May 25, 1929, in ibid., pp. 192–193.

6. THE ASSASSINS AND THE LURS

1. Quoted by James C. Simmons, *Passionate Pilgrims* (New York: William Morrow, 1987), p. 265.
2. FS to Robert Stark, November 14, 1929, in *Freya Stark Letters,* vol. 1, ed. Lucy Moorehead (Compton Chamberlayne, Salisbury, Wiltshire: Compton Russell, 1974), p. 214.
3. E. C. Hodgkin, *Arthur Lionel Forster Smith, 1880–1972* (Oxford: privately printed, 1979), p. 114.
4. FS, *Beyond Euphrates* (London: John Murray, 1951), p. 105.
5. FS to Venetia Buddicom, January 6, 1930, in *Freya Stark Letters,* vol. 1, p. 232.
6. FS to Viva Jeyes, end of November 1929, in ibid., p. 219.
7. FS to Robert Stark, January 10, 1930, in ibid., p. 235.
8. Gertrude Bell, *The Desert and the Sown* (London: William Heinemann, 1907; reprint, London: Virago, 1985), p. 293.
9. Laurence Grafftey-Smith, *Bright Levant* (London: John Murray, 1970), p. 197.
10. Doreen Ingrams, interview, 1993.
11. FS to Viva Jeyes, April 10, 1930, in *Freya Stark Letters,* vol. 1, p. 258.
12. FS to Flora Stark, November 21, 1941, in *Freya Stark Letters,* vol. 4, ed. Lucy Moorehead (Wilton, Salisbury, Wiltshire: Michael Russell, 1977), p. 169. The nationalist was Nashishibi, murdered in Baghdad in 1941.
13. H. C. Bailey remembered living in La Mura, across the street from the villa Herbert Young gave Freya, for two months in 1930. He played badminton almost every day at Herbert's house with Freya and her guest, "the Captain." Bailey remembered clearly that he and his brother both thought of him as "queer."
14. FS, *Beyond Euphrates*, p. 89.
15. FS to Flora Stark, December 17, 1929, in *Freya Stark Letters,* vol. 1, p. 224.
16. This and the following quotations are from a memoir given the author by Veronica Bamfield, whose daughter Julian Morgan was one of Freya's godchildren.
17. Ibid.
18. FS to Venetia Buddicom, February 20, 1932, in *Freya Stark Letters,* vol. 2, ed. Lucy Moorehead (Tisbury, Wiltshire: Compton Russell, 1975), p. 73.
19. FS to Flora Stark, May 6, 1930, in FS, *Beyond Euphrates,* p. 159.
20. FS to Venetia Buddicom, January 6, 1930, in ibid., p. 116.
21. FS to Mrs. Derek Cooper, April 17, 1962, in *Freya Stark Letters,* vol. 8, ed. Caroline Moorehead (Wilton, Salisbury, Wiltshire: Michael Russell, 1982), p. 45.
22. Philip K. Hitti, *The Near East in History* (Princeton, N.J.: D. Van Nostrand, 1961), p. 193.
23. FS to Flora Stark, May 6, 1930, in FS, *Beyond Euphrates,* pp. 159–160.
24. Ibid.
25. Bernard Lewis, *The Assassins* (New York: Basic Books, 1968; New York: Oxford University Press, 1987).
26. Joseph Von Hammer-Purgstall, *The History of the Assassins,* trans. Oswald Charles Wood (1835; reprint, New York: Burt Franklin, 1968), p. 56.
27. FS, *The Valleys of the Assassins* (London: John Murray, 1934), p. 181.
28. Ibid., p. 208.
29. Ibid., p. 192.

30. FS, *Beyond Euphrates,* p. 162.
31. Ibid., pp. 7–8.
32. FS to Herbert Young, January 13, 1928, HRC.

7. The Importance of Friends

1. Interview with Caroline Moorehead, 1993; interview with Xantha ("Bingo") Hardie, 1990.
2. Interview with Xantha Hardie, 1990.
3. Interview with Sheridan Russell, 1989.
4. Interview with Evelyn Lambert, 1990.
5. Malise Ruthven, *Traveller Through Time* (New York: Viking Press, 1986), p. 135.
6. FS, *The Coast of Incense* (London: John Murray, 1953), pp. 7–8.
7. Interview with Xantha Hardie, 1990.
8. Interview with H. C. Bailey, 1993.
9. FS to Flora Stark, November 21, 1930, in *Freya Stark Letters,* vol. 2, ed. Lucy Moorehead (Tisbury, Wiltshire: Compton Russell, 1975), p. 3.
10. FS to Flora Stark, December 23, 1930, in ibid., p. 5.
11. Undated letter from Venetia Buddicom that is clearly prompted by Vera's death as it begins, "I've just had your tragic news," HRC.
12. Venetia Buddicom to FS, February 23, 1931, HRC.
13. Information from Venetia's niece, Jennifer Hamilton, Washington, D.C., 1994.
14. FS, *Beyond Euphrates* (London: John Murray, 1951), p. 193.
15. Ibid., p. 55.
16. Dorothy Middleton, *Victorian Lady Travellers* (London: Routledge and Kegan Paul, 1965), pp. 10–14.
17. At this time these were the standard instruments used by surveyors and cartographers. An aneroid is a type of barometer; a prismatic compass is hand-held and allows the user to take a bearing as he reads the numbers refracted through the instrument; an Abney level is a clinometer that measures angles of slope and elevation.
18. FS to Robert Stark, March 31, 1931, in *Freya Stark Letters,* vol. 2, p. 9.
19. FS, *Beyond Euphrates,* p. 62.

8. A Treasure Hunt in Luristan

1. Note of introduction from the Royal Geographical Society (hereafter RGS) Secretary to the First Secretary of the Legation, in *Freya Stark Letters,* vol. 2, ed. Lucy Moorehead (Tisbury, Wiltshire: Compton Russell, 1975), p. 21.
2. FS to Flora Stark, July 18, 1931, in ibid., p. 21.
3. FS, *The Valleys of the Assassins* (London: John Murray, 1934), p. 226.
4. Ibid., p. 304.
5. Ibid., p. 255.
6. FS to Charles Ker, September 22, 1931, in *Freya Stark Letters,* vol. 2, p. 44.
7. C. J. Edmonds, review of *The Valleys of the Assassins, Geographical Journal,* vol. 8, no. 2 (August 1934).
8. FS, *Valleys of the Assassins,* p. 21.
9. Ibid., p. 23.
10. Edmonds, review of *The Valleys of the Assassins.*
11. FS to Venetia Buddicom, February 20, 1932, in *Freya Stark Letters,* vol. 2, p. 73.

12. The scholar was Professor Vladimir Minorsky of the University of Paris, a noted authority on Persian history and archaeology.
13. FS to Venetia Buddicom, December 4, 1931, in *Freya Stark Letters*, vol. 2, p. 67.
14. FS to Venetia Buddicom, April 26, 1932, in ibid., p. 81.
15. FS, *Beyond Euphrates* (London: John Murray, 1951), p. 244.
16. FS to Flora Stark, January 29, 1932, in *Freya Stark Letters*, vol. 2, p. 70.
17. FS to Flora Stark, July 18, 1931, in ibid., p. 21.
18. To this day there is nothing in British law to protect a homosexual from discrimination. A deep homophobia appears still to exist in England.
19. Harold George Nicolson, *Diaries and Letters: 1930–1964* (London: Collins, 1971), p. 381.
20. FS to Venetia Buddicom, August 6, 1932, in *Freya Stark Letters*, vol. 2, p. 96.
21. FS to Flora Stark, August 20, 1932, in ibid., p. 98.
22. FS to Flora Stark, August 20 and August 28, 1932, in ibid., pp. 98–99.
23. FS to Flora Stark, August 31, 1932, in ibid., p. 100.
24. Flora Stark to FS, May 28, 1932, HRC.
25. Flora Stark to FS, January 5, 1933, HRC.
26. FS to Charles Ker, September 22, 1931, in *Freya Stark Letters*, vol. 2, p. 44.
27. Molly Izzard, *Freya Stark: A Biography* (London: Hodder & Stoughton, 1993), p. 77.
28. FS to Flora Stark, September 8, 1932, in *Freya Stark Letters*, vol. 2, p. 100.
29. FS, *Valleys of the Assassins*, p. 54.
30. FS, *Beyond Euphrates,* p. 308.

9. RECOGNITION

1. FS to Flora Stark, May 6, 1930, in *Freya Stark Letters*, vol. 1, ed. Lucy Moorehead (Compton Chamberlayne, Salisbury, Wiltshire: Compton Russell, 1974), p. 269.
2. Interview with Mrs. Norman Walker, 1989.

10. A LONDON WHIRL

1. FS to Flora Stark, June 22, 1933, in *Freya Stark Letters*, vol. 2, ed. Lucy Moorehead (Tisbury, Wiltshire: Compton Russell, 1975), p. 150.
2. FS to Venetia Buddicom, April 24, 1933, in ibid., p. 148.
3. "Meetings: Session 1932–1933," *Geographical Journal*, vol. 82, no. 2 (August 1933), p. 180.
4. Ibid.
5. Minnie Granville to Flora Stark, June 20, 1933, HRC.
6. Ibid.
7. Gwendolen Guinness, Lady Iveagh, to Flora Stark, November 29, 1933, HRC.
8. Minnie Granville to Flora Stark, December 15, 1933, HRC.
9. Minnie Granville to Flora Stark, March 6, 1933, HRC.
10. Minnie Granville to Flora Stark, December 15, 1933, HRC.
11. Elizabeth Monroe, *Philby of Arabia* (London: Faber & Faber, 1973), p. 49.
12. Wilfrid Blunt, *Cockerell* (New York: Alfred A. Knopf, 1964).
13. Ibid., p. 300.
14. Letter from Methuen, n.d., HRC.
15. Interview with John Murray, 1993.
16. C. J. Edmonds, review of *The Valleys of the Assassins*, *Geographical Journal*, vol. 8, no. 2 (August 1934).

17. Thomas Edward Lawrence to Sir Sydney Cockerell, in *Friends of a Lifetime,* ed. Viola Meynell (London: J. Cape, 1940), p. 372.

18. FS to Flora Stark, June 22, 1933, in *Freya Stark Letters,* vol. 2, p. 150.

19. FS, *Perseus in the Wind* (London: John Murray, 1948; reprint, London: Century, 1984), p. 98.

20. Flora Stark to FS, March 4, 1930, HRC.

21. FS, *The Coast of Incense* (London: John Murray, 1953), p. 13.

22. Interview with Margaret Olivier's granddaughter, Barclay Sanders (Mrs. Theo) Larsson, 1989. Herbert Olivier was always reluctant to sell his pictures, but the family has loaned a number of them to be shown on the walls of the British embassy in Paris, where they are considered an important part of the mansion's collection.

23. FS to Venetia Buddicom, December 19, 1933, in *Freya Stark Letters,* vol. 2, p. 165.

24. FS to Flora Stark, December 26, 1933, in ibid., p. 166.

25. FS to Venetia Buddicom, January 23, 1934, in ibid., p. 171.

26. FS to Flora Stark, January 12, 1934, in ibid., p. 168.

27. FS to Flora Stark, February 10, 1934, in ibid., p. 173.

28. FS, *Beyond Euphrates* (London: John Murray, 1951), p. 94.

29. From Veronica Bamfield's unpublished memoir, which she kindly shared with the author.

30. FS, *Coast of Incense,* p. 18.

31. FS to Lionel Smith, September 28, 1934, in *Freya Stark Letters,* vol. 2, p. 191. Lionel, Freya's friend from Baghdad, was now headmaster of a school in Edinburgh.

11. AT LAST, ARABIA

1. G. Wyman Bury, *The Land of Uz* (London: Macmillan, 1911), p. xxi.

2. Wendell Phillips, *Qataban and Sheba* (New York: Harcourt Brace, 1955), p. 162.

3. FS to Venetia Buddicom, July 14, 1934, in *Freya Stark Letters,* vol. 2, ed. Lucy Moorehead (Tisbury, Wiltshire: Compton Russell, 1975), p. 186.

4. FS to Venetia Buddicom, August 5, 1934, in ibid., p. 188.

5. FS to Venetia Buddicom, September 2, 1934, in ibid., p. 190.

6. Sir Akbar Hydar to FS, June 20, 1934, HRC.

7. David Footman, *Antonin Besse of Aden* (Basingstoke, Hampshire: Macmillan Press with St. Antony's College, Oxford, 1986), pp. 26, 57.

8. Evelyn Waugh, *When the Going Was Good* (Boston: Little, Brown, 1934), p. 144.

9. FS to Flora Stark, December 23, 1934, in *Freya Stark Letters,* vol. 2, p. 211.

10. FS, *The Southern Gates of Arabia* (London: John Murray, 1936), p. 127.

11. FS to Flora Stark, December 18, 1934, in *Freya Stark Letters,* vol. 2, p. 207.

12. Doreen Ingrams, *A Time in Arabia* (London: John Murray, 1970).

13. Interview with Doreen Ingrams, June 1993.

14. From John Masefield's poem "Cargoes": "Quinquireme of Nineveh from distant Ophir; /Rowing home to haven in sunny Palestine;/With a cargo of ivory;/ And apes and peacocks; / Sandalwood, cedarwood, and sweet white wine."

15. This quotation and the following narrative come from Freya's letter to her mother, December 26, 1934, in *Freya Stark Letters,* vol. 2, pp. 211–213; translation of French phrases by the author.

16. Antonin Besse (hereafter AB) to FS, January 22, 1935, HRC. This and all other Besse letters written in French were translated by Edmée Firth, New York City.

17. AB to FS, April 25, 1935, HRC.
18. AB to FS, January 31, 1935, HRC.
19. FS, *Southern Gates of Arabia*, p. 49.
20. Ingrams, *Time in Arabia*, p. 94.
21. FS, *Southern Gates of Arabia*, p. 75.
22. FS to Flora Stark, February 4, 1935, in *Freya Stark Letters*, vol. 2, p. 242.
23. AB to FS, January 17, 1935, HRC.
24. AB to FS, January 22, 1935, HRC.
25. Ibid.
26. AB to FS, January 31, 1935, HRC.
27. FS, *Southern Gates of Arabia*, p. 229.
28. Ibid., p. 268.
29. Lady Iveagh to Flora Stark, March 16, 1935, HRC.
30. Lady Woolley to Flora Stark, April 6, 1935, HRC.
31. AB to FS, April 25, 1935, HRC.
32. FS to Venetia Buddicom, March 9, 1935, in *Freya Stark Letters*, vol. 2, p. 269.
33. FS to Venetia Buddicom, September 20, 1936, in *Freya Stark Letters*, vol. 3, ed. Lucy Moorehead (Tisbury, Wiltshire: Compton Russell, 1976), p. 50.
34. FS to Flora Stark, April 3, 1935, in *Freya Stark Letters*, vol. 2, p. 276.
35. Interview with Doreen Ingrams, June 1993.

12. A Passionate Attachment

1. FS to Venetia Buddicom, June 7, 1935, in *Freya Stark Letters*, vol. 3, ed. Lucy Moorehead (Tisbury, Wiltshire: Compton Russell, 1976), p. 3.
2. Venetia Buddicom to FS, May 5, 1935, HRC.
3. AB to FS, June 19, 1935, HRC.
4. FS to Venetia Buddicom, June 2, 1935, in *Freya Stark Letters*, vol. 3, p. 2.
5. AB to FS, November 13, 1935, HRC.
6. AB to FS, June n.d., 1935, HRC.
7. FS, *The Coast of Incense* (London: John Murray, 1953), p. 95.
8. FS to Venetia Buddicom, July 22, 1935, in *Freya Stark Letters*, vol. 3, p. 5.
9. FS to Venetia Buddicom, July 27, 1935, in ibid., p. 6.
10. Interview with one of Venetia Buddicom's nieces, Jennifer Arnold-Forster Hamilton, Washington, D.C., September 1994.
11. Venetia Buddicom to FS, March 20, 1935, HRC.
12. Venetia Buddicom to FS, December 19, 1934, HRC.
13. Venetia Buddicom to FS, December 9, 1934, HRC.
14. FS to Venetia Buddicom, July 5, 1936, in *Freya Stark Letters*, vol. 3, p. 39; *The Coast of Incense*, p. 101, speaks of a mysterious love "with no bite of conscience or regret."
15. FS to Venetia Buddicom, July 5, 1936, in *Freya Stark Letters*, vol. 3, p. 39.
16. FS to Venetia Buddicom, August 13, 1935, in ibid., p. 7.
17. FS to Flora Stark, December 15, 1935, in ibid., p. 14.
18. FS to Venetia Buddicom, September 13, 1936, in ibid., p. 50.
19. AB to FS, March 4, 1936, HRC.
20. David Footman, *Antonin Besse of Aden: Founder of St. Antony's College, Oxford* (Basingstoke, Hampshire: Macmillan Press with St. Antony's College, Oxford, 1986), pp. 138–152.
21. AB to FS, Christmas Eve, 1935, HRC.
22. AB to FS, November 20, 1935, HRC.

23. AB to FS, February 19, 1936, HRC.
24. AB to FS, May 19, 1936, HRC.
25. FS to Flora Stark, May 26, 1936, in *Freya Stark Letters,* vol. 3, p. 31.
26. FS to Jock Murray, May 31, 1936, in ibid., p. 33.
27. FS to Venetia Buddicom, June 12, 1936, in ibid., p. 34.
28. Ibid.
29. Interview with Xantha Hardie, 1990.
30. FS to Venetia Buddicom, June 17, 1936, in *Freya Stark Letters,* vol. 3, p. 36.
31. FS to Venetia Buddicom, July 5, 1936, in ibid., p. 40.
32. Venetia Buddicom to FS, June 27, 1936, HRC.
33. FS to Venetia Buddicom, October 2, 1936, in *Freya Stark Letters,* vol. 3, p. 53.
34. AB to FS, October 8, 1936, HRC.
35. AB to FS, July 8, 1938, HRC.
36. Ibid.
37. FS to Venetia Buddicom, April 29, 1937, in *Freya Stark Letters,* vol. 3, p. 83.
38. Interview with Bingo Hardie, 1990. The author talked with many other friends who agreed they had seen Freya show this propensity, especially in the lonely years of her late sixties and early seventies. One frequently cited example was her attachment to Dulcie Deuchar, the childless wife of a rich Australian businessman who showered Freya with presents and attentions until Freya became dependent on her generosity and compliments and would be jealous if other women vied for Dulcie's time. By contrast, Lady Sybil Cholmondeley, the marchioness of Houghton Hall, an exceptionally good friend over many years who traveled with Freya and saw her behave in a variety of circumstances, never encountered this side of her friend. Instead, Lady Cholmondeley declared herself grateful to Freya for her erudition and years of shared pleasure. In turn, Lady Cholmondeley always made quietly sure that Freya was never financially wanting in her late age.
39. Veronica Bamfield included this comment of Freya's in the memoir she sent the author.

13. THE ARCHAEOLOGISTS

1. Gertrude Caton-Thompson, *Mixed Memoirs* (Gateshead, Tyne, and Ware: Paradigm Press, 1983), p. 159.
2. FS to Harold Ingrams, December 24, 1936, in *Freya Stark Letters,* vol. 3, ed. Lucy Moorehead (Tisbury, Wiltshire: Compton Russell, 1976), p. 64.
3. Caton-Thompson, *Mixed Memoirs,* p. 180.
4. Elinor Gardner letters to an unidentified friend, November 1, 1937, RGS.
5. FS to Lionel and Mary Smith, October 29, 1937, in *Freya Stark Letters,* vol. 3, pp. 112–113.
6. FS to Jock Murray, November 2, 1937, in ibid., p. 114.
7. FS to Flora Stark, November 4, 1937, in ibid., p. 114.
8. FS to Flora Stark, November 9, 1937, in ibid., p. 116.
9. Interview with Doreen Ingrams, June 1993.
10. Ibid.
11. Elinor Gardner letters, November 28, 1937, RGS.
12. FS to Flora Stark, November 22, 1937, in *Freya Stark Letters,* vol. 3, p. 123.
13. FS to Jock Murray, December 3, 1937, in ibid., p. 129.
14. FS to Flora Stark, December 1, 1937, in ibid., p. 127.

15. Notes from Sydney Cockerell papers given the author by Molly Izzard, who was given them by Wilfrid Blunt.
16. Elinor Gardner letters, December 14, 1937, RGS.
17. Elinor Gardner letters, December 22, 1938, RGS.
18. Caton-Thompson, *Mixed Memoirs,* p. 192.
19. D. Brian Doe, *Southern Arabia,* Archaeological Series (New York: McGraw-Hill, 1971), pp. 25, 238.
    In 1996 the author had the pleasure of visiting the Wadi 'Amd and locating the area of the dig, which Gertrude Caton-Thompson had reburied in sand, a correct archaeological procedure to preserve from looting or the elements.
20. Caton-Thompson, *Mixed Memoirs,* p. 189.
21. Elinor Gardner letters, February 4, 1938, RGS.
22. Elinor Gardner letters, February n.d., 1938, RGS.
23. Caton-Thompson, *Mixed Memoirs,* p. 194.
24. Elinor Gardner letters, March 22, 1938, RGS.
25. Caton-Thompson, *Mixed Memoirs,* p. 196.
26. Elinor Gardner letters, March 22, 1938, RGS.
27. FS, "An Exploration in the Hadhramaut and Journey to the Coast," *Geographical Journal,* vol. 113, no. 1 (January 1939), p. 13.
28. From a letter describing these events from Doreen Ingrams to Molly Izzard, courtesy of Molly Izzard.
29. FS to Jock Murray, April 7, 1938, in *Freya Stark Letters,* vol. 3, p. 208.
30. FS to Sydney Cockerell, April 5, 1938, in ibid., pp. 206–208.
31. Sydney Cockerell to FS in many letters, beginning in July 1938, HRC.
32. Sydney Cockerell to FS, July 12, 1938, HRC.
33. Sydney Cockerell to FS, July 21, 1938, HRC.
34. FS to Jock Murray, July 16, 1938, in *Freya Stark Letters,* vol. 3, pp. 214–215.
35. FS, *Seen in the Hadhramaut* (London: John Murray, 1938), p. xix.
36. Sydney Cockerell to FS, August 31, 1938, HRC.
37. Draft of a letter written on July 30, 1939, shown to Molly Izzard by Cockerell's biographer Wilfrid Blunt and given by Mrs. Izzard to the author. It is a good thing Cockerell kept a draft of this letter to Freya, because there is no record of it among the letters from him now in the possession of the Humanities Research Center. According to Mrs. Izzard, after Blunt published it in *Cockerell* in 1964—although he did not use Freya's name, only offered it as an example of the kind of help Cockerell gave many writers—Freya cut Blunt dead the next time they met.
38. FS to Sydney Cockerell, August 6, 1939, in *Freya Stark Letters,* vol. 3, p. 267.
39. Sydney Cockerell to FS, August 12, 1939, HRC.
40. FS to Jock Murray, July 28, 1939, in *Freya Stark Letters,* vol. 3, p. 266.
41. Copy of letter Freya wrote Jock Murray from Sana'a in 1940, found in Sydney Cockerell's papers and given to the author by Molly Izzard.
42. Gertrude Caton-Thompson to Sydney Cockerell, October 16, 1944, from Newnham College, Cambridge. From Wilfrid Blunt's papers on Cockerell, in the possession of Molly Izzard, who showed them to the author.

14. LONDON PREPARES FOR WAR

1. FS to Flora Stark, October 29, 1938, in *Freya Stark Letters,* vol. 3, ed. Lucy Moorehead (Tisbury, Wiltshire: Compton Russell, 1976), p. 231.

2. FS to Flora Stark, October 13, 1938, in ibid., p. 229.
3. FS to Flora Stark, November 12, 1938, in ibid., p. 232.
4. FS to Flora Stark, October 29, 1938, in ibid., p. 231; FS to Flora Stark and Herbert Olivier, December 18, 1938, p. 237; FS to Flora Stark, December 21, 1938, p. 237.
5. FS, *The Coast of Incense* (London: John Murray, 1953), p. 42.
6. FS to Flora Stark, December 11, 1938, in *Freya Stark Letters*, vol. 3, p. 136.
7. FS to Flora Stark, November 12, 1938, in ibid., p. 232.
8. Discussion following her November 28, 1938, lecture before RGS, *Geographical Journal*, vol. 113, no. 1 (January 1939), pp. 14–17.
9. Ibid.
10. Flora Stark to FS, December 3, 1938, HRC.
11. FS to Flora Stark, October 5, 1938, in *Freya Stark Letters*, vol. 3, p. 228.
12. Flora Stark to FS, December 3, 1938, HRC.
13. John Moorehead, a godson, described in an interview in 1990 how Freya curtsied to the floor before a son of the deposed king of Italy who was visiting in Ventimiglia. Mr. Moorehead said the display embarrassed him greatly.
14. Donald Lennox-Boyd to FS, March 20, 1939, HRC.
15. FS to Sydney Cockerell, February 22, 1939, in *Freya Stark Letters*, vol. 3, p. 241.
16. FS to Flora Stark, January 6, 1939, in ibid., p. 238.
17. FS to Jock Murray, March 29, 1939, in ibid., p. 246.
18. Donald Lennox-Boyd to FS, March 20, 1939, HRC.
19. FS, *Perseus in the Wind* (London: John Murray, 1948; reprint, London: Century, 1984), p. 48.
20. Bernard Berenson to FS, August 20, 1939, HRC.
21. FS to Sydney Cockerell, October 8, 1939, in *Freya Stark Letters*, vol. 3, pp. 275–276.

15. A RECRUIT IN YEMEN

1. FS to Flora Stark, November 19, 1939, in *Freya Stark Letters*, vol. 3, ed. Lucy Moorehead (Tisbury, Wiltshire: Compton Russell, 1976), p. 279.
2. FS, *The Arab Island* (New York: Alfred A. Knopf, 1945), p. 13.
3. FS to Flora Stark, December 23, 1939, in *Freya Stark Letters*, vol. 3, p. 288.
4. FS to Malcolm MacDonald, January 4, 1940, in *Freya Stark Letters*, vol. 4, ed. Lucy Moorehead (Wilton, Salisbury, Wiltshire: Michael Russell, 1977), p. 1.
5. FS to Stewart Perowne (hereafter SP), February 12, 1940, in ibid., p. 13.
6. FS to Flora Stark, February 13, 1940, in ibid., p. 13.
7. FS Report to SP, February 28, 1940, in ibid., p. 28.
8. FS to Flora Stark, February 13, 1940, in ibid., p. 13.
9. FS to Lionel Smith, February 25, 1940, in ibid., p. 26.
10. Freya learned this from Sir Edward Villiers of the Ministry of Information in June 1942.
11. FS to Sydney Cockerell, May 16, 1940, in *Freya Stark Letters*, vol. 4, p. 56.
12. FS to Jock Murray, June 8, 1940, in ibid., p. 69.
13. FS to Jock Murray, May 26, 1940, in ibid., p. 60.
14. FS to Sydney Cockerell, July 11, 1940, in ibid., p. 79.
15. FS to Laurence Rushbrook Williams, August 27, 1940, in ibid., p. 86.
16. FS to Harold Ingrams, August 22, 1940, in ibid., p. 83.
17. Molly Izzard, *Freya Stark: A Biography* (London: Hodder & Stoughton, 1993), p. 156.

18. FS to Sydney Cockerell, September 7, 1940, in *Freya Stark Letters,* vol. 4, p. 90.
19. FS, *East Is West* (London: John Murray, 1945), p. 47.

16. Glittering Cairo

1. Artemis Cooper, *Cairo in the War, 1939–1945* (London: Hamish Hamilton, 1989), p. 112.
2. Harold Macmillan, *War Diaries* (London: Macmillan, 1984), p. 393.
3. Archibald Wavell, *Allenby: A Study in Greatness* (London: G. G. Harrap, 1940).
4. FS, *Dust in the Lion's Paw: Autobiography, 1939–1946* (London: John Murray, 1961), p. 59.
5. FS to SP, September 18, 1940, in *Freya Stark Letters,* vol. 4, ed. Lucy Moorehead (Wilton, Salisbury, Wiltshire: Michael Russell, 1977), p. 93.
6. Pamela Cooper, *A Cloud of Forgetting* (London: Quartet Books, 1993), p. 126.
7. Flora Stark, *An Italian Diary* (London: John Murray, 1945).
8. A letter from Admiral Sir William Goodenough to John Murray expresses the general doubts over the advisability of publishing Flora's book until the war was over. Included in Wilfrid Blunt letters.
9. Lucy Beach to FS, October 27, 1942, HRC.
10. Lucy Beach letters and cables, HRC.
11. FS to Sydney Cockerell, November 3 and December 4, 1942, in *Freya Stark Letters,* vol. 4, pp. 253, 255.
12. Cooper, *Cairo,* p. 58.
13. R. J. Collins, *Lord Wavell, 1883–1941: A Military Biography* (London: Hodder & Stoughton, 1947), p. 302.
14. FS to Lucy Beach, January 19, 1941, in *Freya Stark Letters,* vol. 4, p. 114.
15. Cooper, *Cloud of Forgetting,* p. 132.
16. Ibid.
17. Interviews with Nigel Clive, Pamela Cooper, and Michael Stewart. FS to Jock Murray, March 2, 1941, in *Freya Stark Letters,* vol. 4, p. 121; FS to Flora Stark, July 4, 1941, vol. 4, p. 138; FS to Flora Stark, November, 17, 1941, vol. 4, p. 167; FS to Flora Stark, February 6, 1942, vol. 4, p. 191.
18. FS to SP, February 7, 1941, in ibid., p. 118.
19. FS to SP, February 26, 1941, in ibid., pp. 119–120.
20. Cooper, *Cloud of Forgetting,* p. 134.
21. FS, *The Arab Island* (New York: Alfred A. Knopf, 1945), pp. 68–69.
22. FS to Sydney Cockerell, February 2, 1941, in *Freya Stark Letters,* vol. 4, pp. 116–117.
23. FS to SP, February 26, 1941, in ibid., pp. 119–120.
24. FS to SP, March 2, 1941, in ibid., p. 121.

17. The Baghdad Siege

1. FS, *Dust in the Lion's Paw: Autobiography, 1939–1946* (London: John Murray, 1961), p. 79.
2. Ibid., p. 127.
3. FS to Sydney Cockerell, April 13, 1941, in *Freya Stark Letters,* vol. 4, ed. Lucy Moorehead (Wilton, Salisbury, Wiltshire: Michael Russell, 1977), p. 130.
4. FS to Jock Murray, April 14, 1941, in ibid., p. 130.
5. Recollections of Mr. Hope-Gill in *Tales of Empire: The British in the Middle East,* ed. Derek Hopwood (London: I. B. Tauris, 1989), p. 195.

6. FS, *Dust in the Lion's Paw*, p. 103.
7. Seton Lloyd, *The Interval: A Life in Near Eastern Archaeology* (Osney Mead, Oxford: Alden Press, 1986), p. 81. Seton Lloyd, the archaeologist, was watching Colonel Patrick Domvile, a distant cousin of Stewart Perowne.
8. *Tales of Empire*, p. 195.
9. Lloyd, *Interval*, p. 81.
10. FS, *Dust in the Lion's Paw*, p. 107.
11. Ibid., p. 103.
12. Pam Cooper, *A Cloud of Forgetting* (London: Quartet Books, 1994), p. 148.
13. FS, *Dust in the Lion's Paw*, p. 103.
14. Ibid., p. 105.
15. FS to Sydney Cockerell, April 13, 1941, in *Freya Stark Letters*, vol. 4, p. 130.
16. Lloyd, *Interval*, p. 82.
17. Gerald de Gaury, *Traces of Travel* (London: Quartet Books, 1983), p. 115.
18. Lloyd, *Interval*, p. 82.
19. FS, "The Background of the Rebellion," *Times* [London], June 27, 1941, p. 3.
20. In 1945 both Lebanon and Syria were finally declared independent, but it took another year for French forces to evacuate.

18. THE BROTHERHOOD

1. Artemis Cooper, *Cairo in the War, 1939–1945* (London: Hamish Hamilton, 1989), p. 89.
2. *The Killearn Diaries, 1934–1946* [the memoirs of Miles Lampson, later Lord Killearn] (London: Sidgwick and Jackson, 1972), p. 192.
3. Molly Izzard, *Freya Stark: A Biography* (London: Hodder & Stoughton, 1993), p. 178.
4. FS to Flora Stark, September 1, 1942, in *Freya Stark Letters*, vol. 4, ed. Lucy Moorehead (Wilton, Salisbury, Wiltshire: Michael Russell, 1977), p. 240.
5. "If you can talk with crowds and keep your virtue, / Or walk with kings—nor lose the common touch," from "If" by Rudyard Kipling.
6. Hermione Ranfurly, *To War with Whitaker: The Wartime Diaries of the Countess of Ranfurly, 1939–1945* (London: Mandarin, 1995), p. 112.
7. FS to Sydney Cockerell, August 5, 1941, in *Freya Stark Letters*, vol. 4, p. 145.
8. FS to Flora Stark, July 4, 1941, in ibid., p. 138; FS to Flora Stark, November 23, 1941, p. 170; FS to Flora Stark, January 30, 1942, p. 189.
9. FS to Flora Stark, June 30, 1941, in ibid., p. 136.
10. Interview with Lord Sherfield, 1989.
11. Interview with Pam Hore-Ruthven Cooper, 1993.
12. Ranfurly, *To War with Whitaker*, p. 122.
13. Gerald de Gaury to FS, undated, HRC.
14. FS to Flora Stark, July 26, 1942, in *Freya Stark Letters*, vol. 4, p. 227.
15. FS to Flora, July 30, 1942, in ibid., p. 228.
16. Seton Lloyd, *The Interval: A Life in Near Eastern Archaeology* (Osney Mead, Oxford: Alden Press, 1986), p. 87.
17. Ibid., p. 86.
18. From a 1979 interview with the late Mrs. Monroe in Izzard, *Freya Stark*, p. 302.
19. Interview with Nigel Clive, 1990.
20. Ibid.
21. Peggy Drower, daughter of Freya's friends from early Baghdad days, kept careful lists of all the contents of the boxes so as to have complete answers to Freya's

challenges about missing items. Freya's letters to her were always grateful and affectionate, but the correspondence was lengthy and exhausting because Freya never forgot a jar, or kilim, or particularly her missing riding boots. Because Peggy, later Mrs. Hackforth-Jones, was a trained archaeologist, the idea of leaving her teaching career to run the tessoria in Asolo was distinctly comical. But Freya was never beyond trying. A less fortunate assistant was Barbara Graham, who was attacked in Freya's garden by an intruder. Freya was not sympathetic, and her dismissive response to the incident went the rounds of Freya tales: "Well, *Pam* never got hit on the head!"

22. Ranfurly, *To War with Whitaker,* p. 161.
23. Ibid.
24. Interview with Pam Hore-Ruthven Cooper, 1993.
25. FS to Flora Stark, October 12, 1941, in *Freya Stark Letters,* vol. 4, p. 159.
26. FS to Sydney Cockerell, October 25, 1941, in ibid., p. 160.
27. Pamela Cooper, *A Cloud of Forgetting* (London: Quartet Books, 1994), p. 150.
28. FS to Flora Stark, June 6, 1942, in *Freya Stark Letters,* vol. 4, p. 216.
29. Interview with Nizar Jawdat, 1993.
30. Seton Lloyd, *Interval,* p. 109.
31. See also a description of Stewart's Anglocentric political reporting in William Roger Louis, *The British Empire in the Middle East, 1945–1951* (Oxford: Clarendon Press, Oxford University Press, 1984), p. 315.
32. FS to Sydney Cockerell, May 21, 1943, in *Freya Stark Letters,* vol. 4, p. 288.
33. FS to Harold Bowen, a high official with the Ministry of Information, London, February 4, 1943, in ibid., pp. 266–277.
34. General Archibald Wavell to FS, in ibid., p. 258.
35. FS to Jock Murray, January 22, 1943, in ibid., p. 263.
36. FS to Nigel Clive and Lady Ranfurly, February 11, 1943, in ibid., p. 269.
37. FS to Jock Murray, April 16, 1943, in ibid., pp. 281–282.
38. Lady Holman was interviewed by Molly Izzard, who gave this account in her *Freya Stark.*
39. Interview with Hugh Leach, 1993.
40. FS, *Dust in the Lion's Paw,* p. 148.
41. See Laurence Grafftey-Smith, *Bright Levant* (London: John Murray, 1970), pp. 222–223: "Her results were extraordinary . . . the organization snowballed to tens of thousands."

19. AN AMERICAN TOUR

1. FS to SP, October 24, 1943, in *Freya Stark Letters,* vol. 5, ed. Lucy Moorehead (Wilton, Salisbury, Wiltshire: Michael Russell, 1978), pp. 7–8.
2. Freya and Stewart clearly had talked about this on previous occasions, calling it a vice consulate in "some little town by the river or seashore." She referred to it again in a letter to him on April 27, 1944, in ibid., p. 88.
3. FS to SP, November 7, 1943, in ibid., p. 17.
4. Charles D. Smith, *Palestine and the Arab-Israeli Conflict* (New York: St. Martin's Press, 1992), p. 114.
5. Conor Cruise O'Brien, *The Siege* (New York: Simon & Schuster, 1986), p. 248.
6. FS to Jock Murray, January 6, 1944, in *Freya Stark Letters,* vol. 5, p. 42.
7. FS to Elizabeth Monroe, November 28, 1943, in ibid., p. 27.
8. FS to Elizabeth Monroe, December 23, 1943, in ibid., p. 36.
9. FS to Elizabeth Monroe, January 14, 1944, in ibid., p. 46.

10. FS to Elizabeth Monroe, April 1, 1944, in ibid., p. 79.
11. FS to Elizabeth Monroe, December 2, 1943, in ibid., p. 29.
12. Interview with Sir Isaiah Berlin, 1989.
13. Smith, *Palestine and the Arab-Israeli Conflict,* p. 119.
14. Betty Walker, "No Man's Land," *Chicago Times,* January 11, 1944.
15. *Newsweek,* January 17, 1944; *Vancouver Sun,* February 29, 1944; *Collier's,* April 8, 1944.
16. *Congressional Record,* March 29, 1944.
17. Memorandum to Lord Halifax from Grant McKensie, British Embassy in Washington, March 29, 1944, HRC.
18. FS to Elizabeth Monroe, April 8, 1944, in *Freya Stark Letters,* vol. 5, p. 80.
19. FS to Sydney Cockerell, April n.d., 1944, in ibid., p. 78.
20. [London] *Times,* April 27, 1944.
21. *Evening Standard,* April 26, 1944.
22. Ibid.
23. Lucy Beach to Lady Lawrence, February 25, 1944. Given to Sydney Cockerell by Lady Lawrence, who with her husband, Sir Alexander Lawrence, had for years during the summers rented the villa called La Mura in Asolo, directly across from Casa Freia in Asolo; they knew both Stark women well.
24. FS to Elizabeth Monroe, May 12, 1944, in *Freya Stark Letters,* vol. 5, p. 92.
25. FS to Elizabeth Monroe, May 14, 1944, in ibid., p. 94.
26. FS to Elizabeth Monroe, January 21, 1944, in ibid., p. 47.
27. FS to Momo Marriot, July 11, 1944, in ibid., p. 105.

20. Mrs. Stark

1. FS to Pam Hore-Ruthven, April 28, 1945, in *Freya Stark Letters,* vol. 5, ed. Lucy Moorehead (Wilton, Salisbury, Wiltshire: Michael Russell, 1978), p. 185.
2. Interview with Caroli Piaser, 1990.
3. FS to Michael Stewart, August 5, 1945, in *Freya Stark Letters,* vol. 5, p. 217.
4. FS to William Henderson, September 8, 1945, in ibid., p. 224.
5. FS to Jock Murray, September 2, 1945, in ibid., p. 223.
6. FS to Jock Murray, January 6, 1946, in ibid., pp. 251–252.
7. Interview with Sir Michael Stewart, 1989, and confirmed in a letter to him written on October 16, 1945.
8. FS to Gerald de Gaury, March 3, 1947, in *Freya Stark Letters,* vol. 6, ed. Lucy Moorehead (Wilton, Salisbury, Wiltshire: Michael Russell, 1981), p. 7.
9. Interview with Jock Murray, 1989.
10. Minnie Granville to Lady Lawrence, September 17, 1945, shown to the author by Molly Izzard.
11. Interview with Jock and Diana Murray, 1990.
12. Interview with Father Donald Harris, 1990.
13. Interview with Leslie Perowne, 1990.
14. SP to FS, September 29, 1949, HRC.
15. FS to SP, July 7, 1947, in *Freya Stark Letters,* vol. 6, p. 17.
16. SP to FS, August 22, 1947, HRC.
17. SP to FS, September 5, 1947, HRC.
18. Stewart described what Freya had responded in this telegram in one of his later letters to her.
19. FS to Nigel Clive, September 14, 1947, in *Freya Stark Letters,* vol. 6, p. 22.
20. Ibid.

21. Pam Hore-Ruthven Cooper allowed the author to see copies of all Freya's letters to her.
22. FS to Bernard Berenson, September 22, 1947, in *Freya Stark Letters,* vol. 6, p. 23.
23. Interview with Diana Murray, 1993.
24. Interview with Jock Murray, 1989.
25. Interview with Wilfred Thesiger, 1990.
26. Interview with Leslie Perowne, 1990.
27. SP to FS, October 26, 1947, HRC.
28. SP to FS, December 19, 1947, HRC.
29. SP to FS, October 30, 1947, HRC.
30. SP to FS, November 4, 1947, HRC.
31. SP to FS, November 10, 1947, HRC.
32. SP to FS, November 12, 1947, HRC.
33. SP to FS, December 12, 1947, HRC.
34. SP to FS, December 30, 1947, HRC.
35. SP to FS, December 24, 1947, HRC.
36. FS to SP, January 13, 1948, in *Freya Stark Letters,* vol. 6, p. 42.
37. FS to SP, January 4, 1948, in ibid., p. 40.
38. SP to FS, January 24, 1948, HRC.
39. SP to FS, January 29, 1948, HRC.
40. FS to Pamela Hore-Ruthven, February 28, 1948, lent by her to the author.
41. Ibid.
42. FS to Jock Murray, February 25, 1948, in *Freya Stark Letters,* vol. 6, p. 47.
43. FS to Field Marshal Lord Wavell, Easter Day, 1948, in ibid., p. 50.
44. FS to Jock Murray, April 19, 1948, in ibid., p. 51.
45. Interview with Hon. Malise Ruthven, 1990.
46. SP to FS, May 19, 1948, HRC.
47. SP to FS, May 26, 1948, HRC.
48. SP to FS, July n.d., 1948, HRC.
49. FS to SP, September 15, 1948, in *Freya Stark Letters,* vol. 6, p. 72.
50. SP to FS, September 9, 1948, HRC.
51. SP to FS, September 15, 1948, HRC.
52. SP to FS, November 1, 1948, HRC.
53. SP to FS, November n.d., 1948, HRC.
54. FS to Sydney Cockerell, October 24, 1948, in *Freya Stark Letters,* vol. 6, p. 77.
55. SP to FS, April 21, 1949, HRC.
56. SP to FS, September 8, 1948, HRC.
57. SP to FS, June 6, 1949, HRC.
58. FS, *Perseus in the Wind* (London: John Murray, 1948), p. 91.
59. SP to FS, September 19, 1949, HRC.
60. Sydney Cockerell to FS, August 3, 1953, HRC.
61. SP to FS, May 14, 1949, HRC.
62. SP to FS, June 3, 1949, HRC.
63. SP to FS, July 26, 1949, HRC.
64. SP to FS, St. Michael and All Angels Day, 1949, HRC.
65. Archie Roosevelt, *For Lust of Knowing: Memoirs of an Intelligence Officer* (Boston: Little, Brown, 1988), p. 123. Roosevelt also told the author how surprised he had been on first meeting Freya that she was so attractive. He added, "You couldn't tell from the photographs."
66. FS to Sydney Cockerell, April 1, 1950, in *Freya Stark Letters,* vol. 6, p. 160.

67. FS to SP, October 4, 1949, in ibid., pp. 133–134.
68. SP to FS, October n.d., 1949, HRC.
69. FS to Bernard Berenson, April 12, 1950, in *Freya Stark Letters,* vol. 6, p. 167.
70. FS to Jock Murray, April 26, 1950, in ibid., p. 172.
71. Interview with Lavender Goddard-Wilson, 1990.
72. Interview with Pam Hore-Ruthven Cooper, 1993.
73. FS to SP, August 18, 1950, in *Freya Stark Letters,* vol. 6, p. 185.
74. FS to SP, March 19, 1951, in ibid., p. 209.
75. SP to FS, March 1951, HRC.
76. FS to SP, April 19, 1951, in *Freya Stark Letters,* vol. 6, p. 216.
77. SP to FS, March 1951, HRC.
78. Vita Sackville-West, "A Letter to Freya Stark," *Spectator,* November 24, 1950.
79. Christopher Sykes, "Self-Portrait," *Observer,* October 8, 1950.
80. Raymond Mortimer, "Odd Upbringing," Sunday *Times,* October 8, 1950.
81. FS to Jock Murray, November 29, 1950, in *Freya Stark Letters,* vol. 6, p. 204.
82. SP to FS, June 17, 1951, HRC.
83. FS to SP, March 20, 1951, in *Freya Stark Letters,* vol. 6, p. 211.
84. FS to Sybil Cholmondeley, November 26, 1951, in ibid., p. 256.
85. FS to Bernard Berenson, November 16, 1951, in ibid., p. 255.
86. FS to Sybil Cholmondeley, November 26, 1951, in ibid., pp. 256–257.
87. Duplicate of letter from John W. Stanton, Esq., Freya's lawyer, to SP, HRC.
88. FS to Jock Murray, March 22, 1952, in *Freya Stark Letters,* vol. 6, p. 261.
89. FS to Bernard Berenson, March 25, 1952, in ibid., p. 264.
90. SP to FS, October 26, 1951, HRC.
91. SP to FS, March 26, 1952, HRC.
92. Interview with John Julius Norwich, 1989.
93. Quoted in "Obituaries: Stewart Perowne: Traveller, writer and scholar of the Orient," *Times* (London), May 15, 1989.

21. THE ENDLESS HORIZON

1. FS to Jock Murray, June 10, 1952, in *Freya Stark Letters,* vol. 6, ed. Lucy Moorehead (Wilton, Salisbury, Wiltshire: Michael Russell, 1981), p. 271.
2. Interview with the former Italian ambassador to the United States Boris Bianchieri, whose family summered at La Mortola and knew both Freya and Ceci, 1994.
3. Freya was invoking John Keats, "On First Looking into Chapman's Homer": "Much have I travelled in the realms of gold / And many goodly states and kingdoms seen . . ."
4. FS to Jock Murray, November 14, 1952, in *Freya Stark Letters,* vol. 7, ed. Caroline Moorehead (Wilton, Salisbury, Wiltshire: Michael Russell, 1982), pp. 32–33.
5. FS to Victor Cunard, May 4, 1956, in ibid., p. 161.
6. Comment on the dust jacket of the American edition.
7. Critics frequently invoked the image of painting with words when reviewing her books.
8. FS to Jock Murray, March 22, 1962, in *Freya Stark Letters,* vol. 8, ed. Caroline Moorehead (Wilton, Salisbury, Wiltshire: Michael Russell, 1982), p. 44.
9. FS to Dulcie Deuchar, January 27, 1963, in ibid., p. 53.
10. Interview with Jock Murray, 1989.
11. Pamela Cooper, Michael Stewart, Diana Murray, Barclay (Mrs. Theo) Sanders

Larsson, and others all quoted Freya's pronouncements on the education of the young.

12. Interview with Damaris and Michael Stewart, 1991.

13. Barclay Sanders (Mrs. Theo) Larsson gave this description of the typewriter she lugged about for Freya, and Caroline Moorehead described the suitcase.

14. Hon. Malise Ruthven, Pamela Hore-Ruthven Cooper's younger son, studied Arabic and writes on Islam and the Middle East. Lord and Lady Iveagh's grandson, Sir Mark Lennox-Boyd, studied Arabic and Turkish and became Prime Minister Margaret Thatcher's parliamentary secretary.

15. FS to Jock Murray, September 15, 1960, in *Freya Stark Letters,* vol. 8, p. 19.

16. FS to Jock Murray, November 28, 1958, in *Freya Stark Letters*, vol. 7, p. 270.

17. Interview with E. C. Hodgkin, 1991.

18. Interview with Evelyn Lambert, 1989.

19. Caroline Moorehead, 1991, gave this description.

20. FS to Dulcie Deuchar, June 7, 1966, in *Freya Stark Letters,* vol. 8, p. 97.

21. Thomas and Evelyn Lambert of Texas.

22. This was the case with the British painter Derek Hill.

23. Bingo Hardie remembered Freya's charming way of describing the behavior of her car, 1990.

24. Interview with Xantha Hardie, 1990, and Contessa Loridon, and Contessa deLord, Asolo, 1990.

25. All were published by Michael Russell (Publishing) Ltd.

26. FS to Jock Murray, May 17, 1972, in *Freya Stark Letters,* vol. 7, p. 204.

27. Jan Morris, review of *Over the Rim of the World: Selected Letters of Freya Stark, Independent,* October 1988.

28. Interview with Richard Waller, 1991.

29. Interview with Evelyn Lambert, 1991.

30. Times Newspapers, 1993.

Illustration Credits

Pages 2, 32, 44, 117, courtesy of Richard Waller; pages 17, 18, *Traveller's Prelude,* courtesy of John Murray; pages 19, 45, 214, courtesy of the author; pages 50, 356 (center), courtesy of Mrs. Theo Larsson; page 66 (top), *Beyond Euphrates,* courtesy of John Murray; page 66 (bottom), courtesy of Clwyd County Council, Flintshire; pages 75, 87, 280 (top), 313, courtesy of the Matson Collection and the Episcopal Home; pages 88, 238, 262 (top), 280 (bottom), courtesy of the Middle East Centre, St. Antony's College, Oxford; pages 97 (top and bottom), 129, 290 (bottom), courtesy of Peggy Hackforth-Jones; page 97 (left), courtesy of Veronica Bamfield; page 154 (top), courtesy of Knopf; page 154 (bottom), courtesy of the Murray family; page 168 (top), 188, courtesy of Antonin B. Besse; page 168 (bottom), 174, 175 (bottom), courtesy of Nancy Clark Smith; pages 175 (top), 248, courtesy of Thomas G. Geniesse; page 211 (top), courtesy of Leila Ingrams; page 211 (bottom), courtesy of Paradigm Press; pages 235, 271 (top), courtesy of John Beach; pages 262 (bottom), 326, 356, (top), Hulton Getty; page 271 (bottom), courtesy of Pamela Cooper; page 280 (center), courtesy of Molly Izzard; page 290 (top), courtesy of E. C. Hodgkin; page 356 (bottom), courtesy of John Murray.

About the Author

JANE FLETCHER GENIESSE has worked as a reporter for the *World Telegram & Sun,* the *Boston Herald,* and *The New York Times.* She is the author of a novel, *The Riches of Life,* and her freelance articles have appeared in many magazines. A dedicated traveler, she has recently made trips to Yemen, Turkey, Lebanon, Syria, Jordan, and Israel. She lives with her husband in Washington, D.C., and Fishers Island, New York.

About the Type

This book was set in Sabon, a typeface designed by the well-known German typographer Jan Tschichold (1902–74). Sabon's design is based upon the original letter forms of Claude Garamond and was created specifically to be used for three sources: foundry type for hand composition, Linotype, and Monotype. Tschichold named his typeface for the famous Frankfurt typefounder Jacques Sabon, who died in 1580.